CW01597856

First published June 1991
Second edition published June 1993
Third edition published April 1995
Fourth edition published November 1997
Fifth edition published June 2000
Sixth edition published October 2002
Seventh edition published July 2005

© The Vegan Society

All rights reserved. No part of this book may be reproduced or transmitted in any way or by any means without the prior permission of the publisher

ISBN 0-907337-28-7

Design by Doughnut Design – www.doughnutdesign.co.uk

Printed on recycled paper by Cambrian Printers

Technical Support by Spirit Quest – www.spiritquest.co.uk

Published by
The Vegan Society
Donald Watson House, 7 Battle Road, St Leonard's-on-Sea,
East Sussex TN37 7AA, United Kingdom
Local rate 0845 45 88244 Tel. 01424 427 393
Fax. 01424 717 064
www.vegansociety.com

Nothing printed should be construed to be Vegan Society policy unless so stated. The Society accepts no liability for any matter in the *Animal Free Shopper*. The acceptance of advertisements does not imply endorsement of either the advertiser or its products/service. The inclusion of product information should not be construed as constituting official Vegan Society approval for the product, its intended use, or its manufacturer/distributor. The listing of products under 'health care' is not intended to take the place of advice provided by health care professionals.

CONTENTS

GUIDELINES

• Although, as far as is practical, the publisher has taken care to ensure the accuracy and reliability of information supplied to it, the reader should bear in mind that manufacturers may make alterations to the constituents, derivation and testing of their products *at any time*. The diligent animal free shopper always checks a product's ingredients listing (where one is provided!) before making a purchase.

• The absence of an (apparently) animal free product does not necessarily mean it does not meet the Society's **ANIMAL FREE CRITERIA** (page 292). Product categories that are obviously or typically animal-free (tinned fruit, tea, coffee, nuts, dried pulses, beans, peanut butter etc) have been excluded. Additionally, despite repeated approaches, some manufacturers/distributors (including a number whose products have appeared in previous editions) failed, or simply refused to supply the information requested.

• In order to make effective use of this guide, it is suggested that the new reader familiarises him/herself with the location of the **KEY** (page iii) and **CONTENTS** (page i) — and, at least initially, regularly consults the **PRODUCT INDEX** (page 336).

• The inclusion of a product should not be construed as constituting Vegan Society approval for the product, its intended use, or its manufacturer/distributor (see **OTHER ETHICAL CONSIDERATIONS**, page 299).

• The listing of products under 'Healthcare' is not intended to take the place of advice provided by health care professionals.

• The guide is also now online at ***www.animalfreeshopper.com*** and is updated frequently. All you have to do is register free of charge, log in and search under manufacturer, product type or product name.

KEY

The entire range of the company's products is animal-free (see **ANIMAL FREE CRITERIA**, page 292)	☺
The company is an authorised user of the Vegan Society Trade Mark (but not all its animal-free products may be registered) (see **VEGAN SOCIETY TRADE MARK**, page 6)	TM
The company has at least one vegan proprietor	❶
The company's entire product range is organic	☼
The company has a policy of ensuring that (as far as is possible and practical) the production of its products has not involved the use of genetically modified material (see **GENETICALLY-MODIFIED ORGANISMS**, page 299)	⊘
The company has a policy of not conducting nor commissioning animal testing	🐈
The company has signed up to the Humane Cosmetics Standard (see **ANIMAL TESTING CRITERIA**, page 298)	👁
The company has a policy of using only ingredients which have not been tested on animals by, or at the initiative of, the company or its suppliers since a specified date (Note: In the product listings, the year follows this symbol — eg a 1976 cut-off date appears as ✂1976) (see **ANIMAL TESTING CRITERIA**, page 298)	✂

Food and Drink products in **bold** are registered to use The Vegan Society Trade Mark

w = with (product listings only)

Vegan SOCIETY

people ▪ animals ▪ environment

WWW.VEGANSOCIETY.COM

Log on to the website of the world's premiere vegan organisation.

- Shop securely online for Vegan Society goods
- View listings of all Vegan registered products
- Become a member
- View Factsheets
- Information
- News and developments
- 'Why Go Vegan' section
- Links to other great vegan/veggie web pages

Return for updates and latest information

THE NO. 1 SITE FOR VEGAN SURFING

INTRODUCTION

Welcome to the seventh edition of the *Animal Free Shopper*, The Vegan Society's indispensable guide to each and every vegan product we are aware of on sale in the UK. The Vegan Society has now been established for more than 60 years, and animal-free products have never been easier to get hold of! With a government that has woken up to the fact that good health is easily available from increased consumption of fruits and vegetables, veganism is increasingly mainstream and no longer viewed as a bizarre 'fad' diet. An increased awareness of the realities of factory farming has meant that many people who are not yet vegetarian or vegan are cutting down on their consumption of animal products, searching for cruelty-free alternatives.

With all of this happening, a pocket-sized guide to all of the products that are not just suitable for vegetarians and vegans, but are entirely free from any animal ingredients whatever and from many increasingly common allergens such as milk protein, is an invaluable tool. While labelling of products is improving all the time, there are few things worse than scrutinising an ingredients list, only to be confronted with obscure names, arrays of E numbers, or the dreaded unspecified 'flavourings'. By carrying the *Animal Free Shopper* with you, it's easy and hassle-free to choose from thousands of animal-free products.

With the *Shopper*, the hard work is already done for you. We've contacted hundreds of manufacturers, not just of food and drink but also toiletries, cosmetics, clothing, healthcare products and anything else you care to think of, requesting information on which of their products are animal-free and compiling that information into this easy-to-use guide. With more supermarkets listed than ever before, in addition to a vast array of smaller independent producers, you should be able to find products regardless of your preference for shop type. And even if something isn't listed, our guide to E numbers and additives should help to allay any fears as to ambiguous ingredients in seemingly vegan products.

In terms of background information on veganism, the *Animal Free Shopper* also includes a section on nutrition and some facts and figures about animal exploitation. There are so many reasons to go vegan, for the benefit of people, animals and the environment, that the question is no longer 'why vegan?', but rather 'why not?'

MISSING, PRESUMED VEGAN

Although we've tried to make the *Animal Free Shopper* as comprehensive as possible, you may still come across products that are vegan but are not listed. There are a number of reasons for this, the main ones being:

- companies failing to respond to our requests for information;
- lack of confidence on the part of the compilers that the manufacturers/ suppliers really understand the ANIMAL-FREE CRITERIA (see page 292);
- companies supplying incomplete or inadequate product information;
- claims that the information requested is 'commercially sensitive'.

PLAYING DETECTIVE

Though experienced in investigating the animal-free credentials of a product, there are limits to The Vegan Society's capabilities. Food processing technology is a vast, complex and rapidly changing subject. At the end of the day, unless it obtains evidence to the contrary — or the details provided are clearly suspect - The Vegan Society has to accept the information provided to it (normally in the form of a written declaration) in good faith.

However, playing detective isn't the sole province of the Society. An increasing number of companies understand a vegan's requirements, and enquiries from members of the public are often at least as effective as those from an organisation. Use the ANIMAL-FREE CRITERIA (see page 292) as the basis for your approach and check ADDITIVES (see page 293) to identify E numbers that could be animal derived. You will quickly be able to determine whether the person responding to your enquiry is sufficiently knowledgeable to provide you with plausible product information. Confirming the animal-free status of a product can be thrilling, but be prepared also for frustration and disappointment! That said, discovering that an apparently animal-free product is not suitable certainly isn't wasted effort. Manufacturers take note of consumer interest and will, sooner or later, act. Recent examples of companies deciding to alter their products in response to demand for animal-free goods include: Green & Blacks removing honey from the ingredients of their mint chocolate bar, Granovita developing a vegan Worcestershire sauce, and even a vegan sporran from Freerangers.

ADVOCATES FOR
ANIMALS
Giving voice, taking action

Advocates for Animals is one of the UK's leading animal protection organisations, campaigning against all animal abuse. We envision a world in which people change their relationship with animals from one of exploitation and harm to one of respect and compassion. We promote the protection of all animals through investigations, scientific reports, high-profile campaigns, public education and political lobbying.

For further information contact:

Advocates for Animals
Freepost SCO6143
Edinburgh
EH2 4PG
Tel: 0131 225 6039
Fax: 0131 220 6377
info@advcoatesforanimals.org
www.advocatesforanimals.org

VEGAN TRAVEL GUIDES

www.vegetarianguides.co.uk

Features about vegan travel.
Extracts from Vegetarian Guides.
Links to vegan travel websites from
Australia to Vietnam.

Mapping the vegan world

Available from the Vegan Society, bookshops and online at

www.vegetarianguides.co.uk

Vegetarian Guides Alex Bourke

In addition to drawing the attention of manufacturers to the unmet needs of animal-free shoppers, it is equally important to tell them that you buy their products precisely because they are animal-free!

It is all too easy to complain and accuse companies of 'discriminating against vegans' or 'condoning animal suffering', but letters and phone calls of an encouraging nature are more likely to elicit a receptive response and, ultimately, produce the desired outcome.

LOOKING AHEAD . . .

Research for the *Animal Free Shopper* never ceases and The Vegan Society needs you to be part of this process! If you stumble across a new animal-free product, or discover that a manufacturer has introduced an animal ingredient into a product that was previously animal-free, please share your findings by providing feedback through *www.animalfreeshopper.com* or contacting us at: The Vegan Society, Donald Watson House, 7 Battle Rd, St Leonards-on-Sea, East Sussex TN37 7AA **t** 01424 427393 **f** 01424 717064 **e** info@vegansociety.com

A LITTLE BIT ABOUT THE VEGAN SOCIETY

The Vegan Society promotes ways of living free from animal products for the benefit of people, animals and the environment.

Established in November 1944, the Society was founded by a group of vegetarians who had recognised the ethical compromises implicit in lacto-vegetarianism. Among the founding members was Donald Watson, who coined the word 'vegan' by taking the first three and last two letters of 'vegetarian'.

Today, The Vegan Society continues to highlight the problems caused by an unhealthy dependence on animal products. We are a registered educational charity, focused on the provision of information on all aspects of veganism. We publish a quarterly magazine, which is free to members, as well as several books, a variety of leaflets and information sheets and websites. The message throughout all of these is simple: **go vegan - for people, animals and the environment.**

If you would like to join The Vegan Society and support the work we do, you can do so using the membership form at the back of this book. You can also join through our online shop at *www.vegansociety.com/shop* or by calling 01424 427 393. Thank you for your support.

LOCAL CONTACTS

In addition to our central offices in St Leonards-on-Sea, The Vegan Society has a large network of local contacts throughout the UK. These are members who have offered to act as a point of contact for those interested in the Society's work. So if you are interested in becoming more involved on a local campaigning level, or if you need any advice on being vegan in your area, they are the people to speak to.

Details of Vegan Society Local Contacts and Local Groups are published on *www.vegansociety.com* and are available on request.

OUR TRADEMARK

You will notice that some of the products listed in the *Animal Free Shopper* are highlighted in bold. These are all of the products that, at the time of going to press, were registered to use The Vegan Society's trademark sunflower logo.

This trademark was conceived as a way of helping people to shop for animal-free products. Only Vegan Society authenticated products carry the trademark, and each one has been independently checked by us.

The trademark allows consumers to make easy, informed choices about the suitability of purchases and enables us to work with companies who are willing to recognise their vegan customers. With thousands of items now bearing our familiar logo, and through international recognition of the trademark, our influence has never been greater. We have registered vegan alternatives to just about everything: vegan ice cream, margarine, cheese, fish fingers, wines, chocolate and even champagne. The trademark covers household items such as cosmetics and bath products, cleaners and soaps, and has attracted a lot of interest from producers of remedies and supplements.

'SPECIAL VEGETARIAN FOOD'

A range of frozen, soya–based **vegan** products that are approved by **The Vegetarian Society**. They are GMO free, Kosher, and Shudda. Cholesterol free, no preservatives or colourants and no hydrogenated oil.
Excellent source of protein.

Available from your local independent health food shop.
For further information or to place an order please contact...

BEANIE'S HEALTH FOODS (WHOLESALE) LIMITED

Unit 6, Cherry Tree Industrial Park, 312 Botley Road,
Burridge, Southampton SO31 1BQ
Tel: 01489 574593 Fax: 01489 582003
email: info@beanieshealthfoods.co.uk
www.beanieshealthfoods.co.uk

DOLMA
Vegan Perfumes, Skin Care & Toiletries

Dolma offer an exclusive range of high quality vegan perfumes, skin care and toiletries based on pure essential oils, herbal extracts, floral waters and vegetable oils. All products are carefully blended from safe, long established vegan ingredients and a fixed cut-off date of 1976 applies.

Send S.A.E. for free mail order catalogue or £15.95 for a boxed set of ten trial size perfumes. An ideal gift. Pack of three trial size Aftershave/Colognes also available for £6.50. Cheques/postal orders to be made payable to DOLMA.

The perfumes include a large proportion of natural essential oils with quality perfumery synthetics and ethyl alcohol.

DOLMA, 19 ROYCE AVENUE, HUCKNALL, NOTTINGHAM. NG15 6FU
Tel/Fax: 0115 963 4237 dolma@tinyworld.co.uk
www.veganvillage.co.uk/dolma

NEW FAIRTRADE TROPICAL BAR & FLAPJACKS

A new cereal bar and two flapjacks bearing fairtrade, organic and vegetarian certification. They are Tropical Bar, Original Butter Enriched Flapjack and Apple & Sultana Flapjack.

The brightly packaged Tropical Bar is made with fairtrade fruits, (mango, banana and pineapple) fairtrade brazil nuts, oats and crisp rice. The Apple & Sultana Flapjack and Original Flapjack are both made with fairtrade sugar from Paraguay.

Doves Farm Foods
01488 684880 www.dovesfarm.co.uk

Have a flick through the guidebook to see the huge number and variety of animal-free products that are registered with us, and remember to ask the manufacturer of your favourite products whether they have registered with us yet!

VEGAN SOCIETY TRADEMARK STANDARD

no animal ingredients
The manufacture and/or development of the product, and where applicable its ingredients, must not involve, or have involved, the use of any animal product, by-product or derivative.

no animal testing
The development and/or manufacture of the product, and where applicable its ingredients, must not involve, or have involved, testing of any sort on animals conducted at the initiative of the manufacturer or on its behalf, or by parties over whom the manufacturer has effective control.

genetically modified organisms
The development and/or production of genetically modified organisms (GMOs) must not have involved animal genes or animal-derived substances. Products put forward for registration which contain or may contain GMOs must be labelled as such.

AND A LITTLE BIT ABOUT VEGANISM

Veganism is very much on the rise. The Food Standards Agency's 2001 'Consumer Attitudes to Food Standards Report' showed that around 5% of the population would describe themselves as vegetarian and 0.4% were vegan. This means that around a quarter of a million people in the UK alone are choosing to avoid all animal products, more than double the figure found by the Realeat/Gallup Poll in 1993.

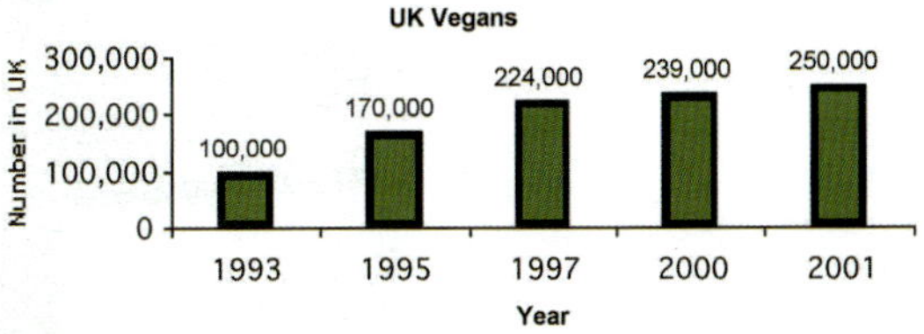

(Source: The Vegan Research Panel www.imaner.net/panel)

Similar polls conducted in the USA suggest that as many as 1% of Americans are vegan.

But that is only part of the story. Even among the meat-eating masses, consumption of animal products has been declining for the better part of fifty years.

Statistics show that the average person is now drinking around two-thirds less wholemilk than they were in the 1940s. Although there has been a corresponding increase in milk consumed in other forms, with it often being 'hidden' in processed foods, the decline of wholemilk intake suggests that many people no longer view it as the essential part of a healthy diet that it was once assumed to be. At the same time, the popularity of plant-based alternatives to dairy milk, such as soya milk, has been steadily increasing.

An even more dramatic change has been observed in egg consumption. The average number of eggs eaten in 2002/03 was 1.66 per person per week, compared with 4.78 in 1965.

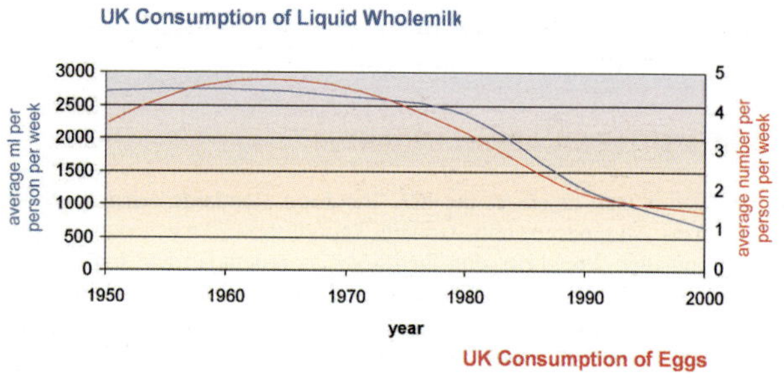

(Source: DEFRA National Food Survey, June 2004)

The clear overall trend is a decreasing dependence on animal products. This is happening for a number of reasons, some of which are explored in the following pages.

A Selection from the Dr Hadwen Trust's Vegan and Cruelty-Free Catalogue

The Dr Hadwen Trust works to find alternatives to animal experiments.

In Britain alone 2½ million animals are used in experiments every year. These include cats, dogs, rabbits, monkeys and mice.

In contrast our research into cancer, diabetes, heart disease, dementia and other illnesses doesn't cause a single animal to suffer. By finding superior, non animal alternatives we can save animals from experiments.

By making a purchase or simply sending a donation, your support will contribute directly to our wholly positive work.

Just two of the options from our range of over 400 vegan and cruelty-free gift ideas,

including Daniel Field hair colours, the new all-vegan Beauty Without Cruelty range, flying lessons!, and a fabulous choice of fair trade gifts, all from our catalogue.
Call 01462 436819 to receive yours now.

www.drhadwentrust.org.uk/
www.crueltyfreeshop.com

Vegan Chocolate Assortment (225g). An irresistible selection of delicious favourites in a ballotin box. £6.25

Animal-free Cosmetics Set 12 eyeshadows, 5 blushers, 4 lip glosses, one mascara (black) and no animal ingredients. Just £5.95.

Dr Hadwen Trust
Humanity in Research

£2 off your very first order!
Just cut out this coupon and enclose with your order to claim your discount.
THIS OFFER IS AVAILABLE TO NEW, FIRST-TIME CUSTOMERS ONLY.
UK orders only.
Photocopies of this voucher cannot be accepted.

Animal-free footwear
Freerangers

Freerangers footwear FOR life

Wherever life takes you it's comforting to know that there's been no animal involvement in producing your footwear. Our shoes, boots and sandals are all individually handmade in the UK with love, and licensed by the Vegan Society.

Step out in lasting comfort with a clear conscience.

Send now for your FREE colour catalogue, or order online at www.freerangers.co.uk

Freerangers AFS05, 87 Derwent Street, Chopwell, NE17 7HZ
Tel: 01207 565957 email info@freerangers.co.uk

Vegan
all products registered by the Vegan Society

WHY ANIMAL-FREE?

Well, why not? By adopting a vegan diet you can:

- help prevent animals from suffering unnecessarily
- reduce your individual environmental impact
- avoid contributing to the hunger of the world's poorest people
- improve your physical wellbeing
- start to feel good about the choices you make every day

Let's start with the most common reason for going vegan...

ANIMAL WELFARE

Animals slaughtered for meat in the UK in 2004:	
Cattle	4,620,000
Pigs	9,367,000
Sheep	15,194,000
Broilers (chickens raised for meat)	881,060,000
Boiling Fowl (spent laying hens)	36,480,000
Turkeys	28,200,000

(Source: DEFRA)

In total, over 900 million animals were slaughtered in the UK in 2004, but even this was not enough to meet UK demand. When we add in the number of animals killed abroad for consumption in the UK, the number of deaths is closer to one billion. These animals all died unnecessarily, but it's how they lived that's the real tragedy.

The popular vision of cattle grazing undisturbed in lush green fields or pigs snuffling happily in the earth, blissfully unaware of their intended fate, has long been defunct. The myth of the 'short but happy' lives of the animals that end up on the plates of 95% of British consumers may help to ease the collective conscience, but it also provides a façade to hide some of the most inhumane and appalling treatment of our fellow creatures.

POULTRY

Chickens raised for meat are known as 'broilers'. The majority of those reared each year in the UK are factory farmed. They are kept permanently indoors in huge windowless sheds so overcrowded that the floor can barely be seen.

A major welfare problem is that the birds have been selectively bred to reach their slaughter weight in 42 days, which is half the time taken 35 years ago. While the muscle grows quickly enough, the supporting structure of legs, joints, heart and lungs fails to keep pace. As a result, every year millions of chickens suffer from painful, sometimes crippling leg disorders, while millions more die of heart disease. By the time they reach slaughter weight, many of them can barely walk to their feeding areas.

PIGS

Pigs raised for meat are often kept indoors in overcrowded, ill-lit, barren conditions. More than half of the fattening pigs raised in the UK are not provided with straw, but are forced to sleep on bare floors, leading to extreme discomfort and stress.

Sows kept for breeding normally give birth to their piglets and nurse them in farrowing crates. These small cramped containers, designed to stop the mother from rolling on to her piglets, allow the sow very little room to turn

Divine Frog
Web Services

Websites by design:

- design
- development
- implementation
- maintenance
- hosting

Phone: 07981 057697
Email: i.nicoll@divinefrog.co.uk
Web: http://www.divinefrog.co.uk

Foods For Life
Cookbook
"vegan food has reinvented itself"
Heres Health
With recipes featured on
www.bbc.co.uk/food
vegan
By Hamlyn £12.99 ISBN 0600609154
www.foodsforlife.org.uk
Consultancy - Training - Marketing - Development
Nutrition
Yvonne Bishop-Weston
BSc Dip ION mBANT
London Clinics
Food Consultancy
Health Writer
Allergy Testing
Tel/Text 07944 068432
yvonne@foodsforlife.org.uk

around or lie down comfortably. Until recently, most breeding pigs in the UK were kept in these conditions all year round. In 1999, this was banned in the UK; since then, British pork production has dropped by almost half, but unfortunately British pork consumption has actually gone up using imported pork from areas where no ban is in force. The ban will become EU-wide in 2006.

Piglets would naturally be weaned at about 4 to 5 months, but they are often removed before 4 weeks, causing great stress to both mother and child. The piglets' traumatic existence has only just begun: in their short life they will endure painful procedures such as tail docking to prevent the distressed animals from biting each others tails, often carried out by unqualified persons and without anaesthetic.

BEEF CATTLE

Beef cattle have been gradually becoming dissociated from life on the range for some time now. Whilst twenty years ago the average cow raised for beef could expect to spend roughly two years roaming the fields, the average time spent outside is now around six months, before they are rounded up to be transported (often over long distances in cramped, badly ventilated conditions) to large buildings or yards for 'finishing'. They stay here for an average of about one year, during which time they are fed on a rich mixture of grain and whatever else comes cheaply and will fatten them up. This unnatural diet can lead to a number of illnesses, not least of which is BSE.

They are often also subjected to a range of painful procedures. Male calves are castrated either surgically, or using tight rubber rings that restrict blood flow, or by crushing the spermatic cord of each testis. When they are 4 to 6 weeks old, they are 'disbudded' with a hot iron to prevent their horns from growing. This is done to stop the distressed, closely confined animals from injuring each other. If this is not done straight away, the cattle will often be de-horned later in life. This can involve the use of saws, horn shears or cutting wire.

At the end of their short lives (a cow's natural lifespan is about 25 years; most are allowed to live for less than three) they are loaded into lorries for their final journey. When they reach the slaughterhouse, they are herded along cramped corridors and into pens where their heads are restrained and a bolt is shot through their skull destroying part of the brain. The cow is then stuck and allowed to bleed to death. All too often the initial stunning is inadequate and the animals may be conscious as they bleed to death.

DAIRY

If the lot of the cow raised for beef alone is to be pitied, the dairy cow deserves even more of our concern. To bring milk to the breakfast tables of the West, cows are kept in a constant cycle of pregnancy and lactation. This unnatural breeding regime results in painful udder infections such as mastitis, affecting 35 to 40% of the UK dairy herd. This condition is aggravated by unsanitary living conditions: for at least six months of the year cows often have no choice but to stand and sleep in their own filth, while some herds never leave the milking shed at all.

Frequent milking stimulates feed intake, increasing milk yields, so cows are often milked three times a day, usually by machines. The average dairy cow produces 5,915 litres per year, more than twice the amount produced by her ancestors in the 1950s. With milk yields increasing all the time, each cow's body is forced to work harder and harder.

> "The amount of work done by the cow in peak lactation is immense...To achieve a comparably high work rate a human would have to jog for about 6 hours a day, every day." (Professor AJF Webster, Dept of Animal Husbandry, Bristol University)

The strain is such that after only a very few years her fertility decreases, her milk levels drop, and she is quickly replaced with a more profitable animal. As with all other intensively farmed animals, she is destined for the dinner plate: the white stuff is inseparable from the red stuff.

HONESTY

A comprehensive mail order collection of vegan products from companies with compassionate policies

Honesty skin & hair care, BWC make-up, Daniel Field hair colours and styling products, Dolma perfumes, Bio D household cleaners, E-cloths, Fleur essential oils, Natracare, Weleda, soaps, toothpastes and more…….

Visit our website & online shop

www.honestycosmetics.co.uk

or for a free catalogue tel. 01629 814 888

Honesty, Units 8-10 Lumford Mill, Riverside Business

organic base from Green People

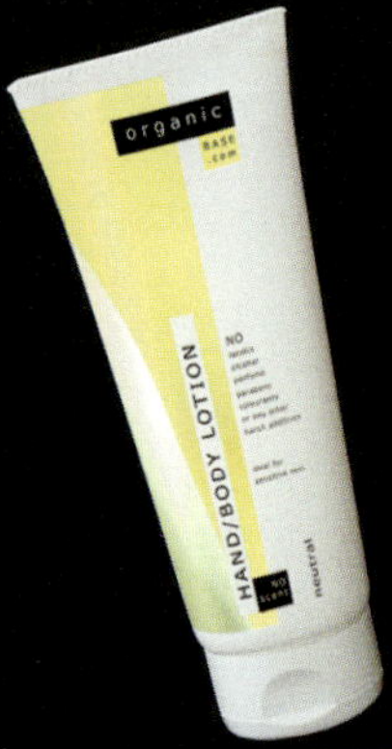

Neutral and Scent-Free

designed for
sensitive and irritated skin

No Scent Cleanser
No Scent 24 hour Cream
No Scent Hand & Body Lotion
No Scent Shampoo
No Scent Conditioner
No Scent Shower Bath
No Scent Liquid Soap
No Scent Deodorant

NO lanolin NO alcohol NO perfume NO parabens NO petrochemicals
NO sodium lauryl sulphate NO unnecessary synthetic additives

call 08702 401444 for a FREE Catalogue

www.greenpeople.co.uk

And it is not only the cow that suffers. Male calves are of the wrong breed to be raised for beef, so their only economic worth is as veal. Quotas and subsidy systems mean that each pint of milk is worth much more to the farmer than its market value, so little can be spared for the calf and they are often ripped from their mothers after just a few hours, causing enormous distress to both mother and child. The notorious veal crates are now being phased out throughout Europe, but legal recommendations for the housing and feeding of veal calves still fall well below recognised welfare requirements.

EGGS

In the European Union around 90% of laying hens are kept in battery cages so small that they cannot stretch their wings, peck, scratch the ground or perform most of their other natural behaviours. Up to 90,000 caged hens may be crammed into one windowless shed, with cages often stacked up to 9 storeys high.

This close confinement not only causes major psychological stress, but can also cause physical damage to the birds. The lack of exercise and the unnatural diet lead to brittle bones that are easily broken. This problem has become so bad that it is now thought to be responsible for around 35% of premature deaths in battery systems: the injured birds are unable to reach food or water and simply starve to death.

Battery systems are to be outlawed in Europe from 2012, but the so-called 'enriched cages' that will replace them are little better. Each hen will have roughly a postcard-sized piece of extra space. This may be an improvement of sorts, but evidence (and common sense) suggests that birds will continue to suffer both physical and psychological stress.

"But," says the ethical egg-lover, "I only buy free-range eggs." The myth of the free-range egg continues to salve the consciences of many British consumers. Images of fat, feathery farmyard chickens pecking and scratching in the dust couldn't be further from the reality of the majority of "free-range" systems. The birds are often kept in flocks of up to 16,000 to a shed, and although there must be access to the outside, this is often through a hole so small and so difficult to reach that up to half the birds in large scale so-called free-range units never see the light of day.

After a year of egg production, fertility decreases and most laying hens are sent for slaughter: worth as little as two pence per bird, they end up in soups, pasties, pies, etc where the pathetic condition of their bodies will not put consumers off their meal.

As with dairy calves, laying hen chicks are of the wrong strain to be raised for meat. Male chicks are therefore completely worthless and are killed when they are just one day old; common slaughter methods include gassing, neck dislocation and the 'homogeniser,' a device that minces chicks alive.

FISH

Fish farming is now the world's fastest growing sector of animal production. Up to 50,000 salmon can be crowded together in a single sea cage, resulting in each 75cm long salmon having the equivalent of a bathtub of water to swim in. Trout are usually stocked at even higher densities (as many as 27 trout to one bathtub). The stress caused by these unnatural conditions (a wild salmon will swim thousands of miles to return to its spawning ground) leads to physical injuries and increased susceptibility to disease. Official figures show that disease-related death rates among farmed fish are as high as 10 to 30%.

Parasites are another devastating problem for intensively farmed fish. The large concentrations of fish attract sea lice that feed on the host salmon, often causing such severe damage to the fish that the skull becomes visible, a condition that has become known as the 'death crown.' The highly toxic products used to treat these infestations cause considerable environmental damage.

Veganicity™

suitable for everyone

VEGAN GLUCOSAMINE
High strength, 750mg glucosamine hydrochloride

- 28 products
- 100% vegan friendly
- Vegan Society registered
- Includes VEGAN Glucosamine
- Brand new
- Gelatin free
- Sugar free
- Lactose free
- Yeast free
- Wheat free
- Vegetarian
- Suitable for everyone
- EXCELLENT VALUE

Look out for a Veganicity display stand in your local, independent health store

Vegan®
Registered with the Vegan Society

Veganicity from Health Plus

Call
01323 872277
for your nearest stockist or more information

Dolphin House, 27 Cradle Hill Ind Est Seaford East Sussex BN25 3JE
www.veganicity.com

NON-FISH OILS

Omega Nutrition
Vegan

*The Best Organic Oils in the world – Vegan Society registered**

Omega Oils are big news these days.

Omega 3 oils provide a precursor for the essential fatty acids, EPA and DHA, which are vital for nerves, brain, eyesight, heart and circulation, balanced pain control and good mood.

Omega 6 oils provide the precursor for GLA, an important fatty acid for skin, hormone balance, immunity, balanced pain control and good mood.

The Vegan Society registered* Omega Nutrition range provides these all-important oils from flax seeds, virgin hemp seeds, sunflower and pumpkin seeds, and other seed sources.

What's more, they are a great alternative to use in food preparation, as salad dressings, as a spread or to go into puddings.

**Excludes Pumpkin Seed Butter, Flax Seed Capsules and Essential Balance Capsules.*

HIGHER NATURE
Nutritional Excellence

For your free full product catalogue call freephone
0800 458 4747

And it is not only the fish themselves that suffer. Every year hundreds of fish-eating species (notably seals, birds, mink, and otters) are attracted to these vast stocks of fish and are shot by fish farmers attempting to protect their livelihoods.

HONEY

Non-vegans are often surprised to learn that honey and other bee-products are unsuitable for vegans. One of the commonest queries we get at The Vegan Society is "I'm a vegan, but I don't really understand why I can't eat honey." Again it's the old storybook image that confuses us: we see honey bees flying around, gathering nectar and taking it back to their hives – what cruelty could possibly be involved?

In fact, bees are manipulated in similar ways to other farmed animals to provide a whole range of products, including honey, beeswax, propolis, bee pollen, bee brood, royal jelly and venom.

A bee will, on average, fly about 800km to provide half a teaspoon of honey.

The major welfare problems associated with bee keeping are centred around the egg-laying process. The queen is routinely artificially inseminated by sperm from decapitated bees (they would normally mate in flight). She is usually killed after 2 years, when her egg-laying abilities begin to decline, and replaced by a new queen, often purchased by mail order from specialist breeding companies. The queens' wings are clipped to force the hives to remain in a single location.

Honey, stored by the bees for the lean winter months, is removed for human use and replaced with nutrient-deficient glucose or corn syrup. Synthetic pesticides and antibiotics are also used.

SHELLAC

Lac are insects (*Lacifer lacca*) living on lac trees, where the female secretes a protective resin over herself. It is this resin, along with encrusted live insects, that is scraped from the trees and manufactured into shellac. 300,000 lac insects are killed for 1kg of shellac.

Shellac is used as a glaze for fruit (such as those surprisingly shiny supermarket apples), nuts, coffee beans; in paint, varnish, tablets, cosmetics, confectionery, floor polish; and in hats as a stiffener. Whilst synthetic resin could easily replace shellac entirely, public demand for 'natural' products may actually be encouraging greater production.

COCHINEAL

Cochineal, also known as carmine, is a red dye used in clothing and foodstuffs. It consists of the dried bodies of *Dactylopius coccus*, an insect indigenous to Central and South America. The female insects are picked by hand after mating and dried in shade for 20 to 30 days. To produce 1 kg of raw cochineal requires about 100,000 to 150,000 insects. Total world production is estimated at 150 to 180 tonnes per year, with Peru producing about 90% and the rest coming from the Canary Islands.

SILK

The most common species of silkworm (moth larvae) used in commercial silk production, *Bombyx mori*, has been 'cultivated' over many centuries and no longer exists in the wild. The female annually lays 300-400 eggs on mulberry trees, secreting a sticky substance to fasten them to the surface.

The silkworm secretes a fine thread to make a cocoon around itself consisting of about 300,000 figure of eight movements. The pupa stage would then be followed by the production of an alkaline substance that would eat through the threads, allowing the moth to emerge, but as the industry requires the threads intact, the pupa is killed by immersing the cocoon in boiling water, steaming, oven drying or exposure to the hot sun.

Only a tiny amount of usable silk is obtained from each cocoon: it takes around 200kg of cocoons and 11.25 tonnes of mulberry leaves to produce

illside Animal Sanctuary

Hillside is home to hundreds of rescued animals and campaigns on behalf of the millions
ho suffer every day within the factory farming industry. We promote a vegan lifestlye while educating the public to the plight of farm animals.
For further details of our work including our farm animal investigations, adopt an animal scheme and gifts, please write, phone or e-mail for our Newletters.

illside Animal Sanctuary
ll Top Farm Hall Lane
ettenham Norwich NR12 7RW
)ff the B1150 North Walsham Road)
l: 01603 736200 Fax: 01603 738520

Hillside Open Days... Visitors are welcome to meet our rescued animals 1-5pm EVERY SUNDAY between Easter and the end of October. Also Bank Holiday Mondays & every MONDAY during JUNE, JULY & AUGUST.
website: www.hillside.org.uk
e-mail: contact@hillside.org.uk

HIPPO

Feeding the World with Compassion

Registered Charity No. 1075420

MAKE A DIFFERENCE WITH HIPPO!

A vegan charity that helps animals and people.

HIPPO is working around the world to help hungry people to obtain and where possible produce their own high protein foods to overcome malnutrition. Whilst many overseas aid agencies encourage the expansion of livestock production we emphasise the value of vegetable proteins. This reduces the pressure on land and water-supplies that keeping livestock inevitably causes, and also saves animals from the cruelty of being exploited for food. In the developing world we support projects run by local people and supply food for orphanages and the homeless. Our staff are volunteers and our costs are very low.

Please send donations and/or enquiries to:

HIPPO, LLANGYNOG, CARMARTHEN SA33 5BS

Tel: 01267 241547

email: hippocharity@aol.com

just 40kg of silk. The dead pupae are typically composted to feed the mulberry trees.

WOOL

The majority of sheep are shorn for the first time at 14 to 15 months and thereafter annually. Early season shearing in wet, windy and cold conditions can result in severe chilling, a high incidence of mastitis and even death.

Australia is the world's largest wool-producing country with around 100 million sheep. 20 to 25% of Australian lambs die either at birth or before the age of 8 weeks, from exposure to extreme weather conditions or starvation. An estimated 1 million Australian sheep die of exposure every year after shearing. Following cruel procedures such as castration, tail docking and mulesing (in which farmers carve strips of flesh (not wool) from around the anal and vaginal area of sheep without anaesthetic or any training or qualification requirements), lambs are susceptible to shock, blood poisoning, tetanus, dislocated joints and arthritis.

Raw wool contains 10 to 25% grease or lanolin, which is recovered during the scouring process. Lanolin consists of a highly complex mixture of esters, alcohols, and fatty acids and is used in adhesive tape, printing inks, motor oils, and machine lubrication. It can also be refined for use in cosmetics and pharmaceuticals.

FUR

The trade in wild furs is responsible for the decline of many species and the extinction of some. As the larger cats became commercially extinct or protected, the fur trade turned to the smaller ones. Thousands of lynx and bobcat are still being trapped each year in North America using steel leg-hold traps (now banned in Europe) which do not kill the animal outright and cause immeasurable suffering.

Worldwide, more than 30 million mink and foxes are imprisoned in row upon row of wire cages to produce fur, although in the UK long-term campaigning has led to the farming of animals exclusively for their fur being outlawed since 1st January 2003. Animals kept in fur factory farms (with small, barren cages averaging at about 90cm by 30cm by 40cm) show stereotypical behaviour, self-mutilation and cannibalism. They are killed by gassing, neck-breaking, lethal injection, or anal electrocution.

LEATHER

Vegans don't eat the inside and, increasingly, they also don't wear the outside. Leather is simply fur with the hairs scraped off one side and the flesh scraped and chemically removed from the other side. The sale of leather makes a sizeable contribution to the viability of the meat industry – it is not a by-product of animal suffering, it is a contributing factor.

Synthetic alternatives such as Lorica, from which vegetarian shoes and jackets are made, are now widely available.

See the clothing section of the *Animal Free Shopper* for a range of vegan footwear suppliers.

VIVISECTION

Home Office statistics show that the total number of procedures on animals in the UK in 2003 was 2,791,781 and 61% of these were conducted without anaesthetic.

There are three main areas of research in which these experiments are claimed to be useful: to increase scientific knowledge, to aid the development of new products, and to test the safety of new products and their ingredients.

Some of the more common experiments are the LD-50 (now banned in the UK, but common throughout the rest of the world), the Draize test, and skin irritancy tests. LD-50 (Lethal Dose 50%) involves giving animals increasing amounts of a chemical or drug to find the dosage required to kill 50% of the test group. The Draize test is performed on rabbits – substances such as laundry products, bleaches and washing-up liquids are dripped into their eyes, which are then examined for signs of damage such as ulcers, bleeding, swelling, or discharge. In skin irritancy tests, the skin of the rabbit or other rodent is shaved and the substance is applied to the area, which is then examined for adverse reactions.

Animal Aid

Campaigning for all animals

Animal Aid is the UK's biggest national animal rights group campaigning against vivisection, factory farming and all other animal abuse. We also promote vegetarianism and cruelty-free living.

We have a wide range of vegan, cruelty-free merchandise, including toileties, books, cards, chocolates, wine, clothes and shoes.

Send for your free merchandise catalogue and support our campaign work

Animal Aid, The Old Chapel,
Bradford St, Tonbridge, Kent TN9 1AW

Tel: (01732) 364546
email: info@animalaid.org.uk
web: www.animalaid.org.uk

ANIMAL AID

THEY CALL IT TESTING. TO HER IT'S TORTURE

You could help end animal testing forever

In the UK nearly three million animals suffer in laboratories every year. The BUAV opposes all animal experiments and campaigns peacefully and effectively to end them. Visit www.buav.org to find out more.

Call the BUAV on 020 7619 6963 or email fundraising@buav.org

- To ask for a free copy of our *Little Book of Cruelty Free* products
- To support the BUAV with a donation
- To adopt an ex-laboratory monkey

British Union for the Abolition of Vivisection, 16a Crane Grove, London, N7 8NN

BUAV
campaigning to end animal experiments

While household products such as bleaches are still routinely tested on animals, animal testing of cosmetics was banned in the UK in 1998. However, many companies continue to test products and ingredients in mainland Europe and elsewhere. There is no legislation to prevent these products being sold in the UK.

Draft legislation that would require the testing or retesting of more than 30,000 commonly used chemicals is currently being discussed by the European Union. This would constitute the largest animal-testing programme in Europe's history.

HEALTH

HEART DISEASE AND CANCER

Replacing animal foods with plant foods and thus reducing intakes of saturated fat and cholesterol and increasing intakes of fibre, vitamin C, folate and carotenoids promotes good health.

Meat has around 40% of calories from fat and cheese has around 70% of which more than 60% is the dangerous saturated fat. Eggs are the richest source of cholesterol: more than one egg a day would exceed recommended cholesterol intakes even if no other animal products were consumed.

Dietary guidelines across the world, including the meat-guzzling USA, now acknowledge the vegan alternative. Fortified plant milks are accepted as an alternative to dairy products as a source of calcium, and beans and nuts are accepted as an alternative to meat and fish as a source of protein. Recommended vegetable and fruit intakes continue to rise, with many experts replacing the familiar five-a-day advice with nine-a-day or more. Research strongly suggests that a diet rich in fruit and vegetables can decrease the risk of having a heart attack or stroke, protect against a variety of cancers, lower blood pressure, reduce risk of intestinal ailments and guard against loss of vision in the elderly.

Compared with lacto-ovo-vegetarians and meat eaters, vegans usually have significantly higher intakes of nutrients associated with reduced risk of cardiovascular disease - including fibre, vitamin C, potassium, magnesium, and folate - as well as lower intakes of sodium. They also consume less total fat and less saturated fat, and have lower levels of total cholesterol as well as a better ratio of total cholesterol to HDL cholesterol.

Research has confirmed reduced risk of heart disease in vegans and other vegetarians. This is believed to be due to lower intakes of saturated fat and cholesterol and higher intakes of fruit and vegetables. However, research has also indicated that some vegans are not getting the full potential benefit of their diet, due to less than optimal intakes of vitamin B12 and omega-3 fatty acids. This is easily remedied by getting at least 3 micrograms of B12 per day from fortified foods or supplements and including some omega-3 rich foods such as rapeseed oil or flaxseed oil (see HEALTHY EATING FOR VEGANS page 49). We look forward to even better results from studies of vegan health once this advice becomes widely adopted.

Evidence is also growing that diets high in milk and dairy products increase the risk of prostate cancer and that diets high in processed meats and low in fibre increase the risk of colon cancer. In this context, it is good news that plant protein sources are now almost universally accepted as providing all the protein we need: when it comes to health, there is nothing second rate about plant foods.

DAIRY ALLERGY AND INTOLERANCE

Dairy products are a common trigger for eczema in infants and can also cause chronic constipation. Among those over the age of five, 90-95% of Black individuals and 20-25% of Caucasians are lactose intolerant (source: Dr Harris Steinman *Milk Allergy and Lactose Intolerance*, 2002): milk sugar causes digestive problems such as bloating and diarrhoea because they lack the enzymes to break it down.

It should therefore come as no surprise that in the UK 31% of all consumers (17 million people) are attempting to reduce their consumption of dairy products, 13% (more than 7 million people) never or hardly ever eat dairy foods, and 22% claim to purchase 'regularly' non-dairy products such as soya milk (Source: 1998 Granose Survey into Lactose Intolerance and non-dairy foods).

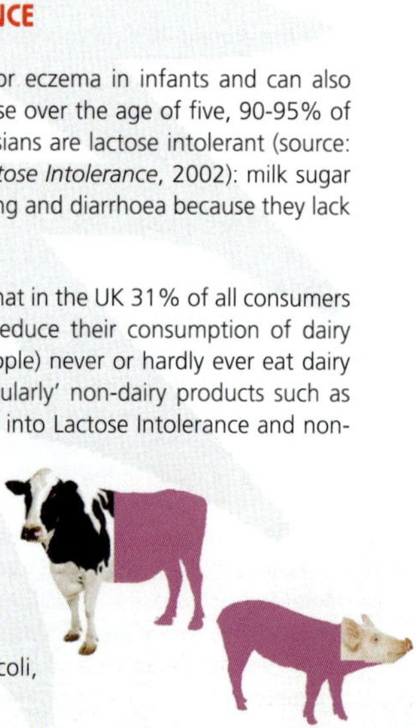

FOOD POISONING

Studies have demonstrated that 53% of bovine carcasses and 83% of pig carcasses were contaminated with E-coli,

mooncup®

eusable menstrual cup for women & our world

he Mooncup is hygienic, comfortable and convenient. One Mooncup lasts for years
naking it the cheapest and most eco-friendly sanitary protection you can buy.

lanufactured in the UK for Mooncup Ltd, 125 Maresfield Road, Brighton, BN2 5ES, UK
elephone: +44 (0) 1273 673845 Email: info@mooncup.co.uk www.mooncup.co.uk

VINTAGE Roots
the organic wine specialists

Order our free List and try the healthier option

Organic wine & beer

Choose from our worldwide range of **vegan** wines, beers, ciders, spirits, juices, oils and chocolates

Fast nationwide delivery

Trade enquiries welcome

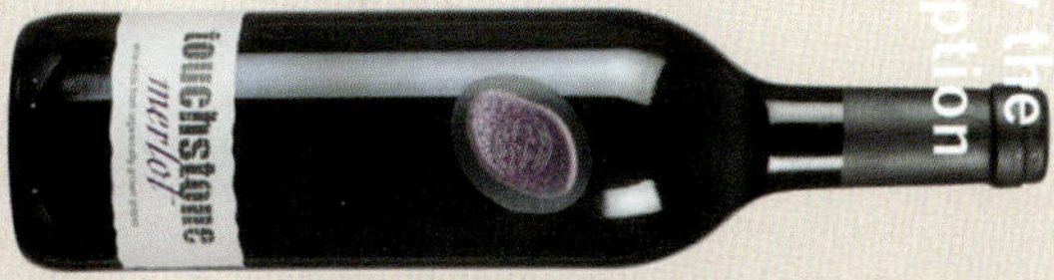

Freephone 0800 980 4992
www.vintageroots.co.uk

Fresh Raw Organic Nut & Seed Butters

Low temperature ground to retain Life Energy, Flavour, Vitamins and Minerals!
13 Varieties including: Pistachio, Almond, Cashew, Tahini, Pumpkin Seed, Hemp Seed and Brazil Nut Butter.
High in Protein, Fibre and Essential Fatty Acids, each product is highly nutritious and delicious!

www.red23.co.uk

t: 01992 815 859 m: 07957 192 430 Info@red23.co.uk

while 18% of raw chicken from Britain and 64% of imported poultry contained Salmonella. In a 1996 study, more than half of UK-bred chickens purchased from retail outlets contained Campylobacter. Eggs and egg-containing foods were involved in 10% of outbreaks of food poisoning in England and Wales between 1992 and 1999. Almost 17,000 cases of Salmonella infection in humans were confirmed in 1999. In fact, food poisoning from eggs has become such a problem that in 2001 the Government's Food Standards Agency stated that eating raw eggs may pose a health risk. They went on to advise that vulnerable groups, "should only consume eggs that have been cooked until the white and yolks are solid." Diarrhetic, paralytic and amnesic shellfish poisoning has also been found in several areas of the UK.

CJD

There is now convincing evidence that the agent that causes BSE is the same as that which causes new variant Creutzfeld Jacob disease (nvCJD) in humans. More than 100 people have now died in the UK. There is still a real possibility that the final death toll will be over 10,000, but earlier estimates of millions of deaths now seem unlikely. This is a matter of luck, as the difficulty of controlling the recent foot and mouth disease epidemic illustrates how easily and quickly infections can spread in modern factory farms: anyone continuing to consume animals is therefore taking a major gamble on their health and that of their family.

Prions, the 'rogue' proteins believed to be responsible for BSE and CJD, have not been found in milk or milk products, but the prion agent is contained in white blood cells ('pus') which are legally permitted in milk at levels up to 2 million per teaspoon!

ANTIBIOTICS

British farmers are some of the heaviest users of antibiotics in Europe, accounting for more than 20% of the 1225 tonnes of antibiotics used annually on farm animals. Antibiotic-resistant bugs have resulted from the use of antibiotic growth promoters in farm animals, not the overuse of antibiotics in hospitals. For example Vancomycin, which is used on humans, is chemically identical to Avoparcin which from 1976 until 1997 was the most widely used antibiotic growth promoter in the UK being fed to most chickens, turkeys, pigs and about 30% of all cattle. DNA sequencing showed that Vancomycin resistance in bugs infecting humans has come entirely from the use of Avoparcin and not from the use of Vancomycin. Approximately 1000kg of Avoparcin was used for every 1kg of Vancomycin.

ECOLOGY

More and more people are becoming aware of the direct correlation between what they eat every day and the health of the planet. Environmentally conscious consumers are concerned not only with food miles, over-packaging, pesticide use and GM foods, but increasingly question the environmental sustainability of modern animal husbandry. Farmers used to be seen as 'custodians of the countryside,' but the overriding image of modern industrial farming is one of destruction and waste.

The meat-intensive diets of the West contribute, among other things, to global warming, deforestation, desertification, water pollution, and loss of fossil fuels.

GLOBAL WARMING

Global temperatures continue to rise at an alarming rate. Whilst no-one can say for certain what the consequences may be, sea level rise, climate change, and species loss are just a few of the possibilities that we face.

Intensive animal husbandry contributes to this environmental crisis in a number of complex ways. The most straightforward statistic is that 16% of anthropogenic emissions (i.e. those caused by human activities) of methane come from cattle. Methane is one of the three gases thought to be responsible for global warming; it is produced by bacteria in the stomachs of ruminants such as sheep, cattle, and goats and is farted and belched out by the animals. Dairy cows have been calculated to produce roughly 30kg more methane per year than free-range beef cattle (84kg and 54kg respectively), largely because of differences in diet and levels of exercise.

FULL OF FLAVOUR
not of animals
THE Redwood Co
caring for all naturally
Cheatin'
Cheezly
Vegideli
Vegetarian and vegan
Meat, egg & dairy free
Cholesterol free
No hydrogenated fats
No artificial colours or preservatives
You can find THE Redwood Co foods in your local independant health store, Holland & Barrett and selected branches of Waitrose, Safeway, Morrisons and Tesco. If you are having problems finding your nearest stockist please phone 01536 400557 for help
theredwoodwholefoodcompany NN17 4DT
t:01536 400557 f:01536 408878 www.redwoodfoods.co.uk

VEGETARIAN SHOES

ANIMAL FRIENDLY FOOTWEAR

Send name and address for free colour brochure, range includes mens' and ladies' shoes and boots, leisure shoes, walking boots, safety boots, jackets, belts etc . . .

12 Gardner Street, Brighton, East Sussex BN1 1UP Tel: 01273 691913
email: information@vegetarian-shoes.co.uk

ORDER DIRECT ON-LINE

www.vegetarianshoes.com

When manure is kept in anaerobic conditions (as in the liquid systems commonly used on intensive farms), even more methane is produced. Manure is also responsible for 7% of emissions of nitrous oxide (a more aggressive greenhouse gas).

In addition to these direct impacts on global warming, animal husbandry also has some more well hidden costs. The felling of forests to provide land to grow food for cattle (see below) means that there are fewer and fewer trees to absorb carbon dioxide, the major greenhouse gas. The feed crops are then grown using artificial fertilisers that release nitrous oxides. Their processing, transport and storage use up fossil fuels, releasing carbon dioxide.

Changing to a vegan diet will not stop global warming, but if you worry about using your car, having baths, turning on the heating, and using energy saving light bulbs, you should also be worrying about the amount of damage the food you eat is causing.

DEFORESTATION

We need forests. They store large amounts of carbon dioxide, release oxygen, protect soils, and harbour millions of plant and animal species. Yet they are being destroyed at an alarming rate. The United Nations Food and Agriculture Organisation estimates that the net loss of forests for the 1990s as a whole was 94 million hectares. This represents an area larger than Venezuela. Forests are being destroyed not only to provide wood, paper and fuel, but also to provide land for grazing cattle and for growing crops to feed to animals (see 'Resource Use' below).

DESERTIFICATION

The felling of forests and over-grazing also contribute to soil loss and desertification. Thin layers of topsoil previously protected by a fine network of roots are extremely vulnerable when the forest cover is removed and are often simply washed away or compacted and broken down by heavy cattle.

The UN estimates that more than 250 million people are directly affected by desertification, and around one fifth of the world's population of 6.5 billion in more than a hundred countries, are at risk from famine and malnutrition as a result of the rapid decrease in the fertile land available for growing crops for humans.

WATER POLLUTION

Every year farmers spread about 200 million tonnes of animal manures and other organic farm wastes on to the land as fertiliser. Slurry and silage effluent can pollute a nearby river or stream by encouraging algal blooms that block sunlight and encourage bacteria that deplete the water of oxygen, in the worst cases killing all the fish and endangering the health of other animals in the area. This process is known as eutrophication, and farming is the major cause of the problem.

Slurry, which is made up of manure and urine, contains high levels of ammonia. This encourages bacteria that produce acid that directly contributes to acid rain. Slurry can be up to 100 times more polluting than raw untreated domestic sewage. Silage effluent, the liquid produced when preserving crops for fodder, is up to 200 times more polluting.

TANNERIES

In its natural state as hide or skin, leather would be totally unsuitable for its current uses and would rot rapidly. To make it pliable and longer lasting, hide is treated with a wide range of environment damaging chemicals such as lime, sodium sulphate solution, emulsifiers, non-solvent degreasing agents, salt, formic acid, sulphuric acid, chromium sulphate salts, lead, zinc, formaldehyde, fats, alcohol, sodium bicarbonate, dyes, resin binders, waxes, coal tar derivatives and cyanide-based finishes. Tannery effluent contains large amounts of other pollutants such as proteins and hair. Overall, the production of leather is far more polluting than modern synthetic versions.

ENVIRONMENT EMERGENCY HOTLINE

The Environment Agency's emergency hotline number 0800 807060 operates 24 hours a day, 365 days a year, for people to report pollution, fish in distress, illegal disposal of waste, poaching and danger to the natural environment.

Over 120 Different Vega Vitamin, Mineral & Herbal Supplements Suitable For A Vegan Diet
Developed by Pharmacists & Nutritionists
Vega Nutritionals
Harnessing Nature Through Science
Vegan
Vegan
HAIR-SKIN-NAILS
VITAMINS, MINERALS & AMINO COMPLEX
Formula
COMPLEXION Care
ECHINACEA
Standardised
1000-COMPLEX
FULL SPECTRUM Erbe
PHYTO-IMMUNE
GINKGO
BILOBA
Standardised
3400-COMPLEX
FULL SPECTRUM Erbe
PHYTO-MEMO
ZM3 Formula™
MULTI VITAMINS & MINERALS
HIGH STRENGTH
Quality
Purity
Innovation
vega
VITAMINS & HERBALS
Vega products are free from artificial additives, colourings, flavours & preservatives. In addition we avoid the use of gelatin, corn, gluten, wheat, salt, sugar, starch, soy, yeast, dairy products & GM ingredients in the product range.
Vega products are available from Tesco & Lloyds Pharmacies, leading Independent Chemists & Health Stores & by mail order from the Nutricentre on 0800 587 2290
Vega Nutritionals, 41 Central Avenue, West Molesey, Surrey, KT8 2QZ
Tel: 08452 267300 Fax: 08452 267400 Email: info@vegavitamins.co.uk

You may be veggie – but is your veg?

Support vegan-organics: for people, animals and planet

» Chemical pesticides and fertilisers kill wildlife and damage the soil » Organic food usually produced using manure from animal farms, supporting the meat industry » Traditional organic systems waste land and water to feed farm animals

Vegan-Organics is the answer!

» Vegan-Organic growers both here and in the developing world make the most efficient use of the earth's resources

Support the Vegan-Organic Network

» We have produced the world's first Stockfree Organic Standards, and are working to ensure their uptake by organic farmers

» We support a wide and growing network of gardeners and small scale growers and help you to 'grow your own' vegan-organically

» We provide farm visits, courses, our biennial magazine Growing Green International, bulletins, email group, information sheets

Join us now!

» Vegan-Organic Network, 10 Charter Rd, Altrincham, Cheshire WA15 9RL, tel 0845 223 5232, **www.veganorganic.net**
Registered charity number 1080847

RESOURCE USE

LAND

Meat and dairy production is a notoriously inefficient use of energy. All animals use the energy they get from food to move around, keep warm and perform their day to day bodily functions. This means that only a small percentage (around 10%) of the energy that farmed animals obtain from plant foods is converted into meat or dairy products.

Yet livestock use roughly 3.4 billion hectares of grazing land, and the production of around one quarter of all croplands. In all, the raising of livestock takes up more than two-thirds of agricultural land, and one third of the total land area (*Food and Agricultural Organisation*)

Quite simply, we do not have enough land to feed everyone on an animal-based diet. So while we continue to waste two-thirds of agricultural land by obtaining only 10% of its potential calorific value, almost 1 billion people are undernourished. A third of the children in the world suffered from malnutrition during the 1990s. More than 24,000 people still die every day from hunger-related causes. These statistics are deeply disturbing, especially when enough plant foods are grown to feed everyone. It has been estimated that 10 acres of land could feed just 2 people on a diet of cattle meat, but 61 people on soya beans.

Access to food is an extremely complex issue, and all too often war, corruption and lack of infrastructure mean that even when food is available people starve. However, with a rapidly increasing world population the fact remains that a plant-based diet is the most environmentally sustainable option available.

WATER

Only a very small percentage of the earth's water is fresh and even less than this is available as drinking water. Yet we continue to squander vast amounts of this most precious of natural resources on farmed animals.

There has been much disagreement over precisely how much water is wasted in this way. Professor David Pimentel of Cornell University's Ecology

Department has calculated that it takes 500 litres of water to produce 1kg of potatoes, 900 litres per kg of wheat, 3,500 litres per kg of digestible chicken flesh and a massive 100,000 litres for 1kg of beef.

A more conservative estimate comes from Beckett and Oltjen of the University of California's Department of Animal Science. In a study partly financed by the California Beef Council, they concluded that wheat production requires 120 litres per kg and beef 3,700 litres per kg

Whichever figures you chose to trust, it is clear that a diet based on animal products is wasteful in the extreme.

UNICEF investigations suggest that approximately 1.1 billion people have no access to safe water.

SPIRITUAL

Central to the beliefs of many of those following an animal-free lifestyle is the conviction of harmlessness or reverence for life, embodied in the spirit of *ahimsa*, the Sanskrit word for non-killing and non-injury championed by Mahatma Ghandi.

Some animal-free shoppers are allied to a particular church such as the pacifist Society of Friends (Quakers) or Seventh Day Adventists, to a particular faith such as Buddhism, Jainism or Christianity or empathise with Paganism (Wicca or Druidry, for example) or Humanism.

Many consider that their animal-free lifestyle, its practical application and sense of inner peace, provide for most of their spiritual needs and there is a tendency towards vegetarianism and veganism within the modern spiritual/personal growth movements.

Liberation of animals from human exploitation, health benefits for humans, resource use, and ecological and spiritual considerations, are five very good reasons for adopting an animal-free lifestyle. With the *Animal Free Shopper* in your pocket, it's never been easier or more fun to GO VEGAN!

Veganstore
It's Faux Real – go on...
treat your feet!
with our fabulous leather free Vegan shoes
ones for the ladees, brash brogues, trendy trainer sandals,
turbo sneakers, kitten heels to make you squeal, fill your boots!
& Vegan Sweeties!
Honey-free Honeycomb, delicious Jelly free Jelly-beans, Jelly free tots, Rhubarb and Custard, gelatine-free Marshmallow and many more...
Over 900 cruelty free vegan products
from faux leather to fanciful food – visit us at
www.veganstore.co.uk
telephone: 01273 302979

VEGGIES

Catering Campaign (Nottingham)

Dedicated Vegan Catering for over 20 years.

- Catering for weddings, meetings, rallies, festivals and gatherings nationwide, including formal and informal buffets.
- Official Caterers to the Social Justice Movement
- Contact Andrew, Patrick or Ronny at Veggies, 245 Gladstone Street, Nottingham NG7 6HX
- Phone number 0845 458 9595 . email veggies@veggies.org.uk
- Visit our vast and extensive website at http://www.veggies.org.uk"
- Freezer supplies to the trade, via Lembas Wholefood Wholesalers : 0845 458 1585

The work of Veggies supports many campaigns and projects, including The Sumac Centre, Nottingham's exclusively vegan cafe, bar, social club and resource centre, where we are based. Volunteer help always welcome.

HEALTHY EATING FOR VEGANS

Sandra Hood BSc(Hons) SRD

One of the most important ways to influence our health is through our diet and as vegans, we often feel that we have to prove that we can be healthy and that we are getting enough of this or that particular nutrient. However, it is all too easy to become obsessed with meeting the nutritional requirements of the general population and forget to look at the other side of the coin and how protective a vegan diet can be.

The mainstay of a healthy diet is plenty of unrefined carbohydrates, such as cereals, pulses and whole grains, plus the important vitamins, minerals and phytochemicals found in fruits and vegetables, and the essential fatty acids found in nuts, seeds and oils. This healthy eating diet has been shown not only to prevent illness but also to treat it. Compared with omnivores, vegetarians have been shown to be at lower risk for conditions such as constipation, diverticular disease, gallstones and appendicitis. Vegan diets have also been used to treat diseases such as angina, diabetes, high blood pressure, rheumatoid arthritis and kidney disease.

In recent years there has been a lot of emphasis on vegans adopting a more raw food oriented or fruitarian diet, and no doubt we should all be including more raw foods in our diet. However, it can also be very bulky and unsuitable for infants and children. Cooking may damage some plant nutrients, but in many cases it alters the structure of nutrients in a way that may actually increase the availability of phytochemicals, resulting in significant health effects. For instance, lycopene (a carotenoid and precursor of vitamin A) is far better absorbed from cooked tomatoes than from raw ones. To maximise benefit from the plant nutrients in the diet, therefore, it is best to include a variety of both raw and cooked foods.

The following paragraphs give a brief outline of nutrients that may be of particular interest to vegans. There are very few rules about what you should or should not eat, but it is important to ensure a reliable source of vitamin B12, and if sun exposure is limited vitamin D supplements or fortified foods should be used.

Aim to eat a variety of whole foods, including the following food groups on a daily basis:

- **Fruits**
- **Vegetables**
- **Nuts and seeds**
- **Cereals**
- **Pulses**

ENERGY

Carbohydrates

These are the main energy foods, and half your energy should come from carbohydrates. There are two types of carbohydrates: starchy foods and sugary foods. Try to choose mainly starchy foods such as whole grain bread, pasta, rice, potatoes and cereals. Vegans generally have a high fibre diet with less reliance on refined carbohydrates; in the refining process, essential nutrients are lost.

Fibre

This is the part of a plant that cannot be digested. All plant foods contain fibre. There are two categories of fibre, soluble and insoluble, and most plants contain a mixture of the two. Insoluble fibre adds bulk to stools and ensures that food passes quickly and easily through the intestinal tract. Soluble fibre, found in peas, beans, oats and lentils, has been shown to reduce blood cholesterol levels. Vegans have been shown to consume 40 to 50g of fibre per day compared with 30 to 40g per day for vegetarians and 10 to 20g per day for omnivores. Recommended minimum intakes are 18g per day and the World Health Organisation (WHO) recommends an upper limit of 54g per day. It has been suggested that intakes comparable with those of vegans would be beneficial for health.

It has been reported that excess fibre may reduce the absorption of certain minerals, but high fibre whole foods provide enough extra minerals to more than compensate for any losses incurred. When fibre does bind with minerals, they can be partly released during the fermentation of fibre by bacteria in the large bowel.

This sow will try to feed and mother her young for 28 days in a cage only inches bigger than her body.

Her piglets will be torn away, kept in filthy, concrete pens and given drugs daily until being killed at six months old.

This is normal, this is factory farming, this is animal abuse.

Viva! works to protect animals, people and the planet from greed and exploitation.

We do it through energetic campaigning, by exposing the sickening conditions in which farmed animals are kept and by encouraging people to become vegetarian or vegan.

Add your voice to ours and help *Viva!* throw open the cages.

Viva!

For a FREE *Go Vegan* pack, including our new merchandise and book catalogues, contact:

Viva!, 8 York Court, Wilder St, Bristol BS2 8QH
T: 0117 944 1000 E: info@viva.org.uk W: www.viva.org.uk

vinceremos
Organic Wines

VEGAN AND ORGANIC WINES

by mail order

Also juices, beers and ciders

Free list from

Vinceremos

74 Kirkgate, Leeds, LS2 7DJ

info@vinceremos.co.uk

www.vinceremos.co.uk

0800 652 2060

Fats

Fats provide vitamins and energy, are essential for the manufacture of hormones and are important for insulation and protection. Fat should provide approximately 30% of adult energy requirements while infants need a higher intake. Most people are confused about the type and quantity of fats. Whether a fat is solid or liquid at room temperature, it will contain the same amount of calories. The main constituents of all fats are fatty acids, which may be saturated, monounsaturated or polyunsaturated, depending on the number of double bonds between the carbon atoms in the molecule. As the number of double bonds increases, the fats become more unsaturated or oily. There are more than 40 fatty acids found in nature.

There is no physiological requirement for dietary fat, only for essential fatty acids. These are the polyunsaturated fats:

- Linoleic – sunflower, corn, safflower and soya oils
- Alpha-linolenic – linseed, walnut and rapeseed oils

Humans and other mammals lack the enzyme to synthesise them, so they are essential in the diet.

Saturated fats

Saturated fat has been linked with heart disease; it raises cholesterol levels in the blood, and the higher your cholesterol level the greater the risk of suffering a stroke or heart attack. Meat and saturated fat go hand in hand, and animal products are the greatest sources of saturated fat in the Western diet. Milk fat is more than 60% saturated fat, compared with 6 to 25% for plant fats, most being in the 10-15% range. The exceptions are tropical oils such as coconut and palm oil.

Monounsaturated fat

Studies have shown that monounsaturated fats (MUFAs) can reduce the risk of heart disease. Vegan dietary sources include olives and olive oil, rapeseed oil, nuts (such as almonds, cashews, hazelnuts, macadamias) and avocados. MUFAs should provide the main source of fat intake.

Polyunsaturated fat

The main dietary sources are vegetable oils, seeds, nuts, grains, legumes and other plant foods. Studies regarding their health effects are inconsistent, but when they replace saturated fats and trans fatty acids in the diet there is no doubt that they are beneficial. The two essential fatty acids are linoleic and alpha-linolenic acid. Linoleic acid is found in vegetable seeds and oils such as soya, corn, sunflower, safflower, walnuts and grains. Alpha-linolenic acid is found in linseed, rapeseed and walnuts. A high ratio of linoleic to alpha-linolenic acid inhibits the production of eicosapentaeonic acid (EPA) and docosahexaenoic acid (DHA), so it is important that vegans achieve a good balance of polyunsaturated fatty acids to ensure adequate levels of EPA and DHA.

Trans fatty acids (hydrogenated oils)

People believe that they are making healthier choices by changing from butter to margarine, but trans fatty acids produced in the manufacture of margarine have been shown to be as harmful as saturated fat. Therefore, choose margarines which do not contain hydrogenated oils and avoid processed foods such as crackers, chips, biscuits, pastries and crisps.

PROTEIN

Protein provides the building blocks for new tissue and is vital for the growth and repair of all cells. It can also be used for energy production, if needed, or stored as fat. Protein is made up of 22 amino acids, the building blocks of protein; 8 of these are essential amino acids because the human body cannot make them, but they are easily supplied by plants. Plant sources can provide adequate amounts of essential and non-essential amino acids. Good sources of protein include nuts, seeds, grains (wheat, oats, rice, barley, buckwheat, millet, pasta, bread) and pulses (peas, beans, lentils).

Many people erroneously believe that animal protein is necessary for human health and that plant protein is inferior. Omnivores tend to have protein intakes above recommendations while vegan intakes meet the recommendations. Combining amino acids is unnecessary as they are stored in protein pools which can be drawn upon as needed.

Summary

- Use whole grains in preference to refined grains.
- Ensure a good balance of polyunsaturated fatty acids.
- Monounsaturated fatty acids should provide the main source of fat intake.
- Avoid hydrogenated oils.

yaoh

ORGANIC HEMP PRODUCTS

HEMP SEED OIL BODYCARE

- ✓ Rich in Organic Hemp Seed Oil
- ✓ Free from Sodium Lauryl Sulphates, Parabens and Petroleums
- ✓ Vegan – not tested on Animals
- ✓ No unnecessary Chemical Additives or Preservatives
- ✓ Suitable for all Skin and Hair types

RAW FOOD HEMP BARS

- ✓ Vegan, Organic and Gluten-free
- ✓ Rich in Essential Fatty Acids
- ✓ Uncooked to preserve Full Nutritonal Status
- ✓ No added Sugar, Oats or Margarine

Also available:

250ml and 500ml Organic cold pressed Chinese Hemp Seed Oil – mild flavour

125gm packs dehulled Organic Hemp Seed
250gm packs Organic Hemp Seed

Available from your local independent health store or online from www.lemonburst.net or by mail order from Yaoh, PO Box 333, Bristol BS99 1NF.
A full list of ingredients for all Yaoh products is available on our website www.yaoh.co.uk

Vegan

yaoh
Tel. 0117 9239053
info@yaoh.co.uk
www.yaoh.co.uk

Bunny Hugger
VEGAN
Loved & used by VIVA!
Vegan
Registered with the Vegan Society
BUAV Approved
Approved by the Vegetarian Society
The world's best supermodels insist on using Red Star Natural Liquid Soaps!
Red Star
Tel: 01922 712691 • Email: redstar@gn.apc.org • www.redstarnaturalliquidsoaps.co.uk

VITAMINS

Vitamins are found in small quantities and are essential for normal body functioning. Fat soluble vitamins are A, D, E and K. Water soluble vitamins are B and C. With few exceptions, vitamins cannot be synthesised by the body and must be obtained from the diet. A vegan diet can provide all the vitamins necessary for good health. The following are of particular interest to vegans:

Vitamin C

Vitamin C is a powerful water soluble antioxidant, neutralising harmful reactions in the blood and the fluid inside the surrounding cells. Vegans and vegetarians are at a distinct advantage here and need to lead the way in the health revolution.

Vitamin D

Vitamin D3 is normally obtained from lanolin, which is derived from sheep's wool and not acceptable to vegans. However, most people get sufficient vitamin D through the action of sunlight on the skin. Spending time outside reduces your need for foods fortified with vitamin D. When sun exposure is limited, a vitamin D supplement may be necessary. Vitamin D promotes the absorption of calcium and is essential for bones and teeth. Foods fortified with a vegan source of vitamin D (vitamin D2, ergocalciferol) include margarine, fortified cereals and some fortified non-dairy milks.

Vitamin B12

This vitamin is essential for the formation of red blood cells and a healthy nervous system. Some plant foods may contain vitamin B12 on their surface from soil residues, but this is not a reliable source. Much of the vitamin B12 present in spirulina, sea vegetables, tempeh and miso has been shown to be an inactive form rather than the active vitamin. So if you are not taking foods fortified with vitamin B12, ensure that you take a supplement. The UK government recommends 1.5 micrograms per day as sufficient to reliably prevent clinical deficiency, but higher intakes are required to avoid elevated homocysteine and associated increased mortality. The Vegan Society therefore recommends that all vegans get at least 3 micrograms of B12 every day to maximise the health benefits of their diet. (For further details, see www.vegansociety.com or contact The Vegan Society for a B12 information sheet.)

GuideMeGreen.com

GuideMeGreen is a growing resource for the ethically and environmentally conscious shopper that cares about what they eat and what they buy!

The GuideMeGreen directory has listings in all of the following areas:

* vegan * organic * fair trade *
* special diet * ethical goods *
* environmentally friendly *

Summary

- Ensure regular exposure to sunlight for adequate vitamin D.
- Ensure a daily source of vitamin B12.

MINERALS

There are a number of minerals essential for health, but most are only needed in small amounts which come from a varied diet of whole grains, fruits, vegetables, nuts and seeds. The two main minerals needed in larger amounts which are of some interest to vegans are iron and calcium.

Calcium

Studies have found that vegan diets may be below current recommendations for calcium. Claims are commonly made that vegans require less calcium than omnivores, based on the lower acid production resulting from metabolism of plant proteins. This has not been resolved. Although oxalates, phytates and fibre in plant foods decrease calcium availability, research shows that absorption of calcium from many plant foods is excellent. Calcium absorption from low oxalate vegetables such as broccoli and kale is better than for cow's milk while absorption from beans,

Vegan SOCIETY

people ■ animals ■ environment

WWW.VEGANSOCIETY.COM/SHOP
Tel. 01424 448832

Browse through pages of great vegan products including a comprehensive range of animal-free cookbooks, nutrition guides and the complete selection of Vegan Society publications and leaflets

Includes:

- **Travel** ■ **Music**
- **Clothing** ■ **Soaps**
- **Books** ■ **Gifts** ■ **Special Offer packs**
- **Candles and much, much more**

All a vegan could wish for....

nuts and seeds is lower. Good vegan sources of calcium include dark green leafy vegetables such as spring greens and kale, calcium-set tofu, baked beans and fortified foods.

Iron

Vegan diets are higher in total iron content than omnivorous diets, but iron stores are lower in vegans because the iron from plant foods, known as non-haem iron, is less well absorbed than the haem iron found in meat. However, iron deficiency anaemia is no more common in vegans than in omnivores. Vitamin C and other organic acids commonly found in vegetables strongly enhance the absorption of non-haem iron. Vitamin C intakes of vegans are frequently high and this, in conjunction with generous levels of dietary iron, may compensate for the lower bioavailability of non-haem iron. Good iron sources include whole or enriched grains and grain products, iron-fortified cereals, legumes, green leafy vegetables and dried fruits.

Zinc

Diets of vegans and non-vegans often contain similar amounts of zinc. However, zinc from plant foods is less well absorbed as some plant foods contain phytate which interferes with zinc absorption. However, no reports of zinc deficiency in vegans have been found. Zinc is an essential component of a number of enzyme systems within the body and is widely distributed in plant foods. Good sources include nuts, seeds, beans and cereals.

Iodine

Iodine is needed by the thyroid gland to produce the thyroid hormone which regulates physical and mental development, including growth, reproduction and other essential functions. Iodine deficiency is rare in the UK. The main source of iodine in the UK is cow's milk, due to iodine supplemented cattle feed and the contamination of milk from teat dips containing iodophors as sterilising agents. Sea foods are rich sources of iodine, with dried seaweed being a popular choice for vegans. Two kelp tablets (with a declared iodine content between 150 and 250 micrograms) per week will ensure sufficient iodine; more than this is not desirable.

Summary

- Calcium absorption from low oxalate vegetables such as broccoli and kale is good.
- Vitamin C aids iron absorption.
- Good sources of zinc are nuts, seeds, beans and cereals.
- Seaweed is rich in iodine.

PHYTOCHEMICALS

It has been known for a long time that fruits and vegetables, grains, seeds, nuts and pulses are good for you, being rich in vitamins, minerals and fibre, but in the past few years there has also been interest in the phytochemicals, which have been shown to have many health benefits.

Some phytochemicals are strong antioxidants which mop up free radicals (active harmful molecules circulating in the body).

A special group of phytochemicals are the plant oestrogens, which block the deleterious action of the potent form of oestrogen either by competing with it for receptor sites or by reducing production of the potent form while increasing production of the less potent form, possibly reducing the risk of osteoporosis and certain types of hormone-dependent cancers. Concerns have been raised regarding the potential adverse effects of phytoestrogens in soya infant formulas, and the best food for babies is certainly breast milk. Nevertheless, where breast feeding is not possible there is a role for soya infant formulas, which have been used for many years without any reports of adverse effects other than occasional allergy. For children and adults, soya should be regarded as another healthy food to be added to the diet in moderation.

Another important group are the plant sterols - a type of fat which has been shown to protect against heart disease. There are no dietary recommendations for sterols, but plant sterols have been shown to be beneficial in lowering cholesterol; high levels of cholesterol in the blood can cause heart disease. The average Western diet contains 180 to 400mg plant sterols per day while the vegan diet contains 600 to 800mg per day.

Useful references

Davis B, Melina V (2000) *Becoming Vegan: the complete guide to adopting a healthy plant-based diet,* Book Publishing Co. Summertown.
Key TJ, Davey GK, Appleby PN (2001) *Health benefits of a vegetarian diet,* Proc Nutr Soc 58 271-275.
Walsh S (2003) *Plant Based Nutrition and Health*, The Vegan Society.

Sandra Hood is a State Registered Dietitian and author of The Vegan Society's Raising your Vegan Infant - With Confidence. *For more information, or to order your copy, go to www.vegansociety.com/shop or call 01424 427 393.*

FOOD

BISCUITS

ASHBOURNE BISCUITS LTD ⃠
Organic Biscuits: Choc Chip, Ginger, Lemon, Oat & Raisin

BARKAT
Ice Cream Cones

BLUE LOTUS PRODUCTS LTD ☺™
Flapjack

BRAKE BROS
Bourbon Creams; Shortcake Biscuits

CLIVE'S
Flapjacks: Almond & Apple, Chocolate Chip, Original, Sultana & Apple

CRAWFORD'S ⃠
Bourbon Creams; Finger Nice; Jam Rings; Marie; Morning Coffee; Nice 250g; Pink Wafer; Shortcake; Thin Arrowroot

DOVES FARM FOODS LTD ⃠™
Fairtrade: **Organic Apple & Sultana Flapjack**; *Organic:* **Apple & Sultana Flapjack**, **Apple & Sultana Flapjack - Individual Bars**, **Chocolate Chip Cookies**, **Digestive Biscuit 200g**, **Digestives 400g**, **Fruity Oat Biscuits**, **Ginger Jazz**, **Lemon Zest Cookies**, **Nice & Nutty Cookies**, **Seven Secrets**

ESSENTIAL TRADING CO-OPERATIVE LTD ™❶⃠✂
Organic Flapjacks: **Almond Fruit**, **Chocolate Chip + Brazil Nut**, **Date + Apricot**, **Vine Fruit**

FIRST QUALITY FOODS ⃠
Ma Baker Giant Bar: Almond, Apple, Apricot, Banana, Cherry, Peanut, Sesame, Walnut; *Ma Baker Organic Bar:* Apple, Apricot

FOX'S BISCUITS ⃠
Biscuits & Herbs; Ginger Crinkles; Ginger Snaps

GLUTANO
Apricot; Chocolate Chip; Chocolate Cream Filled Wafers; Ginger Cookie; Hazelnut Cookies; Ice Cream Cones; Short Cake Ring; Tarteletts; Tea; Wafers; Wizards

GRANOVITA UK LTD ☺⃠☼✂
Castus Bar: Date & Apricot, Raisin; *Organic Flapjacks:* Cranberry, Ginger, Pumpkin, Raisin Apple & Cinnamon, Raisin & Linseed, Traditional Oat

MCVITIE'S ⃠
am Granola Bars - Almond & Raisin & Cranberry; Butter Puffs; Digestive - Lemon & Ginger; Fruit Shortcake; Ginger Nuts; Light Digestive; Lincoln; *Hob Nobs:* Caramel & Hazelnut, Original

ORGRAN ⃠
Cookies: Apricot & Coconut, Sultana & Cinnamon

PANTRI NOLWENN ⃠❶✂☼
Cookie: Almond Roche, Macarwn, Pate

d'Abricots, Pate de Dattes, Pate de Figues, Picen Geirch/Oat Lace Cookie, Teisennan Cri Ffrengig/Walnut Short Bread

R J FOODS LIMITED ☺ ™⃠
Flapjacks: **98% Fat-Free Cherry & Sultana**, **98% Fat-Free Fruit**, **Apple & Apricot**, **Cherry & Coconut**, **Cherry & Sultana**, **Date & Walnut**, **Fig**, **Fruit Bar**, **Mincemeat Bar**, **Muesli**, **Plain**, **Raspberry**, **Rum & Raisin**

THE VILLAGE BAKERY MELMERBY LTD ⃠
Gluten Free Ginger Biscuits - Wheat & Dairy Free; Gluten Free Savoury Biscuits - Wheat & Dairy Free; Savoury Seed Biscuits

TRUFREE (NUTRICIA) ™⃠
Bourbon Biscuits; **Custard Creams**; **Digestive Biscuits**; Ginger Snaps; Nobbles

ZEDZ FOODS ⃠ ✓
Date & Ginger Flapjack

BREADS, ROLLS, PIZZA BASES ETC

BARKAT
Multigrain Bread; *Rice Bread:* Brown, Cinnamon & Raisin, Flax Seed, White; *Rice Pizza Crust:* Brown, White

BELLS OF LAZONBY LTD ⃠
Crusty Cob; Crusty Tin Bread; Farmhouse Bread; Granary Bread; Wholemeal Bread

BLUE LOTUS PRODUCTS LTD ☺ ™
Sourdough Bread

BRAKE BROS
10" Organic Sandwich; 11" Small; 22" Large; 22" Multi Seed; 5" White Floured Baps; 6" Flour Tortilla; 7" Wholemeal Hoagies; 7.5" Sandwich - Petit Pains - Long; 9" Vienna Sandwich Baton; Bakers Basket; Ciabatta Loaves; Ciabatta Selection; English Muffins; Organic White Loaf; Oval Buns; Pitta Bread; Plain Bagels; Pre-Cut Teacakes; Provencette Cracked Black Pepper Panini; *Baguettes:* 10" Harvester, 10" Sandwich, 16", 7.5" Onion Sandwich, 7.5" Tomato Sandwich, Provencette Herb Half; *Medium Sliced Loaf:* White, Wholemeal; *Mini Petit Pains:* Malted Wheat, White; *Petit Pains:* Framhouse Brown, Malted Wheat, White; *Pizza Crust:* Deep Pan 9" 12" 14", Stone Baked w Tomato Sauce 10", Traditional - 9" 12"; *Rolls:* 5" Hot Dog, 7.5" Jumbo Torpedo, Ciabatta, Ciabatta Sandwich, Foccacia, Green Olive Ciabatta Sandwich, Mini Selection, Pain au Levain, Ploughmans Crusty French White, Rye Levain, White Batch; *Sesame Seed Burger Buns:* 4", 5"; *Wraps:* Spinach, Tomato

BUXTON FOODS ⃠
Organic & Wheat-free Bread w Seed Topping: Poppy, Rolled Oat, Sunflower

COOPLANDS LTD ⃠
Breads: All

DEES CARIBBEAN IMPORTS ™
HTB Jamaican Spiced Bun

DISCOVERY FOODS
Tortillas: Bakery, Garlic & Coriander, Gluten Free Corn, Plain Wheatflour

GLUTANO
Bread & Cake Mix; High Fibre Bread Mix; *Organic Rice Bread:* Brown, Flax Seed, White; *Organic, Yeastfree Bread:* Buckwheat, Multi Grain, Sesame; *Par Baked:* Baguettes, Rolls; *Sliced Bead:* White; *Sliced Bread:* Wholemeal

GR WRIGHT & SONS LTD ☺⃠

Bread Mixes: Malty, Mixed Grain, Organic Stoneground Wholemeal, Premium White, Sunflower, Wholemeal

HERON QUALITY FOODS LTD ⃠
Gluten-free Organic Mixes: Bread & Cake, Wheat-Free Bread

HOVIS
Best of Both; Best of Health; Best with Less; Big & Bouncy; Classic Cut; Country Grain; Country Sandwich; Crusty Brown; Crusty White; Granary; Hearty Wholemeal; Heavenly Wholemeal; Square Cut; Wheatgerm; White; White Farmhouse; White Granary; Wholemeal Farmhouse; *Organic:* Brown Seeded Rolls, White Rolls, Wholemeal

MOTHERS PRIDE
Brown; Burger Buns; Danish; Finger Rolls; Large White Baps; Scottish Pan; Scottish Plain; Stays Fresh Longer; White; White Baps; White Split Rolls; *Muffins:* White, Wholemeal

NIMBLE
Amazing Grain; Carbs so Low; White; Wholemeal

ORGRAN ⃠
Bread Mix; Gourmet Pesto Bread Mix; Pizza & Pastry Mix

PANTRI NOLWENN ⃠❶ ✄ ☼
Bread: Afalau Ffogsen Cardamom/Apple Fig Cardamom, Banette aux Noix, Bara Olifau/Olive Bread, Bara Pupur/Pepper Bread, Bara Resin/Raisin Bread, Bricyllen a Almon/Apricot Almond, Cnau Cyll a Syltanas/Hazelnut Sultana, Datys-Cnau Ffrengig/Date Walnut, Rhyg Gwledig/Rustic Rye, Rhyg Winwns/Onion Rye, Rhyg/Rye, Spelta, Tomatos Heulsych/Sundried Tomato

PATAKS FOODS LTD ⃠
Chapattis

PAUL'S TOFU ™☺⃠ ☼
Breads: **Brown Rice Bread**, **Foccacia**, **Four Seed**, **Fruit Rye**, **Gluten Free Number One Sourdough**, **Gluten Free Number Three Sourdough**, **Gluten Free Number Two Sourdough**, **La Tabatiere**, **Light Rye**, **Melton Loaf**, **Olive Bread**, **Organic**

Herb Bread, **Organic Individual Baguette**, **Organic Melton Loaf**, **Organic Rolls**, **Organic Sesame Rolls**, **Organic Tea Cakes**, **Organic Unbleached White**, **Organic Yeast Free Wheat Free Rye Bread**, **Organic Yeasted Bread**, **Organic Yeasted Malthouse**, **Organic Yeasted Mixed Seed**, **Organic Yeasted Spelt Bread**, **Organic Yeasted Stoneground Wholemeal**, **Pain de Campagne**, **Pane Basilicum**, **Rye & Sweetcorn Sourdough**, **Sechskorn**, **Sourdough 4 Seed Bread**, **Sourdough Bread Yeast Free**, **Sourdough Rice**, **Spelt Sourdough**, **Sprouted Kamut Wheat Sourdough**, **Tempeh**, **Tomato Bread**, **Tsampa Sourdough**, **Unbleached White Bread**, **White Rolls**

STAMP COLLECTION ⃠
Wheat-free, Organic Sliced Bread: New York Deli, New York Deli w Caraway; *Wheat-free, Organic w Extra Virgin Olive Oil:* Panini

THE VILLAGE BAKERY MELMERBY LTD ⃠
Baltic Bread; Borodinski Bread; Brazil Nut & Linseed Bread; Campagne; Gluten Free Bread; Hadrian; Pane Toscano; Rossisky Bread; Sunflower Bread; Ten Seed Bread; Wholemeal Bread

TRUFREE (NUTRICIA) ™⃠
Bread Mix; **Part Baked White Bread**; **Sliced White Bread**

WARBURTONS ⃠
Fruit Loaf: Summer, w Orange, Winter; *Morning Goods:* 4 & 12 Fruity Teacakes, 4 Oven Bottom Muffins, 6 Crumpets, 6 Round Potato Cakes, Muffin Toast; *Raisin Loaf:* w Cinnamon; *Rolls:* 2 Wholemeal Sandwich Sub, 3 Seeded Sandwich, 4 & 12 Large Sandwich, 4/6/12 Sandwich, 6 Batched Sandwich, 6 Wholemeal; *Weight Watchers Danish Bread:* Brown 400g, Malted 400g, White 400g; *Weight Watchers Rolls:* 2 Malted, 2 White; *White Bread:* Batch 800g, Crusty 400g, Danish 400g, Good Health 400g, Medium 400g & 800g, Organic 400g, Soft Farmhouse 400g & 800g, Super Toastie 800g, Toastie 400g & 800g; *Wholemeal Bread:* Good Health 400g & 800g, Medium 400g & 800g, Organic 400g, Seeded Batch 400g & 800g, Stoneground 800g, Tasty 800g

BREAKFAST FOODS

BIOFORCE
Muesli

BRAKE BROS
Brakes Oatflakes

DOVES FARM FOODS LTD ⃠™
Organic Bio Bran; Organic Swiss Style Muesli; *Organic:* **Bio-Biz Breakfast Biscuits**, **Cornflakes**; *Organic Easy Cereal:* **Chewy Fruity Corn Flake Cakes - Individual Bars**; *Organic Easy Cereal Bar Boxes of 5:* **Chewy Fruity**

Corn Flake Cakes; *Organic Tasty Cereal:* **Chewy Rice Pop & Chocolate Cakes**, **Chewy Rice Pop & Chocolate Cakes - Individual Bars**

ESSENTIAL BRAND ™❶⊘♞✂
Muesli (Organic & Conventional): **Cereal Base**, **Date + Apricot**, **Deluxe**, **Fine Organic**, **Fruit + Nut**, **Harvest**, **Organic**, **Organic Apple + Cinnamon Cereal**, **Organic Cereal Base**, **Organic Date + Apricot**, **Organic Deluxe**, **Organic Fruit Crunch**, **Organic Strawberry + Cashew Crisp**, **Sultana Crunch**, **Sunflower**, **Super Hi-fibre**, **Tropical**

FRESH FOODS CO LTD ⊘☼
Cornflakes; Maple Frosted Flakes; Swiss Style Muesli

GLUTANO
Cornflakes; Swiss Style Muesli; *Organic:* Breakfast Pops, Cornflakes, Muesli

GRANOVITA UK LTD ☺⊘☼♞✂
Classic Flakes

HEALTHY AND ESSENTIAL ™
Omega Porridge

HERON QUALITY FOODS LTD ⊘♞
Gluten-free Muesli; *Gluten-free Organic Mixes:* Porridge

JORDAN (CEREALS) LTD ⊘
Country Crisp: Absolutely Apricot, Four Nut Combo, Real Raspberry, Real Strawberry, Wild About Berries; *Crunchy:* Luxury Maple & Pecan, Luxury Summer Fruits, Organic; *Flakes & Clusters:* Maple Pecan, Organic Crisp Maple & Pecan; *Muesli:* Natural, Organic, Special, Special Fruit

KELLOGGS ⊘
Apricot Bites; Just Right; Luxury Muesli; Raisin Wheats; *Coco Pops:* Crunchers, Hot Oat Cereal, Original; *Corn Flakes:* Banana Crunch, Original; *Frosties:* Choco, Original; *Fruit 'n Fibre:* Hot Oat Cereal, Original; *Rice Krispies:* Muddles, Original

LITTLE SALKELD MILL ☺⊘☼
Muesli Base; Watermill Muesli

MARIGOLD HEALTH FOODS ❶⊘
Organic Sultana Crunch; Super Muesli

NESTLÈ
Force; *Breakfast Cereals:* Cheerios, Cinnamon Grahams, Nesquik, Shredded Wheat, Shredded Wheat Bitesize, Shredded Wheat Fruitful

ORGRAN ⊘
Breakfast Cereals: Muesli Gluten Free, Rice Porridge

SHEPHERDBOY ™⊘♞
Organic Muesli w Hempseed 500g

SPOFF (SCOTLAND) LTD ™
Highland Muesli: **Almond & Marigold Petal**, **Apricot & Elderflower**, **Blueberry & Cornflower Petal**, **Chocolate & Peppermint**, **Cranberry**

& Sweet Cicely, Date Walnut & Sunflower Seed, Gluten Free Date Walnut & Sunflower Seed, Gluten Free Pineapple & Ginger, Hazelnut & Lemon Verbena, Organic Coconut & Hemp Seed, Organic Wheat Free Cashew Nut & Pumpkin Seed, Pineapple & Ginger, Wheat Free Apricot & Elderflower

SUMA WHOLEFOODS ⃠ ™ ◉ ❶ ✂ 1985
Branflakes; Bransticks; *Crunch:* Cranberry; *Muesli:* Base, Gluten Free, Luxury Tropical, Roast Hazelnut, Super; *Organic Muesli:* Base, De Luxe, Standard

TROPICAL WHOLEFOODS
Mixes - Muesli: Tropical 5 Fruit Salad, Tropical Fruit Mix

WEETABIX LTD ⃠
Alpen: Crunchy Bran, Wheat Flakes; *Nature's Own Organic:* Malt Wheat Squares; *Ready Brek:* Original; *Weetabix:* Mini Crunch Fruit & Nut, Organic, Original

YORKSHIRE HEMP LTD ™
Fruit Hemp Muesli; **Nut Hemp Muesli**

'BURGERS', 'SAUSAGES', 'MEAT' SLICES ETC

AMBROSIAN VEGETARIAN FOODS ™☺ ⃠ ❶ ☼
Organic Burgers: **Chilli Bean**, **Savoury**, **Sesame & Sunflower Seed Vegetable**; *Organic Dry Mixes:* **Organic Savoury Burger Mix**, **Sesame & Sunflower Seed Vegetable**, **Sosage**; *Organic Sosages:* **Plain**, **Savoury Herb**, **Tomato & Garlic**

BRAKE BROS
Crispy Crumbed Vegetable Quarter Pounder; Nut Cutlettes; Vegebanger; *Burger:* Crispy Crumbed Vegetable, Spicy Vegetarian

CAULDRON FOODS LTD ⃠
Burgers: Chilli, Savoury, Spicy Bean

DIRECT FOODS ⃠
Dry Mixes: Beef Style Mince, Burgamix, Chicken-Style Savoury Bake, Sosmix, Sosmix Country Herb

DRAGONFLY FOODS ⃠ ☼
Original Soysage (Soya-Based Sausages); *Organic Beany Savoury (Soya-Based Burger):* Baked, Curry, Fennel, Mushroom, Natural, Nut, Olive, Smoky, Spicy, Tomato, Vegetable; *Organic Beany Sweet (Soya-Based Burger):* Apple, Apricot, Chocolate, Date, Fig, Fruity

FRY'S ☺❶⊘
Special Vegetarian Frozen Foods: Braai (BBQ) Sausages, Cutlets, Hot Dogs, Nuggets, Polony Slicing Sausage, Schnitzels, Spiced Burgers, Traditional Burgers, Traditional Sausages

GRANOSE ⊘
Vegetarian Sausages

GRANOVITA UK LTD ☺ ⊘☼ ✂
Vitamix: Sausage

HALDANE FOODS LTD ⊘
Organic Dry Mixes: Burgamix, Sosmix, Soya Mince

HOLLAND AND BARRETT RETAIL LTD
Meat Free Linc Sausage

JUST WHOLEFOODS ☺ ⊘
Mixes: Banger, Burger

LIFE FOOD GMBH - TAIFUN-TOFUPRODUKTE ☺ ⊘☼
Tofu Green-Spelt Hazelnut Cutlet; Tofu-Spelt Cutlet; *Tofu Rice Cutlets:* Corn-Pepper; *Tofu Sausages:* Grill, Herb, Party, Sombreros, Wiener

LINDA MCCARTNEY PRODUCTS ⊘™
Sausage: Original, Sundried Tomato

NATUREMADE OASIS ⊘ ✂☼
Oasis: Tofuburgers

PAUL'S TOFU ™☺⊘ ☼
Savouries: **Five Grain Tofu & Herb Burgers**, **Five Grain Tofu & Nut Burgers**, **Ganmodoki Tofu Mock Goose**, **Organic Five Grain Tofu Bengal Burger**, **Organic Five Grain Tofu Mexican Chilli Burger**

REALEAT ⊘
Fishless Fish Cake; Herb & Vegetable VegeBurger (Dry Mix); VegeMince; *VegeBangers:* Herb (Dry Mix), Meaty Style (Frozen), Spicy (Dry Mix)

REDWOOD WHOLEFOOD COMPANY ❶⊘☺ ™
Bio Curry Wurst; **Fishless Steaks**; **Organic Coated Nuggets**; **Organic Coated Schnitzels**; **Organic Frankfurter Sausage**; **Organic Gyros Sausage**; **Organic Merguez Sausage**; **Scampi**; **Tuna**; **Vegetarian Breaded Fish-Style Fingers**; *Cheatin' Bites:* **Chicken Style**, **Chicken Style Barbeque**, **Chicken Style Tikka**, **Chicken w 5-spice**; *Cheatin' Roasts:* **Beef**, **Celebration**, **Turkey**; *Cheatin' Slices:* **Beef**, **Chicken**, **Garlic Sausage**, **Ham**, **Pepperoni**, **Sage & Onion**, **Turkey**, **Wafer Thin Chicken**, **Wafer Thin Ham**, **Wafer Thin Turkey**; *Organic:* **Frankfurter Style Sausages**, **Lincolnshire Style Sausages**, **Vegetarian Rashers**; *Rashers:* **Streaky-Style**, **Tempeh**; *Vegi-Deli:* **Boston Baked Bean Style**, **Oregano & Basil Sausages**, **Provencal Style**, **Ready to Eat Lincolnshire Sausage**, **Sage & Marjoram Sausages (Ready to Eat)**, **Spicy Chilli Style**, **Spicy Thai Style**, **Thai Fish Style Cakes**

SUMA WHOLEFOODS ⃠™👁❶✂1985
Burger Mix; Sausage Mix; *Pre-Packs:* **TVP Chunks**, **TVP Flavoured Chunks**, **TVP Flavoured Mince**, **TVP Mince**

TOFURKY ™
Beer Brats; **Deli Slices**; **Jurky**; **Kielbasa**; **Roast**; **Sweet Italian Sausage**

TURTLE ISLAND FOODS ™
SuperBurgers

VEGANSTORE.CO.UK ™☺⃠❶
Dixie: Beef Not Strips, Carvers Roasted Mock Meats, Chicken Not Breasts, Chicken Not Nuggets, Chicken Not Strips, Lasagne Complete Kit, Primo Pizza Mix Pepperoni Not; *Harvest:* Seitan Quick Mix, Veggie Ribs

VEGETARIANS CHOICE ™☺❶⃠
Vegetable Protein: **Burgers**, **Sausage Mix (400g tube)**, **Sausages**

VEGGIEMASTER ™
Vegan: **Chicken-free Tender Chunks**, **Fish-free Steak**, **Hot Dog**, **Nuggets**, **Poultry-free Breast**

VEGGIES CATERING CAMPAIGN ™☺❶⃠
Burger Mix: **Hemp-Seed**, **Veggies**; *Burgers:* **Chilli**, **Hemp**, **Veggies**; *Sosage Mix:* **Veggies**; *Sosages:* **Savory**, **Tomato**, **Veggies**

WICKEN FEN ⃠
Lime Coriander & Garlic Fillets; Meaty Style Burger; Mini Nuggets; *Sausages:* Country Herb, Crumbed Cumberland Style, Cumberland Style Meaty, Mediterranean Roasted Vegetable, Mushroom & Tarragon, Seasonal (Thai Spinach), Tasty Mexicana, Tomato & Garlic

ZEDZ FOODS ⃠
Burgers: Herb & Aubergine, Sage & Onion, Tofu & Ginger

CAKES & CAKE MIXES

AROMAFOODS ™☺✂

Carrot & Orange Cake; **Fabulush Bread Pudding**

BELLS OF LAZONBY LTD ⃠
Cherry Shortbread; Currant Slice; Raspberry Crumble

BLUE LOTUS PRODUCTS LTD ™☺
Date & Pecan Cake; **Millet Munchie Slice**; **Organic Stem Ginger Cake**; *Gluten Free:* **Organic Cherry Cake**, **Organic Chocolate Chip Cake**, **Organic Fruit Cake**, **Organic Stem Ginger Cake**; *Vegan:* **Banana & Pecan Tofu Cheesecake**, **Chocolate Cake**, **Date Slice**, **Passion Cake**, **Passion Loaf**, **Pear & Nut Cake**

BRAKE BROS
Iced Finger Bun; Mini Baked Apple Pies

MOTHERS PRIDE
Crumpets; Currant Buns; Derby Scones; Teacakes; *Pancakes:* Scotch, Syrup & Sultana

NATUREMADE OASIS ⊘ ✂ ☼
Ploughshares: Fridge Cakes

OK FOODS LTD ⊘
Fruit Fingers: Apricot & Cinnamon, Wild Blueberry

ORGRAN ⊘
Gluten-free Pancake Mixes: Apple & Cinnamon, Buckwheat

PANTRI NOLWENN ⊘❶ ✂ ☼
Cake: Apricot-Cognac-Chocolate, Bara Banana/Banana Bread, Bara Brith, Fruit, Fruit Cake Cognac, Teisen Moron/Carrot

PATISSERIE ORGANIC ™
Banana Pecan 'Cheesecake'; **Chocolate Cake**; **Passion Cake/Loaf**; **Pear & Nut Cake/Loaf**

PAUL'S TOFU ™☺⊘ ☼
Cakes: **Apple Strudel**, **Fruit Pie w Kuzu**

STILETTO FOODS ⊘
Mrs Crimble's: Dutch Apple Cake, Dutch Fruit Loaf, Stem Ginger Cake

THE VILLAGE BAKERY MELMERBY LTD ⊘
4 Fruit Bars; 4 Nut Bars; 4 Seed Bars; Apricot Slices; Date Slices; Gluten Free Fruit Nut & Seed Bars - Wheat & Dairy Free

TRUFREE (NUTRICIA) ™⊘
Cake Mix

VEGANSTORE.CO.UK ™☺⊘❶
Dixie: Brownie Mix, Donut Mix, No Bake Cheesecake, Sticky Bun Mix

ZEDZ FOODS ⊘
Rich Fruit Cake Slices; Spiced Apple Mirabel Sweet Pasty; *Flapjacks:* Date & Ginger; *Muffins:* Apple & Cinnamon; *Sweet Muffins:* Apricot & Ginger, Banana, Banana Coconut & Date, Carrot & Orange, Carrot & Orange - Sugar-free, Carrot & Raisin, Carrot & Raisin - Sugar-free, Cherry & Coconut, Chocolate, Chocolate & Orange, Coffee & Walnut, Poppy Seed & Lemon

'CHEESE' & CHEESE SPREADS

FLORENTINO ™⊘
Parmazano

REDWOOD WHOLEFOOD COMPANY ❶⊘☺ ™
Cheezly: **Cream Style - Garlic & Herb Flavour**, **Cream Style - Original**, **Cream Style - Sour Cream & Chive Flavour**, **Feta Style**, **Garlic & Herb Flavoured**, **Mature Cheddar Style**, **Mature Cheddar Style w Cranberries**, **Nacho Style**, **Smokey Style w Added**

Bacon Style Pieces; *Cheezly Melting:* **Cheddar Blocks**, **Cheddar Slices**, **Edam Blocks**, **Gouda Blocks**, **Mozzarella Blocks**, **Mozzarella Slices**

SCHEESE ™☺
Blue Flavour; **Cheddar Style**; **Cheddar w Chives**; **Cheshire Style**; **Edam Style**; **Emmental Flavour**; **Gouda Style**; **Hicory Smoked Style**; **Mozzarella Style**

TOFUTTI ⃠☺ ❶ ✂
Soul Supreme; *Creamy Smooth Slices:* Cheddar, Mozzarella; *Soft Cheese:* Creamy Smooth Country Vegetable, French Onion, Garlic & Herb, Herb & Chives, Original

VEGANSTORE.CO.UK ™☺⃠❶
Roads End Chreese: Mozarella, Original

VEGERELLA ™⃠☺
Cheddar; **Italian**; **Mexican**

WICKEN FEN ⃠
Dairy Free Soft Cheese: Garlic + Herb (Organic), Natural (Organic)

CHOCOLATE

ANIMAL AID ☺❶⃠ ✂1976
Blackcurrant Creams; Coffee Cremes; Eggs; English Elderflower Creams; Marzipan Assortment; Mint Truffles; Orange Cremes; Organic Plain Chocolate Brazils; Pecan Parfait; Peppermint Fondant Cremes; Rose & Violet Creams; Stem Ginger; Triple Truffle Selection; Vegan Chocolate Box 175g; Vegan Chocolate Box 350g; Violet Cremes; *Booja Booja Truffles:* All

BENDICKS OF MAYFAIR
Bittermints

BRAKE BROS
Brakes Choc Mint Creams; Brakes Mint Crisp; Chocolate Special Shapes; Dark; Dark Bitter; Plain Belgian Chocolates; Plain Dark Bitter Calets

CHOCOLATE SOCIETY
New Chocolate Society Bars: 100%, Hot Chocolate Dark, Prune & Orange Dark

D & D CHOCOLATES ☺⃠
Dark Chocolate: Bar, Dinosaur Shapes, Flower Shapes, Peppermint Fondant Creams, Plain Chocolate Chips for Cooking/Eating, Praline Hearts

DIVINE (THE DAY CHOCOLATE COMPANY)
Darkly Divine (70% Cocoa Solids); *Divine Delights:* Apricot, Brazils, Mango

DR HADWEN TRUST ☺❶⃠
After Dinner Mint Cream Thins; Chocolate Brazils; Chocolate Covered Stem Ginger; Chocolate Mango Slices; Classic Gold Vegan Assortment; Coffee Crème Dream; Jaffa Orange Thins; Marzipan Truffles; Maya Gold Gift Box; Organic Champagne Truffles; Organic

Gourmet Chocolate Truffles Selection; Organic Hazelnut Crunch Rocher; Velvet Moments Luxury 525g Assortment; *Choc Bars:* Golden Coconut, Hazelnut Nougat, Organic Swiss-Made Dark; *Liqueurs:* Brandy, Grand Marnier

ELIZABETH SHAW LTD ⃠
Afterdinner Mints; Coffee Crisp; Mint Crisp; Orange Crisp; Twist Wrapped Mint Creams (Pick 'n' Mix)

GREEN & BLACKS ⃠ ☼
Organic Dark Chocolate Bars: 70%, Cherry, Espresso, Fairtrade Maya Gold, Ginger, Hazelnut & Currant, Mint; *Organic Dark Chocolate Pocket Pack:* Dark, Maya Gold; *Organic Dark Chocolate Squares:* Espresso, Mint

HUMDINGER LTD ™
Dairy Free Rice Crackle Bar; **Dairy Free Tangerine Bar**

JUNGLE CHOCOLATE ™☺☼⃠
w Brazil Nuts & Essence of Coffee; w Coconut & Raisin; w Macadamia Nuts; w Pineapple

LINDT & SPRUNGLI ⃠
Excellence: 85% Cocoa; *Excellence 100g bar:* 70% Cocoa; *Excellence Thins 125g carton:* 70% Cocoa

LYME REGIS FINE FOODS LTD ⃠
Marzipan Bar - Plain Chocolate Coated

MONTEZUMAS CHOCOLATES ™
Dark Buttons; **Marzipan Snails**; **Omacatl Dos**; **Omacatl Uno**; **The Big Boy - Kilo Bar**; **The Challenge**; **The Hot Boy - Kilo Bar**; **Tubby Teddy**; **Turtlely Nuts**; *Choco-Block:* **Date & Walnut**, **Orange Peel**, **Pecan & Raisin**, **Whole Brazil**; *Dainty Dollops:* **Bergamot**, **Crunchy Peppermint**, **Mandarin**; *Dark Bar:* **100g**, **48g**; *Dark Chocolate:* **Apricots**, **Brazils**, **Dates**, **Ginger**, **Lemon**, **Mango**, **Orange**, **Prunes**; *Emperor Bar:* **Chilli**, **Orange & Cardamom**; *Speciality Bar:* **Gourmet Gorilla**, **Orangutang**, **Spice it Up**

NESTLÈ
After Eights: Dark, Orange - GB Produced ONLY - check ingredients for butterfat

ORGANICA ⃠
Golden Coconut & Dark Chocolate Bar; Hazelnut Nougat & Dark Chocolate Bar

OSCAR ™⃠
Chocolate Coated: **Coconut Ice Bar**, **Date & Hazelnut Bar**, **Peanut & Raisin Bar**

PLAMIL FOODS LTD ™☺❶⃠
Confections: **Martello (Dairy Milk Chocolate Alternative)**; *Confections - Chocolate w Soya:* Hazelnut, Mint, Orange, **Plain**; *Organic Confections:* **Organic Cayenne Chocolate (70% Cocoa)**, **Organic Chocolate**, **Organic Chocolate Drops**, **Organic Dark Chocolate 87% Cocoa**, **Organic**

Expressions, **Organic Ginger Chocolate**, **Organic Mint Chocolate**, **Organic Orange Chocolate**, Organic Orange Chocolate Drops

RITTER SPORT ⦸
Marzipan; Peppermint; Plain

STAMP COLLECTION ⦸
Orange Bar; Peppermint Bar; Plain Bar

SUMA WHOLEFOODS ⦸™👁➊✂1985
Dark Chocolate Coated: **Ginger**, Peanuts, Raisins

SUPERCOOK
Belgian Luxury Chocolate Dark; Dark Continental

THE BOOJA BOOJA COMPANY LTD ™☺⦸✿
Hazelnut Crunch Rocher; *Truffles:* **Around Midnight Espresso**, **Champagne**, **Cognac Flambed Banana**, **Ginger Wine**

THE COCOA TREE (1657) LTD ™☺➊⦸✓✂
Marzipan; *100g Chocolate Bars:* **Almond**, **Fruit & Nut**, **Ginger**, **Hazelnut**, **Orange**; *Boxed Chocolates:* Chocolate Ginger, Coffee Creams, Elderflower Creams, Marzipan Selection; *Chocolate Easter Eggs:* **Almond Truffle**, **Fruit & Nut Truffle**, **Ginger Truffle**, **Hazelnut Truffle**, **Marzipan**, **Orange Truffle**; *Truffles:* **Almond**, **Fruit & Nut**, **Ginger**, **Hazelnut**, **Orange**

TROPICAL WHOLEFOODS
Fruits: Apricots in Chocolate, Brazil Nuts in Chocolate, Mango in Chocolate

VEGANSTORE.CO.UK ™☺⦸➊✓
Holy Cow: After Dinner Chocolates, Golden Vegan Crunchie, White Chocolate Crunch; *Mrs Mudd:* Chocolate Decadance Truffle Bar; *Vegan Sweets:* White Chocolate Chips

VIVA! ☺➊⦸✓
Gourmet Truffle Selection; Handmade Vegan Chocolate Selection; Hazelnut Crunch Rocher; Mint Pounds; Orange Crèmes; Pecan Parfait; Plain Chocolate Bar; *Tropical Source:* Fair-Trade Chocolate-Dipped Mango

WHIZZERS ™⦸
Chocolate Beans; **Chocolate Footballs**; **Chocolate Mint Balls**; **Speckled Eggs**

CONFECTIONERY & SWEET SNACKS

ANIMAL AID ☺➊⦸✓✂1976
Crunchy Almond Crisp; *Vegan Fudge:* Bars, Box

AROMA CRYSTAL THERAPY ⦸✓✂
Rebar

AUSTRALIAN NOUGAT COMPANY ™⦸
Macadamia Bliss Nougat w Pistachio

BASSETTS
American Hard Gums; Cherry Drops; Fruit Bonbons; Mint Creams; Pear Drops; Sherbet Lemon; *Bassetts & Beyond:* Black Jack & Fruit Salad Lollies, Dip Dab, Refresher Lollies, Sherbet Fountain

BRAKE BROS
Brakes Mint Imperials

CADBURY
Fundays: Chocolate Limes

CLEARSPRING ™☺❶⊘
Ginger Sweets; **Peppermint Sweets**; **Sour Plum Sweets**; **Vanilla Sweets**; *Organic Snack Bars:* **Almond**, **Sesame**, **Sesame & Raisin**

D & D CHOCOLATES ☺⊘
Siesta Carob Confectionary: Animal Shapes (Original/Orange/Peppermint), Bar (Original/Orange/Peppermint), Carob Drops (Original/Orange/Peppermint), Carob Flakes for Cooking, Dinosaur Shapes (Original/Orange/Peppermint), Flower Shapes (Original/Orange/Peppermint), Heart Shapes(Original/Orange/Peppermint)

DOVES FARM FOODS LTD ™⊘
Organic: **Rice Pops**

DR HADWEN TRUST ☺❶⊘
Fudge: Strawberries & Creme, Vanilla; *Turkish Delight:* Rose & Lemon, Strawberry

EMPIRE FOODBROKERS LTD ⊘ ✂
Stretch Island Fruit Leather

GRANOVITA UK LTD ☺⊘✡ ✂
Castus Snack Bar: Pear, Strawberry; *Oskri Snack Bar:* Sesame w Date Syrup, Sesame w Date Syrup & Black Cumin, Sesame w Date Syrup & Fennel, Sesame w Molasses, Sesame w Molasses & Black Cumin, Sesame w Molasses & Fennel; *Snack Bars:* Wild Fruit

JORDAN (CEREALS) LTD ⊘
Organic Cereal Bars; *All Fruit Bars:* Apple & Passionfruit, Apple & Strawberry; *Fruit Pockets:* Chunky Fruit & Nuts, Cranberry Fruit & Nuts, Exotic Mix

JUST WHOLEFOODS ☺⊘
VegeBears: Frooty Fruits, Fruit Jellies

KELLOGGS ⊘
Screamin' Fruit Winders: Apple, Blackcurrant, Lemon, Orange, Raspberry, Strawberry

LIFESTYLE HEALTHCARE LTD ™⊘
Silhouette Dark Carob Bar

LYME REGIS FINE FOODS LTD ⊘
Fruit 4 U: Apple, Cherry, Raspberry; *Fruitus:* Apple, Apricot, Marzipan Bar, Sultana & Hazelnut; *La Fruit:* Apricot, Banana, Date & Fig, Ginger & Pear, Raspberry; *Zaps:* Apricot, Orange

MOTHER HEMP LTD ™⊘
Organic Motherhemp Bar: **w Apple & Cranberry**

NATIONAL TRUST ENTERPRISES LTD ⦸ ✂1998
Kendal Mint Cake White

NESTLÈ
Jellytots; Tooty Frooties; *Polo:* Berrylicious, Clear Cool, Clear Spearmint, Fruits, Original, Spearmint, Sugar-free

ORGRAN ⦸
Gluten-free Fruit Bars: Apricot, Blueberry-Filled

PATISSERIE ORGANIC ™
Date Slice; **Millet Munchies**

PLAMIL FOODS LTD ™☺❶⦸
Carob Confections: **Carob Spread - Sweetened or No Added Sugar**; *Confections:* **Carob Drops**, Carob Drops (No Added Sugar), **Carob (No Added Sugar)**, **Carob Orange**, **Carob Plain**, **Carob w Hazelnuts**

QUEENSLAND GOVERNMENT ❶⦸
Buderim Ginger; Leda Health Bar

SHEPHERDBOY ™⦸
Apple Bars 40g; **Carob Fruit & Nut 38g**; **Coconut/Pineapple Fruit & Nut 38g**; **Cranberry Bar**; **Fruit Bars Organic Sunflower 50g**; **Ginger Fruit & Nut 38g**; **Hempower Bar 50g**; **Multi Fruit 38g**; **Sunflower Fruit & Nut 50g**; *Just/So:* **Crispy Carob 45g**, **Ginger Carob**, **Mint Carob 45g**, **Orange Carob 45g**

SPOFF (SCOTLAND) LTD ™
Snackpack: **Ginger Fruit & Nut**, **Luxury Fruit & Nut**

SUMA WHOLEFOODS ⦸™❶ ✂1985
Carob Drops: **No Sugar**

SWIZZELS MATLOW LTD ⦸
Candy Cone Shakers; Climpies; Fr-ooze pops; Mr Fruits; Rainbow Drops; Snerdles; Super Baby Bottles; *Deposited:* Barley Sugar, Menthol Eucalyptus; *Deposited Crystal:* Fruits, Licorice, Mints; *Lolly:* Fruity Pops, Ice-Cream Pops, Swizz Kid Fruity

THORNTONS PLC ⦸
Mint Crumbles; Real Fruit Jellies; *Gifts:* Marzipan Fruit Box; *Jelly:* Orange Fish; *Mr Men:* Assorted Jelly Bag; *R Dahl:* Frobscottle, Jellies

TREBOR
24-7 Mighty Mints; Mighty Mints; Soft Fruits; *Soft Mints:* Peppermint, Spearmint

TROPICAL WHOLEFOODS
Bars - Snack: Tropical Fruit Bar; *Fruits:* Bogoya Banana, Chewy Banana Chips

UNCLE JOE'S ™⦸
Mintballs

VEGANSTORE.CO.UK ™☺⦸❶
ABC: Cookies; *Boston:* Chocolate Brownie; *Holy Cow:* Chocolate Limes,

Cola Cubes, Dew Drops, Fudge, Honeynotcomb, Ice Creme Lollies, Jelly Babies, Jelly Beans, Lemon Sherberts, Rhubarb & Custard, Strawberries & Cream; *Vegan Sweets:* Chocolate Donuts, Marshmallows

VIVA! ☺❶⊘✓
Dairy-free Fudge; Vegebear's Frooty Fruits; Vegebear's Fruit Jellies; *Tuck Shop Sweets:* Cola Cubes, Rhubarb & Custard, Strawberries & Creme

WHIZZERS ™⊘
Mint Humbugs

WRIGLEY CO LTD ☺⊘✓
Doublemint; Juicy Fruit; Spearmint; *Airwaves:* Blackcurrant, Cherry Menthol, Menthol & Eucalyptus; *Extra:* Cool Breeze, Mountain Frost, Peppermint, Spearmint, Winterfresh; *Extra Mints:* Peppermint, Spearmint; *Extra Thin Ice Breath Freshening Strips:* Peppermint, Spearmint; *Hubba Bubba:* Atomic Apple, Cool Cola, Seriously Strawberry; *Hubba Bubba Bubble Tape:* Snappy Strawberry, Sour Apple; *Hubba Bubba Mix & Match:* Sour Cherry & Lemon, Strawberry & Vanilla Ice Cream; *Orbit:* Ice White Pellet, Ice White Stick, Peppermint, Professional, Spearmint

YAOH ™☺❶⊘✓
Raw Food Hemp Bar: **Apple & Cinnamon**, **Date & Walnut**, **Tropical**

YORKSHIRE HEMP LTD ™
Hemp Nibbles: **Sweet**

COOKING AIDS - SAVOURY

ALLERGYCARE ™⊘
GF Baking Powder; **GF Gravy Mix**; **Herb & Onion Stuffing Mix**

BRAKE BROS
Sage & Onion Stuffing; Vegetarian Suet; *Breadcrumbs:* Golden, Natural; *Cooking Wine:* All; *Herbs in Oil:* Basil, Coriander, Lemongrass

CLEARSPRING ™☺❶⊘
Johsen Shoyu; **Kuzu - 100g Bag/100g Jar/1 kg**; **Mansan Tamari - 150ml/500ml**; **Organic Soksen Shoyu**; **Shiso Condiment**; **Shoyu - Soya Sauce**; **Sushi Soy Sauce**; **Teriyaki Sauce**; **Ume Plum Seasoning - 150ml/500ml**; *Danival:* **Coarse Sea Salt**, **Fine Sea Salt**; *Organic:* **Kagisa Shoyu - 150ml/500ml/2.5l**, **Mansan Tamari - 150ml/500ml/2.5l**; *Traditional Japanese Soya Sauces:* Organic Johsen Shoyu

CYTOPLAN ™
Nutritional Support: **Linseeds**

DOVES FARM FOODS LTD ™⊘
Buckwheat Flour 1kg; **Gram Flour 1kg**; **Rice Flour 1kg**; *Gluten-free:* **Brown Bread Flour**, **Plain White Flour 1kg**, **White Bread Flour**; *Organic:* **Fine Plain Wholemeal Flour**

1kg, Malthouse Flour 1kg, Pasta Flour 1kg, Plain White Unbleached Flour 1kg, Self Raising White Unbleached Flour 1kg, Self Raising Wholemeal Flour 1kg, Spelt Flour 1kg, Strong 100% Wholemeal Flour 1.5kg, Strong White Unbleached Flour 1.5kg, Wessex Brown Flour, Wholemeal Rye Flour 1kg

ESSENTIAL BRAND ™❶ ⃠
Flours: **All (Organic & Conventional)**; *Herbs:* **All (Organic & Conventional)**

ESSENTIAL TRADING CO-OPERATIVE LTD ™❶ ⃠
Organic Yeast Extract; **Yeast Extract**; *Soya Sauce:* **Organic Shoyu, Organic Tamari, Shoyu, Tamari**

HERON QUALITY FOODS LTD ⃠
Gluten-free Organic Mixes: Stuffing Mix - Gluten Free/Wheat Free

HIGHER NATURE PLC ™⃠
Omega Nutrition Organic: **Cold Milled Flax Seeds**

JARROW FORMULAS INC.
Garlic, Fibers, Digestive Enzymes: Flax Seeds - Cold Milled

JUST WHOLEFOODS ☺⃠
VegeRen; *Stuffing Mixes:* Apple & Sage, Mushroom & Sweet Pepper, Sage & Onion

LIVING EARTH EUROPE ™
UK Organic Soya Beans; **UK Soya Beans**

MARIGOLD HEALTH FOODS ❶⃠
Engevita Nutritional Yeast Flakes

MOTHER HEMP LTD ™⃠
Hempso

NATURE'S OWN LTD ™
Nutritional Support: **Linseeds NO VAT**

ORGRAN ⃠
All Purpose Gluten-Free Crumbs

SEAGREENS ™☺⃠
Ascophyllum Pieces: **Table Condiment Grinder**; *Medium Granules:* **Culinary Ingredient, Culinary Ingredient Shaker**, Food Granules

SPA HOUSE LTD ™
Blend of Herbs for Roast Vegetables; Chinese Spice Mix; **Dried Mixed Herbs**; Garam Masala; Garlic Sea Salt; Mixed Herb Blend; **Mixed Peppercorns**; Pasta Herb Blend; Provencal Herbs; **Pure Mint**; Tandoori Masala; Thai Spice Mix

YORKSHIRE HEMP LTD ™
Bread Baking Mixture w Hemp; **Hemp Flour**; **Hemp Pancake**

COOKING AIDS - SWEET

BRAKE BROS
Baby Apples in Syrup; Baby Figs in Rum; Baby Pears in Syrup; Crumb Base; Crumble Mix; Custard Powder; Dark Chocolate Vermicelli; Whole Poached Pears; *Flavouring:* Almond, Brandy, Chocolate, Lemon, Orange, Peppermint, Raspberry, Rum, Vanilla; *Food Colouring:* Apple Green, Blue, Bright Red, Brown, Cochineal (artificial), Orange, Yellow; *Pie Filling:* Apple & Blackberry, Black Cherry, Blackcurrant, Red Cherry, Strawberry

CLEARSPRING ™☺❶⃠
English Barley Malt Syrup; **Japanese Brown Rice Syrup**; **Ume Concentrate**; *Organic:* **Barley Malt Syrup**, **Corn & Barley Malt Syrup - 350g/1kg**, **Japanese Millet Malt Syrup**, **Rice Malt Syrup**

GREEN & BLACKS ⃠☼
Organic 72% Cooking Chocolate

JIF
All Lemon & Lime Juices

JUST WHOLEFOODS ☺⃠
All Natural Custard Powder

MENIER ™⃠
Cooking Chocolate

MERIDIAN FOODS
Natural Sweeteners: Malt Extract, Mince Pie Filling

RYVITA ⃠
Allinson Organic Wholemeal Crispbread

SUMA WHOLEFOODS ⃠™👁❶✂1985
Cherries: All

SUPERCOOK
100's & 1000's; Angelica; Real Chocolate Flakes; *Butterice:* Vanilla; *Strands:* Chocolate, Sugar

WEIKFIELD ™
Jelly Crystals: **Banana**, **Cherry**, **Mango**, **Orange**, **Pineapple**, **Raspberry**, **Strawberry**

CRACKERS, CRISPBREADS ETC

ASHBOURNE BISCUITS LTD ⃠
Crispbread: Mixed Seed Crisp; *Wafers:* Chive, Rye

BRAKE BROS
Brakes Cream Crackers

CLEARSPRING ™☺❶⃠
Double Sesame Rice Cakes ; **Rice Cakes - Sea Vegetable**; **Sesame Garlic Rice Cakes**; **Tamari Brown Rice Crackers**; **Teriyaki Rice Cakes**; *Brown Rice:* **Sesame Wafers**; *Courtney's*

Organic Crackers: **Classic**, **Cracked Pepper**, **Savoury Herb**, **Sun-Dried Tomato**; *Organic:* **Rice Cakes - Multi-grain**, **Rice Cakes - Plain**, **Rice Cakes - Salted**, **Rice Crackers - Tamari**

CRAWFORD'S ⃠
Cream Crackers (Portion Pack); Oat & Wholemeal (Portion Pack)

DEES CARIBBEAN IMPORTS ™
Homemade Special Cream Water Crackers; HTB Crackers

DOVES FARM FOODS LTD ™⃠
Organic: **Rye Crackers**

EMPIRE FOODBROKERS LTD ⃠ ✂
No-No Flatbreads

GEO ORGANICS ⃠
Croutons: Garlic, Lightly Salted

GLUTANO
Cracker Bread; Crackers; Crispbread; Organic Sesame Crackers

MILLERS DAMSEL ⃠
Wafers: Celery, Charcoal, Poppy, Sesame, Wheat

NETWORK OF WHOLEFOOD WHOLESALE CO-OPERATIVES ⃠☺❶☼ ✂
NOW Oatcakes: Low Salt, No Salt; *Organic Oatcakes:* Low Salt, No Salt

ORGRAN ⃠
Gluten-Free Corn Cakes; Organic Rice Cakes; *Gluten-free Crispbreads:* Corn, Rice, Rice & Cracked Pepper, Rice & Garden Herb, Salsa Corn

RYVITA ⃠
Allinson Crackerbread: Wholemeal; *Crispbreads:* Dark Rye, Multigrain, Original Rye, Sesame; *Organic Rice Cakes:* Original, Sesame

SANCHI ⃠
Arare: Five Flavour, Quinoa & Tamari; *Crackers:* Black Sesame, Brown Rice, Brown Rice Mini, Tamari, White Sesame

SUMA WHOLEFOODS ⃠™👁❶✂1985
Japanese Rice Crackers

THE VILLAGE BAKERY MELMERBY LTD ⃠
Oatcakes

TRUFREE (NUTRICIA) ™⃠
Crisp Breads; **Herb & Onion Cracker**; **High Fibre Crackers**; **Spicy Cracker**

CREAM REPLACERS

ALPRO UK LTD ™⃠
Soya Dream

GRANOSE ⃠
Soya Creem

OAT SUPREME ™☺⃠
Cream

DESSERTS

ALPRO UK LTD ™⃠
Dairy Free Custard; Fruits of the Forest; **Fruits of the Orchard**; **Organic Chocolate**; **Organic Vanilla**; *Pot Desserts:* Caramel, **Chocolate**, **Vanilla**

BLUE LOTUS PRODUCTS LTD ™☺
Plum Pudding (fruit pudding); *Gluten Free:* **Plum Pudding (fruit pudding)**

BRAKE BROS
Plum & Port Pudding; Raspberry Dessert Sauce; Spotted Dick; Summer Fruits Pudding; *Coulis:* Apricot, Blackcurrant, Mango, Raspberry, Strawberry, White Peach; *Crumble:* Apple, Apricot (Baked), Rhubarb & Strawberry; *Crunchy Bake:* Apple, Plum; *Terrine:* Mulled Wine, Summer Fruit

CLEARSPRING ™☺❶⃠
Danival: **Almond Dessert**, **Almond/Chocolate Dessert**, **Hazelnut Dessert**, **Hazelnut/Chocolate Dessert**; *Danival Ready-to-Eat Foods Organic:* Almond Dessert, Almond/Chocolate Dessert, Hazelnut Dessert, Hazelnut/Chocolate Dessert; *Organic:* **Brown Rice Amazake - 380g/740g**, **Millet Amazake**

CLIVE'S
Sweet Pies: Apple Pie

H J HEINZ CO LTD ™⃠
Strudel: Apple & Sultana, Wildfruit

JAMES WHITE ☺
Fruit Coulis: 3 Red Fruits, Apricot, Blackcurrant, Blueberry, Mango, Raspberry, Strawberry, Wild Blackberry

JUST WHOLEFOODS ☺⃠
Jelly: Lemon, Raspberry, Strawberry, Tropical; *Vegetarian Jelly Crystals:* Lemon, Raspberry, Strawberry, Tropical Fruits

NATURALLY ME INC ™
Chocolate Mousse Pie; **Gourmet Apple Struesel Pie**; **Gourmet Blueberry Struesel Pie**

NESTLÈ
Dessert Sauce: Caramel, Chocolate

SILVER SPOON
Treat Toppings: Dark Chocolate, Monster Crackin'

TRUFREE (NUTRICIA) ™⃠
Chocolate Sponge Pudding; **Treacle Sponge Pudding**

DIPS & DRESSINGS

AARHUS UNITED UK LTD ⃠
Organic Midsummer: French Dressing, Italian Dressing, Low Fat Vinaigrette, Sun Dried Tomato Dressing

ALAVON ™⃠☺✓
Egg-Free Mayonnaise: **Cajun**, **Garlic**, **Plain**

BRAKE BROS
French Dressing; Guacamole; Humous; Mango Salsa; Peanut Sauce; Salsa; Salsa Sauce; *Balsamic:* Glaze/Reduction

CARB OPTIONS
Dressings: French

DISCOVERY FOODS
Ranch Style Salsa: Hot, Medium

DRAGONFLY FOODS ⃠ ☼
Organic Tofu: Tofupot (Organic Tofu Dip)

GRANOVITA UK LTD ☺ ⃠ ☼ ✂
Mayola!: Garlic, Lemon, Original

HELLMANN'S
Vinaigrette Light

JETHROS ☺
'Spirits of Summer' Vinaigrettes: Cranberry Pepper & Vodka, Irish Whiskey & Grain Mustard, Orange & Bourbon

KETTLE FOODS ❶ ⃠
Kettle Mediterranean: Presto Bean Salsa Dip, Sweet Red Pepper w Sun Dried Tomato Dip

KITCHEN GARDEN PRESERVES
Salad Dressings: Apple & Mint, Balsamic, Hot Chilli, Orange & Cardamom, Tomato & Tarragon

LEEORA VEGETARIAN FOOD ™ ⃠
Mediterranean Cuisine: **Babaganush**, **Deli Chilli**, **Greek Aubergine Dip**, **Lebanese Style Humous**, **Tunisian Style Harissa**

LIFE ™ ⃠
Mayonnaise Style Sunflower Oil Dressing - Egg Free

MARY BERRY & DAUGHTER
Dressing: French Herb, Salad

PHILEAS FOGG COMPANY ⃠
Dips: Barbecue, Chunky Salsa, Sweet Chilli

PLAMIL FOODS LTD ™☺❶ ⃠
Egg-Free Mayonnaise: **Chilli**, **Garlic**, **Plain**, **Tarragon**; *Organic Egg-Free Mayonnaise:* **Plain**, **w Lemongrass**

SOURCE FOODS ☺☼
Organic Miso Mustard

THRESHERS+ FOOD
Houmous; Tomato Salsa

WALKERS SNACK FOODS LTD ⃠
Dippas: Extra Hot Salsa, Hot Salsa Dip, Mild Salsa Dip; *Doritos:* Latinos Smooth Red Pepper & Tomato Dip; *Sensations:* Mango Chutney Dip

EGG REPLACERS

ALLERGYCARE ™ ⃠
Vegan Egg Replacer

ORGRAN ⃠
No Egg - Egg Replacer (Gluten-Free)

VEGANSTORE.CO.UK ™☺ ⃠ ❶
Fantastic: Tofu Eggless Scramble

GRAVIES & STOCKS

BRAKE BROS
Gravy Granules; Vegetable Stock; *Mari-Base:* Fajita, Tropical; *Vegetable Stock:* Light, Mediterranean

JUST WHOLEFOODS ☺⊘
Instant Gravy Granules

MARIGOLD HEALTH FOODS ❶⊘
Marigold Swiss Vegetable Bouillon Powder: Organic, Original, Reduced Salt

ORGRAN ⊘
Gluten-Free Gravy Mix

'ICE CREAMS', SORBETS ETC

BRAKE BROS
Lollies: Assorted Fruit, Orange; *Sorbet:* Champagne, Lemon, Mango, Orange, Raspberry

CALYPSO SOFT DRINKS ⊘
Freezepops: Calypso, Safari, Simpsons

ESSENTIAL TRADING CO-OPERATIVE LTD ™❶⊘🐈✂
Organic Fruit Lollies

FAYREFIELD FOODS
Swedish Glace: Mocha & Coffee Ripple, Raspberry, Rich Chocolate, Smooth Vanilla, Smooth Vanilla w a Rich Chocolate Flavoured Coating, Soft Caramel, Strawberry

MOTHER HEMP LTD ™⊘🐈
Hemp Ice: **Double Choc Chip**, **Mint Chocolate Chip**, **Strawberry**, **Vanilla**

OAT SUPREME ™☺⊘
Low Fat Sugar Free Diabetic Oat Ice: **Lite**; *Non-Dairy Choc Ice's on a Stick:* **Supreme**; *Oatbased Ice Cream:* **Chocolate Supreme**, **Classic Vanilla**, **Strawberry**, **Vanilla Chocolate Fudge Swirl**

SOYA HEALTH FOODS LTD ☺❶⊘🐈✂
Sunrise: Carob Ices, Ice-Dream

TOFUTTI ☺❶⊘🐈✂
Non Dairy Frozen Soya Organic Desserts: Chocolate, Mango & Passionfruit, Strawberry, Vanilla; *Rock & Roll:* Cakes, Cones; *Supreme Ice Cream:* Better Pecan, Chocolate Cookies, Madagascan, Strawberry, Vanilla

MARGARINES, FATS, OILS ETC

AARHUS UNITED UK LTD ⊘
Bread Dipping Oil: Balsamic Vinegar, Garlic & Chilli; *Collection Prestige:* Groundnut, Stirfry, Toasted Sesame, Walnut; *Cooking Oils:* Again & Again, Harry Ramsdens Traditional Tasting;

Extra Virgin Olive Oil Vinegar Dressing w: Balsamic, White Wine; *Infused Olive Oil:* Basil, Chilli, Garlic, Lemon; *Spray n Cook:* Olive Mist, Vegetable Spray

BRAKE BROS
Sunflower Spread Portion Size 10; Truffle Flavoured Oil - White; *Infused Oil:* Basil, Garlic, Lemon

BROADLAND FOODS ⊘
Shredded Vegetable Suet

BRUNEL HEALTHCARE ⊘ 1992
Vertese: Flaxseed Oil

CLEARSPRING ™☺⊘
Toasted Sesame Oil - 150ml/500ml; *Organic:* **Extra Virgin Olive Oil - 500ml/1l/2.5l**, **Hazlenut Oil**, **Omega Oil**, **Safflower Oil - 500ml**, **Sesame Oil - 500ml**, **Soybean Oil - 500ml/1 litre**, **Sunflower Frying Oil - 500ml/1l/2.5l**, **Sunflower Oil - 500ml/1l/2.5l**, **Toasted Pumpkin Seed Oil - 250ml**, **Toasted Sesame Oil - 250ml/500ml**, **Walnut Oil**

COOKEEN
100% Vegetable Fat

CRISP 'N'DRY
Vegetable Oil: Solid 100% Vegetable Fat, Spray

CYTOPLAN ™
Organic Flax Oil 300ml; **Organic Flaxseed Oil 200ml**; *Nutritional Support:* **Organic Flaxseed Oil - High in Omega 3 500ml**

ESSENTIAL BRAND ™ ⊘
Organic Oils: **All**

FLORA
White Flora - 100% Vegetable Fat

FRY LIGHT ™⊘
Cooking Non-Stick Spray: **Extra Virgin Olive Oil**, **Sunflower Oil**

GRANOVITA UK LTD ☺ ⊘
Flax Oil; Hemp Oil; Pumpkin Oil; Speciality Omega Blend Oil

HEALTHY AND ESSENTIAL ™
Lignan Flax Oil

HIGHER NATURE PLC ™⊘
Omega Nutrition Organic: **Coconut Oil**, **Essential Balance Oil**, **Flax Seed Oil**, **Garlic-Chilli Flax Seed Oil**, **Virgin Hemp Seed Oil**

HOLLAND AND BARRETT RETAIL LTD
Oils: Flaxseed

JARROW FORMULAS INC.
Lipid Fatty Acid, Lecithin, Vinegar: Coconut Oil, Flaxseed Oil, Garlic-Chilli Flaxseed Oil, Hi-Lignan Flax Oil, Pumpkin Seed Butter, Super Flaxseed Oil

KOBASHI ™☺⊘
Misc: **Hempseed Oil**

LAWNCOURT HARVEST LTD ™
Roasted Sunflower & Pumpkin Seed Oil

LIFEPLAN PRODUCTS LTD ™⊘✓
Flaxseed Oil; **Wheatgerm Oil**

MOTHER HEMP LTD ™⊘✓
Bottled Hempseed Oil; **Hempseed Oil**

NATURE'S OWN LTD ™
Organic Linseed (Flaxseed) Oil 200ml; *Nutritional Support:* **Organic Linseed (Flaxseed) Oil**

OPTIMA HEALTH & NUTRITION ⊘✓ ✂1995
Organic Choice Balanced Oil Blend

PURE ™⊘
Organic Reduced-Fat Spread; **Soya Spread**; **Sunflower Spread**

RAKUSEN'S ™⊘
Tomor: **250g Block Margarine**, **500g Sunflower Tub**

SMILDE ™⊘
Sunflower Spread

SUMA WHOLEFOODS ⊘™◉❶✂1985
Suma Spreads: **100% Sunflower - 2kg/1Kg/500g**, **Low Fat - 500g**, **Organic Sunflower 500g**, **Soya - 2kg & 500g**

TREE-HARVEST ⊘✓
Hempseed Oil

UDO'S CHOICE ™
Ultimate Oil Blend: **Coconut Oil**, **Flax Seed Oil**, **Oat Bran Oil**, **Oat Germ Oil**, **Rice Bean Oil**, **Sesame Seed Oil**, **Soy Lecithin**, **Sunflower Seed Oil**, **Toco Trienols**

VITAQUELL ™
Margarine: **Extra**, **Organic**, **Organic Light**

YAOH ™☺✓ ⊘❶
Hemp Oil 250ml; **Hemp Oil 500ml**

YORKSHIRE HEMP LTD ™
Hemp Oil

PASTRY

AMBROSIAN VEGETARIAN FOODS ™☺ ⊘❶☼
Organic Pastries: **Cheez' n' Chive**, **Cheezy Bean**, **Savory Herb Sosage Rolls**, **Tomato & Garlic Sosage Rolls**

BAKERS DELIGHT ⊘
Gluten Free: Assorted Jam Tarts, Bramley Apple Pies, Cherry Bakewell Tarts

BRAKE BROS
4cm Cocktail Cups; 6cm Savoury Tartlets; 8.5cm Quiche Cases; Barquette Boat Shapes; Chinese Pancakes; Cream Horn Cases; Filo Pastry; Mini Barquettes; Puff Pastry; Ragout Cocktail Cups; Short Crust Pastry Mix; Short Pastry; Tartlets (Mignardises); Tulip Baskets; *Puff Pastry:* Lids, Sheets, Squares; *Vol au Vents:* 2 5/8" Medium, 2" Party, 3 3/4" King Size

JUS-ROL
Frozen: Filo Pastry Sheets, Puff Pastry Blocks, Puff Pastry Sheets, Shortcrust Pastry Blocks, Shortcrust Pastry Sheets, Vol-au-Vent Cases

TRUFREE (NUTRICIA) ™⃠
Pastry Mix

PICKLES, SAUCES, VINEGARS ETC

AARHUS UNITED UK LTD ⃠
Midsummer Organic Balsamic Vinegar; *Chalice Tapenade:* Green Olive, Kalamata Olive, Sun Dried Tomato, Sweet Red Pepper

BAXTERS OF SPEYSIDE LTD ⃠
Beetroot in Redcurrant Jelly; Beetroot Pickle; *Chutney:* Albert's Victorian, Mango w Ginger, Spiced Fruit, Tomato w Red Pepper; *Chutneys:* Crushed Pineapple & Sweet Pepper, Spanish Tomato & Black Olive; *Jelly:* Cranberry, Mint, Redcurrant, Wild Rowan; *Sauce:* Apple, Cranberry, Mint

BERTOLLI
Sauces: Vine-Ripened Tomato & Black Olive; *Sauces w Olive Oil:* Grilled Vegetable, Tomato & Basil, Tomato Roasted Garlic & Mushroom

BRAKE BROS
Bramley Apple Sauce; Dijon Mustard; Redcurrant Jelly; Sweet Pickle; Tomato Ketchup; Vinegar; *Balsamic:* Vinegar, Vinegar of Modena, White Condiment; *Chutney:* Autumn Fruit, Caramelised Onion, Country Tomato, Lemon, Mango, Plum & Apple; *Mustard:* English, French, Green Peppercorn, Powder; *Piccalilli:* All; *Portions:* Brown Sauce, English Mustard, French Mustard, Tomato Ketchup; *Sachets:* Brown Sauce, English Mustard, French Mustard, Malt Vinegar, Tomato Ketchup; *Sauce:* Arrabbiata, Barbeque, Brown, Cranberry, Mint, Tomato, Tomato & Basil, Tomato & Herb, Tomato Mushroom & Garlic; *Sweet Pickle:* All

CALEDONIAN CURRY CO. ™⃠
Beetroot & Chilli Relish; Hot Garlic & Chilli Relish; **Hot Rhubarb & Chilli Relish**; **Red Pepper & Chilli Relish**; Saltire Sauce; **Tomato & Chilli Relish**; *Hot Pepper Sauces:* 'After Burns' Chilli Sauce, 'Kilt Lifter' Chilli Sauce, 'Nessie's Revenge' Chilli Sauce, 'Sporran Splitter' Chilli Sauce

CARB OPTIONS
Dressings: Italian; *Sauces:* BBQ Table, Chilli Con Carne, Tomato for Bolognese

CARMEL FOOD LTD ™⃠
Carmel Wine Vinegar: **Red Wine Vinegar**

CLEARSPRING ™☺❶⃠
Natto Miso Chutney; **Tsuyu**; **Umeboshi Puree**; **Wasabi**; *Danival:* **Ketchup**; *Danival Organic:* **Seitan 'Bolognaise' Sauce**; *Danival Ready-to-Eat Foods:* Ketchup; *Organic:* **Apple Balsamic Vinegar**, **Balsamic Vinegar**,

Balsamic Vinegar - Vintage Aged, **Brown Rice Vinegar - 150ml/500ml/2.5l**, **Red Wine Vinegar**, **Tofu 'Bolognaise' Sauce**, **White Wine Vinegar**; *Sushi:* **Vinegar**

COLMAN'S
Mustards: Dijon, DSF, English, Mild, Wholegrain; *Sauces:* Apple

DISCOVERY FOODS
2-Step: Chilli Con Carne, Texan Fajita Sauce; *Dressing:* Sweet Chilli & Sesame; *Instant Marinade:* Jalapeno & Lime, Roasted Cumin & Coriander; *Pasta Sauce:* Tomato & Basil, Tomato & Chilli, Tomato & Garlic, Tomato & Roasted Peppers; *Sauce:* Buffalo Wings, Enchilada, Hot & Smoky BBQ, Mexican, New Orleans Creole

DUERRS
Apple Sauce; Cranberry Sauce; Mint Jelly; Mint Sauce; Redcurrant Jelly

ESSENTIAL BRAND ™● ⊘ ✂
Bottled, Jarred, Canned: Organic Dijon Mustard, Organic Wholegrain Mustard

FRESH FOODS CO LTD ⊘ ☼
Organic Tomato Ketchup

GEO ORGANICS ⊘
Malt Vinegar; Piccalilli; Sweet Pickle; Tomato Burger Relish; Worcestershire Sauce; *Chutneys:* Mango, Spicy Tomato; *Mex-Select:* Mexican BBQ Sauce, Mexican Salsa, Tomato Fajita Cooking Sauce; *Tastes of the East:* Balti Curry Paste, Black Bean Cooking Sauce, Brinjal Pickle, Garlic Pickle, Korma Curry Paste, Lime Pickle, Madras Curry Paste, Mango Chutney in Apple Juice, Sweet & Sour Stir Fry Sauce, Szechuan Stir Fry Sauce, Thai Green Curry Paste, Thai Massaman Curry Paste, Thai Red Curry Paste, Thai Satay Curry Paste, Thai Yellow Curry Paste, Tikka Masala Curry Paste, Vindaloo Curry Paste

GO ORGANIC
Curry Sauce: Jalferezi w Bell Peppers, Tomato & Coriander; *Italian:* Tomato & Aubergine, Tomato & Black Olive, Tomato & Red Chilli, Tomato & Sweet Basil, Tomato & Sweet Pepper

GRANOVITA UK LTD ☺ ⊘ ☼ ✂
Organic Brown Sauce; Organic Tomato Ketchup; *Savoury Sauces:* Vegetarian Worcestershire Sauce

H J HEINZ CO LTD ™⊘
Apple Sauce: Jar; *BBQ Sauce:* Hot 'n' Sizzling, Original; *Ketchup:* Chilli, Curry, Hot, Mexican Tomato, Tomato; *Pickles:* Tangy Tomato

HARBOURNE VINEYARD ☺⊘
Cider Vinegar; Wine Vinegar

HELLMANN'S
Curry Sauce

HENDERSONS (SHEFFIELD) LTD ☺
Hendersons Relish

HOLLAND AND BARRETT RETAIL LTD
Cyder Vinegar

JARROW FORMULAS INC.
Lipid Fatty Acid, Lecithin, Vinegar: Apple Cider Vinegar

JEREMY'S SOUPS ⊘ ✓ ✂
Smokin' BBQ Sauce; Sunny Sombrero - Tomato & Herb Sauce; Tasty Tomato - Tomato & Garlic Sauce

JETHROS ☺
Glazes - for Roast & Grill: Balsamic Ginger, Blackcurrant Chilli; *Marinades:* Amadou Barbecue Sauce, Cajun Lime & Jalapeno, Lemon Bay & Rosemary, Lemon Chilli & Coriander, Lime Chilli & Oregano, Orange Chilli & Cumin, Pineapple Chilli & Basil, Red Wine Orange & Juniper; *Sauces - for Dipping & Basting:* 12 Days of Christmas, Ginger Chilli, Ginger Lime, Ginger & Orange, Green Chilli & Coriander, Red Chilli & Garlic

KITCHEN GARDEN PRESERVES ✓
Chutneys: Autumn Apple, Beetroot, Caramelised Onions w Red Wine, Curried Apple Banana & Apricot, Old Spot Real Ale, Spiced Apricot & Orange, Spiced Tomato & Apple, Sweet Plum & Date; *Exotic Chutneys:* Hot Mango; *Exotic Pickles:* Lime; *Hotheadz! Sauces:* Green Devil Salsa, Smokin Satan, Yellow Belly Piccalilli; *Mustards:* English, Hot & Sweet Spiced, Tewkesbury, Wholegrain, Wholegrain w Garlic & Herbs; *Organic Chutneys:* Beetroot, Country Fruit, Pear & Date, Piccalilli, Red Pepper & Chilli Relish, Spiced Apple & Mint, Spiced Apricot & Orange, Tomato; *Organic Sauces:* Cranberry; *Pickles:* Lemon, Ploughmans, Sweet Mustard; *Sauces:* Cranberry, Horseradish; *Savoury Jellies:* Apple w Mint, Apple w Sage, Lime w Chillies, Redcurrant; *Vinegars:* Raspberry

KNORR
Ragu Sauces: Basil & Oregano, Onion & Garlic, Original, Spicy Bolognese, Tomato for Lasagne, Traditional

LEEORA VEGETARIAN FOOD ™⊘
Sauces: **Vegetarian Style Ragu**, **Vegetarian Thai Style Curry**

LIFE ™⊘ ✓
Fish Free Worcestershire Sauce

MERIDIAN FOODS
Organic Cool Salsa; *Free From Range:* Hot Salsa, Korma Sauce, Sundried Tomato Sauce, Tikka Masala Sauce, Tomato Ketchup, White Wine & Mushroom Sauce; *Pasta Sauces - Organic:* Mushroom, Red Pepper & Sweet Chilli, Spanish Olive, Tomato & Herb; *Soya Sauces:* Shoyu, Tamari; *Table Sauces - Organic:* Cranberry Sauce, Tomato Ketchup

OCEAN SPRAY
Cranberry Jellied Sauce; Cranberry Jelly; Redcurrant & Cranberry Sauce; *Gourmet Cranberry Sauces:* w Extra Fruit, w Mulled Wine, w Orange Liqueur

PASTA KING (UK) LTD ™
Arrabiata; **Basilico**; **Mushroom Thyme**; **Peperonata**; **Pomodoro**; **Ratatouille**; **Tuscan Bean**; **Veggie-Bol**

PATAKS FOODS LTD ⦸
Chutneys: Hot Mango, Mango; *Cooking Sauces in Cans:* Balti (Medium/Hot/Mild), Delhi, Madras, Rogan Josh, Vindaloo; *Cooking Sauces in Jars:* Balti, Jalfrezi, Madras, Rogan Josh, Vindaloo; *Pickles:* Brinjal, Chilli, Garlic, Lime (Hot/Medium), Lime Mild Dip Pot, Mango (Hot/Medium), Mixed Pickle; *Spice Express:* Kashmiri Chilli & Peppers

SACLA
Gratinata: Roasted Yellow Pepper & Smoked Garlic, Sauteed Sweetcorn & Rocket, Tomato Mushroom & Red Chilli; *Stir-In Sauce:* Mushroom & Marsala Wine, Olive & Tomato, Sun-Dried Tomato & Garlic; *Whole Cherry Tomato Sauces for Pasta:* Basil, Chilli, Roasted Peppers

SANCHI ⦸
Furikake; *Sauces:* Mirin, Organic Shoyu, Organic Tamari, Ponzu, Shoyu, Tamari, Teriyaki; *Vinegars:* Organic Brown Rice, Ume Su Plum

SEEDS OF CHANGE ⦸ ☼
Cooking Sauces: Chilli w Jalapeno Peppers, Sweet & Sour; *Pasta Sauce:* Bolognese, Cherry Tomato & Olive, Mediterranean Vegetable, Slow Roasted Garlic & Chilli, Spicy Roast Garlic, Tomato & Basil; *Stir & Serve Sauces for Pasta:* Roasted Peppers, Sundried Tomato & Basil

SIKELIA LTD ™
Hot Chilli Peppers in Oil; *Nonna's:* **Artichokes**, **Sliced Aubergine**, **Tomatoes**; *Sicilian:* **Antipasto**, **Chilli Peppers**

SIMPLY ORGANIC ⦸ ☼
Pasta Sauces: Spicy Tomato, Tomato & Basil, Tomato Olives & Capers, Tomato & Red Pepper

SOMA ☺⦸ ☼
Nomato: Ketchup, Pasta Sauce

SUMA WHOLEFOODS ⦸™ ❶ ✂ 1985
Pasta Sauces: Affumicata, Arrosta, Romana, Rustica

TASTE OF ITALY ⦸
Tomato/Basil Cooking Sauce; Tomato/Mushroom Cooking Sauce; Tomato/Pepper Cooking Sauce

VEGGIEMASTER ™
Vegan: **Beijing Spicy Orange Sauce**, **Black Pepper Sauce**, **Original Black Bean Sauce**, **Original Sweet & Sour Sauce**, **Sweet Lemon Sauce**, **Teriyaki BBQ Sauce**

VINTAGE ROOTS ⦸
Ravarino: Balsamic Vinegar

PIES & PASTRIES

AMBROSIAN VEGETARIAN FOODS ™☺ ⃠ ❶ ✡
Cheeze 'n' Onion Pie; Porkless + Apple Pie; **Porkless Pie**

BRAKE BROS
Vegetable Pasties; Vegetable Pasties - 50% Wholemeal Pastry

CLIVE'S
Organic Gluten Free Pies: Vegetable Chilli; *Organic Pies:* Aloo Matar, Arabian Chickpea, Chestnut Cassoulet, Creamy Mushroom, Greek Olive & Lentil, Hungarian Goulash, Mexican Chilli

GAIA ™⃠
Organic Bakery Products: **Apple Raisins Puff-Pastry Cake**, **Apricot Tart**, **Blueberry Tart**, **Strawberry-Raspberry Tart**

GET REAL ORGANIC FOODS ⃠ ✡
Sutaki Pies

HOLLAND AND BARRETT RETAIL LTD
Low Fat Veg Sausage Roll; Porkless Pie; *Low Fat Veg Pasty:* Cornish, Tandoori

LINDA MCCARTNEY PRODUCTS ™⃠
Cocktail Sausage Rolls; Deep Country Pie; Sausage Rolls; Vegetable Slice

PAUL'S TOFU ™☺⃠ ✡
Savouries: **Mushroom & Nut Parcels**, **Organic Mushroom & Tofu Pie**, **Tofu Arame Pasty**, **Tofu Vegetable Pasty**

VEGAN PASTY CO ™
Pasties: **Popeye**, **Small Mixed Veg**, **SPF**, **Vegan**, **Vegan 'Cheese'**, **Vegan 'Cheese' & Mushroom**

ZEDZ FOODS ⃠
Pasties: Bolog-No-No - Soya Mince & Tomato Filling, Vegetable & Split Pea; *Savoury Muffins:* Olive & Oregano, Sundried Tomato & Oregano; *Savoury Pasties:* Coconut Curry, 'Pizza'

SAVOURIES CANNED / BOTTLED

BRAKE BROS
Spaghetti Hoops in Tomato Sauce; Spaghetti in Tomato Sauce; *Baked Beans:* All; *Marinated Olives:* Campagnola Green, Rustica Black

CLEARSPRING ™☺❶⃠
Mugwort Mochi; **Takuan (Pickled Daikon Radish)**; **Umeboshi Plums**; *Brown Rice:* **Mochi**; *Danival Organic:* **Lentils & Smoked Tofu w Vegetables**, **Ratatouille**, **Seitan Ravioli**, **Tofu Ravioli**; *Danival Ready-to-Eat Foods:* Hot Vegetarian Chilli; *Organic:* **Umeboshi Plums - 200g/1kg**; *Sushi:* **Cucumber**, **Daikon**, **Garlic (w Umeboshi)**, **Ginger**

DISCOVERY FOODS
Refried Beans; Spicy Refried Beans

ESSENTIAL BRAND ™❶ ⃠
Bottled, Jarred, Canned: **Organic**

Apples, **Organic Apricots**, **Organic Baby Carrots**, **Organic Blackberries**, **Organic Blackeye Beans**, **Organic Button Mushrooms**, **Organic Cherries**, **Organic Chickpeas**, **Organic Chopped Peeled Tomatoes**, **Organic Chopped Tomatoes**, **Organic Cranberries**, **Organic Forest Fruits**, **Organic French Beans**, **Organic Gherkins - Sour**, **Organic Grapefruit Segments**, **Organic Green Peas**, **Organic Green Peas + Carrots**, **Organic Green Peas + Mint**, **Organic Haricot Beans**, **Organic Mango Chunks**, **Organic Mixed Beans**, **Organic Passata**, **Organic Peach Slices**, **Organic Pineapple**, **Organic Plums**, **Organic Prunes**, **Organic Puy Lentils**, **Organic Raspberries**, **Organic Red Kidney Beans**, **Organic Sauerkraut**, **Organic Spinach**, **Organic Strawberries**, **Organic Sweetcorn**, **Organic Tomato Puree**, **Organic Tropical Fruits**, **Organic Whole Tomatoes**

FRESH FOODS CO LTD ⃠ ☼
Organic Baked Beans

GRANOSE ⃠
Lentil & Vegetable Casserole; Meatless Mince & Onion; Mock Duck; Nuttolene; Sausalatas

GRANOVITA UK LTD ☺ ⃠ ☼ ✂
Nut Luncheon; Vegetable Hotpot

H J HEINZ CO LTD ™⃠
Baked Beans: Barbecue, Curried, Healthy Balance in Tomato Sauce, In Tomato Sauce, Organic in Tomato Sauce, Reduced Sugar & Salt, Weight Watchers in Tomato Sauce; *Pasta Shapes in Tomato Sauce:* Bill & Ben, Clifford the Big Red Dog, Disney Princess, Fimbles, Pokemon, Sabrina, Simpsons, Spiderman, Teletubbies, Thomas the Tank Engine, Tweenies, Winnie the Pooh, X Men; *Spaghetti:* Hoops in Tomato Sauce, In Tomato Sauce, Meat Free Bolognese; *Weight Watchers Pasta:* Spaghetti in Tomato Sauce w Parsley

OIL IN THE RAW ☺ ⃠ ☼
Organic Hand-Picked Kalamon Table Olives in Sea Salt

ORGRAN ⃠
Gluten-Free Tinned Spaghetti

PATAKS FOODS LTD ⃠
Canned Vegetable Curries: Black-eyed Bean Dhal, Bombay Potato, Chickpea Dhal, Lemon Dhal, Lentil Dhal, Mixed Vegetable, Potato & Pea

SOMA ☺ ⃠ ☼
Nomato: Baked Beans, Veg Chilli

WESTLER FOODS LTD ⃠
Chesswood: Chilli No Carne, Vegetable Balti Curry, Vegetable Casablanca, Vegetable Chilli; *Chesswood Organic:* Vegetable Chilli, Vegetable Curry, Vegetable Hot Pot; *Wayfarer:* Spicy Vegetable Rigatoni, Vegetable Curry

SAVOURIES CHILLED / FRESH

AROMAFOODS ™☺✓✂
Aromatic Braised Red Cabbage; **Greek Spinach Falafel**; **Lemon & Coriander Falafel**; **Masala Veget-Apple Pakora**; **Mexican Bean Burger**; Mildly Spiced Mini Bhajia; **Spinach & Onion Bhajia**; **Sweetcorn & Pineapple Bhajia**

BRAKE BROS
Chargrilled Vegetable Terrine; Gnocchi; *Salad:* Beetroot & Onion, Provencale Bean, Roasted Mediterranean Vegetable, Roasted Vegetable Cous Cous, Spicy Tomato & Penne Pasta

CAULDRON FOODS LTD ⃠
Crunchy Carrot Peanut & Onion Nut Burgers; Falafel; *Organic:* Falafel

CLIVE'S
Soysage Roll

DIPAK FOODS LTD ™⃠☺❶✓✂
Dal Kachori; **Mixed Vegetable Spring Rolls**; **Onion Bhaji**; **Peas Kachori**; **Peas Petis**; **Soya Chunks Curry**; **Soya Mince Curry**; **Spinach Bhaji**; **Spinach Pakora**; **Sunder Curry Sauce**; **Vegetable Curry Sauce**; *Samosas:* **Mixed Vegetable**, **Soya**

HOUSE OF LIFE ™
Veggie Cutlets

LEEORA VEGETARIAN FOOD ™⃠
Meal Centres: **8 Koobbe**, **8 Swedish Style Veggie Balls**; *Mediterranean Cuisine:* **Falafel**, **Teboula w Sundried Tomato**; *Ready Meals:* **3 Koobbe w Pasta & Sundried Tomato**, **3 Koobbe w Rice**, **Vegetarian Italian Style Ragu w Pasta**, **Vegetarian Thai Style Curry w Mejadra Rice**, **Veggie Balls w Mushroom Rice**

MACSWEEN OF EDINBURGH ⃠
Vegetarian Haggis

MCCAIN FOODS GB LTD ⃠
Chilled Chips: Fresh, Friers Choice, Harvest Choice

PAUL'S TOFU ™☺⃠✓☼
Savouries: **Tofu & Vegetable Samosa**

REDWOOD WHOLEFOOD COMPANY ❶⃠☺ ™
Vegi-Deli: **Falafel**

SACLA
Char Grilled Mushrooms; Red & Yellow Peppers in Balsamic Vinegar

SIMPLY ORGANIC ⃠☼
Pure & Pronto Ready Meals: Lentil & Vegetable Stew, Mediterranean Vegetable & Bean Casserole, Mixed Bean Chilli, Moroccan Vegetable Tangine, Roasted Vegetables w Quinoa, Thai Vegetable Curry w Green Lentils

THRESHERS+ FOOD
Olives; Red Onion Bhaji; Vegetable Samosa

WICKEN FEN ⃠
Cakes: Bangkok Noodle, Bubble & Squeak Potato, North African Cous Cous

SAVOURIES - DRIED

BARKAT
Pot Meal: Mexican Rice, Rice & Tomato

CLEARSPRING ™☺❶⃠
Lotus Root Slices - Dried; **Maitake Mushrooms**; **Shiitake Mushrooms - 50g/150g**; **Shredded Daikon - Dried**; **Udon - Brown Rice Noodles**; **Udon - Wholewheat Noodles**; *Danival:* **Hot Vegetarian Chilli**; *Organic:* **Brown Rice Udon Noodles**, **Lomein Noodles**, **Soba - Jinenjo Noodles**, **Soba Noodles**, **Udon Noodles**, **Udon - Wholewheat**; *Soba Buckwheat Noodles:* **100%**

DISCOVERY FOODS
Traditional Tacos Shells; *Kit:* Cajun Fajita, Gluten Free, Mexican Fajita, Nachos; *Wrap & Roll:* Garlic & Coriander, Original, Tomato & Chilli

ESSENTIAL BRAND ™❶⃠
Pre Packs (Organic & Conventional): **Apple Rings**, **Apricots**, **Cereals Flakes & Grain Meals**, **Cranberries**, **Crystalised Ginger**, **Currants**, **Dates**, **Figs**, **Flours (All)**, **Fruit Salad**, **Grains (All)**, **Herbs + Spices (All)**, **Mango Slices**, **Mixed Fruit**, **Nuts**, **Papaya**, **Pear Halves**, **Pineapple Rings**, **Prunes**, **Pulses + Beans**, **Raisins**, **Rice (All)**, **Seeds (All)**, **Sugars (All)**, **Sultanas**, **Textured Vegetable Protein - Plain**, **Tomatoes (All)**

FIRST QUALITY FOODS ⃠
Sammy's Falafel Mix; *Sammy's Couscous:* Moroccan, Roast Garlic & Olive Oil, Salad, Sundried Tomato, Wild Mushroom

GLUTANO
Pot Meal: Mexican Rice, Organic Potato & Onion, Rice & Tomato

GRANOSE ⃠
Roast: Cashew, Cashew Mix, Nut, Nut Mix, Sunflower & Sesame Mix

GRANOVITA UK LTD ☺⃠☼
Organic Grains: Bulgar Wheat, Quinoa, Red Quinoa

H J HEINZ CO LTD ™⃠
Weight Watchers Pasta: Curry Flavour Noodles, Spicy Thai Flavour Noodles

JUST WHOLEFOODS ☺⃠
Mixes: Biriyani, Chow Mein, Cous Cous & Lentils, Falafel, Hummus; *Organic World Mixes:* Biriyani, Chow Mein, Falafel, Houmous & Cous Cous & Lentil

MOTHER HEMP LTD ™⃠
Hemp/Spelt Pasta

ORGRAN ⃠
Falafel Mix

PAUL'S TOFU ™☺⊘♞☼
Savouries: **Organic Nut Roast**

SANCHI ⊘
Organic Noodles: 40% Soba, Green Tea, Someh, Thai Rice, Udon; *Organic Ramen:* Ginger; *Organic Ramen Noodles:* Mushroom, Seaweed; *Organic Udon Noodles:* Brown Rice; *Soba Noodles:* 100% Buckwheat, 40% Buckwheat; *Udon Noodles:* Brown Rice (Genmai), Quinoa

SUMA WHOLEFOODS ⊘™◉❶✁1985
RSPB Organic & Wildlife Friendly: **Spanish Brown Short Grain Rice**, **Spanish Short Grain Rice**

TRUFREE (NUTRICIA) ™⊘
Lasagne; **Pasta Penne**; **Pasta Shells**; **Spaghetti**

VEGANSTORE.CO.UK ™☺⊘❶♞
Roads End: Shells Vegan Macaroni Cheese, Tuna Not Salad

YORKSHIRE HEMP LTD ™
Hemp Pasta; **Hemp Rasta Pasta**; **Hemp Spaghetti**

SAVOURIES - FROZEN

AROMAFOODS ™☺♞✁
Japanese Pulse Salad; Turkish White Cabbage

AUNT BESSIES ™⊘

Hash Browns; Homestyle Chips; Jacket Wedges; Oven Crunchies; Potato Waffles; *Chip Shop:* Chunky Chips, Oven Chips

BRAKE BROS
Battered Onion Rings; Battered Pepper Rings; Carrot & Coriander Goujons; Chargrilled Vegetable Terrine; Cracked Black Pepper Battered Potato Skins; Crispy Vegetable Parcels; Eastern Variety Pack; Flaming Fire Fingers; Giant Whole Battered Onion Rings; Golden Vegetable Crown; Hash Browns; Indian Appetiser Selection; Leek & Lentil Pie; Mediterranean Vegetable Tartlet; Mini Indian Savoury Selection; Mini Vegetable Samosas; Nutty Vegetable Crumble - Mini Multi; Raj Vegetable Curry; Rice & Vegetable Mix; Sag Aloo & Bombay Potato Mixed Box; Savoury Bean Casserole; Spicy Tortilla Bites; Stacks; Sweet Pepper & Chilli Tart; Vegetable Chilli; Vegetable Pakora; Vegetable Samosas; Vegetable Smiles; Vegetable Spring Rolls; *Bhaji:* Moghlai Onion, Onion; *Breaded:* Mushrooms, Onion Rings; *Chargrilled Vegetables:* All; *Fries:* All; *Potato:* Baked Jacket, Cooked Baby Charlotte, Crushed, Dice, Garlic & Rosemary Roasting, Jacket Wedges, Letters, Long Boat Shells, Mini Waffles, Saute, Skins - Pre-fried, Ted Heads, Waffles; *Seasoned Fries:* All; *Vegetable Mix:* Mexican Stir Fry, Oriental, Roasted Mediterranean

CALEDONIAN CURRY CO. ™⃠
Baigan Nariyal (Hot Aubergine & Chilli); **Baigan Tamatar (Spiced Aubergine & Tomato)**; **Bombay Potato**; **Caledonian Chickpea**; **Channa Dhal Masala**; **Highland Beetroot Curry**; **Palak Choley (Spinach & Chickpea Curry)**; **Saag Aloo**; **Tarka Dal**

DRAGONFLY FOODS ⃠ ☼
Cabbage; Original Tatty (Potato-Based Pattys)

MCCAIN FOODS GB LTD ⃠
Potato Flake; *Appetisers:* Aromatic Thai Babycorn, Baby Corn Firesticks; *Foodservice Southern Fries:* Garlic & Oregano Wedges, Piri Piri Wedges, Savoury Herb Dice, Spicy Lattice Fries, Spicy Spiral Fries, Spicy Wedge Fries; *French Fry Products:* Beefeater, Chippy Chips, Crispy French Fries, Freeze Chill, Gold Standard Crinkle Cut, Gold Standard Straight Cut, Harvest Choice, Homefries Crinkle Cut, Homefries Straight Cut, Julienne, Lights, Lumberjacks, Original Oven Chips Crinkle Cut, Original Oven Chips Straight Cut, Sous Chef, Stay Crisp, Supervalue; *Microwave Products:* Fries to Go, Mega MicroChips, MicroChips Crinkle Cut, MicroChips Straight Cut; *Potato Specialities:* 1/2 Cut Potato Skins, 1/4 Cut Potato Skins, Chunky Wedges, Country Style Dice, Crunchy Potato Bites, Hash Brown Nuggets, Hash Browns, Hash Rounds, Home Roast, Jacket Wedges, Mini Waffles, Nicely Spiced Wedges, Pomme Noisettes, Roast Potatoes, Rosti, Saute Potatoes, Sea Salt & Cracked Black Pepper, Smiles, Smoulderin Vibes, Speedsters

SEASONAL FOODS

BAKERS DELIGHT ⃠
Gluten Free (seasonal): Mince Pies

BRAKE BROS
Baked Mince Pies; Christmas Pudding Loaf; Hot Cross Buns; Individual Christmas Pudding; *Matthew Walker:* Christmas Pudding Logs, Individual Puddings

DR HADWEN TRUST ☺❶⃠
Animal-Free Christmas Pudding

GREEN & BLACKS ⃠ ☼
Organic Fairtrade Maya Gold Easter Egg

KITCHEN GARDEN PRESERVES
Christmas Range: Christmas Chutney, Luxury Mincemeat w Brandy

KP NUTS ⃠
Luxury Roasted Cashews (Xmas)

PAUL'S TOFU ™☺⃠ ☼
Breads: **Organic Hot x Buns**; *Cakes:* **2 Organic Mince Pies w Miso & Kuzu**, **2 Organic Mince Pies w Miso & Kuzu (Gluten Free)**, **Gluten Free Christmas Cake**, **Gluten Free Christmas Pudding**, **Gluten Free**

Mince Pies, **Organic Christmas Cake**, **Organic Christmas Pudding**

THE VILLAGE BAKERY MELMERBY LTD ⃠
Gluten Free Christmas Pudding - Wheat & Dairy Free; Gluten Free Mince Pies - Wheat & Dairy Free

WALKERS SNACK FOODS LTD ⃠
Doritos: Christmas Dip

WARBURTONS ⃠
Morning Goods: Hot Cross Bun Loaf

SEAWEED & SEAVEG

CLEARSPRING ™☺❶⃠
Agar Agar Flakes - 28g/100g; **Arame - 50g/250g**; **Dulse - Atlantic Coast USA - 50g/250g**; **Green Nori Flakes**; **Hijiki**; **Kombu**; **Kombu - Breton**; **Nori**; **Nori-Flavoured Strips**; **Sea Salad**; **Sea Vegetable Salad**; **Wakame**; *Brown Rice:* **Sea Vegetable Snacks**; *Sushi:* **Nori Toasted**

LIVING EARTH EUROPE ™
Flaked Nigari

QUALITY SEA VEG ™☺
Quality Sea Veg

SANCHI ⃠
Seaweed: Arame, Kombu, Nori, Sushi Nori, Wakame

SEAGREENS ™☺⃠✡
Dulse Granules; *Ascophyllum Pieces:* **Seaweed Table Condiment**; *Pelvetia Pieces:* **Pelvetia Seaweed Salad**

SETALG ™
Les Algues Gastronomes: **Agar Agar**, **Dulse**, **Haricot de Mer**, **Kambu**, **Laitve de Mer**, **Noiu**, **Salade de la Mer**, **Wakame**

SOURCE FOODS ☺✡
Herbs of the Sea

XYNERGY HEALTH PRODUCTS ⃠✓
Seagreens: Wild Seaweed Food

SNACKS - SAVOURY

BRAKE BROS
Crisps; Salted Peanuts

BUXTON FOODS ⃠
Sweet Potato Chips; Vegetable Chips

CLEARSPRING ™☺❶⃠
Quinoa Black Sesame Snacks; **Roasted Pumpkin Seeds**; **Roasted Snack Mix**; **Roasted Soya Snack - Onion**; *Japanese Rice Snacks:* Traditional Rice Snacks - Black Sesame, Traditional Rice Snacks - White Sesame; *Organic:* **Rice Crackers - Extra Virgin Olive Oil & Sea Salt**; *Organic Snack Mixes:* Roasted Soya Snack - Onion; *Traditional Rice Snacks:* **Black Sesame**, **White Sesame**

CRAZY JACKS ⦸
Bombay Mix

DISCOVERY FOODS
Tortilla Chips

ESSENTIAL BRAND ™❶ ⦸ ✂
Mixes: **Fruit Salad**, **Organic Fruit + Nut Mix**, **Organic Fruit Salad**

GLUTANO
Pretzels: Salted, Sesame Rings

GOLDEN WONDER ⦸
Crisps: Pickled Onion Flavour, Quite Hot Curry Flavour, Ready Salted, Salt + Vinegar Flavour, Sausage + Tomato Flavour, Tomato Ketchup Flavour; *Crunchy Fries:* Salt + Vinegar Flavour; *Ringos:* Pickled Onion Flavour, Salt + Vinegar Flavour

HEARTY'S ⦸
Soy Nuts: BBQ, Salted

HULA HOOPS ⦸
Original; Salt & Vinegar

JONATHAN CRISP ⦸
Crisps: Jalapeno Pepper, Lightly Salted, Sea Salt & Black Pepper, Sea Salt & Malt Vinegar

KETTLE FOODS ❶⦸
Kettle Chips: Golden Parsnip, Jersey Royals Lightly Salted, Lightly Salted, Red Duke of York, Salsa w Mesquite, Sea Salt & Balsamic Vinegar, Sea Salt Rosemary & Garlic, Sea Salt w Crushed Black Peppercorns, Sweet Potato; *Kettle Mediterranean:* Sweet Red Pepper & Sun Dried Tomato; *Kettle Organics Handcooked Chips:* Lightly Salted, Sea Salt w Crushed Black Peppercorns; *Kettle Tortillas:* Louisiana Hot Sauce, Sea Salt Coriander & Garlic; *Peak Baked Crisps:* Lightly Salted

KP CRISPS ⦸
Beef; Ready Salted; Salt & Vinegar; Worcester Sauce

KP IRELAND ⦸
Salted Popcorn

KP NUTS ⦸
Brannigans Peanuts: Dry Roasted, Roasted Salted; *Peanuts:* Dry Roasted, Salt & Vinegar, Spicy Chilli; *Roast Salted:* Cashews, Pistachios

LAWNCOURT HARVEST LTD ™
Chilli Mix; **Original Mix**; **Pumpkin Mix**; **Vanilla Pumpkin**

LIFE FOOD GMBH - TAIFUN-TOFUPRODUKTE ☺⦸☼
Thai Sticks

McCOYS POTATO CHIPS ⦸
Chinese Sizzlin Beef; Mexican Chilli; Salt & Malt Vinegar; Salted

MOTHER HEMP LTD ™⦸
Hemp Seed; **Hulled Hemp Seed**

PHILEAS FOGG COMPANY ⃠
Bagel Chips: Pastrami to Go; *Tortillas:* Classic Mexican, Lightly Salted

QUEENSLAND GOVERNMENT ❶⃠✓
Ajitas Vegetarian Chips

RAINBOW FLAVOURS ™
Rainbow: **Flavours**, **Fruit Crisps**

SANCHI ⃠
Sanchi Nippers (Seasoned Nori Snack); *Chips:* Brown Rice, Hot & Spicy Wasabi, Sea Vegetable

STONEWALLS ™
Cajun Bacon

SUMA WHOLEFOODS ⃠™👁❶✂1985
Bhusu; Bombay Mix; Delhi Mix; Garlic Sticks; Organic Bombay Mix; Spiced Roast Chick Peas; Spicy Noodles; Spicy Sticks

THE VEGE CHIP COMPANY ™
Ajitas Vege Chips: **BBQ Flavour**, **French Onion Flavour**, **Herbs & Garlic Flavour**, **Natural Flavour**, **Sweet Chilli Flavour**, **Sweet & Sour Flavour**

THRESHERS+ FOOD
Crudités

TRUFREE (NUTRICIA) ™⃠
Potato & Vegetable Quicksnack; **Rice & Lentil Quicksnack**

UNITED BISCUITS LTD ⃠
Discos: Pickled Onion, Salt & Vinegar; *Frisps:* Ready Salted, Salt & Vinegar; *Mini Chips:* Beef, Salt & Vinegar; *Space Raiders:* Pickled Onion

VEGANSTORE.CO.UK ™☺⃠❶✓
Tings: Cheesy Nik Naks

WALKERS SNACK FOODS LTD ⃠
Ready Salted Squares; Salt 'n' Shake; Salt & Vinegar Quavers; *Crisps:* Pickled Onion, Prawn Cocktail, Ready Salted, Roast Chicken Flavour, Salt & Vinegar, Worcester Sauce; *Dippas Dipping Chips:* Lightly Salted; *Doritos:* Chilli Heatwave; *French Fries:* Ready Salted, Salt & Vinegar; *Lites:* Ready Salted, Salt & Vinegar; *MAX:* Salt & Vinegar; *Mr Potato Head:* Ready Salted; *Sensations:* Tangy Tomato & Red Pepper Salsa Flavour; *Sensations Oriental Crackers:* Black Bean Flavour, Tangy Malaysian Chutney; *Shots:* Nicely Spicely Flavour; *Smiths:* Ready Salted, Ready Salted Chipsticks, Salt & Vinegar Chipsticks; *Stax:* Ready Salted; *Wotsits:* Flamin' Hot Flavour

YAOH ™☺✓⃠❶
De-Hulled Hemp Seeds

YORKSHIRE HEMP LTD ™
Hemp Seeds; **Shelled Hemp Seeds**; *Cannibis Club:* **Potato Chips**; *Hemp Nibbles:* **Cappuccino**, **Hot & Spice**, **Salt & Herb**

SOUPS

BAXTERS OF SPEYSIDE LTD ⃠
Fresh: Chunky Minestrone, Mediterranean Tomato; *Healthy Choice:* Carrot Onion & Chickpea, Italian Bean & Pasta; *Healthy Helpings:* Chunky Country Vegetable; *Organic:* Vegetable Bean & Pasta; *Traditional:* French Onion, Minestrone, Potato & Leek; *Vegetarian:* Carrot & Butterbean, Mediterranean Tomato, Tomato & Butterbean

BRAKE BROS
Carrot & Coriander; Minestrone; Spring Vegetable; Tomato & Basil

CLEARSPRING ™☺❶⃠
Miso Soup - Red (Sea Vegetables); **Miso Soup - White (Tofu)**; *Organic:* **Instant Miso Soup**

GO ORGANIC
Warming Parsnip; *Italian:* Tomato & Basil

H J HEINZ CO LTD ™⃠
Lentil; Vegetable; *Weight Watchers from Heinz:* Carrot & Lentil, Country Vegetable, Mediterranean Tomato & Vegetable, Tomato & Red Pepper, Vegetable; *Weight Watchers from Heinz - Microwaveable:* Country Vegetable Cup

JEREMY'S SOUPS ⃠ ✂

Bonza Bean; Lip Smakin' Lentil; Mad Melon & Ginger; Voluptuous Vegetable

JUST WHOLEFOODS ☺⃠
Instant Soup Mixes: Carrot & Coriander, Leek & Potato, Minestrone, Tomato & Basil, Vegetable; *Soup in a Mug:* Carrot & Coriander, Leek & Potato, Tomato & Basil, Vegetable & Minestrone

ORGRAN ⃠
Garden Vegetable Soup Mix

SANCHI ⃠
Miso Soup: Instant w Seaweed, Organic, Organic w Mushroom

SEEDS OF CHANGE ⃠ ✿
Spicy Lentil; Three Bean

SIMPLY ORGANIC ⃠ ✿
Chunky Tomato & Lentil; Chunky Vegetable; Lentil & Parsley; Mediterranean Tomato; Minestrone; Yellow Split Pea

SOMA ☺⃠ ✿
Nomato: Nomato Soup

SUMA WHOLEFOODS ⃠™❶ ✂ 1985
Broth Mix; *Organic Soups:* Carrot & Coriander, Minestrone, Pea, Spicy Lentil, Tomato, Tomato & Red Pepper

THORNTONS PLC ⃠
Vegetable & Lentil

SOYA & OTHER 'MILKS'

ALPRO UK LTD ™⃠
Organic Soya Fruity: **Orchard**, **Tropical**; *Organic Soya Milk:* **Sweetened**, **Unsweetened**, **Vanilla Flavour**; *OY! Flavoured Soya Milk:* **Banana**, **Chocolate**, **Strawberry**, **Vanilla**; *Rice Drink:* **Organic**, **w Calcium + Vitamins**; *Soya Milk:* **Sweetened**, **Unsweetened**, **w Calcium**, **w Calcium & Vitamins**; *Soya Soleil:* **Sweetened**, Unsweetened

CAM INTERNATIONAL ™⃠
The Soy Milker

CLEARSPRING ™☺❶⃠
Graindrops: **Oat Drink**, **Rice Drink**, **Spelt Drink**; *Graindrops Organic Dairy-Free Beverages:* Oat Drink, Rice Drink, Spelt Drink

GRANOSE ⃠
Soya 'Milk': Calcium Enriched, Calcium Enriched - Sweetened, Organic

GRANOVITA UK LTD ☺⃠☼
Soya Drink: Calcium Enriched, Organic Sugar Free

HOLLAND AND BARRETT RETAIL LTD
Rice Delight; *Soya Alternative to Milk:* Calcium Enriched, Unsweetened

LIFE FOOD GMBH - TAIFUN-TOFUPRODUKTE ☺⃠☼
Soya-Drink: Harmonie, Natur

LIVING EARTH EUROPE ™
Digital Multi Function Milk Maker

OAT SUPREME ™☺⃠
Milk

PLAMIL FOODS LTD ™☺❶⃠
Organic Soya Milk; *White Sun - Pea Based Alternative to Milk:* **White Sun w Vitamins & Calcium**

SANCHI ⃠
"Bonsoy" Soya Milk

SOYA HEALTH FOODS LTD ☺❶⃠
Soya Milk 'Sunrise': Calcium & Vitamin Enriched, Organic Sweetened, Organic Unsweetened

TOM SOYA ☺⃠
Childrens Soya Drinks: Tom's Banana Shakes, Tom's Chocolate Shakes, Tom's Strawberry Shakes; *Soya Drinks:* Chocolate Flavoured Soya Drink, Organic Soy Drink

TREE OF LIFE UK LTD ⃠
Vitasoy Organic Soya Drink: Chocolate Delight, Creamy Original, Vanilla Delight

VEGANSTORE.CO.UK ™☺⃠❶
Dixie: Moo Not Powdered Soy Milk; *Tam Tov:* Coffee Creamer

WHITEWAVE ⃠
Calcium Enriched - Sweetened; No Added Sugar

SPICES

CHIMANS ™☺⃠
Aloo Gobi; **Balti Pasta**; **Bean Curry**; **Bombay Potatoes**; **Dal**; **Spicy Chick Peas**; **Spicy Vegetable Soup**; *Organic:* **Aloo Gobi**, **Bean Curry**, **Bombay Potatoes**, **Dal**, **Spicy Chick Peas**, **Spicy Vegetable Soup**

DISCOVERY FOODS
Seasoning Mix: Cajun, Fajita, Taco

PATAKS FOODS LTD ⃠
Curry Pastes: Balti, Bhuna, Biryani, Extra Hot Curry, Garam Masala, Jalfrezi, Kashmiri Masala, Korma, Madras, Mild Curry, Rogan Josh, Tikka, Tikka Masala, Vindaloo

SCOTTISH HERBAL SUPPLIES ™⃠☺❶
Dried Organic Herbs

THE ORGANIC HERB TRADING COMPANY ⃠☼
Organic Herbs & Spices

SPREADS - SAVOURY

ALAVON ™⃠☺
Coleslaw; **Garlic Coleslaw**; **Potato Salad**

CAULDRON FOODS LTD ⃠
Chickpea & Black Olive Paté; *Vegetable Paté w:* Herbs, Mushrooms

ESSENTIAL BRAND ™❶ ⃠ ✂
Tahini (Organic & Conventional); *Peanut Butters:* **All (Organic & Conventional)**

FLORENTINO ™⃠
Pesto: **Basil - Cheese Free**, **Red - Cheese Free**

FRESH FOODS CO LTD ⃠☼
Nut Butters: All

GRANOVITA UK LTD ☺⃠☼ ✂
Tangy Tomato Pate (Yeast Free); *Organic Ready Spready:* Garlic & Herb, Herb, Mushroom, Original; *Pateole:* Mushroom; *Ready Spready:* Herb Provence, Mushroom, Original

LEEORA VEGETARIAN FOOD ™⃠
Mediterranean Cuisine: **Moroccan Style Matbucha**; *Pate:* **Carrot & Chive**, **French Style**, **Green Lentil**, **Mushroom & Garlic**, **Spicy**, **Sundried Tomato**

MARMITE
Yeast Extract

MERIDIAN FOODS
Free From Range: Green Pesto, Red Pesto; *Savoury Spread:* Yeast Extract, Yeast Extract-Low Salt

MOTHER HEMP LTD ™⦸✓
Hemp Pesto: Green, **Red**

PANTRI NOLWENN ⦸❶✓✂☼
Spread: Babaganouj, Ensalada Pimiento, Guacamole, Hummous, Pate de Champignons/Mushroom Pate, Pate Ffa Gwyn/White Bean Pate, Rouille/Red Pepper Spread, Tapenade

RED23 ™☺
Chunky Almond Butter; Hempini - Hemp Seed Butter; Luscious Nut & Seed Spread; Pistachio Nut Butter; *Fresh Raw:* Almond Butter, Brazil Nut Butter, Cashew Butter, Pumkin Seed Butter, Sunflower Seed Butter, Tahini

REDWOOD WHOLEFOOD COMPANY ❶⦸☺ ™
Smoked Salmon Pate; *Cheatin' Pate:* **Forestier Pate**, **Pate de Campagne**, **Provencal Pate**

SIKELIA LTD ™
Pate: **Artichoke & Pistachio Nut**, **Aubergine**; *Pesto:* **from Mount Etna**, **Green Olive & Almond**, **Green Olive & Chilli**; *Sicilian Pesto:* **Artichoke**, **Aubergine**, **Caper**, **Pistachio**, **Tomato & Black Olive**

SUMA WHOLEFOODS ⦸™👁❶✂1985
Organic Tomato Paste; *Organic Pate:* Herb, Mushroom; *Organic Peanut Butter:* Crunchy, Crunchy - No Salt, Smooth, **Smooth - No Salt**; *Organic Pesto:* **Green**, **Red**; *Pate:* Herb; *Peanut Butter:* Crunchy, Crunchy - No Salt, Smooth, Smooth - No Salt

SPREADS - SWEET

BAXTERS OF SPEYSIDE LTD ⦸
Reduced Sugar Jam: Blackcurrant, Raspberry, Rhubarb & Ginger, Strawberry; *Reduced Sugar Marmalade:* Orange Lemon & Grapefruit, Thick Cut Seville Orange, Thin Cut Seville Orange

CLEARSPRING ™☺❶⦸
Fruit Puree - Apple/Banana; **Fruit Puree - Apple/Orange**; **Fruit Puree - Apple/Strawberry**; **Fruit Puree - Pear**; **Fruit Spread - Blackcurrant**; *Organic:* **Apricot Fruit Spread**, **Blueberry Fruit Spread**, **Orange Fruit Spread**, **Prune Fruit Spread**, **Pumpkin Puree**, **Sour Cherry Fruit Spread**, **Strawberry Fruit Spread**; *Organic Fruit Purées:* Apple & Orange Fruit Purée, Pear Fruit Purée; *Organic Puree:* **Apple**, **Apple/Apricot**, **Apple/Blueberry**, **Apple/Plum**

DUERRS
'Fruit Farm' Preserves: Apple & Blackcurrant, Apple & Strawberry, Apricot, Blackcurrant, Fine Cut Orange, Mixed Fruit, Raspberry, Strawberry, Thick Cut Orange; *Fruit Jams:* Apricot, Blackcurrant, Bramble, Ginger, Raspberry, Seedless Raspberry, Strawberry; *Low Carb High Fruit Spreads:* Apricot, Fine Cut Orange, Raspberry, Strawberry;

Marmalades: Coarse Cut, Fine Cut (w 3% Teacher's Scotch Whisky); *Organic Marmalades:* Fine Cut Orange, Thick Cut Orange; *Organic Preserves:* Apricot, Raspberry, Strawberry; *Seriously Fruity Jams:* Pure Fruit Apricot, Pure Fruit Blackcurrant, Pure Fruit Seedless Raspberry, Pure Fruit Strawberry; *Traditional Marmalades:* Fine Cut Grapefruit, Fine Cut 'Half Sugar' Orange, Fine Cut Orange, Ginger, Medium Cut Orange, Shredless Orange, Thick Cut Orange

ESSENTIAL TRADING CO-OPERATIVE LTD ™❶⊘🌱✂
Fruit Spreads: **Organic Cherry**, **Organic Four Fruit**, **Organic Raspberry**, **Organic Strawberry**, **Organic Wild Bilberry**; *Spreads:* **Organic Apricot**, **Organic Blackberry**, **Organic Blueberry**

KITCHEN GARDEN PRESERVES 🌱
Extra Jams: Apricot w Almonds, Blackberry & Apple, Blackcurrant, Gooseberry & Orange, Pear & Ginger, Plum, Raspberry, Rhubarb, Strawberry, Summer Berry; *Marmalades:* Coarse Cut Lemon & Ginger, Fine Cut Grapefruit, Fine Cut Orange & Cranberry, Fine Cut Three Fruit, Rough Cut Lime, Rough Cut Orange; *Organic Extra Jams:* Apricot w Almonds, Blackcurrant, Plum, Raspberry, Strawberry, Wild Blueberry & Apple; *Organic Marmalades:* Fine Cut Three Fruits, Rough Cut Grapefruit, Rough Cut Seville Orange

PANTRI NOLWENN ⊘❶🌱✂☼
Spread: Siytni Bricyllen/Apricot Chutney, Siytni Datys/Date Chutney

PLAMIL FOODS LTD ™☺❶⊘
Organic Chocolate Spread: **Crunchy Nut**, **Orange**, **Plain**

TOFU, TEMPEH, MISO ETC

CAULDRON FOODS LTD ⊘
Tofu: Marinated, Marinated Pieces, Organic Original, Organic Smoked, Original

CLEARSPRING ™☺❶⊘
San J Tamari 2.5l; **Snow Dried Tofu**; **Tekka (Miso Condiment)**; *Danival Organic:* **Barley Miso**, **Brown Rice Miso**, **Tempeh**; *Organic:* **Hatcho Miso**, **Johsen Genmai (Brown Rice) Miso**, **Johsen Genmai (Brown Rice) Miso (Pasteurised)**, **Marukura (Sweet White) Miso (Pasteurised)**, **Onozaki Mugi (Barley) Miso - 300g/1kg**

DRAGONFLY FOODS ⊘☼
Organic Tofu: Deep-Fried, Natural, Smoked

LEAFCYCLE ™☺⊘
LEAF CURD (Pure Dried Leaf Curd)

LIFE FOOD GMBH - TAIFUN-TOFUPRODUKTE ☺⃠☼
Tofu: Plain, Plain "Demeter", Ragout Classic, Ragout Curry, Rosso, Silken, Smoked, Smoked "Demeter", Smoked w Almonds & Sesame Seeds; *Tofu Terrine:* Country-Style, Graffiti

LIVING EARTH EUROPE ™
Tofu Kit

MARIGOLD HEALTH FOODS ❶⃠
Braised Tofu

NATUREMADE OASIS ⃠ ✂ ☼
Oasis: Tempeh, Tofu

OHSO MISO ☺☼
Yummo Sesame; *Organic Instant Soup:* Beetroot, Ginger, Original, Spirulina

PAUL'S TOFU ™☺⃠ ☼
Savouries: **Abura Age Marinated Tofu**, **Nigari Tofu**

PHYTOFOODS ☺⃠❶ ✂☼
Tempeh Kit

QUINOVA ™⃠☺
Chunks; **Mince**; *Banyan:* **Indian Spice**, **Mediterranean**, **Plain**, **Welsh Onion & Chives**

SANCHI ⃠
Miso: Genmai (Brown Rice), Hatcho (Soya Bean), Mugi (Barley), Organic Mugi (Barley), Organic Unpasteurised Barley (Mugi), Shiro

SOURCE FOODS ☺☼
Low Sodium Rice & Soy Organic Miso: Mellow Brown, Sweet Brown; *Organic Miso:* Ginger, Hemp, Mellow Field Bean Barley, Mex Chilli; *Rice & Soy Organic Miso:* Mellow Brown, Sweet Brown

SOYA HEALTH FOODS LTD ☺❶⃠ ✂
Sunrise Tofu

TURTLE ISLAND FOODS ™
Turtle Island Tempeh

'YOGHURTS'

ALPRO UK LTD ™⃠
Alpro Dairy Free Alternative to Yogurt Raspberry & Vanilla Flavour; **Alpro Dairy Free Chocolate Flavoured Custard + Calcium**; **Exotic Fruits**; **Forest Fruits**; **Peach**; **Strawberry**; *Organic Yofu:* Peach/Mango, **Plain**, Red Cherry, **Summer Fruits**; *Yofu Junior:* **Peach & Pear**, **Strawberry & Banana**

GRANOVITA UK LTD ☺⃠☼ ✂
Deluxe Soyage: Banana, Black Cherry, Mango, Peach & Apricot, Plain, Raspberry, Strawberry, Tropical; *Organic Soyage:* Fruits of the Forest, Peach & Apricot, Strawberry

SO GOOD ⃠
Black Cherry; Peach & Passion Fruit; Pineapple; Plain; Strawberry

NOTES

■ **Banana chips** may be dipped in honey.

■ **Bread:** a few pre-packed loaves contain either skimmed milk powder or vitamin D3. Most large producers use vegetable-based emulsifiers (E471, E472 etc). When buying bread from local bakers check ingredients and type of fat used to grease tins.

■ **Breakfast cereals** fortified with vitamin D will often contain the animal-derived D3.

■ **Chocolate:** unfortunately, plain chocolate is not always animal-free. For UK-produced chocolate, reading the ingredients listing is not always sufficient. Continental plain chocolate is less likely to contain animal substances.
All of the chocolate products listed here have been made without animal-derived ingredients or processing aids, but may have been produced on the same lines as milk chocolate products, see **contamination**, below.

■ **Contamination:** the *Animal Free Shopper* only lists products that we have been informed meet our ANIMAL-FREE CRITERIA. However, many of the foods listed will have been produced on the same lines as products containing animal-based ingredients. Although health and hygiene, and product quality, requirements mean that machines are cleaned thoroughly between different products, there is a very slight, theoretical, risk of contamination. This means, for example, that some listed products may not be suitable for dairy allergy sufferers.

■ **Crisps** may contain lactose or whey. Even if no animal ingredients are named in the ingredients list, animal-derived processing aids may have been used as a flavour carrier.

■ **Di-calcium phosphate** may be sourced from bone and may be used as a growth medium for yeast used to manufacture bread. However, the most common yeast food used in the UK baking industry is calcium sulphate (animal-free).

■ **Fruit** may be glazed with animal (commonly beeswax or shellac), vegetable (usually carnauba) or mineral waxes. Contact manufacturers for further details as information changes regularly (according to season, supplier, etc).

■ **Gelatine carrier:** beta-carotene and vitamin D2 may be 'carried' in gelatine to maintain stability. In the case of beta-carotene, vegetable oil carriers are available and are generally animal-free; however, when sold as a supplement it is typically encased in capsules made of gelatine.

■ **Peanut butter** has been omitted as being obviously vegan

■ **Processing aids** may be animal derived. There is no statutory requirement for these to be listed on products.

■ **Salt** is usually vegan, except some low salts which contain a milk derivative. Centura Foods produce a variety of different types of salt which are vegan, including iodised salt.

■ **Sugar:** bone char is sometimes used as a decolourant in sugar production. However, the largest suppliers of sugar to companies in the UK - British Sugar, Tate & Lyle and Billington - do not use any animal-derived ingredients (except for Tate & Lyle Traditional Royal Icing, which contains dried egg white powder). Most supermarkets' own-brand sugars are made for them by one of these companies.

■ **Vinegar:** although malt and spirit vinegars are generally animal-free, the production of wine, cider and sherry vinegars may involve the use of a fining agent of animal origin.

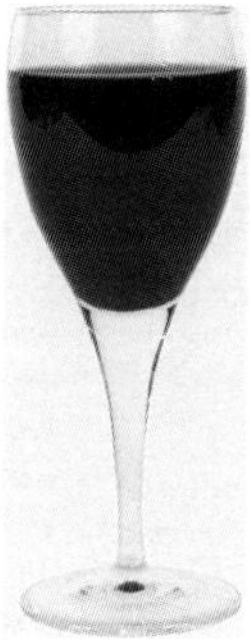

DRINK

BEER

ANHEUSER-BUSCH EUROPE LTD
Budweiser; Michelob; Michelob Ultra

ANIMAL AID ☺❶⊘✓ ✂1976
Organic Pinkus Special Lager Case

ASTON MANOR BREWERY CO LTD
Bottled Ales: Piddle in the Hole; *Bottled Beers:* Davenports Ale, Englands Glory, Fox's Nob, Highgate Best Bitter, Highgate Dark Mild, Highgate Export Lager, Highgate Lager, Highgate Old Ale

BLACK SHEEP BREWERY PLC ✓⊘
Bottled Ales: Black Sheep, Emmerdale, Golden Sheep Ale (Tesco Finest Range), Monty Python's Holy Grail, Riggwelter Strong

BRAKSPEAR
Organic Ale

CALEDONIAN BREWING CO
Bottled Beers: Caledonian 80, Deuchars IPA (not 330ml bottle), Golden Promise Organic

CARLSBERG UK LTD ⊘✓
Carlsberg (3.8% ABV Lager in Keg & Bottle - 4.0% ABV Lager in Can); Carlsberg Export (5.0% ABV Premium Lager in Keg Bottle & Can); Carlsberg Special Brew (9.0% ABV Strong Lager in Bottle & Can)

DR HADWEN TRUST ☺❶⊘✓
Golden Promise Bitter; Mixed Beer & Lager Case; Special Mixed Beer Case

DUCHY ORIGINALS
Organic Ale

FULLERS
Bottled & Keg (NOT Draught): All except Honey Dew

GEORGE BATEMAN & SON ™⊘✓
Bottled Beers: **Combined Harvest Multigrain Beer**, **Dark Lord Premium Ale**, **Rosey Nosey Premium Ale**, **Victory Ale**, **XXXB Classic Bitter**, **Yella Belly Organic Beer**

INTERBREW ⊘✓
Hoegaarden; Rolling Rock

PITFIELD BREWERY ™⊘✓☼
Bottled Beers: **Amber Ale**, **Black Eagle**, Christmas Ale, **East Kent Goldings**, **Eco Warrior**, **Hoxton Heavy**, **Imperial Stout**, **India Pale Ale**, **London Porter**, **Mild Ale**, **N1 Organic Wheat Beer**, **Pitfield Organic Lager**, **Pitfield Original** , **Shoreditch Stout**, XX Stout, **XXXX Stock Ale**

ROBERT CAIN & COMPANY LIMITED ⊘✓
Canned: Dark Mild, FA, Finest Bitter, IPA

SAMUEL SMITH ™⊘✓
Celebrated Oatmeal Stout; **Cider Reserve**; **Extra Stout**; **Famous Taddy**

Porter; **Imperial Stout**; **India Ale**; **Nut Brown Ale**; **Old Brewery Pale Ale**; **Organic Best Ale**; **Organic Lager**; **Pure Brewed Lager**; **Sovereign Bitter**; **Winter Welcome Ale**; *Ayingerbrau:* **D Pils Lager**, **Hefeweiss Lager**, **Lager**, **Low Alcohol Lager**, **Prinz Lager**

THE DURHAM BREWERY LTD
Bottle-Conditioned: Benedictus, Cloister, Evensong, St Cuthbert, Temptation, White Magic

THE INNIS & GUNN BREWING COMPANY LTD. ☺⊘✓👁✂
Oak Aged Beer

TRAQUAIR
Traquair Ale: Bear, House, Jacobite

VINCEREMOS ORGANIC WINES ™⊘✓
Broughton Ales: Border Gold

VINTAGE ROOTS ⊘
Cool Blonde Lager - The Beer Station; Dupetit Cannabia; Freedom Organic Pilsener; O'Hanlons Brewing Co Organic Rye Beer; Organic Beer; Organic Lager; *Black Isle Brewery:* Black Isle Porter, Black Isle Yellow Hammer; *Riedenburger:* Organic Lager (Helles), Weisse Wheatbeer

VIVA!☺❶⊘✓
Beers: All

WDB BRANDS ⊘✓
Marston's Resolution

YORKSHIRE HEMP LTD ™
Cannibis Club: **Beer**

CHAMPAGNE

ANIMAL AID ☺❶⊘✓✂1976
Champagne Case

DUVAL-LEROY UK LTD ™
Vegan Champagne

PURE WINE COMPANY ⊘✓☼
Jose Ardinat: Non Vintage Carte d'Or Brut, Non Vintage Rose

VINTAGE ROOTS ⊘
Fleury Champagne: AOC Champagne - Vintage 1996, Carte Rouge, Fleur de l'Europe, Rosé Brut; *Georges Laval:* Champagne Premier Cru Reserve Special Brut; *Serge Faust Champagne:* Carte d'Or, Cuvée Reserve

VIVA!☺❶⊘✓
Champagnes: All

CIDERS & PERRIES

ANIMAL AID ☺❶⊘✓✂1976
Organic Sparkling Cider Case

ASTON MANOR BREWERY CO LTD
Bottled Ciders: Frosty Jacks, Hereford Orchard, Kingstone Press Cider, Polaris White

AVALON VINEYARDS ⃠
Pennard Organic: Dry Cider (Draught)

DUNKERTON'S CIDER COMPANY ⃠☺ ☼
Ciders: Black Fox Sparkling Medium Dry, Kingston Black, Premium Organic Sparkling, Sparkling Extra Dry; *Perries:* Sparkling, Still; *Still Blended Ciders:* Dry, Med, Med Sweet, Sweet

LUSCOMBE ORGANIC DRINKS ☺⃠
Devon Cider

SEDLESCOMBE ORGANIC VINEYARD ™⃠ ☼
Dry Cider

SHEPPY'S CIDER ⃠
Draught Cider - Dry/Medium/Sweet; Gold Medal Vintage Cider - Dry/Medium/Sweet; Oakwood Draught Cider - Dry & Medium; Organic Cider - Dry or Medium; *Oakwood Special - Sparkling:* Dry, Medium; *Single Variety Ciders:* Dabinett, Kingston Black, Taylor's Gold, Tremlett's Bitter; *Sparkling:* Bullfinch (Medium), Goldfinch (Dry)

VINTAGE ROOTS ⃠
Domaine des Cinq Autels Normandy Cider; *Eric Bordelet:* Poiré Granit, Sydre Brut Tendre

VIVA!☺❶⃠
Ciders: All

WESTON & SONS LTD ☺⃠
Henry Weston's Vintage Reserve; Scrumpy Supreme; *Oak Conditioned Cider:* Medium Sweet, Strong Medium Dry; *Organic:* Cider, Perry, Spritzer, Vintage Cider; *Stowford Press Cider:* Dry, LA, Medium Dry, Medium Sweet

'HOT'

BIOFORCE
Bambu

BOVRIL
Vegetarian

BRAKE BROS
Drinking Chocolate

CLEARSPRING ™☺❶⃠
Mu Tea - 16 Herbs; *Organic:* **Bancha (Hojicha) Tea Bags**, **Genmaicha Green Tea/Roasted Brown Rice - Loose**, **Genmaicha - Green Tea/Roasted Brown Rice Tea Bags**, **Genmaicha Tea Bags**, **Hojicha Roasted Bancha Leaf Tea Bags**, **Hojicha Roasted Bancha Leaf Tea - Loose**, **Kukicha (Bancha) Twig Tea Bags**, **Kukicha (Bancha) Twig Tea - Loose 125g**, **Kukicha (Bancha) Twig Tea - Loose 500g**, **Kukicha Twig Tea Bags**, **Sencha Green Tea Bags**, **Sencha Green Tea - Loose**

ESSENTIAL BRAND ™❶ ⃠ ✂
Organic Coffee: **All**; *Organic Demeter Teas:* **All**

FRESH FOODS CO LTD ⃠ ☼
Organic: Nocaf, Wakecup

GREEN & BLACKS ⃠ ☼
Organic Cocoa; Organic Hot Chocolate

NESTLÈ
Caro: Extra, Instant

THE COCOA TREE (1657) LTD ™☺❶⃠
Drinking Chocolate

YORKSHIRE HEMP LTD ™
Hemp Tea: **Turkish**, **w Blackcurrant & Blackberry Leaf**, **w Elderberry**, **w Fruit**, **w Lemon Verbena & Blackberry Leaf**, **w Nettle & Blackberry Leaf**

SOFT

AME ⃠
Dry; Red; Rose; White

AQUA LIBRA ⃠
Berry Fruit Drink w Spring Water & Botanical Extracts; Dry Fruit Drink w Spring Water & Botanical Extracts; Original Fruit Drink w Spring Water & Botanical Extracts

AVALON VINEYARDS ⃠
Pennard Organic: Apple Juice

BASS ⃠
Shandy Lemon Flavour Soft Drink w Beer

BELVOIR FRUIT FARMS ☺⃠
Cordials: Autumn - Plum & Damson, Elderflower, Fruits of the Season, Ginger, Lime, Passion Fruit & Mango, Spiced Winter Berries, Spring - Gooseberry & Mint, Summer Berries, Summer - Cherry; *Crush:* Apple & Blackberry, Apple & Quince, Pear & Redcurrant, Rhubarb & Ginger; *Organic Cordials:* Blackcurrant, Cranberry, Elderflower, Ginger; *Organic Pressés:* Elderflower, Ginger Beer, Hand-made Lemonade; *Pressés:* Apple & Elderflower, Cranberry, Elderflower, Ginger & Lime, Lime & Lemongrass, Summer Berries

BIONADE ☺❶⃠
Organic Isotonic Fruit Drinks: All

BOTTLEGREEN DRINKS CO ™⃠
Bon Grape: **Red Grape Juice Drink**, **Rose Grape Juice Drink**, **White Grape Juice Drink**; *Cordial:* **Apple & Elder**, **Dandelion & Burdock**, **Elderflower**, **English Summer**, **Ginger & Lemongrass**, **Raspberry & Lovage**, **Spiced Berry**; *Presse:* **Apple & Elder**, **Blackcurrant**, **Blueberry**, **Citrus**, **Cranberry**, **Elderflower**, **Elderflower - Light**, **Ginger & Lemongrass**, **Limeflower**

BRAKE BROS
Adult Soft Drinks: All; *Bottled Drinks:* All; *Canned Drinks:* All; *Energy Drinks:* All; *Flavoured Mineral Water:* All; *Juice:* All; *Ready to Drink Soft Drinks:* All; *Squash & Cordial:* All

BRITVIC SOFT DRINKS LTD ⃠
American Ginger Ale; Bitter Lemon Drink; Grapefruit Juice; Indian Tonic Water; Iron Brew; Lime Juice Cordial; Low Calorie Bitter Lemon Drink; Low Calorie Indian Tonic Water; Norfolk Punch; Orange Juice; Orange Squash; Organic Lemon Refresher Soft Drink; Peppermint Flavour Soft Drink; Pineapple Juice; Tomato Juice Cocktail; *Britvic 55:* Apple Juice Soft Drink, Apple Raspberry & Cranberry Juice Soft Drink, Orange Juice Drink, Orange Juice Soft Drink; *Citrus Spring:* Lemon Drink, Lime Drink, Orange Drink; *Quencher:* Orange Drink

CALYPSO SOFT DRINKS ⃠
Cup Drinks: Sugar-Free; *Flavoured Natural Mineral Water:* Sparkling, Still; *Juice Drinks:* Simpsons

CARMEL FOOD LTD ™⃠
Carmel Grape Juices: **Muscat**, **Rose**

CHEGWORTH VALLEY JUICES ☺
Certified Organic Juices: Cox Apple, Pear; *Classic Apple Juices:* Bramley, Cox & Bramley, Discovery, Discovery & Bramley, Russet, Worcester & Bramley; *Pear Juice & Special Variety Juices:* Apple & Blackberry, Apple & Cranberry, Apple & Raspberry, Apple & Rhubarb, Apple & Strawberry, Pear

CORONA ⃠
Lemonade

ELLA DRINKS ☺⃠
Bouvrage: Blaeberry Drink, Raspberry Drink

ESSENTIAL BRAND ™● ⃠ ✂
Organic Apple Juice; **Organic Beetroot Juice**; **Organic Carrot Juice**; **Organic Vegetable Juice**

FRESH FOODS CO LTD ⃠ ☼
Organic Soft Drinks: Cola, Cranberry, Lemonade, Orange

GRANOVITA UK LTD ☺⃠ ☼ ✂
Eden Organic Juice Products: Beetroot, Carrot, Fitness Cocktail, Prune, Purifying Cocktail, Red Grape, Slender Blend, Tomato, Vegetable

IDRIS ⃠
Cream Soda; Dandelion & Burdock; Ginger Beer; Traditional Style Cream Soda; Traditional Style Dandelion & Burdock; Traditional Style Ginger Beer

INNOCENT DRINKS ⃠
Innocent Juicy Waters: Blackcurrants, Cranberries & Limes, Lemons & Limes, Mangoes & Passion Fruits; *Innocent Pure Fruit Smoothies:* Blackberries & Blueberries, Cranberries & Raspberries, Mangoes & Passionfruits, Oranges Bananas & Pineapples, Pineapples Bananas & Coconuts, Strawberries & Bananas; *Innocent Really Lovely Juices:* Oranges Mangoes & Lime

J2O ⃠
Apple & Mango Juice Soft Drink; Apple & Melon Juice Soft Drink; Orange & Cranberry Juice Drink; Orange & Passionfruit Juice Soft Drink

JAMES WHITE ☺
Classic Juices - Freshly Pressed: Apple & Blackberry - Wild & Fruity, Apple & Cinnamon - Gently Spiced, Apple & Elderflower - Light & Fragrant, Bramley - Dry & Crisp, Cox - Deliciously Fruity, English Pear - Blended w Cox, Russet - Dessert; *Great Uncle Cornelius:* Finest Spiced Ginger, Ginger Beer, Lemon Refresher; *Organic Juices - Unfiltered:* Apple, Apple & Ginger, Carrot & Apple, Cranberry & Apple, Pear, Raspberry & Pear

JARROW FORMULAS INC.
Protein, Diet & Food Formulas: Pomegranate Juice

LIPTON
Ice Tea: All

LUSCOMBE ORGANIC DRINKS ☺⊘
Apple & Apricot; Apple & Ginger; Apple Juice; Apple w Elderflower; Elderflower Bubbly; Pear & Apple; Sicilian Lemonade; St. Clements; *Ginger Beer:* Cool, Hot

MERIDIAN FOODS
Fruit Juice Concentrates: Apple, Apple & Blackcurrant, Organic Apple, Pear

PURDEY'S ⊘
Activation Multivitamin Energy Drink; Rejuvenation Multivitamin Drink

QUEENSLAND GOVERNMENT ❶⊘
Bundaberg Ginger Beer

R. WHITES ⊘
Cloudy Lemonade; Lemonade; Low Calorie Premium Lemonade; Premium Lemonade

RDA ORGANIC ☺⊘ ✡
Fresh Organic Juice: Cranberry Orange & Apple, Guava Apple & Grape, Mango Apple & Grapefruit, Passionfruit Grape & Orange, Pink Grapefruit & Orange; *Fresh Organic Smoothie:* Berry Special (Seasonal), Blueberry & Apricot, Kiwi & Banana

RED BULL COMPANY LIMITED ☺⊘
Red Bull: Stimulation, Sugar Free

RED CARD⊘
Orange Fruit Soft Drink

RED DEVIL ⊘
Energy Drink

ROBINSONS ⊘
Barley Water: Lemon Soft Drink, Orange Soft Drink; *For Milk:* Peachy Banana Soft Drink; *Fruit & Barley:* Apple & Blackcurrant Soft Drink w Barley, Citrus Soft Drink w Barley, Orange Soft Drink w Barley, Peach Soft Drink w Barley, Pink Grapefruit Soft Drink w Barley, Strawberry & Kiwi Soft Drink w Barley, Summer Fruits Soft Drink w Barley; *Fruit Shoot:* Apple Soft Drink, Blackcurrant & Apple Soft Drink, No Added Sugar Apple Soft Drink, No Added Sugar Blackcurrant & Apple Soft Drink, No Added Sugar Orange &

Peach Soft Drink, No Added Sugar Strawberry Soft Drink, Orange & Peach Soft Drink, Strawberry Soft Drink; *Fruit Spring:* Apple & Cranberry Juice Drink, Apple & Lime Juice Drink, Raspberry & Lemon Juice Drink; *Fruit Squash:* Apple & Blackcurrant Soft Drink, Lemon Soft Drink, Orange & Pineapple Soft Drink, Orange Soft Drink, Summer Fruits Soft Drink; *High Juice:* Apple Cherry & Raspberry Drink, Apple Drink, Orange Drink, Peach Drink, Pink Grapefruit Drink, Summer Fruits Drink; *No Added Sugar:* Apple & Blackcurrant Soft Drink, Lemon Soft Drink, Orange & Mango Soft Drink, Orange & Pineapple Soft Drink, Orange Soft Drink, Summer Fruits Soft Drink

ROCKS ORGANIC CORDIALS ⃠ ☼
Juice Drinks: Bella Blackcurrant; *Organic Cordials:* Blackcurrant, Cranberry, Elderflower, Fruit Punch, Ginger, Lemon, Lime, Summer Fruit, Tangerine; *Squashes:* Lizzy Lemon, Olly Orange

SEDLESCOMBE ORGANIC VINEYARD ™ ⃠ ☼
Apple Juice; **Blackberry & Apple Juice**; **Bramley Apple Juice**; **Cox Apple Juice**; **Pear Juice**

SMOOTH BROTHERS ™
Juices: **Orange**; *Smoothies:* **A Little Tart**, **Luuv Juice**, **Peace Punch**, **Raspberry Rush**

SOMA ☺ ⃠ ☼
Formula 5: Barefoot Doctor Drink; *Gusto:* Lemonade, Original; *Smoothies:* Blueberry Chill, Fruity Roots, Jungle Juice, Tropical C

TANGO ⃠
Apple Soft Drink; Cherry Soft Drink; Fruit Fling Soft Drink; Orange Soft Drink; *Ice Blast:* Bubblegum Flavour Sorbet, Cherry Flavour Sorbet, Lemon Flavour Sorbet, Raspberry Flavour Sorbet; *Low Calorie:* Apple Soft Drink, Orange Soft Drink

THE CREOLE DRINKS COMPANY ☺
Big Tom - Rich & Extra Spicy Tomato Juice

THORNCROFT ☺ ⃠
Healthy Thirst: Sparkling Carnival Spirit, Sparkling Cranberry & Hibiscus, Sparkling Detox, Sparkling Elderflower, Sparkling Kombucha, Sparkling Pink Ginger; *Well-Being Cordials:* Carnival Spirit, Detox, Ginkgo Green Tea, Kombucha

TOM SOYA ☺ ⃠
Huckleberry Finn Natural Fruit Drinks: Boysenberry Juice, Cranberry Juice, Cranberry & Raspberry Smoothie, Detox Drink, Mango Smoothie, Peach & Passionfruit Smoothie; *Soya Fruit Drinks:* Tropical Soya Smoothie, Wildberry Soya Smoothie

VINTAGE ROOTS ⃠
Organic Kicking Kola; Organic Lively Lemonade; Vitamont Apple Juice; Vitamont Orange Juice; *Domaine de*

Saoubis: Pure White Grape Juice; *Loupas d'Estrech:* Pure Red Grape Juice; *Robinvale Vineyards:* Sparkling Grape Juice; *Sedlescombe Vineyard:* Organic Apple Juice, Organic Pear Juice

VIVA! ☺❶⊘

Cordials: All; *Juices:* All

WESTON & SONS LTD ⊘☺

Organize: Apple

YORKSHIRE HEMP LTD ™

Cannibis Club: **Energy Drink**

SPIRITS & APÉRETIFS

AVALON VINEYARDS ⊘

Pennard Organic: Fortified Raspberry Liqueur

CARMEL FOOD LTD ™⊘

Carmel Brandies & Spirits: **Arack 50%**, **Brandy 100**, **Brandy 777**, **Brandy Orange**, **Partom 10 years**, **Vodka Citron 40%**, **Vodka Regular 40%**; *The Well Known Sabre Liquers:* **Orange Chocolate**, **Orange Coffee**

DOMECQ'S ⊘

Sherry: All

HARVEYS ⊘

Sherry: All

SEDLESCOMBE ORGANIC VINEYARD ™⊘ ☼

Blackberry Liqueur; **White Grape Liqueur**

THE ORGANIC SPIRITS COMPANY ☺⊘ ☼

Juniper Green: Organic London Dry Gin; *Papagayo Organic Rum:* Spiced, White; *UK5:* Organic Vodka

VINCEREMOS ORGANIC WINES ™⊘

Casal dos Jodoes (Portugal): **Majara Finest Reserve Port Quinta da Esteveira**; *Organic Spirits Company:* Juniper Green Organic London Dry Gin; *Roland Seguin:* Cassis au Cognac

VINTAGE ROOTS ⊘

Alain Verdet: Crème de Cassis (Blackcurrant), Crème de Framboise (Raspberry), Crème de Mure (Blackberry), Crème de Pêche (Peach); *Casal dos Jordoes:* Finest Reserve Port, Tawny Port, Vintage Port 2000; *Clos St Martin:* AOC Muscat de Rivesaltes; *Destillerie Dwersteg:* Amaretto Liqueur; *Domaine de Saoubis:* Bas Armagnac; *Fasoli Gino:* Grappa di Chardonnay; *Guy Pinard:* Cognac ***, Cognac Napoleon, Cognac VSOP; *Jacques & Dany Brard Blanchard:* AOC Pineau des Charentes; *Michel Beucher:* Calvados

VIVA! ☺❶⊘

Fortified Wines & Ports: All wines

ANIMAL AID ☺❶⊘ ✂1976

Mixed Wine Case; Organic Fine Wine

Case; Organic Sampler Case; Special Occasion Case

ASTON MANOR BREWERY CO LTD
Chardolini; Chardolusco

CARMEL FOOD LTD ™⃠
King David Sweet Kiddush Wines: **Chat. Richon Rouge**, **Concord**, **Muscat King David**, **Old Treasure Muscat**, **Richon Vin Blanc**, **Sacramental**; *Palwin Sweet Kiddush Wines:* **10**, **11**, **4**, **4A**; *Private Collection Eblends:* **Cabernet Sauvignon/Sauvignon Blanc**; *Private Collection Varietals:* **Emerald Riesling**, **Muscat Late Harvest**, **Sweet Muscat**; *Semi-Sparkling Wines:* **Fantasia White or Rose**; *Vineyards Selected:* **Dry Muscat**, **Moscato Di Carmel**, **Petite Sirah**

CLEARSPRING ™☺❶⃠
Mikawa Mirin; **Mirin**; **Sake**; *Organic:* **Mikawa Mirin**

MATTHEW CLARK PLC ⃠
Armadillo; QC Fortified British Wine; VP Fortified British Wine

SOLANO TRADING ™⃠
Domaine de Farlet, Meze, France: **Voignier**

WINES - FRUIT

ANIMAL AID ☺❶⃠ 1976
Organic Fruit Wine Case

AVALON VINEYARDS ⃠
Pennard Organic: Apple, Dry Gooseberry, Elderberry, Folly, Ginger, Plum, Raspberry, Red Gooseberry, Tayberry

BROUGHTON PASTURES ORGANIC FRUIT WINE ⃠ ☼
Blackberry; Blackcurrant; Elderberry; Elderflower; Ginger (Fairtrade); Sparkling Elderflower

MATTHEW CLARK PLC ⃠
Stones Ginger Wine; *Whiteways Fortified British Wine:* Apricot, Cherry, Damson

SEDLESCOMBE ORGANIC VINEYARD ™⃠ ☼
Black Cherry Wine; **Blackberry Wine**; **Elderberry Wine**; **Elderflower Wine**; **Ginger Wine**; **Golden Apple Wine**; **Plum Wine**

SPLASH ENGLISH WINES ™
Apricot Wine; **Elderberry Wine**; **Elderflower Wine**; **Peach Wine**; **Rhubarb Wine**

VINTAGE ROOTS ⃠
Broughton Pastures: Blackberry, Blackcurrant, Elderberry, Elderflower, Ginger, Sparkling Elderflower

WINES - RED

ANIMAL AID ☺❶⃠ 1976
Red Wine Case

CARMEL FOOD LTD ™⦸
Private Collection Eblends: **Cabernet Sauvignon/Merlot**, **Cabernet Sauvignon/Shiraz**; *Private Collection Varietals:* **Cabernet Sauvignon**, **Merlot**; *Vineyards Selected:* **Cabernet Sauvignon**, **Dry Red**

DR HADWEN TRUST ☺❶⦸
Mixed Cases; Mixed Red Sparkling Case

HARBOURNE VINEYARD ☺⦸
English Wines

MATTHEW CLARK PLC ⦸
Seventh Moon Cabernet Sauvignon; *Rougemont Light British Wine:* Red; *Stowells:* Merlot, Tempranillo

PURE WINE COMPANY ⦸ ✡
Chateau de Boisfranc (France) Beaujolais Superior AC; J. & F. Lurton (France) Terra Sana Red; Jacques Frelin (France) Crozes Hermitage AC 1999/2000; Jasci (Italy) Montepulciano d'Abruzzo Rosso; Parra Jiminez (Spain) Caballero de Mesarubias DOC; Sonop Wine Farm (South Africa) Shiraz; *Alicia Rojas (Spain):* Red Rioja Solarce Crianza, Red Rioja Solarce Tinto; *(Australia):* Eden Collection Shiraz/Cab; *Badger Mountain (USA):* Cabernet Franc/Merlot, Cabernet Sauvignon; *Bon Cap Winery (South Africa):* 'The Ruins' Pinotage; *Bucaro Doc (Italy):* Montepulciano d'Abbruzzo Reserva; *Cantina Pizzolato (Italy):* Cabernet Piave DOC, Il Vacanziere IGT - Rosso Da Tavola, Merlot del Piave DOC; *Castello Di Arcania (Italy):* Cabernet DOC, Merlot DOC; *Chateau Barrail des Graves AC (France):* St Emillion; *Chateau Corsou AC (France):* Red Bordeaux; *Chateau Moulin de Peyronin AC (France):* Red Bordeaux; *Domaine De Balazut (France):* Cabernet Sauvignon AC, Merlot AC, Syrah AC; *Domaine de la Grande Bellaine AC (France):* Côtes du Rhone Village; *Domaine de Valescure (France):* Merlot, Rose, Vin Rouge; *Era (Italy):* Montepulciano d'Abbruzzo, Nero d'Avola IGT, Sangiovese IGT; *Erbaluna (Italy):* Barolo DOCG; *Jacques Frelin (France):* Cabardes AC, Cotes de Ventous, Côtes du Rhone; *La Corte Del Pozzo DOC (Italy):* Bardolino Classico DOC; *La Fortuna (Chile):* Malbec; *Las Lomas (Chile):* Las Lomas; *Michael Bettili (Italy):* Merlot DOC, Serenel - Rosso da Tavola, Valpolicella DOC; *Montirius AC (France):* Vaqueras; *Navarsottilo (Spain):* Rioja Commisatio, Rioja Magister Bibendi Crianza, Rioja Noemus Tinto; *Penfolds (Australia):* Claire Valley Shiraz Cab; *Pircas Negras (Argentina):* Barbera, Malbec, Syrah; *Pizzolato (Italy):* Cabernet Reserva DOC, Merlot Reserva DOC; *Robinvale Vineyards (Australia):* Cabernet Sauvignon/Merlot/Shiraz, Shiraz; *San Michelle (Italy):* Chianti Colli Fiorentini DOC; *Tenuto San Vito (Italy):* Chianti DOCG; *Wilkie Estate (Australia):* Cab/Merlot

SEDLESCOMBE ORGANIC VINEYARD ™⦸ ✡
Regent Dry Red English Wine

SOLANO TRADING ™⦸
Domaine de Farlet, Meze, France: **Cabernet Sauvignon**, **Merlot**; *Michel*

Delecroix, Theziers, France: **Cabernet, Cote de Rhone**

VINCEREMOS ORGANIC WINES ™

Paul Giboulot (France); *Albet i Noya (Spain):* Can Vendrell Tinto; *Boira:* Pinot Grigio, Sangiovese; *Bon Cap Winery (South Africa):* **'The Ruins' Pinotage**; *Bucaro:* **Montepulciano d'Abruzzo Riserva**; *Domaine de Clairac:* **Cuvee des Cinq Filles**, **French Organic Red**, **Joubio Rouge**, **Marsanne**, **Syrah**; *Domaine Richeaume (France):* Côtes de Provence, Cuvée Columelle Côtes de Provence, Syrah; *Domaine St. Michel (France):* Cabernet Sauvignon Vin de Pays d'Oc, Merlot Vin de Pays d'Oc, Syrah-Malbec Vin de Pays d'Oc; *Eden Collection Wines (Spain):* **Tempranillo**; *Era (Italy):* Inzolia, Montepulciano, Nero D'Avola, **Primitivo**, Sangiovese; *Jacques Frelin (France):* Crôzes Hermitage, **Cuvee Olivier Vin de Table Rouge (10L Box)**, **Merlot Cuvée la Marouette**, **Vin de Pays du Gard**; *La Nature:* Barbera Argentina, Merlot Vin de Pays d'Oc, Rhone Valley Red, Shiraz/Cabernet Sauvignon Australia, Vin de Pays d'Oc, Vin de Pays Rouge; *La Nature Wines (France):* **Cabernet Sauvignon**; *Los Pinos (Spain):* Crianza, Dominio los Pinos Barrica, Seleccion Tinto; *Ottomarzo (Italy):* Bardolino Classico, Schaffer (Italy) Barbera 'Solo per Laura', Valpolicella Classico; *Perlage (Italy):* Cabernet del Veneto, Corte del Giano, Merlot del Veneto, Solatio Rosso; *Pircas Negras (Argentina):* **Torrontes Barbera Malbec Syrah**; *Richmond Plains (New Zealand):* Escapade Nelson, Pinot Noir Nelson, Reserve Pinot Noir Nelson; *San Michele (Italy):* Chanti Classico Riserva, Chianti Classico, Chianti Colli Fiorentini; *San Vito (Italy):* Chianti, Chianti Vigna la Reina, Fior di Selva Barrique; *Vignoble Saint Frédéric (France):* Gigondas; *Volpi (Italy):* Era Montepuiciano d'Abruzzo, Era Nero d'Avola, Era Sangiovese; *Wilhelm Zähringer (Germany):* Baden, Spätburgunder, Spätburgunder Spätlese Baden; *Wilkie Estate (Australia):* **Cabernet Merlot**

VINTAGE ROOTS

Domaine Mestre Grotti Vin de Pays d'Oc 1999/2000; *Albet i Noya:* DO Penedès Can Vendrell - Cabernet Sauvignon - Tempranillo, DO Penedès Lignum Negre, DO Penedès Nuria 1999, DO Penedès Reserva Martí 1997/1998, DO Penedès Tempranillo Clàssic, DO Penedès Tempranillo Col.lecció, DO Penedès-Cabernet Sauvignon Col.lecció 1999, DO Penedès-Syrah Col.lecció 1998/1999; *Azienda Agricola Bettili:* DOC Valpolicella 2000, IGT Organic Rosso, IGT Veneto - Merlot; *Azienda Agricola San Polino:* DOC Rosso di Montalcino; *Azienda Biovitivinicola A. de Iuliis:* VQPRD Montepulciano d'Abruzzo - Casanova; *Barra Estate Vineyards:* Mendocino - Petite Sirah, Mendocino - Pinot Noir, Mendocino - Zinfandel; *Bodegas:* Irjimpa DO La Mancha - Caballero de Mesarrubbias, Palmera DO Utiel-Requeña Bobal y

Tempranillo, Ruiz Jimenez DO Rioja - Perseus; *Bodegas Azul y Garanza:* DO Navarra; *Bodegas Fabril Alto Verde:* San Juan - Buenas Ondas - Malbec, Touchstone - Syrah; *Bodegas Parra Irjimpa:* Organic Tinto; *Bodegas Ruiz Jimenez:* DO Rioja - Perseus; *Buondonno:* DOC Chianti Classico 1998/1999, DOC Chianti Classico Riserva 1997; *Cantina Foraci:* IGT Sicilia - Sollatio Rosso; *Château Bousquette:* AOC St Chinian; *Chateau Couronneau:* AOC Bordeaux Supérieur, AOC Bordeaux Supérieur - Cuvée Pierre e Cartier; *Château de Bastet:* AOC Côtes du Rhône - Les Cistes; *Château Falfas:* AOC Côtes de Bourg 1998/1999, AOC Côtes de Bourg 'Le Chevalier' 1996/1998; *Château Le Rait:* AOC Bordeaux Supérieur 1999/2000; *Château Pech-Latt:* AOC Corbières Selection Vielles Vignes; *Château Richard:* AOC Bergerac 1999/2000, AOC Bergerac - Les Charmes; *Clos de Joncua:* AOC Vacqueyras - La Font de Papier; *Clos de Joncuas:* AOC Gigondas 1998; *Clos Plince:* AOC Pomerol; *CVLR:* AOC Organic Corbières, AOC Organic Côtes du Rhône; *D'Heilly-Huberdeau:* AOC Bourgogne Côtes Chalonnaise, AOC Bourgogne Passetoutgrain; *Domaine Bassac:* VDP des Côtes de Thongue - Organic Rouge; *Domaine de Brau:* AOC Cabardès 2000/2001, VDP d'Oc Cuvée Gabriel - Merlot 2000, VDQS Cabardès 'Cuvée Exquise' 1999, Vin de Pays de l'Aude 2000/2001; *Domaine de Buis-Rond:* AOC Beaujolais; *Domaine de l'Isle des Sables:* VDP du Gard; *Domaine de Marcoux:* AOC Châteauneuf-du-Pape; *Domaine de Soulié:* AOC St Chinian 1999/2000; *Domaine du Jas d'Esclans:* AOC Côtes de Provence Cru Classé; *Domaine Jacqueline André:* AOC Châteauneuf-du-Pape; *Domaine Joliette:* AOC Côtes du Rousillon - Cuvée André Mercier, AOC Côtes du Rousillon Villages - Cuvée Romain Mercier; *Domaine Pastouret:* AOC Costières de Nîmes; *Domaine Spiropoulos:* Porfyros; *Domaine St Nicolas:* VDQS Fiefs Véndeens - Biodynamic Rouge; *Fasoli Gino:* DOC Valpolicella Amaroene - Alteo, DOC Valpolicella Classico - La Corte del Pozzo, IGT La Calle, IGT Rosso Veronese - Pinot Noir -Sande; *Jean Claude Rateau:* AOC Beaune Premier Cru - Les Reversés; *Jeriko Estate:* Mendocino - Pinot Noir, Mendocino - Syrah; *M. Chapoutier:* AOC Coteaux du Tricastin; *Mas de Longchamp:* AOC Côteaux d'Aix en Provence - Organic Provence, VDP des Bouches du Rhône; *Mas Igneus:* DO Priorato Costers del Segre, DO Priorato FA206, DO Priorato FA206 1999/2000; *Meinklang:* Qualitätswin - Neusiedlersee - Pinot Noir; *Montalbano:* VDT Rosso - Terre Montalbano; *Organic Cellar:* Western Cape - Merlot, Western Cape - Pinotage, Western Cape - Shiraz; *Perrini:* IGT Primitivo, IGT Salento Rosso; *Podere Biovino di Lorenzo Rizzotti:* DOCG Chianti - San Donato a Lucardo; *Pulmary Familias Vinicultoras:* Mendoza - Cuq, Mendoza - Donaria - Bonarda; *Robinvale Vineyards:* Ruby Cabernet,

Shiraz/Cabernet Sauvignon/Merlot - Victoria 1999; *The Milton Vineyards:* Gisborne - Te Arai - Merlot; *Tsantali:* Merlot; *Villa Conversino di Filippo:* VDT Rosso dell'Umbria; *Viña Ijalba:* DO Rioja - Crianza, DO Rioja - Dionisio Ruiz Ijalba, DO Rioja - Graciano, DO Rioja - Livor; *Viñedos Orgánicos Emiliana:* Colchagua Valley - Adobe - Carmenère, Colchagua Valley - Coyam, Colchagua Valley - Novas - Cabernet Sauvignon/Merlot, Colchagua Valley - Novas - Carmenère - Cabernet Sauvignon, Colchagua Valley - Novas - Syrah/Mourvèdre, Touchstone - Cabernet Sauvignon, Touchstone - Merlot

VIRGIN WINES LTD.
Chile: Novas Cabernet Sauvignon 2001, Novas Carmenere Cabernet Sauvignon 01/02; *France:* Pierre Andre Chateauneuf du Pape 99/00; *Italy:* Colli Berci Vita Pura Organic Merlot 02/03, Ottomarzo Bardolino Classico 02/03; *USA:* Fetzer Bonterra Vineyards Zinfandel 99/00

VIVA! ☺❶⊘✓
Red Wines: All

WINES - ROSÉ

HARBOURNE VINEYARD ☺⊘✓
English Wines

PURE WINE COMPANY ⊘✓☼
Jasci (Italy) Montepulciano d'Abruzzo Cerasuolo; *Cantina Pizzolato (Italy):* Il Vacanziere IGT - Rosato de Tavola, Rossato del Veneto IGT Frizzante

SEDLESCOMBE ORGANIC VINEYARD ™⊘✓☼
English Wine

SOLANO TRADING ™⊘✓
Michel Delecroix, Theziers, France: **Rose**

VINCEREMOS ORGANIC WINES ™⊘✓
Domaine de Clairac: **Cabernet Sauvignon Rosé**, **Joubio Rosé**

VINTAGE ROOTS ⊘
Albet i Noya DO Penedès - Pinot Noir/Merlot Clàssic Rosat; Domaine de Brau VDP de L'Aude - Brau Rosé 2000/2001; Domaine du Jas d'Esclans AOC Côtes de Provence Cru Classé Rosé 2000/2001; *Azienda Agricola Bettili:* IGT Serenel Vivace - Rosato; *Bodegas Fabril Alto Verde:* San Juan Buenas Ondas - Syrah Rosé; *Château de Passavant:* AOC Cabernet d'Anjou; *Domaine Bassac:* VDP des Côtes de Thongue - Organic Rosé; *Domaine du Jas d'Esclans:* AOC Côtes de Provence Cru Classé- Rosé

WINES - SPARKLING

ANIMAL AID ☺❶⊘✓ ✂1976
Organic Celebration Fizz Case

CARMEL FOOD LTD ™⊘
Sparkling Wine: **President E/D**

DAVENPORT VINEYARDS ☺⊘ ✿
All

LIMNEY ESTATE ☺⊘ ✿
All

PURE WINE COMPANY ⊘ ✿
Albert Noya (Spain): Cava Rose

SEDLESCOMBE ORGANIC VINEYARD ™⊘ ✿
Cuvée Bodiam Brut English Sparkling Wine 2001; **Cuvée Pinot Noir Regent Brut Rosé English Sparkling Wine 2002**; **Elderflower Sparkling Wine**

VINCEREMOS ORGANIC WINES ™⊘
Achard Vincent (France): Clairette de Die Brut, Clairette de Die Tradition; *Albet i Noya (Spain):* Cava Brut 21 Can Vendrell, Cava Can Vendrell; *Domaine du Jas (France):* Blanquette de Limoux, Crémant de Limoux; *Perlage (Italy):* Prosecco Frizzante, Prosecco Spumante de Valdobiaddene

VINTAGE ROOTS ⊘
Albet i Noya DO Cava: Brut 21, Brut Reserva, Brut Roast, Can Vendrell; *Bosco del Merlo:* IGT Prosecco del Veneto; *D'Heilly-Huberdeau:* AOC Crémant de Bourgogne; *Ffizz!:* Organic Brut; *Veuve Ambal:* Pierre Delize - Brut Tradition - Chardonnay

WINES - WHITE

ANIMAL AID ☺❶⊘ ✂1976
White Wine Case

AVALON VINEYARDS ⊘
Pennard Organic English White Wine: Dry Seyral 2003, Med Dry Orion 2003, Med Dry Syral 2001

CARMEL FOOD LTD ™⊘
Private Collection Varietals: **Chardonnay**; *Vineyards Selected:* **Chardonnay**, **Emerald Riesling/Chenin Blanc**, **Sauvignon Blanc**, **White Zinfandel**

DAVENPORT VINEYARDS ☺⊘ ✿
All

DR HADWEN TRUST ☺❶⊘
Mixed Cases

HARBOURNE VINEYARD ☺⊘
English Wines

LIMNEY ESTATE ☺⊘ ✿
All

MATTHEW CLARK PLC ⊘
Rougemont Light British Wine: Medium Dry, Medium Sweet; *Stowells:* Chardonnay Pinot Grigio, Chenin Blanc

PURE WINE COMPANY ⊘ ✿
Albet I Noya (Spain) Cava; Bernard Delmas (France) Cremant de Limoux AC; Cantine Foraci (Italy) Sollatio Blanco

IGT; Christian & Nicole Dauny (France) Sancerre AC; Domaine De Balazut (France) Blanc de Blanc AC; Guy Bossard (France) Muscadet de Sevre Et Main Sur Lie AC; J & F Lurton (France) Terra Sana White; Jasci (Italy) Trebbiano d'Abruzzo Bianco; *Alicia Rojas (Spain):* White Rioja Solarce; *Cantina Pizzolato (Italy):* Chardonnay Piave, Il Vacanziere IGT - Bianco De Tavola, Prosecco Valdabbiadene, Spumante Frederik DOC, Spumante Stefany DOC; *Castello Di Arcania (Italy):* Pinot Grigio DOC, Sauvignon DOC; *Chateau Corsou AC (France):* White Bordeau; *Chateau Pourchard Larquey ac (France):* White Bordeau Entre Deux Mers; *Chateay Le Barradis AC (France):* Bordeau Dessert Wine; *Clos St Martin (France):* Muscat Dessert Wine; *Domaine de Farlet (France):* Viognier; *Domaine de la Paretiere AC (France):* Muscadet de Sevre Maine; *Domaine de Mabilliere AC (France):* Vouvray Demi Sec; *Domaine de Valescure (France):* Blanc de Blanc, Chardonnay, Sauvignon Blanc; *Domaine Philippe & Jean Goulley (France):* Chablis AOC, Petit Chablis AOC; *Era (Italy):* Inzolia; *Eugine Meyer AC (France):* Gewurtztraminer, Sylvaner; *Jacques Frelin (France):* Picpoul de Pinet; *La Fortuna (Chile):* Sauvignon Blanc; *Michael Bettili (Italy):* Pino Grigio DOC, Serenel - Bianco Da Tavola, Soave Classico DOC, Soave DOC; *Navarsottilo (Spain):* Rioja Noemus Blanco; *Penfolds (Australia):* Claire Valley Chardonnay; *Pircas Negras (Argentina):* Torrentes; *Robinvale Vineyards (Australia):* Chardonnay, Chenin Blanc, Sauvignon Blanc; *Sonop Wine Farm (South Africa):* Chardonnay, Sauvignon Blanc; *Terre Laviche (Italy):* Frascati Superiore DOC

SEDLESCOMBE ORGANIC VINEYARD ™⊘ ☼
Bodiam Harvest English Wine; **Dry White English Wine**; **Reserve English Wine**

SOLANO TRADING ™⊘
Domaine de Farlet, Meze, France: **Chardonnay**; *Michel Delecroix, Theziers, France:* **Blanc Vin de Pays**

VINCEREMOS ORGANIC WINES ™⊘
Albet i Noya (Spain): Can Vendrell Blanco, Lignum Blanc; *Bonterra (USA):* Chardonnay, Muscat, Roussanne, Viognier; *Ch de Barradis (France):* La Balance Bergerac, Monbazillac; *Clos St Martin (France):* Muscat de Rivesaltes, Muscat Sec Vin de Pays des Pyrenées Orientales; *Dom Garreliere (France):* Chenin Blanc Touraine, Sauvignon Blanc Cuvée Cendrillon Touraine, Sauvignon Blanc Touraine; *Domaine de Clairac:* **Joubio Blanc**; *Domaine de Farlet (France):* Chardonnay Vin de Pays des Collines de la Moure, Viognier Vin de Pays des Collines de la Moure; *Domaine de la Parentiere:* **French Organic White**, **Muscadet de Sevre et Maine sur lie**; *Domaine Richeaume (France):* Blanc de Blanc Côtes de Provence, Viognier Côtes de Provence; *Domaine St. Michel (France):* Chardonnay Vin de Pays d'Oc, Entre Deux Mers, Sauvignon Blanc Vin de Pays d'Oc ; *Eden Collection Wines (Spain):* **La Mancha Blanco**;

Eugène Meyer (France): Gewurztraminer, Pinot Blanc, Sylvaner; *Frick (France):* Gewurztraminer Cuvée Precieuse, Pinot Blanc Cuvée Classique, Pinot Blanc Cuvée Precieuse, Pinot Gris Cuvée Precieuse, Sylvaner Cuvée Classique; *Guy Bossard (France):* Domaine de la Parentière Muscadet de Sèrvre et Maine Sur Lie, Gros Plant Sur Lie Vin de Pays Nantais, Hermine d'Or Muscadet de Sèrvre et Maine Sur Lie, Muscadet de Sèrvre et Maine Sur Lie; *Jacques Frelin (France):* Château Petit Roubie Picpoul de Pinet, Cuvée de Marouette Sauvignon Blanc Vin de Pays de l'Aude, **Cuvee Olivier La Mancha Blanc (10L Box)**, Domaine de Petit Roubie Vin de Pays des Côtes de Thau, Joubio Blanc Domaine de Clairac Vin de Pays l'Herault, Marsanne Vin de Pays de l'Herault; *Jean Goulley (France):* Chablis, Petit Chablis; *Klaus Knobloch (Germany):* Bacchus Kabinett Rheinhessen, Ortega Spätlese Rheinhessen; *La Nature:* Chardonnay Vin de Pays d'Oc, Chardonnay/Sauvignon Blanc Australia, La Mancha Blanco Spain, Sauvignon Blanc Vin de Pays d'Oc, Torrontes Argentina; *La Nature Wines (Spain):* **La Mancha Blanco**; *Millton (New Zealand):* Chardonnay Barrel Fermented Gisborne, **Chardonnay Gisborne**, Chenin Blanc Barrel Fermented Gisborne, Opou Reisling Gisborne, Viognier Tietjen Gisborne; *Paul Giboulot (France):* Bourgogne, Hautes Côtes de Nuits; *Perlage (Italy):* Chardonnay, Solatio Bianco; *Podere Canneta (Italy):* La Luna e Le Torri, Vernaccia di San Gimignano; *Richmond Plains (New Zealand):* Chardonnay Nelson, Sauvignon Blanc Nelson; *San Vito (Italy):* Bianco Colli dell'Etruria Centrale, Verdiglio, Vin Santo; *Volcanic Hills (Hungary):* Dry White Neszmély, Irsai Oliver Neszmély; *Weingut Stefan Sander:* **Kerner Kabinett Lieblich**, **Riesling Kabinett Trocken**, **Riesling Spatlese Trocken**; *Wilkie Estate (Australia):* **Verdelho**

VINTAGE ROOTS ⃠
Albet i Noya: DO Penèdes - Can Vendrell Chardonnay/Xarel.lo, DO Penèdes - Chardonnay Colleccio 1999, DO Penèdes - Lignum Blanco, DO Penèdes - Xarel.lo Clàssic; *André Stentz*: AOC Alsace Gewürztraminer 1999/2000, AOC Alsace - Pinot Blanc 1999/2000, AOC Grand Cru Gewürtztraminer Steingruber; *Azienda Agricola Bettili*: DOC Soave, IGT Veneto - Organic Bianco, IGT Veneto - Pinot Grigio; *Azinda Agrico La Bettili:* IGT Veneto - Serenel Frizzante; *Barra Estate Vineyards*: Mendocino - Pinot Blanc; *Bodegas:* Fabril Alto Verde -Touchstone Chardonnay; *Bodegas Fabril Alto Verde:* San Juan - Buenas Ondas - Chardonnay; *Casale Mattia:* DOC Frascati Superiore - 2000/2001; *Château La Canorgue*: AOC Côtes du Luberon 2000/2001; *Château Le Barradis:* AOC Monbazillac 1997; *Château Petit Roc:* AOC Bordeaux Sec - Petit Roc 1999/2000; *Château Richard:* AOC Bergerac Sec 2000/2001, AOC Bergerac Sec - Les Charmes, AOC Saussignac - Coup de Coeur 1997/1998, AOC Saussignac - Tradition 1998/1999; *Christian Dauny:* AOC Sancerre, AOC Sancerre - Terres Blanches; *Coop Jesus*

del Perdon: DO La Mancha - Organic Blanco 2000/2001; *Davenport Vineyards:* Horsmonden Dry; *Domaine Bassac:* VDP des Côtes de Thongue - Muscat Moëlleux 2000/2001; *Domaine de Brau:* VDP d'Oc - Cuvée Nina Chardonnay, VDP de l'Aude - Blanc de Brau, VDP de l'Aude - Chardonnay Finement Boisé 1999; *Domaine de Jas D'Esclans :* AOC Côtes de Provence Cru Classé 2000/2001; Domaine de L'Ecu: AOC Musadet de Sèvre et Maine sur Lie, AOC Muscadet Sèvre et Maine sur Lie - Hermine d'Or; *Domaine de Pajot:* VDP des Côtes de Gascogne; *Domaine des Maisons Brulées:* AOC Touraine - Sauvignon Blanc; *Domaine Huet:* AOC Vouvray Sec - Haut Lieu; *Domaine Jeandeau:* AOC Pouilly-Fuissé- Les Progues; *Domaine Philippe Goulley:* AOC Chablis 2000, AOC Chablis Premier Cru - Montmains, AOC Petit Chablis 1999/2000; *Domaine Spiropoulos:* VQPRD Mantinia - Orino; *Fasoli Gino:* DOC Soave Borgocetto, DOC Soave Pieve Vecchia, DOCG Recioto di Soave San Zeno, IGT Bianco Veronese - Liber, IGT del Veneto - Perantonie; *Fetzer Bonterra Vineyards:* Medocino - Bonterra Chardonnay; *Guyot et Fils:* AOC Puligny Montrachet; *Holmes Brothers:* Marlborough - Sauvignon Blanc 2000/2001; *Jacques & Francois Lurton:* VDP Charentais - Terra Sana Blanc; *Jeriko Estate:* Mendocino - Chardonnay; *La Vigubor S.A.:* CuricóValley - Ventura - Chardonnay/Sémillon, Curicó Valley - Ventura - Sauvignon Blanc, Touchstone Sauvignon Blanc; *Meinklang:* Qualitätswein - Neusiedlersee - Grüner Vertliner; *Montalbano:* DOC Fruili Grave - Pinot Grigio 2000/2001; *Piroux:* AOC Bordeaux - Organic Blanc; *Richmond Plains:* Nelson - Chardonnay 2000/2001, Nelson - Sauvignon Blanc 2000/2001; *Robinvale Vineyards:* Victoria - Chardonnay/Chenin Blanc/Sauvignon Blanc 1999/2000, Victoria - Oaked Chardonnay; *Sedlescombe:* Dry White 1999/2000; *Sonop Wine Farm:* Chardonnay - Organic Terroir; *St Ursula Weinkellerei:* Qba St Ursula - Organic 2000; *Terre Cortesi Moncaro:* Geos Verdicchio dei Castelli di Jesi; The Milton Vineyards: Gisborne - Chardonnay, Gisborne - Opou Chardonnay, Gisborne - Opou Riseling, Gisborne - Te Arai Chenin Blanc; *Tsantali:* Assyrtiko; *Viberti:* DOC Piemonte Chardonnay 1998/1999; *Viña Ijalba:* DOC Rioja - Genoli; *Viñedos Orgánicos Emiliana:* Casablanca Valley - Adobe Chardonnay, Casablanca Valley - Novas Chardonnay, Casablanca Valley - Novas - Sauvignon Blanc; *Weingut Klaus Knobloch:* QMP Rheinehessen - Reisling Kabinett Trocken

VIRGIN WINES LTD.
France: Guy Bossard Mascadet de Sevre et Maine Sur Lie 02/03; *Italy:* Colli Berici Vita Pura Organic Garganego Chardonnay 02/03; *USA:* Fetzer Bonterra Organic Muscat Bartolucci Vineyard 00/01, Fetzer Bonterra Vineyards Organic Chardonnay 01/02

VIVA! ☺❶⊘✓
White Wines: All

NOTES

■ **Beers:** As a general rule traditional, cask-conditioned beers ('real ales') are usually clarified (cleared) with isinglass finings (see GLOSSARY OF ANIMAL SUBSTANCES page 295). The addition of the finings speeds up a process that would otherwise occur naturally. Keg, canned, beersphere and some bottled beers are usually filtered without the use of animal substances. Lagers are generally chill-filtered but some may involve the use of isinglass. Keg beers may contain the foam-control agent Glyceryl Monostearate (E471), which can be animal-derived; alternatives are available, however, and are widely used.

■ **Fruit juices** may be made from fruit coated with animal-based ingredients. See FOOD NOTES, page 106.

■ **Soft drinks and alcopops** may contain animal-derived colourants, such as cochineal / carmine (see GLOSSARY OF ANIMAL SUBSTANCES page 295). Orange coloured drinks may contain beta-carotene held in a gelatine suspension. For example, some Coca-Cola products contain traces of fish; these include Fanta Orange, Lilt Pineapple and Grapefruit, Alive Orange Cascade and Kia-Ora Orange and Pineapple. Also see FOOD NOTES, page 106.

■ **The production of spirits** does not usually involve the use of animal substances. However, some red drinks may contain cochineal / carmine as a colouring agent.

■ **Wines** are often fined using one of the following: blood, bone marrow, chitin, egg albumen, fish oil, gelatine, isinglass, milk or milk casein (see GLOSSARY OF ANIMAL SUBSTANCES page 295). Non-animal alternatives include limestone, bentonite, kaolin and kieselguhr (clays), plant casein, silica gel, and vegetable plaques.

■ Co-op labels those wines that are suitable for vegans and declares all processing aids used in their manufacture. Several major off-licences now have vegan lists available so do ask.

TOILETRIES & COSMETICS

BATH & SHOWER

ABSOLUTE AROMAS ™⦸✓
Ord River: **Bath & Shower Gel 250ml**

ABSOLUTELY PURE ™⦸✓✂
Fields of Ambrosia - Aromatherapy Mineral Salt Glow Scrub: **Meadow Mist**, **Moonlight**, **Morning Dew**, **Rain Drops**, **Starlight**, **Sunlight**; *Fields of Ambrosia - Floral Garden Salt Glow Scrub:* **Country Roses**, **Lavender Fields**, **Orange Blossom**; *Fields of Ambrosia - Fruit Orchard Fizzy Bath Crystals:* **Lemon Lift**, **Orange Vanilla Marmalade**, **Pink Grapefruit**; *Luscious Skincare:* **Citrus & Almond Body Scrub**; *Luscious Skincare - Silky Salt Scrub:* **w Lavender & Rosemary**, **w Seaweed**; *Mukti Botanicals:* **Face & Body Exfoliant**

AMPHORA AROMATICS LTD ⦸✓ ✂1998
Goodnight Sleeptight Bubble Bath w Lavender & Chamomile; *Aromatherapy Bath Fizz Bombes:* Grapefruit, Juniper, Lavender, Mandarin, Meroli, Ylang Ylang; *Bath Oils:* Anti-Cellulite, Athletic, Fresh Feet, Invigorating, PMT, Pure Pleasure, Relaxing, Sensuous, Skin Nourishing; *Bath & Shower Gel:* Aromatherapy Base, Energising, Gentleman's, Gym & Swim, Relaxing, Sensual; *Bath Soak:* Moisturising, Relaxing; *Cocoa Butter Aromatherapy Bath Bars:* Lavender, Mandarin, May Chang, Ylang Ylang

ANIMAL AID ☺❶⦸✓✂1976
Violet & Almond Foaming Bath Oil; *Body Wash:* Amber, Woodspice; *Foam Bath:* Calendula & Vanilla, Vanilla & Passion Flower; *Shower Gel:* English Rose Moisturing, Tropical

ANNEMARIE BÖRLIND ❶⦸✓
Bodyvital Body Crème Scrub; *Natural Care - For Men:* Revitalizing Shower Gel; *Shower Gel:* Body Lind, Body Lind Sportiv

ARTEL ALLERGY PRODUCTS ✓
Body Cleansers: Fragrant Foaming Body Wash, Moisturising Bath & Shower Gel

BAY HOUSE AROMATICS ⦸✓✂1978
Bubble Bath/Shower Gel; Dispersing Bath Oil; *Bath Milk:* Luxury; *The Bay House Blue Range Bath Oils:* Exotic, Refreshing, Relaxing

BEAUTY NATURALS (MARTHA HILL) ❶⦸✓
Gently Exfoliating Seaweed Body Scrub; *Bath Oil:* Citrus Refreshing, Lavender Relaxing, Rose Geranium Harmonising, Seaweed Therapeutic; *Body Wash:* Citrus Refreshing, Lavender Relaxing, Rose Geranium Harmonising, Seaweed Therapeutic

BEAUTY THROUGH HERBS ☺⦸✓👁✂1990
Galeno Gold Body Scrub; Out Of Africa Bath Essence

BURT'S BEES ⦸✓
Healthy Skin: Vitamin E Body & Bath Oil

CAMILLA HEPPER LTD ⊘ ✂1987
Bath Oil: Herbal; *Bath & Shower Gel:* Cocktail Shower Shaker No 2, Jasmin, Lavender, Lemon Verbena, Rose, Seaweed, White Musk; *Foam/Bubble Bath:* Avocado, Caribbean, Orange Blossom

CAPITELLI OILS ™☺ ⊘
Foam Bath: **Dormi Bene**, **Invigorante**

CELESTIAL DESIGNS AROMATHERAPY ™⊘
Bath Foam/Shower Gel; **Bath Milk**; **Dispersing Bath Oil**

CULPEPER LTD
Aromatherapy Naturals Bath Oils: Elizabethan, Jasmine, Lavender, Rose, Stephanotis; *Aromatherapy Naturals Bath Salts:* Jasmine, Lavender, Rose, Rose Geranium, Sandalwood, Stephanotis; *Aromatherapy Naturals Enriched Foam Bath Elixirs:* Elizabethan, Herb Gold Pine, Lavender, Rose, Rose Geranium, Sandalwood, Stephanotis; *Aromatherapy Naturals Foaming Bath & Shower Gel:* Aftersport, Comforting, Focussing, Refreshing, Relaxing, Sensual

DOLMA ™☺❶⊘ 👁✂
Aromatic Body Shampoos: **Antiseptic**, **Deep Relaxing**, **Invigorating**, **Relaxing**, **Relaxing & Refreshing**

DR HADWEN TRUST ☺❶⊘
Rose Foaming Bath Oil; Sleepytime Splash; Vitalising Splash; *Bath Salts from the Dead Sea:* Geranium, Lavender, Ylang Ylang; *Foam Bath:* Anti-Stress, Easy Breathe, Lavender Geranium & Ylang Ylang, PMT, Tropical Palm; *SLS-Free Foam Bath:* Chamomile & Lemon, Lavender & Pettigrain; *SLS-Free Shower Gel:* Apple & Chamomile, Cherry & Melon, Evening Primrose

DRI-PAK LTD ☺❶⊘ ✂1997
Tara Toiletries: Bath Crystals, Shower Gel

ECOVER ™⊘
Shower Gel - Lavender & Aloe Vera

ESSENTIALLY YOURS LTD ™⊘
De-Stress Shower Gel; **Hypnotic Shower Gel**; **Morning Shower Gel**; **Sports Shower Gel**; **Wellbeing Shower Gel**; *Natural Elements:* **Anti-Fatigue Shower Gel**, **Anti-Stress Shower Gel**; *Therapeutics Range:* **E Bath Oil**

ETHICAL WARES ☺❶
Sea Breeze: Foam Bath, Shower Gel

FAITH PRODUCTS LTD ❶⊘ ✂👁1978
Foam Bath: Lavender & Geranium, Organic Aloe Vera & Ylang Ylang , Organic Chocolate, Seaweed, Tea Tree

FINEMOOD LTD ⊘
Bath Oils: Exotic, Refreshing, Relaxing; *Shower Gel:* Cedarwood & Frankincense, Grapefruit & Palmarose, Lavender & Geranium

FREERANGERS ™
Pamper Products: **Bath Melts**

FUNK BUBBLE ™
Bubble Bath: Lavender/Geranium, Tea Tree; *Organic Bubble Bath:* Aloe Vera, Chocolate; *Organic Shower Wash:* Aloe Vera, Chocolate; *Shower Wash:* Tea Tree

GREEN DOT GUIDES
Golden Lotus Bath & Massage Oils: May Chang, Tantra; *Golden Lotus Bubble Bath:* May Chang, Tantra; *Golden Lotus Exfoliating Body Scrub:* May Chang, Tantra

GREEN PEOPLE CO. ™
Hair & Body Care: **Aloe Vera Shower Gel**, **Rosemary & Pink Clay Shower Gel**, **Vita Min Fix Shower Wash**; *Men's Range:* **Cool Style Hair & Body Wash**; *Organic Base:* **Shower Bath**; *Sugar Scrub:* **Soothing**, **Stimulating**

HIGHER NATURE PLC ™
Alka-Bathe (Powder); **Special Sea Soak**

HONESTY COSMETICS LTD ™ 1976
Foam Bath: **Orange Geranium & Lavender**, **Tangerine & Vanilla**; *Shower Gel:* **Apple & Sandalwood**, **Mandarine Ginger & Ylang Ylang**, **Strawberry & Papaya**

JOPHIEL®
Rejuvanating™ Skincare: Crystal Body Scrub; *Rejuvanating™ Skincare Mineral Bath Salts w Essential Oils & Epsom Salts:* De-Tox, Invigorate, Relaxing

KENT COSMETICS
Australian Organics: Bath/Shower Gel, Exfoliating Body Wash, Shower Gel

KISS MY FACE
Cheap Kisses Shower Gel: Anti Stress, Early to Bed, Early to Rise; *Obsessively Organic - Preservative Free:* Sugar Reef Body Scrub; *Shower Gel:* Active Athletic, Anti Stress, Cold & Flu, Early to Bed, Early to Rise, Peaceful Patchouli, Romance, Rough Thyme, Silky Soft; *Sudz Bodywash:* C-Weed, Close Encounter, In the Pink, Salad Bar, Sports Bar

KOBASHI ™
Bath: **Fragrance Free Bath Base**, **Refreshing Fruit Bath**, **Relaxing Bath**, **Wild Flower Shower Gel**

L'OCCITANE EN PROVENCE
Aromachologie: Relaxing Melting Bath Drops; *Bath Salts:* Lavender Harvest; *Bath & Shower Gel:* Eau d'Azur, Eau des 4 Reines, Eau des Vanilliers, Eau du Val; *Body Treatment:* Almond - Delicious Paste, L'Oranger - Orange Sugar Scrub for Body, Lavender Harvest - Velvet Body Scrub; *Cream Bath:* Shea Butter; *Foam Bath:* Aromachologie, Lavender Harvest, Verbena Harvest; *Mediterranean Bath:* Olive Harvest; *Milky Bath:* Eau des Vanilliers; *Neutral Bath Base:* Aromachologie; *Revitalizing Sugar Cubes:* Aromachologie; *Shower Cream:* Olive Harvest; *Shower Gel:* Aromachologie - Purifying, Aromachologie - Revitalizing, Eau de Contadour, for Men, L'Oranger, Lavender Harvest; *Shower Oil:* Almond

LUSH
Ballistics: Avobath, Big Blue, Blackberry BOMB, Bon Bomb, Butterball, Fairy Jasmine, Fox in the Flowers, Gingerman, Hot Java, Ickle Baby Baff, Rainbow Warrior, Sakura, Softy, Summer Blues, The Sicilian, Tisty Tosty, Uluru, Waving Not Drowning; *Bath Melts:* Ceridwen's Cauldron, Dreamtime, Elixir, Floating Island, Mmm Marshmallow Melt, Nude, Something Wicked, You've been Mangoed; *Bubble Bar:* Amandopondo, Aunty Pamela, Bathos, Blue Skies, Bottle of Bubbly, Double Bubble, French Kiss, Got Milk?, Little Monkey, Play Doze, Two Timing Tart; *Christmas Bath Ballistics:* Christmas Carol, Christmas Party, Jingle Spells, Mr Butterball; *Christmas Bubble Bar Slices:* Christmas Candy Cane, Hot Toddy; *Christmas Glittery Items:* Elixir Bath Melt, Glam Rock Hair Glitter, Golden Glitterbug, Iridescent Glitterbug, Pink Glitterbug, Shimmy Shimmy, Something Wicked This Way Comes; *Skincare, Haircare, etc:* Chai - Bottled, Chai - Frozen, Creamed Alm & Coco Smoothie, Freeze - Bottled, Freeze - Frozen, Happy for SAD - Frozen, Narcotick - Bottled, Narcotick - Frozen, Tramp - Bottled, Tramp - Frozen

MEADOWSWEET LTD ™
Aloe Vera Range: **Foam Bath**; *Bath Products:* **Alpine Foam Bath**, **Herbal Relaxing Bath Soak**, **Lavender/Geranium/Ylang-Ylang**, **Mixed Fruits Foam Bath**, **Oriental Musk Foam Bath**, **Rose Foaming Bath Oil**, **Tropical Palm Foam Bath**, **Ylang Ylang Foam Bath**; *Comfrey+ Range:* **Chickweed Foaming Bath Oil**; *Herbal Aromatic Range:* **Easy Breathe Foam Bath**, **Relaxing Bath Oil**; *Nature Power Range:* **Anti Stress Foam Bath**, **PMT Foam Bath**, **Sleepytime Splash**, **Vitalising Splash**; *Salts From the Dead Sea:* Geranium, Lavender, Ylang Ylang; *Shower Gel:* **Apple**, **Cherry**, **Evening Primrose**; *SLS Free Foam Baths:* Chamomile & Lemon, Lavender & Petitgrain; *SLS Free Shower Gels:* Apple & Chamomile, Cherry & Grapefruit, Evening Primrose

MONTAGNE JEUNESSE
Bath: Aches-Away, Anti-Cold, Dinosaur - 3 Products

MORNY
Bath & Shower Gel: Nature's Oil of Evening Primrose, Nature's Vitamin E, Original Lavender; *Luxury Bath & Shower Gel:* English Rose, French Fern, Sandalwood

NAPIERS HERBAL HEALTH CENTRE
Bath, Skin & Body Products: Bath Tea Bags; *Wash Range:* Aloe Vera Shower Gel, Aloe Vera & Ylang Ylang Body Wash, Seaweed Body Wash

NATURA ORGANICS
Foaming Bath: w Cinnamon, w Shea

Butter & Aloe Vera, w Ylang-Ylang; *Shower Gel:* w Cinchona Sage & Lemon, w Grapefruit & Lavender, w Lavender & Rosemary, w Mandarin & Orange

NATURAL BY NATURE OILS ☺⊘ ✂1974
Bath Oils: All

NATUREWATCH ☺⊘ ✂1976
Clearly Compassionate: Lavender & Geranium Relaxing Bath Soak; *Clearly Compassionate Shower Gel:* Mandarin & Lemongrass Invigorating, Rosemary Pine & Lemon

NEAL'S YARD REMEDIES ⊘
Aromatic Foaming Bath; *Bath Oil:* Baseline, Exotic, Geranium & Orange, Soothing; *Bath Salts:* Citrus, Lavender; *Bath & Shower Gel:* Baseline

NEW SEASONS ☺⊘
Neutral Base: Bath Milk, Foam Bath, Shower Gel

NORFOLK LAVENDER LTD ✂
The English Lavender

NUBIAN CARE ™
Nu Care: **Lavender & Tea Tree Body Wash**

OPTIMA HEALTH & NUTRITION ⊘ ✂1995
Allergenics: Face & Body Shower Wash; *Raw Aloe Shower Gel:* w Tea Tree & Citrus Oils; *Thursday Plantation Tea Trea:* Herbal Skin Wash

ORGANIC BLUE ™⊘
Body Care: **Shower Gel**

ORIGINAL SOURCE ™⊘
Bath Foam: **Basil & Lemongrass**, **Mandarin & Sandalwood**, **Rose & Geranium**, **Tea Tree & Lavender**, **Ylang Ylang & Patchouli**; *Shower:* **Pure Lime**, **Rose & Geranium**, **Spearmint & Lavender**, **Tea Tree & Lavender**, **Tea Tree & Lemon**, **Tea Tree & Mint**

REN ⊘
Monoi Moisturising Body Rinse; *Shower Wash:* High Altitude Lavender, Moroccan Rose Otto, Neroli & Grapefruit, Seaweed & Sage

SEVEN WIVES NATURAL BODYCARE ™⊘
Shower Balm

SIMPLY SOAPS ™❶⊘ ✂
Bath Oils: Invigorating & Detoxifying, Love, Relax; *Bath Salts:* **Citrus**, **Love**, **Relax**, **Woodland Calm**; *Gift Sets:* Citrus, Decadence, Relax, Woodland; *Salt Scrub:* **Aphrodisia**, **Exfoliating**, **Invigorating**, **Stimulating**

TISSERAND AROMATHERAPY PRODUCTS ™
Bath Care: **Awaken Shower Gel**, **Indulge Bath Soak**, **Indulge Soap**, **Mind Unwind Bath Oil**, **Muscle Ease Bath Oil**, **Refresh Bath Soak**, **Refresh**

Soap, **Rejuvenate Shower Gel**, **Relax Bath Soak**, **Relax Soap**; *Clear Breathe:* **Clear Breathe Bath Oil**; *Lavender Products:* **Lavender Bath Soak**

TREE-HARVEST ⊘ ✓
Body & Bath Oils

URTEKRAM ⊘ ✓ ✂
Pure Balance Shower Gel: Aloe Vera; *Shower Gel:* Brown Sugar Shower Gel

WELEDA ⊘ ✓ ✂1985
Bath Milk: Citrus, Citrus Refreshing, Lavender Relaxing, Pine Reviving, Rosemary Invigorating; *Bath Soak:* Chestnut Toning

WOODS OF WINDSOR ☺ ✓
Bath & Body Oil: Aromatherapy Lavender; *Bath & Shower Gel:* for Men; *Bubbling Bath Cream:* Orange Spice; *Exfoliating Shower Puree:* Orange Spice; *Invigorating Shower Gel:* Forget Me Not, Lavender, Lily of the Valley, Mimosa, True Rose; *Moisturising Body Wash:* Forget Me Not, Lavender, Lily of the Valley, Mimosa, True Rose; *Moisturising Cream Bath:* Forget Me Not, Lavender, Lily of the Valley, Mimosa, True Rose; *Relaxing Bath Soak:* Aromatherapy Lavender; *Wide-Awake Shower Gel:* Orange Spice

YAOH ™☺❶ ✓ ⊘
Bubble Bath; Shower Gel

BRUSHES ETC

BEAUTY NATURALS (MARTHA HILL) ❶⊘ ✓
Complexion Massage Brush; *Cosmetic Brushes:* All

CAMILLA HEPPER LTD ⊘ ✓ ✂1987
Hands & Feet Pumice Sponge

ESSENTIAL OIL COMPANY ☺⊘ ✓ 👁
Natural Sisal Body Brush

LUSH ✓
Hair Treatments: The Strokes

NEAL'S YARD REMEDIES ⊘ ✓
Ayate Cloth; Back Brush; Loofah; Massage Mitt; Nail Brush; Sponges

CONDITIONERS & HAIRCARE

ABSOLUTE AROMAS ⊘™ ✓
Ord River: **Conditioner 250ml**

ABSOLUTELY PURE ™⊘ ✓ ✂
Luscious Skincare: **Cocoa Butter Pre Conditioner**, **Jojoba Pre Wash Conditioner**, **Revitalising Hair Treatment**

ALOE PURA ⊘ ✓ ✂1995
Organic Aloe Vera Herbal Conditioner: All Hair Types

AMPHORA AROMATICS LTD ⦸✓ ✂1998
Aromatherapy Conditioner Base

ANIMAL AID ☺❶⦸✓ ✂1976
Coconut Conditioner

ANNEMARIE BÖRLIND ❶⦸✓
Ceramide Cream Rinse; Vital Hair Care Fluid

ARTEL ALLERGY PRODUCTS ✓
Hair Care: Fruit Essence Conditioners

BAY HOUSE AROMATICS ⦸✓ ✂1978
Hair Conditioner

BEAUTY NATURALS (MARTHA HILL) ❶⦸✓
Conditioner: Deep Moisturising

BEAUTY THROUGH HERBS ☺⦸✓ 👁✂1990
Cryotermol Hair Lotion; Hair Masque; Hair Repair Conditioner; Hair Repair Conditioner w Cryotermol

CAMILLA HEPPER LTD ⦸✓ ✂1987
Avocado Treatment Wax; *Conditioner:* Herbal Protein, Natural Orange, Rosemary Scalp

CULPEPER LTD
Aromatherapy Naturals Conditioner: Calendula

DANIEL FIELD DIRECT ☺✓
Classics: Mineral Hair Repair Masque, Plant Remoisturising Treatment; *Classics Conditioner:* Body Builder Detangling, First Aid, Revitalising Mineral; *Supernaturals Conditioner:* Curl Enhancing, Intensive Therapy 5 Spa, Smooth & Shine, Volumising

DOLMA ™☺❶⦸✓ 👁✂
Other Hair Preparations: **Cedarwood & Cypress Hair Conditioner**, **Lavender & Jojoba Hair Conditioner**, **Rosemary Nettle & Marigold Hair Lotion**

DR HADWEN TRUST ☺❶⦸✓
Mineral Hair Repair Masque; Plant Remoisturising Treatment; *Conditioner:* Banana & Vanilla, Body Builder & De-Tangling, Chamomile, Coconut, First Aid, Mango & Apricot, Nettle Herbal Care, Volumising

ETHICAL WARES ☺❶✓
Sea Breeze: Conditioner

FAITH PRODUCTS LTD ❶⦸✓ ✂👁1978
Conditioner: Ginkgo Biloba, Hemp & Meadowfoam, Jojoba, Lavender & Geranium, Organic Aloe Vera, Rosemary, Saw Palmetto, Seaweed, Tea Tree (w 2% oil)

FINEMOOD LTD ⦸✓
Hair & Body Care: Hair Conditioner, Headlice Conditioner, Scalp Tonic

FUNK BUBBLE ™
Conditioner: Jojoba, Lavender/Geranium, Tea Tree; *Organic Conditioner:* Aloe Vera

GREEN PEOPLE CO. ™⊘✓
Hair & Body Care: **Aloe Vera Herbal Conditioner**, **Aloe Vera & Rosemary Styling Gel**, **Intensive Repair Conditioner**, **Rosemary Herbal Conditioner**, **Vita Min Fix Conditioner**; *Men's Range:* **Itch Away Conditioner**; *Organic Base:* **Conditioner**

HERB UK LTD ☺⊘✓
Nature's Essential: Conditioner, Intensive Treatment, Seal & Shine; *Tints of Nature:* Scalp Treatment

HERBS HANDS HEALING LTD ™⊘✓
Morning Rain Hair Water

HONESTY COSMETICS LTD ™☺❶⊘✓ 👁✂1976
Conditioner: **Coconut & Avocado**, **Jojoba & Peach**

KENT COSMETICS ☺⊘✓
Australian Organics Conditioner

KISS MY FACE ⊘✓ 👁 ✂
Conditioned Response; Lightweight Conditioner; *Cheap Kisses:* Lightweight Conditioner

L'OCCITANE EN PROVENCE ✓ 👁
Aromachologie: Angelica Conditioner, Artemisia Conditioner; *Lavender Harvest:* Detangling Conditioner; *Olive Harvest:* Hair Care Oil, Paste for Hair; *Shea Butter:* Hair Conditioner, Ultra Rich Hair Cream

LAVERA ™
Hair: **Repair Conditioner**

LUSH ✓
Hair Treatments: Arabian Bright, Marilyn; *Skincare, Haircare, etc:* Veganese

MARTHA HILL ❶⊘✓
Purely Natural Haircare Conditioner: Mild & Gentle, Moisturising, Reconstructive, Treatment

MEADOWSWEET LTD ™☺⊘✓
Aloe Vera Range: **Conditioner**; *Comfrey+ Range:* **Cade Intensive Conditioner**; *Conditioner:* **Banana & Vanilla**, **Chamomile**, **Coconut**, **Kiwi & Lemon Balm**, **Mandarin & Papaya**, **Mango & Apricot**, **Nettle**; *Men's Range:* **Sandalwood Conditioner**

NAPIERS HERBAL HEALTH CENTRE ✓
Hair Lotion: Eucalyptus, No. 2, Rosemary; *Wash Range:* Aloe Vera Conditioner, Hemp & Ginger Conditioner, Seaweed & Lime Conditioner

NATURA ORGANICS ⊘✓ ☼
Hair Conditioner: w Exotic Vervain Lemon & Sage

NATUREWATCH ☺⊘✓ 👁✂1976
Clearly Compassionate: Jojoba & Lavender Intensive Conditioner for Normal/Dry Hair

NEAL'S YARD REMEDIES ⊘
Rosemary & Cedarwood Hair Treatment; *Conditioner:* Calendula, Chamomile & Jojoba, Rosemary & Jojoba

NEW SEASONS ☺⊘
Neutral Base: Conditioner

NUBIAN CARE ™
Nu Care Conditioner: **For Dry Hair**, **For Normal Hair**

OPTIMA HEALTH & NUTRITION ⊘ ✂1995
Thursday Plantation Tea Tree: Conditioner

ORGANIC BLUE ™⊘
Body Care: **Conditioner**

ORIGINAL SOURCE ™⊘
Conditioner: **Almond & Coconut**, **Rose & Aloe**, **Tangerine & Bergamot**, **Tea Tree & Mint**; *Conditioners:* **Almond & Coconut**

QUINESSENCE AROMATHERAPY ☺❶⊘
Protein Conditioner; Protein Conditioner Base

SERF TO SURF UK ⊘
Afrika Gold

SEVEN WIVES NATURAL BODYCARE ™⊘
Hair Conditioner

SIMPLY SOAPS ™❶⊘ ✂
Hair Care: **Conditioning Oil**, **Strengthening Oil**

TISSERAND AROMATHERAPY PRODUCTS ™
Tea Tree Products: **Tea-Tree Lemon & Rosemary Conditioner**

URTEKRAM ⊘ ✂
Conditioner: Aloe Vera, Camomile, Lavender, Rose, Tea Tree; *Pure Balance Conditioner:* Lavender, Wild Rose

WELEDA ⊘ ✂1985
Rosemary Hair Lotion; *Bottled Conditioner:* Calendula, Lemon Balm, Rosemary

YAOH ™☺❶ ⊘
Conditioner

DEODORANTS & ANTIPERSIRANTS

ABSOLUTELY PURE ™⊘ ✂
Kettlecare: **Herb & Mineral Deodorant Spray**; *Miessence:* Ancient Spice Roll On Deodorant, Tahitian Breeze Roll On Deodorant; *Mukti Botanicals:* **Deodorant**

AMPHORA AROMATICS LTD ⊘ ✂1998
Thai Deodorant Stones

ANIMAL AID ☺❶⊘ ✂1976
White Musk Body Spray

ANNEMARIE BÖRLIND ❶⊘
Deodorant Spray: Body Lind, Body Lind Sportiv; *Natural Care - For Men:* Deostick

BEAUTY NATURALS (MARTHA HILL) ❶⊘
Herbal; *Deodorant:* Pure

BIOFORCE
Crystal Spring

CAMILLA HEPPER LTD ⊘ ✂1987
Watercress Deodorant

DEODORANT STONE (UK) LTD ☺⊘
Deodorant Stone; *Roll-On Stone:* Aloe & Cucumber, Herbal Spice, Tea Tree, Unscented; *Spray-On Stone:* Aloe & Cucumber, Herbal Spice, Tea-Tree, Unscented

DOLMA ™☺❶⊘ ✂
Miscellaneous Products: **Roll-On Deodorant**

DR HADWEN TRUST ☺❶⊘
Crystal Stone

ESSENTIAL OIL COMPANY ☺⊘
Pure Crystal Deodorant

FINEMOOD LTD ⊘
Push-up Sticks: Eucaplyptus, Lavender, Tea Tree

GREEN PEOPLE CO. ™⊘
Gentle Control: **Aloe Vera Deodorant**; *Hair & Body Care:* **DeoKrystal**, DeoKrystal Spray, **No Scent Deodorant**, **Rosemary Deodorant**; *Men's Range:* **Stay Cool Deodorant**, **Stay Fresh Deodorant**; *Organic Base:* **Deodorant**

KISS MY FACE ⊘ ✂
Active Enzyme Stick: Fragrance Free, Lavender, Scented, Summer Scented; *Cheap Kisses:* Fragrance Free Liquid Rock Deodorant; *Liquid Rock Rollon:* Fragrance Free, Lavender, Patchouli, Scented

L'OCCITANE EN PROVENCE
Aromachologie: Crystal Deodorant Stone, Purifying Deodorant

LAVERA ™
basis sensitiv: **Deo Roll-On**

LUSH
Deodorants: Aromaco, Aromacreme, Aromarant, Fuwari, Krysztal, Lavender, T'Eo

MEADOWSWEET LTD ™☺⊘
Deodorant Stone; *Sprays:* **White Musk Body**, **Wild Dewberry Body**

NEAL'S YARD REMEDIES ⊘
Lemon & Coriander Deodorant

OPTIMA HEALTH & NUTRITION ⊘ ✂1995
Thursday Plantation Tea Tree: Antiperspirant Floral, Antiperspirant Sport, Roll-On Deodorant

ORIGINAL SOURCE ™⦸♞
Antiperspirant Roll-on: Chamomile, Ginger FCL, Lavender, Tea Tree & Mint; *Antiperspirant Spray:* Lavender, Tea Tree & Mint

PASSION FOR LIFE PRODUCTS
Deo-Krystal Spray

PITROK LTD ⦸♞
Crystal Deodorant: Original, Push-up; *Spray Deodorant:* Fragrance, Natural

PURPLE FLAME AROMATHERAPY ⦸♞
Deodorant: Crystal, Roll-On

SEVEN WIVES NATURAL BODYCARE ™⦸♞
Aloe Vera & MSM Natural Deodorant Spray; **Natural Crystal Stick**; *Natural Crystal Hemp Oil Roll-on:* **Active**, **Lavender**, **Powder**, **Unscented**

TISSERAND AROMATHERAPY PRODUCTS ™
Lavender Products: **Lavender Roller Ball**; *Tea Tree Products:* **Tea-Tree Lemon & Rosemary Deodorant**, **Tea-Tree Roller Ball**

TOM'S OF MAINE ⦸♞✂
Natural Anti-Perspirant & Deodorant; *Natural Deodorant Gentle Formula:* Calendula, Woodspice; *Natural Deodorant Original Formula:* Honeysuckle Rose, Unscented

URTEKRAM ⦸♞✂
Liquid Crystal Deodorant: Flower Crystal Deo, Green Crystal Deo, Neutral Crystal Deo; *Solid Crystal Deodorant:* Neutral Crystal Deo

WELEDA ⦸♞✂1985
Deodorant: Citrus, Sage

WOODS OF WINDSOR ☺♞
Body Spray: Forget Me Not, Lavender, Lily of the Valley, Mimosa, True Rose; *Roll-On Deodorant:* for Men

XYNERGY HEALTH PRODUCTS ⦸♞
Aloe & Cucumber Roll-On Deodorant; Deodorant Stone

ESSENTIAL OILS & MASSAGE PRODUCTS

ABSOLUTE AROMAS ™⦸♞
Ord River: **Pure Tea Tree Oil 10ml & 25ml**

ABSOLUTELY PURE ™⦸♞✂
Earthbound Organics: **Muscle Tension**, **Relaxing Oil**, **Uplifting Oil**; *Kettlecare:* **Muscle Rub**; *Pure Essentials - Oils:* **Balancing Facial**, **Relaxation**, **Replenishing Facial**

AMPHORA AROMATICS LTD ⦸♞ ✂1998
Moisturising Body Massage; *Essential Oils:* All; *Massage Oils:* Anti-Cellulite,

Athletic, Fresh Feet, Invigorating, PMT, Pure Pleasure, Relaxing, Sensual, Sensuous, Skin Nourishing; *Organic Essential Oils:* All

ARKOPHARMA (UK) LTD ☺⊘✔
Massage Gels: Litelegs, Phytorhuma

BAY HOUSE AROMATICS ⊘✔ ✂1978
Essential/Carrier/Vegetable Oils: All; *The Bay House Blue Range Massage Oils:* Exotic, Refreshing, Relaxing

BEAUTY THROUGH HERBS ☺⊘✔ 👁✂1990
Complementary, Carrier & Massage Oils: All; *Essential Oils:* All

BIOFORCE
Po-Ho Oil; St John's Wort Oil

CAMILLA HEPPER LTD ⊘✔ ✂1987
Aromatherapy Muscular Massage; *Essential Oils:* All

CAPITELLI OILS ™☺✔ ⊘
Essential Oil Mixtures: **Dormi Bene**, **Prima**, **Versatilita**; *Oils for Special Occasions:* **Testa Fresca**, **Zanzara Via**

CELESTIAL DESIGNS AROMATHERAPY ™⊘✔
Carrier Oils: **All**; *Essential Oils:* **All**; *Infused Oils & Floral Hydrolats:* **All**; *Massage Blends:* **All**

CHIRALI OLD REMEDIES
Relaxation Massage Oil

COTSWOLD HEALTH PRODUCTS ☺⊘✡
Essential Oils: All

DOLMA ™☺❶⊘✔ 👁✂
Massage Oils: **Anti-Cellulite**, **Invigorating**, **Relaxing**, **Soothing**

DR HADWEN TRUST ☺❶⊘✔
Massage Oil: Body-Firming Contouring, Cellulite & Thigh; *Therapy in Blue Body Oil:* Balancing/Calming, Detox/Tone, Stress Ease, Uplifting/Refreshing; *Therapy in Blue Face Massage Oil:* Nourishing, Rejuvanating

ESSENTIAL OIL COMPANY ☺⊘✔ 👁
Carrier Oils: All; *Pure Essential Oils:* All

ESSENTIALLY YOURS LTD ™⊘✔
For Play: **Anticipation Penis Cream**, **Discovery Cream**, **Divine Nipple Gel**, **Everlasting Gel**, **Fantasy Massage Oil**, **Interplay Lubricating Gel**, **Yin-Yang Lubricating Oil**; *Natural Elements:* **Facial Massage Oil**, **Refreshing Massage Oil**, **Relaxing Massage Oil**

FAITH PRODUCTS LTD ❶⊘✔ ✂👁1978
Skin Care: Essential Body Oil

FINEMOOD LTD ⊘✔
Aromatic Waters: Chamomile, Jasmine, Lavender, Melissa, Neroli, Rose; *Blended Essential Oils:* Benzoin, Jasmine - 25% Blend w Jojoba, Jasmine - 5% Blend w Jojoba, Melissa - 25% Blend w Jojoba, Melissa - 5% Blend w Jojoba, Neroli - 25% Blend w Jojoba, Neroli - 5% Blend

w Jojoba, Rose Otto - 25% Blend w Jojoba, Rose Otto - 5% Blend w Jojoba; *Care for - Pure Essential Oil Mix:* After Flight, Always, Cellulite, Circulation, Clear Head, Easy Breathe, Fatigue, Joints, Muscles, Respiratory System, Rest, Stresses & Strains, Stretch Marks, Visible Veins, Women; *Care for - Ready Mixed Lotion:* Always, Cellulite, Clear Head, Joints, Muscles, Problem Skin, Stresses & Strains, Women; *Care for - Ready Mixed Oil:* Cellulite, Circulation, Fatigue, Joints, Muscles, Stresses & Strains, Stretch Marks, Visible Veins; *Care for - Spray:* Women; *Carrier Oils:* Almond, Apricot, Avocado, Calendula, Carrier Oil Mix, Carrot, Evening Primrose, Grapeseed, Hazelnut, Hypericum, Jojoba, Lime Blossom, Macadamia, Melissa, Peachnut, Rosehip, Sunflower, Wheatgerm, White Lotion; *Essential Oils:* All; *Hair & Body Care - Aromatic Body Oil:* Jasmine, Neroli, Rose; *Massage Oils:* Cellulite, Exotic, Facial, Hair & Scalp, Muscle Fatigue, Refreshing, Relaxing

GREEN DOT GUIDES ⃠ ✓
Sensitile Natural - Natural Sensual Pleasures; *Golden Lotus:* Gold Frankincense & Myrrh Opulent Organza Gift Set

HEALTHY HERBS ✓ ⃠ ☼
Arnica Cream; Burned Cream; Herb Oil; Vit E Cream

HERBS HANDS HEALING LTD ™ ⃠ ✓
Base Oils: Castor, Nutmeg Kernel, Sweet Almond, Wheatgerm; *Massage Oils:* Bud & Berry, Deep Tissue, Earth Song, Flower, Hot Zing, Intimate, Relaxing; *Pure Essential Oils:* All

HERBS OF GRACE ™ ⃠ ✓
Essential Oils: **All**; *Organic Carrier Oils:* **All**

HERMITAGE OILS ☺ ❶ ⃠ ✓
All; *Fixed Oils:* Jojoba, Peach Kernal, Sweet Almond BP, Wheatgerm

HIMALAYA UK LTD ☺ ✓ ✂
Spa Aromatherapy: All

JOPHIEL® ☺ ❶ ⃠ ✓
Carrier Oils: Almond Sweet, Apricot Kernal, Arnica, Avocado (Unrefined), Borage (Starflower), Calendula, Carrot, Coconut, Comfrey, Grapeseed, Hazelnut, Hempseed, Jojoba, Macadamia, Peach Kernal, Rosehip, Safflower, St. John's Wort, Wheatgerm; *Essential Oils:* All; *Lifestyle Oils:* Calming & Balancing, Invigorate, Lavender & Geranium, Relaxation, Tranquility; *Therapeutic Oils:* Cold Relief, Hay Fever, Muscular Aches & Pains, Rheumatism & Arthritis, Sinusitis, Sports

KOBASHI ™ ☺ ⃠ ✓ 👁 ✂
Rosehip Oil Organic; Seabuckthorne Oil; *Blended Massage Oils:* **Anti-Cellulite**, **Relaxing**, **Sensual**, **Sports**; *Misc:* **Carrier Oils**, **Essential Oils**, **Poster**, **Vitamin E**

L'OCCITANE EN PROVENCE ✓ 👁
Aromachologie: Essential Oil, Neutral Vegetable Oil, Purifying Bath & Massage Oil, Relaxing Bath & Massage Oil, Revitalizing Bath & Massage Oil; *Olive Harvest:* Olive Massage Oil; *Shea Butter:* Massage Balm, Pure Shea Butter 'Limited Edition'

LAVERA ™
basis sensitiv: **Body Oil**

LUSH ✓
Massage Bars: Amazonians, Baby Face, Black Magic, Cosmic Dreamcatcher, Each Peach, Fever, Glitterbug - Iris, Scalp Massage Bar, Shimmy Shimmy, Sweet Japanese Girl, Therapy, Wiccy Magic Muscles

MEADOWSWEET LTD ™☺⊘✓
Aromatherapy (Carrier Oils): **Avocado**, **Carrot**, **Evening Primrose**, **Grapeseed**, **Jojoba**, **Peach Kernel**, **Sweet Almond**, **Wheatgerm**; *Aromatherapy (Pure Essential Oils):* **Basil**, **Bergamot**, **Black Pepper**, **Camphor**, **Cedarwood**, **Chamomile (Roman)**, **Citronella**, **Clary Sage**, **Clove**, **Cypress**, **Eucalyptus**, **Frankincense**, **Geranium** , **Ginger**, **Grapefruit**, **Juniper**, **Lavender (High Altitude)**, **Lemon**, **Lemon Grass**, **Lime**, **Mandarin**, **Manuka**, **Marjoram (Sweet)**, **Myrrh**, **Niaouli**, **Orange**, **Patchouli**, **Peppermint**, **Petitgrain**, **Pine**, **Red Thyme**, **Rosemary**, **Rosewood**, **Sandalwood**, **Sweet Fennel** , **Tea Tree**, **Vetivert**, **Ylang-Ylang**; *Herbal Aromatic Range:* **Relaxing Massage Oil**; *Men's Range:* **Comfrey After Sports Massage Oil**; *Nature Power Range:* **Body Firming Contouring Massage Oil**, **Cellulite Thigh Intensive Massage Oil**; *Therapy in Blue™ Face Oil:* **Nourishing**, **Rejuvenate**; *Therapy in Blue™ Massage Oil:* **Balance/Calm Body**, **Detox/Tone Body**, **Exotic/Sensual Body**, **Stress Ease**, **Uplifting/Refresh Body**

NAPIERS HERBAL HEALTH CENTRE ✓
Essential & Massage Oils: All; *Organic Essential Oils:* All

NATIONAL TRUST ENTERPRISES LTD ⊘✓✂1998
Muscle Rub: Gardeners

NATURAL BY NATURE OILS ☺⊘✓👁✂1974
Base/Carrier Oils: All; *Essential Oils:* All; *Organic Essential Oils:* All; *Special Oils & Creams:* Aromatherapy Base Cream, Body Tone, Cellulite, Evening Primrose, Muscle Fatigue

NATURALLY GIFTED ™
Bath & Massage Oil: **Citrus & Lavender**, **Neroli & Rose**

NEAL'S YARD REMEDIES ⊘✓
Essential Oils; *Essential Oil Burner:* Bodo Sperlein; *Massage Oil:* Aromatic, Base, Baseline, Geranium & Orange, Mother's, Sandalwood

NEW SEASONS ☺⊘♞
Absolute Oils: All; *Carrier Oils:* All; *Essential Oils:* All; *Organic Oils:* All

ORGANIC BLUE ™⊘♞
Massage Oils: **Muscle Rub**, **Relaxing**, **Sensual**; *Mood Blends:* **Easy Breathe**, **Energising**, **Meditation**, **Relaxing**, **Restful Night**, **Sensual**

ORGANIC COLOUR COMPANY ™
Rosemary Herbal Oil

OSHADHI LTD ☺♞
Essential Oils, Massage Oils etc: All

PHYTO PRODUCTS LTD ☺
Carrier Oils: Almond Sweet B.P., Apricot Kernel, Borage (21.5% GLA), Grapeseed, Jojoba, Peach Kernel, Wheatgerm; *Infused Oils:* Arnica

PURPLE FLAME AROMATHERAPY ⊘♞
Carrier Oils: All; *Concentrated Oil Blends:* Energise, Head Clearing, Muscle, Relaxation, Unwind; *Precious Oils in Jojoba:* Chamomile Blue/German, Jasmine Maroc, Melissa, Neroli, Rose Maroc; *Pure Essential Oils & Absolutes:* All; *Synergistic Skin & Massage Oil Blends:* Ascension, De-tox, Energise, Inner Calm, L'Homme Sensuel, La Femme Sensuelle, Post-workout, Pre-workout, Unwind

QUINESSENCE AROMATHERAPY ☺❶⊘♞👁
Essential Oils: All; *Massage Oils:* Athletic, Cellulite, Invigorating, Joint Mobility, Muscle Ease, Relaxing, Stress, Stretch Marks; *Organic Oils:* All

SCENT BY NATURE ☺⊘♞✂1986
Aromatherapy: Apricot Carrier Oil, Discounted Essential Oil Multi-Packs, Dispersable Vegetable Bath Carrier Oil, Essential Oil Collections, Grapeseed Carrier Oil, Self-Selection Gift Packs, Sweet Almond Carrier Oil, Tea Tree Antiseptic Cream; *Essential Oils:* All

SCOTTISH HERBAL SUPPLIES ™⊘♞✂👁
Organic & Non-Organic Essential Oils; **Vegetable Creams**; **Vegetable Oils**

SIMPLY SOAPS ™❶⊘♞✂
Oils: **Aphrodisia**, **Invigorating**, **Relaxing**

THE ORGANIC HERB TRADING COMPANY ⊘☼
Organic Macerates & Flower Waters

TISSERAND AROMATHERAPY PRODUCTS ™
After Treatment Products: **After Wax Oil**, **Tinted After-Electrolysis Cream**; *Blended Essential Oils:* **Jasmine/Jojoba**, **Linden Blossom/Jojoba**, **Orange Blossom/Jojoba**, **Rose/Jojoba**; *Blended Massage Oils:* **Cellulite Treatment Oil**, **Facial Treatment Oil**, **Muscle Fatigue Treatment Oil**, **Nourishing Facial Lotion**, **Refreshing Body Lotion**, **Relaxing Body Lotion**, **Relaxing Body Oil**, **Sensual Body**

Oil; *Clear Breathe:* **Clear Breathe Concentrate**, **Clear Breathe Inhaler** , **Clear Breathe Vapour Rub**; *Essential Oils:* **Basil (Herb)**, **Benzoin (Trees)**, **Bergamot (Rind of the Fruit)**, **Black Pepper (Peppercorns)**, **Camomile German (Flowers)**, **Camomile Roman (Flowers)**, **Cardomon (Seeds)**, **Carrot Seed (Seeds)**, **Cedarwood Atlas (Trees)**, **Cedarwood (Virginian) (Trees)**, **Citronella (Grass)**, **Clary Sage (Herb)**, **Coriander (Dried Fruits)**, **Cypress (Leaves of the Tree)**, **Eucalyptus (Leaves of the Tree)**, **Fennel (Herb)**, **Frankincense (Tree Resin)**, **Geranium (Leaves)**, **Ginger (Root of the Plant)**, **Grapefruit (Rind of the Fruit)**, **Immortelle (Flowers)**, **Jasmine Absolute (Flowers)**, **Juniper (Berries)**, **Kanuka (Foliage)**, **Lavender (Flowers)**, **Lemon (Rind of the Fruit)**, **Lemongrass (Grass)**, **Lime (Rind of the Fruit)**, **Linden Blossom Absolute (Flowers)**, **Mandarin (Rind of the Fruit)**, **Marjoram French (Herb)**, **Marjoram Spanish (Herb)**, **May Chang (Fruit)**, **Melissa (Leaves & Flowers)**, **Myrrh (Tree Resin)**, **Niaouli (Leaf of the Tree)**, **Orange Blossom (Neroli) (Flowers)**, **Orange (Rind of the Fruit)**, **Palmarosa (Grass)**, **Patchouli (Herb)**, **Peppermint (Herb)**, **Petitgrain (Orange Tree Leaf)**, **Pine (Trees)**, **Rose Absolute (Flowers)**, **Rose Otto (Flowers)**, **Rose Phytol (Flowers)**, **Rosemary (Herb)**, **Rosewood (Tree)**, **Sandalwood (Tree)**, **Tea-tree (Leaves of the Tree)**, **Vetiver (Grass)**, **Violet Leaf Absolute (Flowers)**, **Yarrow (Milfoil) (Flower Heads)**, **Ylang-Ylang (Flowers)**; *Lavender Products:* **Lavender Gel**, **Lavender Lotion**, **Lavender Moist Tissues**, **Lavender Water**; *Massage Oil Base:* **Avocado**, **Body Massage Oil Base**, **Evening Primrose w Vitamin E**, **Face Massage Oil Base**, **Grapeseed**, **Jojoba**, **Massage Lotion Base**, **Peach Kernel**, **Soya Bean**, **Sweet Almond**, **Wheatgerm**; *Masterblends:* **Energy**, **Euphoria**, **Passion**, **Serenity**; *Tea Tree Products:* **Natural Antiseptic Cream**, **Tea-Tree & Kanuka Blemish Stick** , **Tea-Tree & Kanuka Gel**, **Tea-Tree & Lime Cream Body Wash**, **Tea-Tree Lotion**, **Tea-Tree & Manuka Cream**, **Tea-Tree Moist Tissues**

TREE-HARVEST ⊘ 🐈
Essential Oils: All

URTEKRAM ⊘ 🐈 ✂
Body Oil: Apricot, Jojoba

WOODS OF WINDSOR ☺ 🐈
Lavandula Angustifolia: Aromatherapy Lavender

YAOH ™☺❶ 🐈 ⊘
Massage Oil

YORKSHIRE HEMP LTD ™
Chanvre Hemp Body Care: **Aromatherapy Cool Mind**, **Aromatherapy Hemp Emotion**, **Aromatherapy Hempflower**, **Aromatherapy Mindbalance**, **Aromatherapy Pure Hemp**, **Havanna**

Massage Oil, **Pure & Natural Massage Oil**, **Stress Easing Massage Oil**, **Woman Eau de Toilette**; *Hemp Massage Oil:* **Chanvre**

EYE PRODUCTS

ABSOLUTELY PURE ™⊘✔✂
Earth's Beauty: Eye Pencil, Loose Eye Liner, Mineral Colours Matte Eye Shadow; *Luscious Skincare:* **Rosehip Eye Gel**; *Monave:* Mineral Shimmer Eye Shadow; *Mukti Botanicals:* **Rosehip Eye Gel**

ANNEMARIE BÖRLIND ➊⊘✔
Eye Make Up Remover; Kohl Crayons; Powder Eye Shadow; Pura Soft Q10 Eye Area Care

ARTEL ALLERGY PRODUCTS ✔
Facial Skincare: Gentle Eye Make Up Remover, Touch of Youth Mandarin Eye Elixir

BARRY M COSMETICS ✔✂1985
Dazzle Dust; *Kohl Pencils:* All

BEAUTY NATURALS (MARTHA HILL) ➊⊘✔
Eye Care: Contour Balm, Elderflower Contour Gel, Gentle Cleansing Gel; *Eye Colours:* Eye Crayon, Eye Liner Pencil, Herbal Silky 'Diamonds' Shadow, Powder Eye Shadow Duos; *Gentle Cleansing for Eyes:* Lotion

BEAUTY THROUGH HERBS ☺⊘✔◉✂1990
Galeno Gold Nourishing Eye Cream Gel; Phyto Marine Eye Contour Gel

BEAUTY WITHOUT CRUELTY ™☺
Eye Defining Pencil; **Liquid Eyeliner**; **Soft Kohl Pencil**; *Eyeshadow:* **Satin Finish Duos**; *Mascara:* **Full Volume**, **Waterproof**

CAMILLA HEPPER LTD ⊘✔✂1987
Cucumber Eye Gel; Eye Make-Up Remover Lotion; Herbal Eye Cream

DOLMA ™☺➊⊘✔◉✂
Skin Care: **Aloe Vera Eye Gel**, **Chamomile & Aloe Vera Eye Cream**, **Chamomile & Fennel Eye Make-up Remover**

DR HADWEN TRUST ☺➊⊘✔
Eye Make-up Remover Cream; Eye Shimmers Colour Set; Herbal Leg & Vein Cream Gel; Liquid Eyeliner; Luxury 48-Eyeshadow Set; Satin Finish Eyeshadow Duos; *Eye Gel:* ComfreyPlus Cucumber, Elderflower, Unfragranced; *Eye Pencils:* Defining, Soft Kohi; *Mascara:* Full Volume, Waterproof

ESSENTIAL OIL COMPANY ☺⊘✔◉
Eyezone Massager

ESSENTIALLY YOURS LTD ™⊘✔
Natural Elements: **Eye Cleansing Liquid**, **Eye Cream**, **Eye Firming Serum**

FAITH PRODUCTS LTD ❶⊘♞ ✂👁1978
Skin Care: Aloe Vera Eye Gel

GREEN PEOPLE CO. ™⊘♞
Hair & Body Care: Chamomile Eye Care; *Skin Care:* Superlight Eye Cream, **Eye Cream (Night), Eye Cream (Night), Eye Gel (Day)**

HERBS HANDS HEALING LTD ™⊘♞
Eyebright & Goldenseal Eyewash; *Allergies:* Eyebright & Goldenseal Eyewash Formula

HERBS OF GRACE ™⊘♞
Eyewash Powder

JOPHIEL® ☺❶⊘♞
Rejuvanating™ Skincare: Gentle Eye Protection Cream

KISS MY FACE ⊘♞ 👁 ✂
Obsessively Organic - Preservative Free: Eye Witness (A C & E)

L'OCCITANE EN PROVENCE ♞ 👁
Immortelle: Eye Balm; *Verbena Harvest:* Ice Eye Pads

MEADOWSWEET LTD ™☺⊘♞
Cleansers: **Eye-Make-Up Remover Cream**; *Comfrey+ Range:* **Cucumber Eye Gel**; *Fragrance Free Range:* **Eye Gel**; *General Bodycare:* **Elderflower Eye Gel**

NEAL'S YARD REMEDIES ⊘♞
Eye Gel: White Tea

SEVEN WIVES NATURAL BODYCARE ™⊘♞
Eye Cream; Eye Gel

TREE-HARVEST ⊘♞
Elderflower Eye Gel; Eye Gel

VEGANSTORE.CO.UK ™☺⊘❶♞
Vizulize: Contact Lens Cleaner

FEMININE HYGIENE

ARKOPHARMA (UK) LTD ☺⊘♞
Phyto Soya: Feminine Wash, Vaginal Gel

HIGHER NATURE PLC ™⊘♞
VagiClear

MOONCUP LTD. ™
Mooncup

NATRACARE ☺❶⊘♞
Organic Cotton Feminine Wipes; *Natural Pads:* Curved Regular, Slender, Super; *Natural Panty Liners:* Breathable, Curved; *Organic All Cotton Applicator Tampons:* Regular, Super; *Organic All Cotton Tampons:* Regular, Super, Super-Plus; *Pads:* Night Time, Ultra w Wings

NATURAL WOMAN ⊘♞
Lunapads: Washable Organic Sanitary Towels

PASSION FOR LIFE PRODUCTS
Bio-Fem Actigel - Instant Relief from Intimate Female Problems

PURPLE FLAME AROMATHERAPY ⊘✔
Moon Cup: After Child Birth, Before Child Birth

FOOT & LEG CARE

AMPHORA AROMATICS LTD ⊘✔ ✂1998
Herbal Relaxing Foot Spray

ANIMAL AID ☺❶⊘✔ ✂1976
Cool Mint Foot Lotion; Peppermint Foot Powder

ARTEL ALLERGY PRODUCTS ✔
Footcare: Peppermint Foot Lotion, Peppermint Foot Powder, Peppermint Foot Scrub, Peppermint Foot Soak, Peppermint Foot Spray, Toe Fungus Relief

BAY HOUSE AROMATICS ⊘✔ ✂1978
Peppermint & Aloe Vera Foot Lotion

BEAUTY NATURALS (MARTHA HILL) ❶⊘✔
Energising Leg Gel; Moisturising Foot Balm

BEAUTY THROUGH HERBS ☺⊘✔ 👁✂1990
Phyto Care: Footbalm Herbal Cream, Legtonic

CAMILLA HEPPER LTD ⊘✔ ✂1987
Aloe Vera Foot Lotion

CAPITELLI OILS ™☺✔ ⊘
Foot & Hand Cream: **Crema Mani**, **Crema Peidi**

DEODORANT STONE (UK) LTD ☺⊘✔
Peppermint Foot Spray-On Stone

DOLMA ™☺❶⊘✔ 👁✂
Hand & Foot Care: **Aromatic Foot Shampoo w Lemongrass & Cypress**, **Aromatic Foot Shampoo w Peppermint & Tea Tree**, **Peppermint Foot Cream**

DR HADWEN TRUST ☺❶⊘✔
Athlete's Foot Oil; Cellulite & Thigh Massage; Deodorising Foot Spray; Skin Softening Peppermint Foot Cream

ESSENTIAL OIL COMPANY ☺⊘✔ 👁
Spa Foot Pamper Pack

ESSENTIALLY YOURS LTD ™⊘✔
Natural Elements: **Anti-Microbial Foot Cream**, **Anti-Microbial Foot Soak**, **Anti-Microbial Foot Spray**, **Foot Massage Cream**, **Refreshing Foot Scrub**, **Refreshing Foot Soak**, **Warming Foot Cream**, **Warming Foot Soak**

FAITH PRODUCTS LTD ❶⊘✔ ✂👁1978
Skin Care: Essential Foot Lotion

FINEMOOD LTD ⊘✔
Hair & Body Care: Foot Reflex Cream

HEALTHY HERBS ✓ ⦸ ☼
Burdock & Chickweed Oil; Calendula Oil; Comfrey Oil

L'OCCITANE EN PROVENCE ✓ ◉
Aromachologie: Purifying Powdered Foot Care, Revitalizing Cream for Tired Legs; *Shea Butter:* Exfoliating Foot Care, Foot Cream

LUSH ✓
Skincare, Haircare, etc: Pied de Pepper, Volcano - Preserved Feb 2004

MEADOWSWEET LTD ™☺⦸ ✓
Comfrey+ Range: **Peppermint Foot Cream**; *Creams:* **Leg & Vein, Peppermint Foot**; *General Bodycare:* **Herbal Foot Soak**; *Nature Power Range:* **Athletes Foot Oil**; *Sprays:* **Deodorising Foot**

MONTAGNE JEUNESSE ⦸ ✓
Foot Cooler; Foot Scrub; Foot Soak Foot Lotion

NEAL'S YARD REMEDIES ⦸ ✓
Pumice Foot Scrub

OPTIMA HEALTH & NUTRITION ⦸ ✓ ✂1995
Thursday Plantation Tea Tree: Anti-Fungal Gel, Foot Powder, Foot Spray

PASSION FOR LIFE PRODUCTS
PediTech - Foot Spray; Wartner - Wart & Verruca Removal (Not Suitable for Diabetics)

PURPLE FLAME AROMATHERAPY ⦸ ✓
Sweet Feet Reflexology Wipes

QUINESSENCE AROMATHERAPY ☺❶⦸ ✓ ◉
Foot Balm

SEVEN WIVES NATURAL BODYCARE ™⦸ ✓
Foot Cream Tea Tree

TISSERAND AROMATHERAPY PRODUCTS ™
Hand & Foot Care: **Foot Lotion**, **Foot Soak**, **Foot Spray**, **Footbar**

GIFT BOXES & PACKS

DR HADWEN TRUST ☺❶⦸ ✓
Essential Spa Set; Neroli & Sandalwood & Grapefruit & Kiwi Aquatherapy Set

GREEN PEOPLE CO. ™⦸ ✓
Skin Care: **Organic Face Pamper Pack**

KOBASHI ™☺⦸ ✓ ◉✂
Misc: **Starter Baskets/Gift packs**

LUSH ✓
Christmas Gifts: Angel's Delight Balsa Box, Christmas Soap Stack, Fairy Christmas, Happy Christmas, Purple Haze, Snowcake Balsa Box

SEVEN WIVES NATURAL BODYCARE ™⦸ ✓
3 Soaps Gift Set: Care Range, Castille Range

WOODS OF WINDSOR ☺✔
Overnight Gift Bag: Lavender, Lily of the Valley, True Rose; *Relaxation Kit Bag:* Lavender, Lily of the Valley, True Rose

HAIR DYES

CAMILLA HEPPER LTD ⃠✔ ✂1987
Natural Henna Hair Colours: Black, Chestnut Brown, Copper Gold, Natural Auburn

COLORA HENNA ☺⃠✔ ✂
All

COTSWOLD HEALTH PRODUCTS ☺⃠✪
Henna: Neutral, Sahara Blonde; *Henna Powder:* Black, Red

DANIEL FIELD DIRECT ☺✔
Watercolour: Black (this is not a true black), Chestnut Brown, Chestnut Darker Brown, Copper Beech - Radiant Rich Copper, Copper Darker Brown, Dark Blonde, Dark Brown, Dark Copper Blonde, Dark Warmer Bonde, Ebony - Super Dark Brown, Lightest Chestnut Brown, Lightest Warm Brown, Mahogany - Richest Red Brown, Maple - Rich Red Brown, Mid Golden Blonde, Mid Golden Copper Blonde, Natural Darker Brown, Natural Lightest Brown, Natural Mid Blonde, Neutal Dark Blonde, Neutral Lightest Brown, Oak - Natural Brown, Pale Natural Soft Blonde, Radiant Bordeaux Brown (Violet Red), Radiant Burgundy Brown (Red Violet), Rosewood - Radiant Light Red Brown, Sycamore - Radiant Golden Copper, Walnut - Darkest Warm Brown, Warm Brown, Warm Darker Brown

DR HADWEN TRUST ☺❶⃠✔
Cruelty-free Hair Water Colours Available in 30 Shades

HERB UK LTD ☺⃠✔
Changes Semi Permanent Hair Colour: Allamanda, Dianthus, Felicia, Genista, Inula, Jasminum, Kalmia, Morina, Nerine; *Tints of Nature Permanent Hair Colour:* Black, Dark Blonde, Dark Brown, Dark Henna Red, Darkest Brown, Light Blonde, Light Brown, Light Golden Brown, Light Henna Red, Medium Blonde, Medium Brown, Medium Golden Blonde, Medium Mahogany Blonde, Medium Mahogany Brown, Medium Red Copper, Platinum Blonde, Rich Copper Brown, Soft Copper Blonde

LUSH ✔
Hennas: Caca Brun, Caca Marron, Caca Noir, Caca Rouge

MONTAGNE JEUNESSE ⃠✔
Davinci Hair Colour: Dark Brown, Light Brown, Medium Brown; *One Night Stand Hair Colors:* All

NAPIERS HERBAL HEALTH CENTRE ✔
Hair Care: Henna (Black/Red/Blonde/Brown)

NEAL'S YARD REMEDIES ⃠✔
Henna

ORGANIC COLOUR COMPANY ™
Herbatint; Vegetal

HAIRSPRAYS,GELS ETC

ABSOLUTELY PURE ™
Kettlecare: 100% Natural Hair Spray

BEAUTY NATURALS (MARTHA HILL)
Natural Style Conditioning Hair Gel

CAMILLA HEPPER LTD 1987
Jojoba Hair Gel

DANIEL FIELD DIRECT
Classics: Anti Frizz Protector Hairspray, Body Builder Spray, Cactus Sap Styling Gel, Curl Hold & Shine, Pump up the Volume!, Smooth & Shine Serum, Styling Wax; *Supernaturals:* Curl Enhancing Spritz, Glossing Gel, Polishing Wax, Volumising Air-o-Foam; *Supernaturals Serum:* Mirror Finish, Smooth & Shine

DR HADWEN TRUST
Curl Enhancing Spritz; Polishing Wax; Pump Up the Volume Mousse; Straighten & Smooth Balm; Styling Gel; Texture & Define Paste; *Serum:* Mirror Finish, Smooth & Shine; *Spray:* Anti-Frizz, Body Builder, Curl Hold & Shine

ESSENTIALLY YOURS LTD ™
Natural Elements: **Anti-Tangle Spray, Hair Oil, Hair & Scalp Fluid**

KISS MY FACE
Upper Management Style Gel; *Cheap Kisses:* Styling Gel

LAVERA ™
basis sensitiv: **Special Hair Treatment**

MONTAGNE JEUNESSE
Davinci: Hair Thickening; *Hair Spray:* Frizz Killer, Style Slave, Ultra Shine; *Miracle Hair:* Frizz, Moisture, Volume

HAND & NAIL PRODUCTS

ABSOLUTELY PURE ™
Luscious Skincare: **Frankincense & Myrrh Nail Oil**

ANIMAL AID 1976
Marigold & Marshmallow Handcream

ANNEMARIE BÖRLIND
Hand Balm

ARTEL ALLERGY PRODUCTS
Body Cleansers: Gentle Liquid Hand Cleanser; *Hand Care:* Calendula Hand Moisturiser, Hand Repair Treatment

ASTONISH
Liquid Hand Wash: Blueberry, Coconut, Kiwi, Waterlilly

BARRY M COSMETICS 1985
Nail Paints: All

BAY HOUSE AROMATICS ⃠ ✂ 1978
Hand Cream: for Gardeners w Sandalwood & Benzoin, Jojoba Base, Luxury w Rose Oils

BEAUTY NATURALS (MARTHA HILL) ➊ ⃠
Gardener's Cream; Nourishing Nail Oil; Skin Smoothing Hand Scrub; *Cuticle Cream:* Gentle, Nourishing

BEAUTY WITHOUT CRUELTY ™☺
High Gloss Nail Colour

CAMILLA HEPPER LTD ⃠ ✂ 1987
Evening Primrose Hand Cream

CELLANDE MIDLANDS ☺⃠
Hand Cleaner: Coconut, Lavender & Avocado Oil, Pine

CULPEPER LTD
Aromatherapy Naturals Hand Wash: Lavender, Tea Tree w Grapefruit

DOLMA ™☺➊⃠ ✂
Hand & Foot Care: **Lemongrass Hand Cream**, **Nail & Cuticle Oil**, **Wild Poppy Hand Cream**

DR HADWEN TRUST ☺➊⃠
High Gloss Nail Colours; *Hand Cream:* Peach & Apricot, Rich Rose; *Hand Lotion:* Orange & Lavender, Rose & Glycerine

ESSENTIALLY YOURS LTD ™⃠
Natural Elements: **Extra Rich Hand Cream**; *Passion to Garden:* **Luxury Hand Lotion**, **Luxury Hand Wash**

FAITH PRODUCTS LTD ➊⃠ ✂ 1978
Hand Wash: Lavender & Geranium, Tea Tree

FINEMOOD LTD ⃠
Hair & Body Care: Hand Lotion

GROOMERS LTD ⃠
Germaway Hand Disinfectant

HONESTY COSMETICS LTD ™☺➊⃠ ✂ 1976
Hand Cream w Comfrey

KENT COSMETICS ☺⃠
Australian Organics Hand Cream

L'OCCITANE EN PROVENCE
Immortelle: Young Hands; *Lavender Harvest:* Cleansing Hand Wash, Lavender Hand Cream, Moisturizing Hand Lotion; *Shea Butter:* Extra Gentle Lotion for Hands & Body, Hand Cream, Milk Extra Gentle Wash for Hands & Body, Mini Hand Cream, Nail & Cuticle Cream, Softening Hand Scrub; *Verbena Harvest:* Ice Hand Cream Gel, Refreshing Towlettes

LIBERON WAXES LTD
Liquid Glove

MEADOWSWEET LTD ™☺⃠
Hand Care: **Lemon & Hawthorn Barrier Cream**, **Peach & Apricot Hand Cream**, **Rich Rose Hand Cream**, **Rose & Glycerine Hand Lotion**

NAPIERS HERBAL HEALTH CENTRE ✔
Bath, Skin & Body Products: Bath Grains; *Wash Range:* Lavender & Geranium Handwash, Neem & Propous Handwash

NATIONAL TRUST ENTERPRISES LTD ⊘ ✔ ✂1998
Hand Cream: Gardeners, Lavender; *Hand & Nail Cream:* Rose

NATURA ORGANICS ⊘ ✔ ☼
Hand Cream: w Shea Butter Olive Oil & Lavender

NATUREWATCH ☺⊘ ✔ 👁✂1976
Clearly Compassionate: Lavender & Lemon Hand & Nail Cream

NEAL'S YARD REMEDIES ⊘ ✔
Citrus Hand Wash

NEW SEASONS ☺⊘ ✔
Neutral Base: Hand Cream

QUINESSENCE AROMATHERAPY ☺❶⊘ ✔ 👁
Hand Cream

SEVEN WIVES NATURAL BODYCARE ™⊘ ✔
Hand Cream

TISSERAND AROMATHERAPY PRODUCTS ™
Hand & Foot Care: **Hand & Nail Cream**

WOODS OF WINDSOR ☺ ✔
Conditioning Hand & Nail Cream: Forget Me Not, Lavender, Lily of the Valley, Mimosa, True Rose

LIP PRODUCTS

ANNEMARIE BÖRLIND ❶⊘ ✔
Lip Liner

ARKOPHARMA (UK) LTD ☺⊘ ✔
Sore-Lip Stick

BARRY M COSMETICS ✔ ✂1985
Lip Liners: All

BEAUTY NATURALS (MARTHA HILL) ❶⊘ ✔
Aloe Vera Lip Balm; Herbal Enriched Lip Twist; Herbal Lip Primer; Vitamin E Lip Treatment

BEAUTY WITHOUT CRUELTY ™☺
Lip Defining Pencil; **Lip Gloss**; **Moisturising Lipstick**

CAMILLA HEPPER LTD ⊘ ✔ ✂1987
Lip Smoothies: Banana, Mint, Passionfruit

DOLMA ™☺❶⊘ ✔ 👁✂
Miscellaneous Products: **Mandarin Lip Salve**, **Spearmint Lip Salve**

DR HADWEN TRUST ☺❶⊘ ✔
Clear Lip Gloss Pen; Lip Defining Pencils; Lip Shimmers Colour Set;

Moisturising Lipstick in 24 Shades; *Lip Balm:* Banana, Coconut, Green Apple, Peppermint, Red Cherry, Rich Plum, Strawberry, Wild Dewberry

FINEMOOD LTD ⃠ ✓
Skin Care: Lip Balm

GREEN PEOPLE CO. ™ ⃠ ✓
Lip Care: **Soft Lips ("No Scent")**

HONESTY COSMETICS LTD ™☺❶⃠ ✓ 👁 ✂1976
Lip Balm

L'OCCITANE EN PROVENCE ✓ 👁
Immortelle Lip Lift; *Lip Gloss:* Eau des 4 Reines, Eau des Vanilliers; *Shea Butter:* Lip Balm Cream SPF15, Lip Balm Stick, Tinted Balm

MEADOWSWEET LTD ™☺⃠ ✓
Lip Balms: **Banana**, **Coconut**, **Green Apple**, **Peppermint**, **Red Cherry**, **Rich Plum**, **Strawberry**

OPTIMA HEALTH & NUTRITION ⃠ ✓ ✂1995
Thursday Plantation Tea Tree: Lip Fix Cream

SEVEN WIVES NATURAL BODYCARE ™ ⃠ ✓
Ecolips

TISSERAND AROMATHERAPY PRODUCTS ™
Lavender Products: **Lavender & Raspberry Lip Balm**; *Tea Tree Products:* **Tea-Tree & Mandarin Lip Balm**

VEGANSTORE.CO.UK ™☺⃠❶ ✓
Beep Balm Lip Balm

XYNERGY HEALTH PRODUCTS ⃠ ✓
Trilogy Rosehip Oil Skin Care: Intensive Lip Treatment

YAOH ™☺❶ ✓ ⃠
Salve; *Lip Balm:* **Coconut**, **Mango**, **Spearmint**

PERFUMES ETC

ABSOLUTELY PURE ™ ⃠ ✓ ✂
Cheri's Country Cottage: Cologne Spray; *Luscious Skincare - Solid Cream Perfume:* **Apple Blossom**, **Jasmine**, **Luscious**; *Miessence:* Pump Spray Perfume, Roll On Perfume

AMPHORA AROMATICS LTD ⃠ ✓ ✂1998
Exotic Essential Oil Perfumes: Tranquil & Calming

ANNEMARIE BÖRLIND ❶⃠ ✓
Pur Arôme Fragrance: Green Leaf, Purple Velvet, Tropical Sun, White Satin

BEAUTY THROUGH HERBS ☺⃠ ✓ 👁 ✂1990
Out of Africa: Cologne, Perfume

DOLMA ™☺❶⊘✓👁✂
Vegan Perfumes: **Amethyst Mist, Anahita, Calista, Cushie B, Keltina, Prelude, Raga, Sarabande, Sonata, Vegamusk**

DR HADWEN TRUST ☺❶⊘✓
Perfume & Eau de Parfum Sprays: Amethyst Mist, Anahita, Calista, Cushie B, Keltina, Prelude, Raga, Sarabande, Sonata, Vegamusk

ESSENCE SERENE ™☺⊘✓✂
Karmarny: **Eau de Toilette**; *Purity:* **Water Based Perfume**

JOPHIEL® ☺❶⊘✓
LingQiessence® Perfume Oil: Jasmine, Neroli, Rose

L'OCCITANE EN PROVENCE ✓👁
Eau de Parfum: for Men, L'Oranger - Eau de Cologne, L'Oranger - Eau de Parfum Neroli; *Eau de Toilette:* Almond, Eau d'Azur, Eau de 4 Reines, Eau de Val, Eau des Vanilliers, for Men, Lavender Harvest, Verbena Harvest; *Eau des 4 Voleurs:* for Men; *Solid Perfume:* Eau des Vanilliers, Eau du Val, Verbena Harvest

LUSH ✓
Fragrance: Ginger, Karma; *Skincare, Haircare, etc:* Ginger Lotion, Karma Lotion

MEADOWSWEET LTD ™☺⊘✓
Men's Range: **Jaztec Aftershave, Sandalwood Aftershave**

MORNY ⊘✓
Eau de Toilette Spray: Original Lavender

NATIONAL TRUST ENTERPRISES LTD ⊘✓✂1998
Cologne: Lavender Roll On, Lavender Spray, Rose

NEAL'S YARD REMEDIES ⊘✓
Cologne

NORFOLK LAVENDER LTD ✓✂
The English Lavender

PERFUMERS GUILD LTD, THE ☺❶⊘✓
Anniversary Woman; Bespoke Signature Scents (Personalised Perfume); Eau de Parfum for Women; Marine Blend - Diana; The Scent of Flowers; The Scent of Friendship - Amitie; *Chypre Blends:* Christina, Margot; *Citrus Blends:* Louisa, Twenty One; *Floral Blends:* Alice, Gabriella, Lily of the Valley, Margaret, Provence Lavender; *For Men:* Anniversary Man, Eau de Toilette for Men, Kensington, St John, Twenty One; *Oriental Blends:* Amber, Georgina, Sophie; *Scents of Romance:* Original, St Valentine, Unforgettable, w Love; *The Rose Collection:* English, Heritage, Millennium, Society

TREE-HARVEST ⊘✓
Tree Cologne: Birch, Cypress, Elder, Juniper, Mosses, Rowan

VEGANSTORE.CO.UK ™☺⊘❶✓
Ecco Bella: Perfume

WELEDA ⦸ ✔ ✂ 1985
Mens Range: Eau de Cologne

WOODS OF WINDSOR ☺ ✔
Eau de Toilette: for Men; *Parfum de Toilette:* Forget Me Not, Lavender, Lily of the Valley, Mimosa, True Rose

SHAMPOOS

ABSOLUTE AROMAS ™⦸ ✔
Ord River: **250ml**

ALOE PURA ⦸ ✔ ✂ 1995
Organic Aloe Vera Herbal Shampoo: Dry/Damaged Hair, Normal/Frequent Use

AMPHORA AROMATICS LTD ⦸ ✔ ✂ 1998
Aromatherapy Base; Gym & Swim Conditioning; Strong Tea Tree

ANIMAL AID ☺❶⦸ ✔ ✂ 1976
Amber; Jojoba Orange & Rosemary; Sea Spray; Tea Tree & Coconut; Woodspice

ARTEL ALLERGY PRODUCTS ✔
Hair Care: Fruit Essence

BAY HOUSE AROMATICS ⦸ ✔ ✂ 1978
Cream

BEAUTY NATURALS (MARTHA HILL) ❶⦸ ✔
Deep Moisturising; Gentle Balancing; Protein Enriched

BEAUTY THROUGH HERBS ☺⦸ ✔ 👁 ✂ 1990
Ginseng; Ginseng w Cryertomol

BIOFORCE
Neemcare; Neemcare Riddance

CAMILLA HEPPER LTD ⦸ ✔ ✂ 1987
Coconut Oil; Herbal; Natural Orange; Rosemary; Ti-Tree & Thyme

CAPITELLI OILS ™☺ ✔ ⦸
Bene; **Invigorante**

CAURNIE SOAPERIE ☺⦸ ✔ 👁 ✂
Avocado; Nettle; Pure; Rosemary Teatree

CULPEPER LTD
Aromatherapy Naturals Herbal Shampoo: Calendula, Chamomile, Rosemary, Soapwort, Tea Tree

DANIEL FIELD DIRECT ☺ ✔
Classics: Plant Remoisturising, Revitalising Detox Frequent Wash, Spring Water Everyday, Two-in-One w Conditioner; *Classics Therapy:* Body Builder, Dandruff Scalp, First Aid; *Supernaturals:* Curl Enhancing, Dandruff Scalp Therapy, Intensive Therapy 5 Spa, Smooth & Shine, Volumising

DOLMA ™☺❶⦸ ✔ 👁 ✂
Nettle & Pectin Hair Shampoos: **Bitter Orange & Tangerine**, **Cedarwood & Cypress**, **Lavender & Sage**, **Rosemary**, **Tea Tree & Thyme**; *Other*

Hair Preparations: **Jojoba & Sandalwood**

DR HADWEN TRUST ☺❶⊘✓
Banana & Vanilla; Chamomile; Coconut; ComfreyPlus Nettle All-Purpose; Herb & Protein Deep Conditioning; Lavender; Mango & Apricot; Wild Thyme & Mint; *Hair & Body (for Men):* Jaztec, Sandalwood; *Men's Hair & Body Shampoo:* Jaztec, Sandalwood; *SLS-free:* Bergamot & Orange, Rose & Geranium

ESSENCE SERENE ™☺⊘✓✂
Hair & Body

ESSENTIALLY YOURS LTD ™⊘✓
Natural Elements: **Conditioning**; *Therapeutics Range:* **E Hair & Body**

ETHICAL WARES ☺❶✓
Sea Breeze

FAITH PRODUCTS LTD ❶⊘✓ ✂👁1978
Gingko Biloba; Hemp & Meadowfoam; Jojoba; Lavender & Geranium; Organic Aloe Vera; Organic Chocolate; Rosemary; Saw Palmetto; Seaweed; Tea Tree (w 2% Oil)

FINEMOOD LTD ⊘✓
Hair & Body Care: Dry Hair, Greasy Hair, Headlice, Normal Hair

FUNK BUBBLE ™
Jojoba; Lavender/Geranium; Tea Tree; *Organic:* Aloe Vera

GREEN PEOPLE CO. ™⊘✓
6 Vitamin Boost Hair & Body Wash; *Hair & Body Care:* **Aloe Vera Herbal**, **Intensive Repair**, **Rosemary Herbal**, **Vita Min Fix**; *Men's Range:* **Itch Away**; *Organic Base:* **Shampoo**

HERB UK LTD ☺⊘✓
Nature's Essential; Sulfate Free

HERBS HANDS HEALING LTD ™⊘✓
Head & Hair

HONESTY COSMETICS LTD ™☺❶⊘✓👁✂1976
Apple & Rosemary Conditioning; **Chamomile & Orange**; **Hair & Body**; **Lemon & Vanilla**; **Nettle & Lavender**; **Peach & Coconut**

KENT COSMETICS ☺⊘✓
Australian Organics

KISS MY FACE ⊘✓👁✂
Big Body; Misstreated; SaHaira; Whenever; *Cheap Kisses:* Whenever

KOBASHI ™☺⊘✓👁✂
Shampoo: **Fragrance Free Base**, **Wild Tea Tree & Mandarin**, **Wild Thyme & Lime**

L'OCCITANE EN PROVENCE ✓👁
Aromachologie: Angelica, Artemisia, Juniper, Mint; *for Men:* Cade; *Lavender Harvest:* Clarifying; *Olive Harvest:* Extra Gentle; *Shea Butter:* Milk

LAVERA ™
basis sensitiv: **Balm**, **Regenerative**, **Shower**, **Vital**; *Neutral:* **Shower**

LUSH ✓
Shampoo Bars & Truckles & Solid Conditioners: Irresistible Bliss, Jumping Juniper, Karma Comba, New (Hair), Re Incarnate, Seanik, Soak & Float, The Blonde, Trichomania, Tropical Fruit Jungle, Ultimate Shine; *Skincare, Haircare, etc:* Big, Cynthia Sylvia Stout, Daddyo, I Love Juicy, Rehab

MARTHA HILL ❶⊘✓
Purely Natural Haircare: Enhancing, Mild & Gentle, Moisturising, Treatment, Volumising

MEADOWSWEET LTD ™☺⊘✓
Aloe Vera; **Fragrance Free**; *Comfrey+ Range:* **Nettle All Purpose**; *Men's Range:* **Jaztec**, **Sandalwood**; *Shampoo:* **Banana & Vanilla**, **Chamomile**, **Coconut**, **Herb & Protein**, **Kiwi & Lemon Balm**, **Lavender/Geranium/Ylang-Ylang**, **Mandarin & Papaya**, **Mango & Apricot**, **Nettle**, **Seaweed**, **Wild Thyme & Mint**; *SLS Free:* Bergamot & Orange, Rose & Geranium

NAPIERS HERBAL HEALTH CENTRE ✓
Quassia; Tonic; *Wash Range:* Aloe Vera, Hemp & Ginger, Seaweed & Lime

NATURA ORGANICS ⊘✓☼
w Karate Jojoba & Aloe Vera

NATURAL ORGANICS ™
Shampoo/Conditioner Bars: **Anti Headlice**, **Chamomile & Orange Blossom**, **Kilimanjaro**, **Marigold & Rhubarb**, **Nettle & Horsetail**, **Seaweed & Sage**, **Seaweed & Vetiver**, **Specially for Mums - Orange Blossom**, **Vetiver & Patchouli**

NATUREWATCH ☺⊘✓👁✂1976
Clearly Compassionate: Cypress & Tea Tree Conditioning for Normal/Oily Hair, Jojoba & Lavender Protein for Normal/Dry Hair, Lemon & Ylang Ylang Conditioning for Normal/Oily Hair, Rosemary Bay & Cedarwood Conditioning for Normal/Dry Hair

NEAL'S YARD REMEDIES ⊘✓
Baseline; Calendula; Chamomile & Orange Flower; Coconut & Jojoba; Nettle & Sage; Rosemary & Thyme; Seaweed

NEW SEASONS ☺⊘✓
Neutral Base: Conditioning

NUBIAN CARE ™
Nu Care: **Lemon Grass**

OPTIMA HEALTH & NUTRITION ⊘✓✂1995
Allergenics: Medicated; *Thursday Plantation Tea Tree:* Anti-Dandruff, Deep Cleansing

ORGANIC BLUE ™⊘✓
Body Care: **Normal/Dry**, **Normal/Greasy**

ORGANIC COLOUR COMPANY ™
Luminous; **Nettle & Burdock**; **Normalizing**; **Super**

ORIGINAL SOURCE ™⊘
Almond & Coconut; **Rose & Aloe**; **Tangerine & Bergamot**; **Tea Tree & Mint**

QUINESSENCE AROMATHERAPY ☺❶⊘
Frequent; Mild Base; Tea Tree

REALLY WORKS ™☺⊘
Hand & Body Soap/Shampoo

SEVEN WIVES NATURAL BODYCARE ™⊘
Shampoo; *Shampoo Bars:* **Chamomile & Geranium**, **Rosemary & Tea Tree**

SIMPLY SOAPS ™⊘❶
Liquid; *Shampoo Bars:* **Chamomile**, **Rosemary & Lavender**

SUMA WHOLEFOODS ⊘™❶ 1985
Cucumber; Mandarin; Pure

TISSERAND AROMATHERAPY PRODUCTS ™
Lavender & Mint Conditioning; *Hair Care:* **Three in One**; *Tea Tree Products:* **Tea-Tree Lemon & Rosemary**

TOM'S OF MAINE ⊘
Aloe & Almond; Honeysuckle

TREE-HARVEST ⊘
Shampoo Soap: Neem, Tropical Coconut

URTEKRAM ⊘
Aloe Vera; Chamomile; Hawthorn; Henna Neutral; Henna Red; Herbal; Nettle Anti Dandruff; Rhassoul; Rosemary; Sage; Seaweed; Tea Tree; Thistle; *Hair & Body Shampoo:* Rose; *Pure Balance:* Aloe Vera & Citrus, Lavender, Wild Rose

WELEDA ⊘ 1985
Bottled Shampoo: Calendula, Lemon Balm, Rosemary; *Shampoo Tube:* Rosemary

WOODS OF WINDSOR ☺
for Men

YAOH ™☺❶⊘
Shampoo

SHAVING PRODUCTS

ABSOLUTELY PURE ™⊘
Cheri's Country Cottage: After Shave Bracer

ANIMAL AID ☺❶⊘ 1976
Aftershave Lotion

ANNEMARIE BÖRLIND ❶⊘
Natural Care - For Men: Aftershave Balm, Aftershave Gel, Caring Shaving Cream,

BEAUTY NATURALS (MARTHA HILL) ❶⊘
David Hill for Men: Cleansing & Shaving Gel, Skin Calming Aftershave Balm,

Skin Calming Shaving Oil, Skin Refreshing Aftershave Gel, Skin Soothing Cream Shave

CAMILLA HEPPER LTD ⊘ ✂ 1987
Daen Depilatory Wax Strips

DOLMA ™☺❶⊘ ✂
Especially For Men: **De-luxe Aftershave Balm**, 'Freedom' Aftershave/Cologne, **'Kwame' Aftershave/Cologne**, **'Sirius' Aftershave/Cologne**, **Wet Shaving Fluid**

DR HADWEN TRUST ☺❶⊘
Pre-Wet Shave Cream; *Aftershave:* Kwame, Sirius; *Aftershave Balm:* Jaztec, Sandalwood; *Men's Shaving/Grooming Kit:* Complete, PLUS

ESSENTIALLY YOURS LTD ™⊘
Natural Elements: **Depilatory Shave Oil**, **Easy Shave for Men**

FINEMOOD LTD ⊘
Hair & Body Care: After Shave Balm, Post Epilation Moisture Cream

GREEN PEOPLE CO. ™⊘
Men's Range: **Pre-Shave Face Wash**, **Shave Now Shaving Gel**

HERBS HANDS HEALING LTD ™⊘
Splash on Toner; Sunrise After Shave Water

KISS MY FACE ⊘ ✂
Cheap Kisses: Fragrance Free Moist Shave; *Moisture Shave:* Cool Mint, Fragrance Free, Jasmine, Key Lime, Marine, Peaceful Patchouli, Peaches & Creme, Summer Melon, Vanilla Earth, Virgin Forest

L'OCCITANE EN PROVENCE
Eau de Toilette: Eau des Bergers for Men; *for Men:* Cade After Shave Balm, Cade Shaving Cream, Cade Shaving Stick, Cade Travel Shaving Oil, Energy Face Gel, Shaving Bowl w Cade Soap, Travel Shaving Brush

MEADOWSWEET LTD ™☺⊘
Men's Range: **Aloe Vera After Shave Skin Gel**, **Pre-Wet Shave Moisturising Cream**

NATURAL BY NATURE OILS ☺⊘ ✂ 1974
Special Oils & Creams: Easy Shave

NATURAL ORGANICS ™
Shaving Soaps: **Argosy**, **Grenada**, **Old Original**, **Patchouli Peculier Shave**, **Tea Tree**

NEAL'S YARD REMEDIES ⊘
After Shave Balm; Lavender & Vitamin E Shaving Soap; Shaving Oil; *Shaving Cream:* Red Clay

NEW SEASONS ☺⊘
Gel Base: After Shave

ORIGINAL SOURCE ™⊘
Shave Gel: Ginger FCL, Lavender, Tea Tree & Mint

QUINESSENCE AROMATHERAPY ☺❶⦸♞👁
Aftershave Balm

REN ⦸
Multi-Vitamin Aftershave Moisturiser; Tamanu High Glide Shaving Oil

SIMPLY SOAPS ™⦸❶♞✂
Shaving Bars: **Eucalyptus & Lavender**

TOM'S OF MAINE ⦸♞✂
Natural Shaving Cream: Gentle Honeysuckle, Refreshing Mint

TREE-HARVEST ⦸♞
Shaving Bowl: Bay, Juniper

WELEDA ⦸♞✂1985
Mens Range: Shaving Lotion

WOODS OF WINDSOR ☺♞
Aftershave: for Men; *Shaving Brush Bristle:* for Men

SKIN CARE - MASKS, WRAPS ETC

ABSOLUTELY PURE ™⦸♞✂
Luscious Skincare: **Floral Water Mask Mix**; *Luscious Skincare - Clay Masks:* **Green Clay & Seaweed**, **Rejuvenating - for Oily Skin**; *Luscious Skincare - Mud Masks:* **Dead Sea Mineral**, **Pink Clay Face & Body**, **White Clay Face & Body**; *Mukti Botanicals:* **Earth Mineral Mask**

ANNEMARIE BÖRLIND ❶⦸♞
Beauty Extras: Anti-Stress Mask, Exfoliating Peel; *LL Regeneration Series:* Moisturising Cream Mask, Vital Cream Mask; *Purifying Care Series:* Cleansing Mask

ARTEL ALLERGY PRODUCTS ♞
Facial Skincare: Anti-Ageing Blue Chamomile Facial Mask, Gentle Herbal Facial Mask, Pure Facial Mask

BEAUTY NATURALS (MARTHA HILL) ❶⦸♞
Facial Care - Treatments: Seaweed Peeling Mask; *Skin Revivals - Refining:* Hydrating Gel Mask

BEAUTY THROUGH HERBS ☺⦸♞👁✂1990
Galeno Gold Face Masque: Anti-Age, Purity

BURT'S BEES ⦸♞
Healthy Treatment: Pore-Refining Mask

CAMILLA HEPPER LTD ⦸♞✂1987
Mask: Herbal Clay

DOLMA ™☺❶⦸♞👁✂
Skin Care: **Rosemary & Seaweed Facial Mask**

DR HADWEN TRUST ☺❶⦸♞
Aloe & Lavender Exfoliating Lotion; *Face Mask:* ComfreyPlus Marshmallow

ESSENTIALLY YOURS LTD ™⦸♞
Natural Elements: **Combination/Oily**

Face Mask, **Dry/Mature Face Mask**, **Normal Face Mask**

GREEN PEOPLE CO. ™⊘✔
Skin Care: Gel Purifying Mask, Revitalising Minute Gel Masque, **Vita Min Mask**

HERBS OF GRACE ™⊘✔
Miscellaneous: **Bentonite Clay**

HONESTY COSMETICS LTD ™☺❶⊘✔👁✂1976
Face Mask w Tea Tree & Lavender

KISS MY FACE ⊘✔👁✂
Obsessively Organic - Preservative Free: Pore Shrink (Deep Pore Mask)

L'OCCITANE EN PROVENCE ✔👁
Lavender Harvest: Face Exfoliating Mask; *Olive Harvest:* Face Scrub Mud; *Shea Butter:* Moisturizing Mask

LUSH ✔
Fresh: Angels on Bareskin, Aqua Marina, Catastrophe, Cupcake, Herbalism

MEADOWSWEET LTD ™☺⊘✔
Cleansers: **Apple Blossom Face Mask**, **Avocado & Cucumber Face Mask**; *Comfrey+ Range:* **Marshmallow Face Mask**

MONTAGNE JEUNESSE ⊘✔
Cellulite Mud; *Chantelle Mask:* Avocado & Walnut Exfoliating, Orange & Vitamin C Peel Off; *Davinci:* Peel Off Masque; *Dead Sea:* Body Mud; *Fab Face:* Kiwi & Vitamin Peel Off Mask, Peach & Elderflower Face Food, Zen Flower Sensitive Masque; *Masque:* Cucumber Peel-Off, Peach Kernel & Walnut Exfoliating, Red Hot Earth Sauna, Strawberry Gel; *Men's Masque:* Dead Sea, Peel Off; *Model Secrets:* Face Lift Mask, Sauna Mud Mask Facial

NEAL'S YARD REMEDIES ⊘✔
Clay Mask

QUINESSENCE AROMATHERAPY ☺❶⊘✔👁
Marine Clay Mask

REN ⊘
F10 Enzymatic Mask; Jioagulan Energising Mask; Multi Mineral Detox Mask

SEVEN WIVES NATURAL BODYCARE ™⊘✔
Masks: Cream, Face & Body Peeling, Gel

TREE-HARVEST ⊘✔
Herbal Face Pack

VIVA! ☺❶⊘✔
Cafe Mask

WELEDA ⊘✔✂1985
Almond Facial Masque; Wild Rose Intensive Facial Masque; *Iris Masque:* Facial, Intensive Treatment

XYNERGY HEALTH PRODUCTS ⊘✔
Trilogy Rosehip Oil Skin Care: Purifying Masque

SKIN CARE - MOISTURISERS & BODY LOTIONS

ABSOLUTE AROMAS ™⊘✓
Ord River: **Hand & Body Lotion 250ml**

ABSOLUTELY PURE ™⊘✓✂
Kettlecare: **Essential Face Cream**, **Essential Facial Serum**, **Meadow Mist Moisturiser**; *Luscious Skincare:* **Exotic Elbow Cream**, **Geranium Barrier Lotion**; *Luscious Skincare - Moisturising Body Mist:* **Aloe Vera & Pink Grapefruit**, **Cucumber & Lime**; *Mukti Botanicals:* **Hydrogel**, **Oil-free Moisturiser**, **Rehydrating Facial Oil**, **Sebogel**

ALOE PURA ⊘✓✂1995
Organic Aloe Vera Gel; Organic Aloe Vera Gel w Tea Tree; Organic Aloe Vera Gel w Vitamins A C & E

AMPHORA AROMATICS LTD ⊘✓ ✂1998
Moisturising Body Oil: for Daily Use, Relaxing, Sensual

ANIMAL AID ☺❶⊘✓✂1976
Apricot & Jojoba Moisturising Cream; Exotic Body Lotion; Natural Source Vitamin E Cream; Vanilla & Macadamia Nourishing Cream; *Moisturising Lotion:* Calendula & Vanilla

ANNEMARIE BÖRLIND ❶⊘✓
Cellulite Gel; *Beauty Extras:* Ceramide Vital Fluid, Facial Firming Gel, Skin Whitening Fluid, Velvet Cream; *Bodyvital:* Body Cream, Caring Body Spray Lotion; *LL Regeneration Series:* Concentrate Ampoules, Decollete Cream, Moisturising Ampoules; *Natural Care - For Men:* Anti-Ageing Revitalizing Cream, Revitalizing Body Lotion; *Purifying Care Series:* Facial Cream; *Young Beauty:* Peach Series Facial Cream

ARKOPHARMA (UK) LTD ☺⊘✓
Mincifit Stretchmarks Cream; Phyto Soya Age Minimising Cream

AROMA CRYSTAL THERAPY ⊘✓✂
Wrinkle Quencher

ARTEL ALLERGY PRODUCTS ✓
Body Moisturisers: Nourishing Body Repair Lotion, Shimmering Body Glow Gel, Shimmering Body Glow Lotion; *Facial Skincare:* Anti-Ageing Blue Chamomile Day Moisturiser, Anti-Ageing Blue Chamomile Eye & Face Elixir, Anti-Ageing Blue Chamomile Night Moisturiser, Anti-Ageing Blue Chamomile Skin Tonic, Gentle Daily Moisturiser, Intensive Skin Care Treatment, Moisturising Facial Gel

BAY HOUSE AROMATICS ⊘✓✂1978
Chamomile Cream; Lavender & Comfrey Healing Cream; Lemon & Rose Revitalising Cream; Marigold & Vitamin E Rich Night Cream; Palmarosa &

Almond Moisturising Cream; *Base Cream:* Calendula, Comfrey, Sweet Almond, Vitamin E; *Face & Body Gel:* Aloe Vera, Lavender, Tea Tree; *Face Cream:* Frankincense & Rosehip; *Hand & Body Lotion:* Lemon & Rose, Tea Tree & Lavender; *Skin Cream:* Avocado & Grapefruit, Carrot & Orange, Tea Tree Antiseptic

BEAUTY NATURALS (MARTHA HILL) ❶⃠

Body Oil: Evening Primrose & Lavender, Orange; *Camomile Skin Care:* Moisture Milk; *David Hill for Men:* Extra Rich Treatment Cream, Skin Soothing Daytime Moisturiser; *Evening Primrose:* Moisturiser; *Herbal Skin Care:* No 3 Day Cream; *Moisturiser:* Enriched Body; *Seaweed:* Body Toning Gel, Enriched Body Treatment Cream; *Skin Revivals - Moisturising:* Pure Skin Treatment, Revitalising Cream

BEAUTY THROUGH HERBS ☺⃠ ✂1990

Out Of Africa Body Lotion; *Galeno Gold:* Anti-Cellulite Body Cream, Cell Renewal Serum, Firming Body Cream, Firming Gel, Hydrating Body Cream, Intensive Hydrating Cream, Intensive Hydrating Lotion, Ultimate Body Contour, Vitalising Day Cream; *Phyto Care:* Calmskin Herbal Gel, Coolskin Herbal Gel; *Phyto Marine:* Intensive Nourishing Cream, Nourishing Cream, Vitalising Lotion

CAMILLA HEPPER LTD ⃠ ✂1987

Anti-Wrinkle Oil; Azufre Lotion; *Body Lotion:* Jojoba Oil, Orange Blossom & Cocoa Butter, Rose; *Cream:* Azufre, Facial Wash, Regenerative, Rich Skin Food, Wheatgerm & Marigold Moisture

CAPITELLI OILS ™☺⃠

Body Lotion: **Luxury**, **Patchouli**; *Facial Moisturisers/Cleansers:* **Extra Rich Moisturiser**

CELESTIAL DESIGNS AROMATHERAPY ™⃠

Exfoliating Lotion; **Moisturising Cream**; **Seaweed Gel w Aloe Vera**; **Vitamin E Cream**; **White Lotion**

DOLMA ™☺❶⃠ ✂

Miscellaneous Body Preparations: **Aloe Vera Hand & Body Lotion**, **Ho-Leaf & Orange Moisturising Body Wash**, **Niamh De-luxe Body Lotion**; *Skin Care:* **Avocado & Ylang Ylang Moisture Cream**, **Carotene Enriched Fragrance Free Moisture Cream**, **Carotene Ho-Leaf & Orange Moisture Cream**, **Chamomile Moisture Lotion**, **De-luxe Facial Oil**, **Facial Oil for Dehydrated Skin**, **Facial Oil for Dry Skin**, **Facial Oil for Mature Skin**, **Facial Oil for Sensitive Skin**, **Facial Oil for Thread Veins**, **Fragrance Free Moisture Lotion**, **Geranium & Evening Primrose Night Cream**, Ho-Leaf Geranium & Lavender Body Cream, **Wheatgerm & Lavender Moisture Cream**

DR HADWEN TRUST ☺❶⊘✓
Avocado & Cucumber Lotion; Body Firming Gel; Olive Oil & Green Tea Skin Softening Body Cream; Watercress Daytime Moisturiser; *Body Lotion:* Lavender Geranium & Ylang Ylang, Luxury; *Cream:* ComfreyPlus Jojoba Complex, ComfreyPlus Vitamin E Moisturising, Extra Enriched Vitamin E, Melon & Jojoba Night, Vitamin-Enriched Melon & Carrot; *Olive Oil & Green Tea Moisturiser:* Hydrating, Intensive; *Serum:* Active Gel, Day, Face Contouring, Night

ESSENCE SERENE ™☺⊘✓✂
Exfoliating Lotion; **Face Wash**; Rejuvanate Exfoliating Cream; Rejuvanate Moisturising Cream; *Aromatherapy:* **Aloe Vera Skin Cleanser**, **Jasmine Skin Tonic**, **Moisturising Skin Cream**; *Serum:* **Contouring Face**, **Eye firming**, **Hydrating Night**, **Rejuvenating Day**; *Suitable for Use by Persons Prone to Eczema & Psoriasis:* Extra Rich Moisturiser

ESSENTIALLY YOURS LTD ™⊘✓
Natural Elements: **Body Lotion**, **Combination/Oily Moisturiser**, **Combination/Oily Night Gel**, **Combination/Oily Serum Gel**, **Day Serum**, **Dry/Mature Cleanser**, **Dry/Mature Moisturiser**, **Dry/Mature Night Cream**, **Eye/Neck Gel**, **Face Contouring Serum**, **Firming Gel**, **Night Serum**, **Normal Moisturiser**, **Normal Night Cream**; *Therapeutics Range:* **E Extra Rich Barrier Cream**, **E Hand & Body Lotion**, **E Moisturising Oil**

ETHICAL WARES ☺❶✓
Sea Breeze: Moisturiser

FAITH PRODUCTS LTD ❶⊘✓ ✂◉1978
Skin Care: Aloe Vera Moisturising Cream, Jojoba Moisturising Lotion, Rose & Wheatgerm Moisturising Cream

FINEMOOD LTD ⊘✓
Hair & Body Care: After Bath Lotion, Avocado Moisture Cream, Facial Treat Rejuvenator, Peppermint Balm, Scar Care Moisture Cream, Sinus Care Moisture Cream, Visible Veins Moisture Cream; *Skin Care:* Clear Skin Moisture Cream, Hand & Body Lotion, Moisture Cream, Moisturising Lotion, Rejuvenating Night Cream, Special E Moisture Cream

FREERANGERS ™☺✓
Pamper Products: **Hand & Foot Balm**

FUNK BUBBLE ™
Body Cream: Aloe Vera/Lemon, Chocolate/Orange, Jojoba/Ylang Ylang

GREEN PEOPLE CO. ™⊘✓
Men's Range: **Cool Down Moisturiser**; *Organic Base:* **Hand/Body Lotion**; *Skin Care:* **Body Comfort (Body Lotion)**, **Body Comfort "No Scent" (Body Lotion)**, **Day Solution (Day Cream)**, **Femme Body Oil**, **Femme Face Oil**, **Fruitful**

Nights (Night Cream), **Vita Min Fix (Day & Night Cream)**, **Vita Min Fix "No Scent" (Day & Night Cream)**

HIGHER NATURE PLC ™⊘
Energys Energy Gel; **Energys Youthful Skin Elixir**; **MSM Lotion**; **The Ultimate Aloe Vera Skin Gel**

HONESTY COSMETICS LTD ™☺❶⊘ 1976
Geranium & Ylang Ylang Moisturising Lotion; **Lavender & Geranium Moisturising Cream**; **Peach & Vanilla Moisturising Lotion**; *Unscented Moisturiser:* **Cream w Vitamin E**, **Lotion w Cocoa Butter**, **Rich Cream w Carrot & Jojoba**

JOPHIEL® ☺❶⊘
Aromatherapy Creams: Frankincense & Rosehip Moisturiser, Lavender & Geranium Face & Body Cream, Sandalwood & Vitamin E Moisturising Cream, Ti-Tree & Litsea Cubeba Cream; *Rejuvanating™ Skincare:* Moisturiser, Rejuvanating™ Body Oil; *Rejuvanating™ Skincare Complexion Boost™:* Day, Night

KENT COSMETICS ☺⊘
Australian Organics Body Lotion

KISS MY FACE ⊘
Cheap Kisses: Lavender & Shea Butter; *Moisturisers:* Alpha & Aloe Fragrance Free, Alpha & Aloe Vanilla, Chinese Botanical, Everyday SPF15, Fragrance Free, Lavender & Shea Butter, Oil Free, Olive & Aloe, Peaceful Patchouli, Peaches & Creme, Vitamin A & E; *Obsessively Organic - Preservative Free:* C the Change (Ester C Serum), Cell Mate 15 Facial Moisturiser SPF15, So Refined (Jojoba & Mint), Under Age (C & A Ultra Rich); *Organic Moisturisers:* C's the Day, Filthy Rich, Tighten Up

KOBASHI ™☺⊘
Aloe Vera: **Gel**, **Liquid**; *Luxury Lotions:* **Fragrance Free Moisturiser**, **Rose Facial**

L'OCCITANE EN PROVENCE
Body Lotion: Eau d'Azur, Eau des 4 Reines, Eau des Vanilliers, Eau du Val, Lavender Harvest, Olive Harvest, Shea Butter, Verbena Harvest; *Body Treatment:* Almond - Milk Concentrate, Eau des Vanilliers, Immortelle - Vitality Serum, Shea Butter - Ultra Moisturizing Body Cream; *for Men:* Energy Face Gel; *Immortelle:* Essential Lotion, Precious Cream, Protective Lotion SPF15; *Lavender Harvest:* Face Cream Gel Moisturiser; *Olive Harvest:* Face Cream, Face Cream SPF 15; *Shea Butter:* Gentle Face Buff, Ultra Moisturizing Day Care SPF 15, Ultra Moisturizing Night Care, Ultra Rich Face Cream

LAVERA ™
basis sensitiv: **Moisturizing Body Lotion**; *Neutral:* **Body Lotion**, **Facial Fluid**

LUSH
Body Butters: Aqua Mirablis 2004,

Buffy the Backside Slayer, King of Skin 2004, Running to the Embassy, You Snap the Whip; *Skincare, Haircare, etc:* Celestial, Dream Cream, Enzymion, Imperialis, Skin Drink, Sympathy for the Skin, Ultra light

MEADOWSWEET LTD ™☺⊘✓
Aloe Vera Range: **Day Cream**, **Moisturising Lotion**, **Night Cream**, **Skin Repair Gel**; *Comfrey+ Range:* **Cocoa Butter Lotion**, **Jojoba Complex Repair Cream**, **Vitamin E Moisturising Cream**; *Creams:* **Carrot Oil**, **Comfrey & Vitamin E Ointment**, **Evening Primrose**, **Melon & Carrot Day**, **Melon & Jojoba Night**, **Vitamin E**; *Fragrance Free Range:* **Day Cream**, **Moisturising Lotion**, **Night Cream**; *Herbal Aromatic Range:* **Problem Skin Lotion**, **Soothing Body Lotion**; *Hydrolats:* Orange, Rose, Witch Hazel; *Lotions & Toners:* **Avocado & Cucumber Moisturising Lotion**, **Evening Primrose Body Lotion**

MORNY ⊘✓
Face & Body Cream: Nature's Vitamin E; *Moisturising Cream:* Nature's Aloe Vera; *Revitalising Cream:* Nature's Oil of Evening Primrose

NAPIERS HERBAL HEALTH CENTRE ✓
Cream: Arnica, Bilberry, Chamomile, Chamomile & Peppermint, Comfrey, Eyebright, Frankincense Night, Neroli Day, Pilewort, Seven Herb, Starflower, Vegan Base, Venatone, Wild Yam; *Lotion:* Base, Neroli, Starflower; *Moisturisers:* Rose

NATURA ORGANICS ⊘✓☼
Body Lotion: Lavender/Orange, Lavender/Rosemary, w Grapefruit & Aloe Vera

NATURAL BY NATURE OILS ☺⊘✓👁✂1974
Natural, Gentle & Kind Range: Luxury Body Lotion, Luxury Cream

NATUREWATCH ☺⊘✓👁✂1976
Clearly Compassionate: Sandalwood & Vitamin E Facial Replenishing Cream; *Clearly Compassionate Body Lotion:* Lavender & Geranium, Mandarin & Lemongrass; *Clearly Compassionate Camomile & Lavender:* Facial Moisturising Fluid

NEAL'S YARD REMEDIES ⊘✓
Chamomile & Aloe Vera Lotion; Cocoa Butter; Frankincense Nourishing Cream; Jasmine Enriching Cream; *Body Lotion:* Frankincense; *Facial Oil:* Rose; *Night Cream:* Vitamin E & Avocado; *Skin Oil:* Exotic, Jasmine Nourishing, Soothing

NEW SEASONS ☺⊘✓
Gel Base: Moisturising Face & Body (w Aloe Vera & Alantoin); *Neutral Base:* Moisturising Cream, Moisturising Lotion

OPTIMA HEALTH & NUTRITION ⊘✓✂1995
Raw Aloe: Advanced Gel w Tea Tree Vitamin E & Shea Butter, Cellulite Massage Gel, Hand Wash; *Thursday Plantation:* Macadamia Face & Body Oil; *Thursday Plantation Tea Tree:* Hand & Body Lotion

ORGANIC BLUE ™⃠
Body Care: **Body Lotion**

PHYTO PRODUCTS LTD ☺
Pure Skin Creams: Arnica, Chamomile German, Chickweed, Comfrey, Echinacea, Garlic, Marigold, Tea Tree, Witch Hazel

QUINESSENCE AROMATHERAPY ☺❶⃠
Aloe Vera & Lavender Gel; *Cream:* Age Defying, Hydrating Day, Hydrating Night, Vitamin E Cream; *Lotion:* After Sun, Base Carrier, Hand & Body, Insect Repellent, Moisture

REALLY WORKS ™☺⃠
Anti-Bacterial Hand Spary

REN ⃠
Cucumber Hydrating Facial Mist; Frankincense Repair Cream; Monoi Nourishing Body Oil; Omega 3 Facial Serum; Wild Yam Omega 7 Body Repair Cream; *Body Balm:* Guerande Salt Exfoliating, Monoi & Shea Butter; *Moisturiser:* Calendula Omega 3/7, Mayblossom & Konjac, Phytostimulene, Rose Complex

RHEMA UK LTD ❶⃠
Cento Per Cento: Hand & Body Lotio, Moisturisers (1/2/4)

SERF TO SURF UK ⃠
Unrefined Shea Butter & Organic Hempseed Oil

SEVEN WIVES NATURAL BODYCARE ™⃠
Body Lotion; Tonic Lotion; *Intensive:* Light, Lotion, Medium, Rich, Tea Tree; *Liposome:* Light, Medium, Super, Tea Tree; *Super Sensitive:* Light, Medium, Rich

SKIN CARE CAFE LTD ™
Dry/Mature Moisturiser - Lavender & Geranium; **Organic Almond & Patchouli Anti-ageing Night Oil**; **Organic Chinese Geranium Anti-Ageing Night Oil**; **Organic Grapeseed & Aloe Vera Cleanser**; **Organic Lavender & Rose Geranium Moisturiser**; **Organic Lemongrass Face Mask**; **Organic Lemongrass & Rosemary Face Mask**; **Organic Orange & Chamomile Body Wash**; **Organic Orange & Vanilla Body Conditioning Lotion**; **Organic Orange & Vanilla Body Lotion**; **Organic Rose Geranium Moisturiser w 5 vitamins**

TISSERAND AROMATHERAPY PRODUCTS ™
Tea Tree Products: **Tea-Tree & Grapefruit Skinwash**

TREE-HARVEST ⃠
Basil; Coconut Butter; Frankincense & Geranium Body Lotion; Henna; Holy Thorn Healing Cream; Horsechestnut & Rowan Gel; Pau d'Arco; Shea Butter

URTEKRAM ⃠
Body Lotion: Aloe Vera, Camomile, Lavender, Rose, Tea Tree

VIVA! ☺❶⊘🐇
Cafe Facial Oil; Cafe Moisturiser

WELEDA ⊘🐇 ✂1985
Almond Facial Oil; *Body Lotion:* Mallow; *Specialist Skin Care:* Aknedoron Lotion

WOODS OF WINDSOR ☺🐇
Body Moisturiser: Forget Me Not, Lavender, Lily of the Valley, Mimosa, True Rose; *Cooling Body Moisturiser:* Aromatherapy Lavender; *Cooling Gel Skin Soother:* Aromatherapy Lavender; *Facial Spritz:* Aromatherapy Lavender; *Fruity Body Moisturiser:* Orange Spice

XYNERGY HEALTH PRODUCTS ⊘🐇
Aloe 99: Vitamin E Cream, Vitamin E Lotion; *Trilogy Rosehip Oil Skin Care:* 100% Pure Rosehip Oil, Nourishing Body Lotion, Vital Moisturising Cream

YAOH ™☺❶🐇⊘
Body Lotion; **Coco Bean Moisturiser**; **Moisturiser**; **Papaya Moisturiser**

SKIN MAKE UP

ABSOLUTELY PURE ™⊘🐇✂
Earth's Beauty: Loose Mineral Blush, Mineral Colours Original Foundation, Mineral Colours Plus SPF15 Foundation; *Monave:* Caramel Bronzer, Face & Body Shimmer, Fudge Bronzer, Loose Mineral Foundation, Loose Powder, Toffee Bronzer; *Real Purity:* Health Glo Foundation

ANNEMARIE BÖRLIND ❶⊘🐇
Compact Powder; Fluid Make-Up; Powder Make-Up; Powder Rouge; *Beauty Extras:* Cosmetic Sponges

BARRY M COSMETICS 🐇 ✂1985
Body Glitter Shaker Pots; Fine Glitter Dust; Natural Dazzle Powder Loose (Not Compact); Translucent Powder Loose (Not Compact)

BEAUTY NATURALS (MARTHA HILL) ❶⊘🐇
Dual Concealer & Eye Stick; Dual Wet & Dry Foundation; Ultra Sheer Liquid Foundation

BEAUTY WITHOUT CRUELTY ™☺
Cream Concealer; **Natural Look Tinted Moisturiser**; **Satin Finish Blusher**; **Superfine Pressed Powder**; **Ultrafine Loose Powder**; *Moisturising Makeup:* **Matte**, **Satin**

BURT'S BEES ⊘🐇
Healthy Treatment: Parsley Blemish Stick; *Natural Remedies:* Doctor Burt's Herbal Blemish Stick

DR HADWEN TRUST ☺❶⊘🐇
Animal-free Cosmetics Set; Blusher Quartet; Cream Concealer; Moisturising Matte; Moisturising Satin; Natural-Look Tinted Moisturiser; Satin Finish Blushers; *Ultra-Fine Powders:* Loose, Pressed

L'OCCITANE EN PROVENCE 🐇👁
Color Cream for Lips & Cheeks; Tinted Day Care SPF15; *Lavender Harvest:* Lavender Vinegar

SEVEN WIVES NATURAL BODYCARE ™⃠
Make up: Beige, Bronze, Dark, Light

VEGANSTORE.CO.UK ™☺⃠❶
Ecco Bella: Lipstick, Mascara skincare - cleansers & toners

ABSOLUTELY PURE ™⃠ ✂
Cheri's Country Cottage: Face Cleansing Gel, Fresh & Fruity Skin Chiffon, Shea Butter Facial Cleanser, Whipped Cream Body Souffle; *Earthbound Organics:* **Cream Cleanser**, **Facial Scrub**, **Orange Blossom Water**, **Rose Tonic Water**; *Kettlecare:* Earth & Sea Mineral Polish, **Scrubs - Dry Normal & Oily Skin**; *Luscious Skincare:* **Moisturising Aloe Vera Makeup Remover**; *Luscious Skincare - Floral Water Spray:* **Chamomile**, **Cucumber Toner**, **Grapefruit**, **Jasmine**, **Lavender**, **Orange Flower**, **Rose**, **Witch Hazel**, **Ylang Ylang**; *Luscious Skincare - Floral Waters:* **Chamomile**, **Cucumber Toner**, **Grapefruit**, **Jasmine**, **Lavender**, **Luscious**, **Orange Flower**, **Witch Hazel**, **Ylang Ylang**; *Mukti Botanicals:* **Floral Hydrating Mist**, **Organic Herbal Toner**, **Refreshing Mist**

ANIMAL AID ☺❶⃠ ✂1976
Fruit & Nut Face & Body Scrub; *Cleansing Lotion:* Aloe & Papaya; *Facial Wash:* Kiwi & Grapefruit; *Toner:* Aloe & Papaya

ANNEMARIE BÖRLIND ❶⃠
Young Beauty - Peach Series Cleanser; *Combination Series:* Cleansing Gel, Day Essence, Facial Toner; *LL Regeneration Series:* Blossom Dew Gel, Cleansing Milk; *Purifying Care Series:* Facial Cleanser, Facial Toner; *Rosedew Series:* Cleansing Milk, Facial Toner; *System Absolute Series:* Beauty Fluid, Cleanser; *Young Beauty - U-Series:* Ultra Stick; *ZZ Sensitive Series:* Cleansing, Facial Toner

ARTEL ALLERGY PRODUCTS
Body Cleansers: Cleansing Bar; *Facial Skincare:* Anti-Ageing Blue Chamomile Facial Cleanser, Anti-Ageing Blue Chamomile Facial Scrub, Foaming Facial Cleanser, Gentle Herbal Facial Cleanser, Gentle Herbal Facial Toner, Gentle Pure Grains Facial Scrub, Purifying Strawberry Leaf Toner, Smooth & Polish Sugar Scrub

BAY HOUSE AROMATICS ⃠ ✂1978
Floral Waters: All; *Unfragranced Lotions & Cleansers:* Chamomile Cleanser, Cocoa Butter Lotion, Exfoliating Face & Body Scrub, White Base Lotion

BEAUTY NATURALS (MARTHA HILL) ❶⃠
Camomile Skin Care: Cleansing Gel; *David Hill for Men:* Deep Cleansing Lotion; *Evening Primrose:* Cleansing Lotion, Toning Gel; *Herbal Skin Care:* No 1 Cleansing & Conditioning Milk, No 2 Toning Gel; *Herbal Skin Tonic:* Cucumber, Rosewater; *Skin Revivals - Reviving:* Harmonising Tonic

BEAUTY THROUGH HERBS ☺⊘♥ 👁✂1990
Galeno Gold Face Scrub; *Phyto Care:* Clearskin Herbal Gel, Coolskin Herbal Gel, Facial Wash; *Phyto Marine:* Facial Cleansing Cream, Mild Exfoliant Wash, Sun & Sea Gel Wash

BURT'S BEES ⊘♥
Healthy Skin: Citrus Facial Scrub, Garden Tomato Toner; *Healthy Treatment:* Rosewater & Glycerin Toner

CAMILLA HEPPER LTD ⊘♥ ✂1987
Elderflower Skin Toner; Mint & Olive Stone Scrub; *Cleanser:* Azufre, T-Zone Foaming; *Cleansing Milk:* Meadowsweet; *Flower Water:* Rose

CAPITELLI OILS ™☺♥ ⊘
Facial Moisturisers/Cleansers: **Anti-Spot Serum Gel**, **Cleansing Lotion & Make-Up Remover**, **Pelle Grassa**, **Pelle Secca**; *Toners:* **Combination/Oily Skin**, **Dry/Mature Skin**

CELESTIAL DESIGNS AROMATHERAPY ™⊘♥
Cleansing Lotion: **Chamomile**, **Cucumber**

DOLMA ™☺❶⊘♥ 👁✂
Skin Care: **Almond & Orange Facial Scrub**, **Aromatic Face Shampoo**, **Astringent Toner**, **Chamomile & Mint Facial Wash**, **Evening Primrose & Marigold Moisture Cream**, **Fragrance Free Cleansing Lotion**, **Freshening Toner**, **Gentle Toner**, **Lavender & Chamomile Cleansing Lotion**, **Oil Free Cleanser**, **Purifying Toner**

DR HADWEN TRUST ☺❶⊘♥
Cleanser: Lavender & Aloe; *Cleansing Milk:* Apricot Smooth, Orchid & Chamimile; *Face Wash:* Active, Lavender & Aloe; *Facial Scrubs:* Passion Fruit; *Hydrolat/Toner:* Orange, Rose; *Toner:* Witch Hazel

ESSENTIALLY YOURS LTD ™⊘♥
Natural Elements: **Combination/Oily Antimicrobial Face Wash**, **Combination/Oily Cleanser**, **Combination/Oily Exfoliating Lotion**, **Combination/Oily Toner**, **Dry/Mature Face Wash**, **Dry/Mature Toner**, **Normal Cleanser**, **Normal Face Wash**, **Normal Toner**

FINEMOOD LTD ⊘♥
Skin Care: Almond Scrub, Essential Facial Wash, Rosewater Toning Lotion, Seaweed Cleansing Lotion, Skin Care Travel Pack, Cleansing Cream, Cleansing Cream, Cleansing Milk, Toning Lotion

GREEN DOT GUIDES ⊘♥
Washable Cleansing Pads

GREEN PEOPLE CO. ™⊘♥
Organic Base: **24-Hour Cream**, **Cleanser**; *Skin Care:* **Body Tuning (Cellulite Lotion)**, **Fruit Scrub**, **Gentle Cleanse**, **Gentle Tone**

HERBS HANDS HEALING LTD ™⃠
Herbs & Flowers Skin Toner; Lavender Water; Rose Water Facial Tonic; Skin Guard Water

HERBS OF GRACE ™⃠
Organic Flower Waters: **All**

HONESTY COSMETICS LTD ™☺❶⃠ 1976
Papaya Facial Wash; Spicy Orange Scrub; *Cleansers:* **Lavender & Geranium**, **Unscented w Chamomile**; *Facial Toners:* **Lavender & Geranium**, **Unscented w Chamomile**

JOPHIEL® ☺❶⃠
Hydrolats & Flower Waters: Cucumber & Aloe Vera Toner, Orange Flower Water, Rosewater; *Rejuvanating™ Skincare:* Cleanser, Toner

KISS MY FACE ⃠
Cheap Kisses: Miniature Pack; *Facial Care:* All Day Creme, Citrus Cleanser, Citrus Essence Astringent, Flower Essence Toner, Lemongrass Souffle Masque, Shea Butter Eyemake-up Remover, Ultra Light Facial Creme; *Obsessively Organic - Preservative Free:* Balancing Act Facial Toner, Break Out (Botanical Acne Gel), Clean for a Day Facial Cleanser, Facial Treats (8 Piece Sample Pack), Startup Exfoliant Facewash - Jumpstart

KOBASHI ™☺⃠
Misc: **Chamomile Water**, **Dill Water**, **Lavender Water**, **Neroli Water**, **Peppermint Water**, **Rose Water**

L'OCCITANE EN PROVENCE
Body Splash: Immortelle - Essential Water Body; *Body Treatment:* Immortelle - Elixir for the Body; *Immortelle:* Brightening Serum, Dermatological Soap, Elixir, Essential Water Face, Foaming Milk; *Lavender Harvest:* Cleansing Face Gel, Face Lotion; *Olive Harvest:* Cleansing Face Oil; *Shea Butter:* Extra Moisturizing Cold Cream Soap, Extra-Gentle Cleansing Milk, Extra-Gentle Cleansing Water

LAVERA ™
basis sensitiv: **Cleansing Gel**, **Cleansing Milk 2 in 1**

LUCIA GOLDSTEIN ™⃠
Cleanser; **Face Cream**; **Toner**

LUSH
Skincare, Haircare, etc: Breeze on a Sea Air, Dream Wash, Eau-Roma Water, Tea Tree Water

MEADOWSWEET LTD ™☺⃠
Cleansers: **Apricot Cleansing Milk**, **Cucumber & Fennel Cleansing Gel**, **Elderflower Wash Cream**, **Lime Blossom & Orange Flower Cleansing Gel**, **Oatmeal Scrub**, **Orchid Cleansing Milk**, **Passion Fruit Facial Scrub**, **Pineapple & Peach Wash Cream**; *Comfrey+ Range:* **Clivers Facial Wash**, **Oatmeal Facial Scrub**; *Creams:* **Cucumber Astringent**, **Facial Blemish**, **Herbal Skin Soothing**; *Fragrance Free Range:* **Cleansing Lotion**; *Lotions & Toners:* **Avocado &**

Cucumber Toner, **Elderflower Toner**, **Lavender/Geranium/Ylang-Ylang**, **Orange Flower Toner**, **Rosemary Herbal Face Lotion**

MONTAGNE JEUNESSE ⦸ ✓
Dead Sea: Anti-Stress Face Tonic

MORNY ⦸ ✓
Face & Body Scrub: Nature's Apricot

NAPIERS HERBAL HEALTH CENTRE ✓
Cleanser: Rose; *Freshener:* Rose

NATURAL BY NATURE OILS ☺⦸ ✓ 👁 ✂ 1974
Natural, Gentle & Kind Range: Cleansing Lotion, Facial Toner, Rose Water, Witch Hazel; *Special Oils & Creams:* Face Treatment

NATUREWATCH ☺⦸ ✓ 👁 ✂ 1976
Clearly Compassionate Camomile & Lavender: Facial Cleanser, Facial Toner, Foaming Facial Wash

NEW SEASONS ☺⦸ ✓
Calendula Cleanser; *Floral Water:* Lavender, Rose; *Flower Water:* Lavender, Orange, Chamomile, Lavender, Orange Flower, Rosewater; *Neutral Base:* Cleanser, Facial & Body Scrub, Solubiliser, Vegetable Glycerine, Witchazel

OPTIMA HEALTH & NUTRITION ⦸ ✓ ✂ 1995
Thursday Plantation Tea Tree: Blemish Gel, Blemish Stick, Cleansing Face Wash

PHYTO PRODUCTS LTD ☺
Floral Waters: Hamamelis, Triple Elderflower, Triple Orange Flower, Triple Rose

PURPLE FLAME AROMATHERAPY ⦸ ✓
Tea Tree Moist Wipes; *Flower Waters/Hydrosols:* Chamomile, Lavender, Orange Flower/Neroli, Peppermint, Rose, Rosemary, Sandalwood, Tea Tree; *Flower/Hydrosols:* Frankincense

QUINESSENCE AROMATHERAPY ☺❶⦸ ✓ 👁
Facial Exfoliator; Problem Skin; Rose Facial; Rose Toner; *Lotion:* Antiseptic, Cleansing

REN ⦸
Damask Rosewater Toning Facial Mist; *Cleanser:* Calendula & Arctic Blackcurrant; *Cleansing Milk:* Zostera Marina; *Facial Scrub:* Jojoba Microbead; *Facial Wash:* Mayblossom & Blue Cypress, Rosa Centifolia

RHEMA UK LTD ❶⦸ ✓ ✂
Cento Per Cento: Skin Tonic, Tone

SEVEN WIVES NATURAL BODYCARE ™⦸ ✓
Cleansing Milk; Face Cleanser

SIMPLY SOAPS ™⦸❶ ✓ ✂
Exfoliating Facial Scrub

TISSERAND AROMATHERAPY PRODUCTS ™
Lavender Products: **Lavender Cream Body Wash**, **Lavender Foaming Face Wash**, **Lavender Hand Cream**

TREE-HARVEST ⊘✓
Floral Waters

URTEKRAM ⊘✓✂
Facial Creme: Cleansing Creme, Day Creme, Night Creme; *Pure Balance Lotion:* Wild Rose; *Skincare:* Brown Sugar Body Scrub

VIVA! ☺❶⊘✓
Cafe Cleanser

WELEDA ⊘✓✂1985
Almond Cleansing Lotion; Iris Facial Toner; *Facial Toner:* Wild Rose

XYNERGY HEALTH PRODUCTS ⊘✓
Aloe 99: Facial Cleanser; *Trilogy Rosehip Oil Skin Care:* Body Cleansing Bar, Cleansing Cream, Hydrating Toner

SOAPS

ABSOLUTE AROMAS ™⊘✓
Ord River: **Ord River Handwash 250ml**, **Tea Tree & Lavender 125g**

ABSOLUTELY PURE ™⊘✓✂
Cheri's Country Cottage: Whipped Mousse Body Wash

AMBER ™
Sandalwood Beauty

AMPHORA AROMATICS LTD ⊘✓ ✂1998
Clear Melt & Pour; Tea Tree Liquid Soap; *Aromatherapy Soap:* Bergamot, Chamomile, Lavender, Neroli, Sandalwood, Tea Tree; *Clear Glycerine Soap:* Citrus Woods, Lavender, Lemon, Red Rose, Tea Tree, Vit E

ANIMAL AID ☺❶⊘✓✂1976
Calder Valley; Glycerine

BAY HOUSE AROMATICS ⊘✓✂1978
Almond Oil; Aloe Vera & Ylang Ylang; Chocolate; Geranium & Rosewood; Hemp w Green Tea & Lemongrass; Lavender; Lavender Olive Oil; Liquid; Rose; Tea Tree & Lavender; Ylang Ylang & Lemongrass; *Liquid Soap:* Tea Tree

BIO-D CO. LTD. ™☺⊘✓✂1983
Aromatherapy; **Aromatic Hemp Oil**; **Hemp Bran**; **Hemp Oil**

BURT'S BEES ⊘✓
Healthy Skin: Wild Lettuce Complexion; *Natural Remedies:* Poison Ivy

CALDER VALLEY SOAP ™☺⊘✓👁
Almond Blossom; **Aloe Vera**; **Anise**; **Avocado & Cucumber**; **Coconut Palm**; **Grapefruit**; **Lavender**; **Lemongrass**; **Minted Lime**; **Oatmeal Scrub**; **Orchard Apple**; **Peppermint & Poppyseed**; **Rose**; **Sandalwood**; **Sea Kelp**; **Tea Tree**; **Vanilla**; **Violet**; **Wild Raspberry**

CAMILLA HEPPER LTD ⃠ ✂1987
Pure Vegetable Oil Soap: Avocado, Grapefruit, Orange Blossom

CAPITELLI OILS ™☺ ⃠
Invigorante; **Sapone Lussuoso**

CAURNIE SOAPERIE ☺⃠ ✂
Whole Soap: Heather Lavender, Lavender, Lemongrass, Nettle, Rose

CELLANDE MIDLANDS ☺⃠
Liquid Soap: Almond, Mint Bactericidal

DOLMA ™☺❶⃠ ✂
Glycerine Soap: **Carrot Ho-Leaf & Orange**, **Hemp Seed Fragrance Free**, **Lavender & Jojoba**, **'Niamh' De-luxe**, **Tea-Tree & Calendula**

DR HADWEN TRUST ☺❶⃠
Aromatherapy Soap: Bergamot & Orange, English Lavender, Grapefruit & Juniper, Lemon & Mint, Neroli & Lemongrass, 'Orange Blossom', Tea Tree w Eucalyptus, Ylang Ylang; *Conditioning Soap:* Olive Oil & Green Tea

ECOLINO ™⃠
Handsoap

ECOVER ™⃠
Hand Soap

ETHICAL WARES ☺❶
Sea Breeze

FAITH PRODUCTS LTD ❶⃠ ✂1978
Pine; *Bulk Soap:* Ginkgo Biloba, Orange, Organic Aloe Vera & Ylang Ylang, Organic Chocolate, Organic Hemp w Lemongrass & Green Tea, Organic Lavender, Organic Tea Tree, Pine, Rosemary, Seaweed; *Pure Vegetable Soap:* Essential Gift, Gingko Biloba, Orange, Organic Aloe Vera & Ylang Ylang, Organic Chocolate, Organic Hemp w Lemongrass & Green Tea, Organic Lavender, Organic Tea Tree, Rosemary, Seaweed

FINEMOOD LTD ⃠
Rosemary; Tea Tree; *Skin Care:* Tea Tree

FREERANGERS ™☺
Pamper Products: **Pack 3 Soaps**, **Single Soap**

FUNK BUBBLE ™
Chocolate/Orange; Cinnamon/Oatmeal; Orange/Lemon; Rose; Tea Tree; Ylang Ylang/Neroli

GREEN DOT GUIDES ⃠
Pack of 6 Egg-Shaped; Wild Collection Set of 6; *Golden Lotus:* May Chang, Tantra

GREEN PEOPLE CO. ™⃠
Hair & Body Care: **Aloe Vera Liquid Soap**, **Hair & Body Shampoo Bar**, **No Scent Liquid Soap**, **Rosemary Liquid Soap**; *Organic Base:* **Liquid Soap**

HIGHER NATURE PLC ™⃠
Omega Nutrition Handmade Soaps: **Flax Orange**, **Rainforest**

HONESTY COSMETICS LTD ™☺❶⊘ 🐇 👁✂ 1976
Apple & Sandalwood; Carrot & Jojoba; Geranium & Lavender; Orange; Strawberry & Papaya

JARROW FORMULAS INC.
Face & Body: Orange, Unscented

KENT COSMETICS ☺⊘ 🐇
Australian Organics Pure Plant

KISS MY FACE ⊘ 🐇 👁✂
Olive & Aloe; Olive & Chamomile; Olive & Green Tea; Olive & Herbal; Olive & Lavender; Olive & Verbena; Pure Olive Oil; *Liquid Moisture:* Almond, Fragrance Free, Melon, Olive & Aloe, Orangeblossom, Patchouli, Peach, Pear, Tea Tree Germaside; *Self Foaming:* Grapefruit & Bergamot, Lavender & Chamomile; *Sudz Bar Soap:* Bare Naked, C-Weed, Close Encounter, In the Pink, Rough Seas, Salad Bar, Sports Bar; *Sudz Self-Forming Liquid Soap:* Salad Bar

KOBASHI ™☺⊘ 🐇 👁✂
Liquid Soap: **Fragrance Free Soap Base**, **Tea Tree & Lemon**

L'OCCITANE EN PROVENCE 🐇 👁
Amande; Eau des 4 Reines; Eau des Vanilliers; Eau du Val; L'Oranger; Lavender Harvest; Lavender Harvest w Lavender Grains; Olive Harvest; Olive Harvest w Olive Leaves; Shea Butter Extra Gentle; Verbena Harvest; Wood for Men; *Liquid Soap:* Shea Butter, Verbena Harvest

LUSH 🐇
Alkmaar; Bohemian; Carmen Miranda; Coalface; Demon in the Dark; Extra Virgin Olive Oil; Figs & Leaves; Fresh Farmacy; I Should Coco; Karma; Middle Earth Turns to Rock; Milky Bar; Ooh La La; Red Rooster; Sandstone; Sea Vegetable; *Christmas Soap:* Angel's Delight, Noriko, Snowcake, Spice Mountain

MEADOWSWEET LTD ™☺⊘ 🐇
Aromatherapy Soaps: **Bergamot & Orange**, **Grapefruit & Juniper**, **Lavender**, **Lemon w Peppermint Leaves**, **Neroli & Lemon Grass**, **Orange & Poppy Seed**, **Tea Tree & Eucalyptus**, **Ylang Ylang**; *Complexion Soaps:* **Dry Skin - Jojoba & Unrefined Avocado**, **Mature Skin - Carrot w Vitamin E Enriched Wheatgerm**, **Normal Skin - Orchid Oil & Cocoa Butter**, **Oily Skin - Fullers Earth & Lemon Juice**, **Olive Oil**, **Rejuvenaid Scrub Bar - Oatmeal & Evening Primrose**; *Fragrance Free Range:* **Liquid Soap**; *Fragrance Soaps:* **Banana & Vanilla**, **Coconut Ice**, **Mango & Apricot**, **Rose & Cinnamon**; *Nature Power Range:* **Antiseptic Hand Wash Cleanser**

MORNY ⊘ 🐇
Fine English Soap: English Rose, French Fern, Original Lavender, Sandalwood; *Fragranced Liquid Soap:* Original Lavender, Sandalwood

NAPIERS HERBAL HEALTH CENTRE 🐇
Wash Range: Lavender Hand Wash

NATIONAL TRUST ENTERPRISES LTD ⊘ ✔ ✂1998
Liquid Soap: Gardeners

NATURAL ORGANICS ™
Adam the Gardener's Tea Tree Scrub; **Aloe Vera & Lavender**; **Bergamot**; **Cheer Up** ; **Frankincense & Myrrh**; **Geranium**; **Geranium & Orange Blossom - Turkish Delight**; **Lavender**; **Lavender & Chamomile**; **Lavender Scrub**; **Lemongrass & Rosemary**; **Patchouli**; **Patchouli Soap**; **Relax & Chill Out**; **Rose Garden**; **Rose & Jasmine**; **Rose & Vanilla**; **Sandalwood**; **Soothing Smoothing**; **Tea Tree & Lavender**; **Vanilla Marble**; *New:* **No Worries**, **Rosemary**, **Soothing Smoothing 1**, **Soothing Smoothing 2**

NATURALLY GIFTED ™
Bed of Roses; **Citrus Grove Bar**; **Hemp & Walnut**; **Herbal Mint**; **Oatmeal & Spice Scrub**; **Seaweed Bar**; **Summer Solstice**; **T Tree**

NEAL'S YARD REMEDIES ⊘ ✔
Calendula; Citrus Glycerine; French Almond; French Lavender; Geranium & Orange; Lavender Glycerine; Lavender & Tea Tree; Lemon & Coriander; Marseille Block; Neem; Rose; Rosemary

NEW SEASONS ☺⊘ ✔
Neutral Base: Liquid Soap

NORFOLK LAVENDER LTD ✔ ✂
The English Lavender

ONE WITH NATURE ™
Soap Range 1: **Base**, **Citronella**, **Gaia**, **Lavender & Marigold**

OPTIMA HEALTH & NUTRITION ⊘ ✔ ✂1995
Olive Oil & Aloe Vera; Olive Oil & Aloe Vera w Lavender Essential Oil; Olive Oil & Aloe Vera w Tea Tree Antiseptic; Olive Oil & Aloe Vera w Vitamin E Moisturiser; *Thursday Plantation Tea Tree:* Deep Cleansing Vegetable

PURPLE FLAME AROMATHERAPY ⊘ ✔
French Lavender; Organic Tea Tree; Revitalising Citrus

REALLY WORKS ™☺⊘ ✔ ✂
Lotion Hand; *Gel Citrus Hand Cleaner:* **w Pumice**, **Without Pumice**

RED STAR NATURAL LIQUID SOAPS LTD ™☺⊘ ✔ 👁 ✂
Hard Bar Soaps: **Smooth as a Baby's Bum**; *Liquid Soaps:* **Lavender**, Tea Tree

REDBUSH TEA CO
Redbush Soaps: Coconut Oil, Olive Oil, Palm Oil, Pure Water infused w Rooibos (Aspalathus Linearis), Shea Butter

RHEMA UK LTD ❶⊘ ✔ ✂
Vegan Soap: All

SCENT BY NATURE ☺⊘ ✔ ✂1986
100% Plant-Based Essential Oil Soap: Tea Tree & Eucalyptus

SEVEN WIVES NATURAL BODYCARE ™⃠✓
Gardeners & Workshop Exfoliating; *Care Range:* **Avocado & Cedarwood, Avocado & Lavender, Lavender & Cocoa, Lavender & Rosewood - Exfoliating Bar**; *Castille Range:* **Hazelnut & Lavender, Shea Butter & Cedarwood, Shea Butter & Hazelnut, Shea Butter & Lavender**

SIMPLY SOAPS ™⃠➊✓✂
3-Soap Gift Box; **All Bar One**; **Banana & Citron**; **Calendula & Lavender**; **Cedarwood**; **Geranium & Rose**; **Hemp**; **Liquid Soap**; **Orange**; **Rosemary & Lavender**; **Seaweed**; **T-Tree**

SOLANO TRADING ™⃠✓
Almond; **Lavender**; **Scented**

SUMA WHOLEFOODS ⃠™👁➊ ✂1985
County Garden: Chamomile, Mixed Pack, Rosemary, Violet; *Exotic:* Cinnamon & Sandalwood, Mixed Pack, Nutmeg & Vanilla, Tea Tree; *Extra Gentle:* Avocado & Cucumber, Desert Aloe Vera, Fragrant Coco Palm, Mixed Pack; *Glycerine Soaps:* Almond, Cucumber, Lavender, Mandarin, Rose, Vitamin E; *Handmade Gifts:* Box of Soaps - Gift Box; *Old English:* Elderflower & Apple, English Lavender Blossom, Mixed Pack, Rose of York

TANJERO ™☺⃠✓
Aloeswood; **Apple & Orchid**; **Aquarius**; **Aries**; **Cancer**; **Capricorn**; **Carrot & Hempseed**; **Chamomile**; **Coconut & Kelp**; **Cucumber & Mint**; **Gardenia**; **Gemini**; **Geranium**; **Geranium & Lime**; **Grapefruit & Orange**; **Jasmine**; **Just Carrot**; **Kitchen Coffee Bar**; **Lavender**; **Lavender & Aloe Vera**; **Lavender & Chamomile**; **Lavender & Oatmeal**; **Lavender w Flowers**; **Leo**; **Libra**; **Litsea Cubeba**; **Musk**; **Patchouli**; **Pisces**; **Pure Aloe Vera**; **Rose**; **Sagittarius**; **Scorpio**; **Tanjero No. 1**; **Tanjero No. 2**; **Tanjero No. 3**; **Taurus**; **Tea Tree & Aloe Vera**; **Tea Tree & Lavender**; **Tea Tree & Lavender w Oatmeal**; **Tea Tree & Mint**; **Tea Tree & Oatmeal**; **Violet**; **Virgo**; **Ylang Ylang**

THE VEGAN SOCIETY ™☺➊✓
Jasmine & Honeysuckle; Ylang Ylang

TISSERAND AROMATHERAPY PRODUCTS ™
Lavender Products: **Lavender & Evening Primrose**; *Tea Tree Products:* **Tea-Tree & Avocado**

TOM'S OF MAINE ⃠✓✂
Natural Deodorant Soap: Calendula, Unscented; *Natural Glycerin Bar Soap:* Herbal Lemon Verbena, Jasmine Rose, Refreshmint, Unscented; *Natural Glycerin Liquid Soap:* Herbal Lemon Verbena, Jasmine Rose, Refreshmint, Unscented; *Natural Moisturising Soap:* Calendula, Lavandin, Unscented

TREE-HARVEST ⊘
Artisan Natural Soap: Bay, Calendula, Cedar & Lemon, Forest Spice, Frankincense & Myrrh, Gardener's, Geranium Chamomile & Lavender, Hemp, Lavender, Pomander, St Clement's, Tea Tree

URTEKRAM ⊘ ✂
Aloe Vera; Camomile; Herbal; Lavender; Rose; Rose Liquid Handsoap; Tea Tree; *Bath Soap:* Lavender; *Hand Soap:* Brown Sugar Liquid; *Pure Balance:* Wild Rose

VIVA! ☺❶⊘
Banana & Citron; Cinnamon & Cedarwood; Geranium & Rose Petal; Lavender & Calendula; Ti-Tree & Calendula

WELEDA ⊘ ✂1985
Iris; Rosemary

WOODS OF WINDSOR ☺
Exfoliating Body Bar: Orange Spice; *Fine English Soap:* for Men, Forget Me Not, Lavender, Lily of the Valley, Mimosa, True Rose; *Glycerine Body Bar w Lavender Flowers:* Aromatherapy Lavender; *Shaped Soaps:* Green Tea Leaf, Lemon

XYNERGY HEALTH PRODUCTS ⊘
Aztec Nopal & Neem: Neem, Nopal

YAOH ™☺❶ ⊘
Liquid Soap

SUN CARE

ABSOLUTELY PURE ™⊘ ✂
Caribbean Blue: **Sun Shield**

ANIMAL AID ☺❶⊘ ✂1976
Suntan Lotion

ANNEMARIE BÖRLIND ❶⊘
After-Sun Gel; Sun Block Balm Factor 30; Sun Lotion Factor 12 & 24; Sun Milk Factors 10 & 12; Sun Spray Factor 15; Sunless Bronze

BEAUTY NATURALS (MARTHA HILL) ❶⊘
Hair Protection Mist; *After Sun:* Skin Calming Gel, Skin Repair Lotion; *Sun Protection Lotion:* SPF 15, SPF 25; *Sun Protection Oil:* SPF 10

FINEMOOD LTD ⊘
Hair & Body Care: Sun Milk

GREEN PEOPLE CO. ™⊘
Self Tan Lotion; *Skin Care:* **Day Solution SPF15 (Day Cream)**; *Sun Care:* **Edelweiss Sun Lotion - SPF8/SPF15**, **Water Lily After Sun**

HONESTY COSMETICS LTD ™☺❶⊘ ✂1976
Aftersun Lotion; **High Protection Sun Lotion (SPF15)**; **Medium Protection Sun Lotion (SPF8)**; **Moisturising Lotion w UVB filter**; **Sun & Sport Shower Gel**

KISS MY FACE ⃠ ✓ 👁 ✂
Swyflotter Insect Repellent; *Aftersun:* Aloe Soother; *Face Factor Face & Neck Moisturiser:* SPF30; *Instant Sunless Tanner:* SPF8; *Oat Protein Sunblock:* SPF18, SPF30; *Spray on Sunblock:* SPF30; *Sunswat + Insect Repellant:* SPF15

L'OCCITANE EN PROVENCE ✓ 👁
Shea Butter: After Sun, Protective Body Oil SPF 12; *Shea Butter Face & Body Balm:* SPF15, SPF30

LAVERA ™
basis sensitiv: **Après Sun Body Lotion, Moisturizing Sun Screen SPF 20**

MALIBU HEALTH PRODUCTS LTD ⃠ ✓
Moisturising Self-Tanning Lotion; Moisturising Self-Tanning Mousse; Smoothing Self-Tanning Gel; *After Sun:* Aloe Vera Moisturising Gel, Glitter Gel, Ice Blue Cooling Gel, Moisturising Spray, Moisturising w Tan Extender, Soothing, Soothing w Insect Repellent; *Dry Oil:* SPF12 Spray For Men, SPF15 Gel, SPF15 Spray, SPF4 Spray, SPF8 Gel, SPF8 Spray; *High Protection Lotion:* SPF15, SPF15 Facial Fluid, SPF20, SPF30, Spray SPF15, Spray SPF30; *Protective Mousse:* SPF12 Sun Protection, SPF20 High Protection; *Protective Sun Lotion:* SPF12, Spray SPF8

NEAL'S YARD REMEDIES ⃠ ✓
Lemongrass Sun Lotion; Shea Nut Natural Sun Screen

NEW SEASONS ☺ ⃠ ✓
Gel Base: After Sun

SEVEN WIVES NATURAL BODYCARE ™ ⃠ ✓
Self Tanning Cream; Sun Gel Factor 8; Sun Lotion Factor 12

URTEKRAM ⃠ ✓ ✂
Solar Crème: Factor 10, Factor 15, Factor 20

YAOH ™ ☺ ❶ ✓ ⃠
AfterSun; **Sun Cream**; **Sunblock 15**; **Sunblock 30**; **Sunblock 50**

TALCUM POWDERS

ABSOLUTELY PURE ™ ⃠ ✓ ✂
Kettlecare: **Bath & Body Powder**

BEAUTY NATURALS (MARTHA HILL) ❶ ⃠ ✓
Body Talc; Lavender

CAMILLA HEPPER LTD ⃠ ✓ ✂ 1987
Avocado; White Musk

LUSH ✓
Dusting Powders: Bare Naked Lady, Candy Fluff, Ginger, Karma, Silky Underwear, T for Toes

MORNY ⃠ ✓
Luxury Body Powder: English Rose, French Fern, Original Lavender, Sandalwood

NORFOLK LAVENDER LTD ✓ ✂
The English Lavender

WOODS OF WINDSOR ☺✓
Dusting Powder: Forget Me Not, Lavender, Lily of the Valley, Mimosa, True Rose; *Talcum Powder:* for Men, Forget Me Not, Lavender, Lily of the Valley, Mimosa, True Rose

TOOTHPASTES & ORAL HYGIENE

ABSOLUTE AROMAS ™⊘✓
Ord River: **Tea Tree Toothpaste 75 g**

ALOE DENT ⊘✓ ✂1995
Aloe Vera Mouthwash: Vitamin K & Tea Tree; *Aloe Vera Toothpaste - Mint Flavour:* Night Time - w Chamomile, Sensitive - w Silica, Wake Up - w Ginseng, Whitening - w Echinacea

AMBER ™
Toothpaste (Sugar Free)

BIOFORCE
Echinacea Toothpaste; *Dentaforce:* Mouthwash, Spray, Toothpaste

BURT'S BEES ⊘✓
Natural Remedies: Doctor Burt's Toothpaste - Lavender Mint

CLEARSPRING ™☺❶⊘
Dentie Toothpaste; **Dentie Toothpowder**

GREEN PEOPLE CO. ™⊘✓
Oral Hygiene: **Citrus Herbal Fresh Toothpaste**, **Mint Herbal Fresh Toothpaste**, **Mint Mouthwash**

HERBS HANDS HEALING LTD ™⊘✓
Ears, Eyes & Mouth: Mouthwash Water

HERBS OF GRACE ™⊘✓
Miscellaneous: **Photodent**

HOLLYTREES ™⊘✓
Deodorant; **Mouthwash**; **Toothpaste**

KINGFISHER NATURAL TOOTHPASTE ☺⊘✓ ✂1981
Aloe Vera Tea Tree Fennel; Aloe Vera Tea Tree Mint; Baking Soda Mint; Fennel; Mint w Lemon; *Fluoride Free:* Fennel, Mint w Lemon

LAVERA ™
Neutral: **Neutral Tooth Gel**

NEAL'S YARD REMEDIES ⊘✓
Lemon & Mint Mouth Freshener; *Toothpaste:* Fennel, Gardenmint

OPTIMA HEALTH & NUTRITION ⊘✓ ✂1995
Thursday Plantation Tea Tree: Mouthwash, Toothpaste

TOM'S OF MAINE ⊘✓ ✂
Natural Alcohol-Free Mouthwash: Cinnamint, Gingermint Baking Soda, Peppermint Baking Soda, Spearmint; *Natural Toothpaste for Sensitive Teeth:* Fennel, Wintermint; *Natural Toothpaste*

w Fluoride: Cinnamint, Fennel, Gingermint Baking Soda, Peppermint Baking Soda, Spearmint, Wintermint

WELEDA ⊘ ✂ 1985
Toothpaste: Aloe Vera Toothpaste, Melisse Toothpaste, Calendula, Calendula, Plant Gel, Ratanhia, Salt

NOTES

■ **Contact lenses** are classed as a medicine under the Medicines Act, all contact lens solutions and associated products have been safety-tested (which invariably entails animal testing at some point). Such products are listed *only* if the company under whose name they are sold meets our animal testing criterion (see **ANIMAL-FREE CRITERIA**, page 292).

■ **Dental floss** may contain beeswax or propolis.

■ **Disposable razors** are often manufactured by companies involved in animal testing, and if they have moisturising strips, may even contain animal-tested or animal-derived ingredients. Veganstore.co.uk sells a range of shaving products that are free from animal ingredients and animal testing, including disposable and refillable razors and shaving brushes.

■ **Mascara** usually contains silk, as do many other types of make-up.

■ **The Body Shop** cannot state that any of their products are free from animal derived ingredients.

■ **Toothpastes and mouthwashes** often contain glycerine, which may be animal-derived.

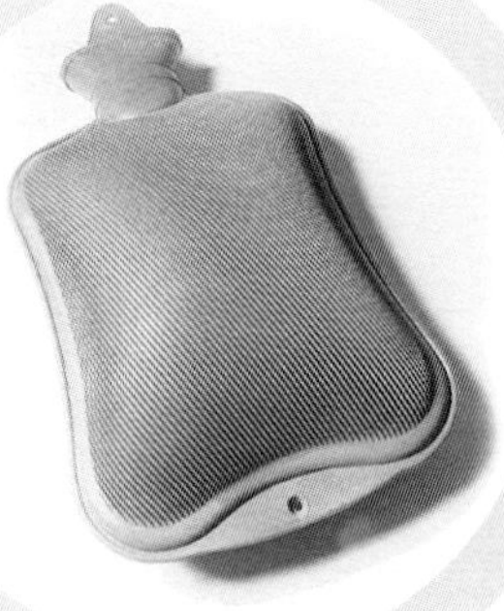

HEALTHCARE

CONTRACEPTIVES

CONDOMI HEALTH UK LTD ™☺✓⊘
Condoms: **Condomi**, **Condomis**, **Mondos**

FOOD SUPPLEMENTS

ACE NUTRITION LTD. ☺⊘✓✂995
Tablets: Green Synergy, Hawaiian Spirulina, Japanese Yaeyama Chlorella, Klamath Lake Algae

ALL SEASONS HEALTH ™
Chlorella Powder; **Chlorella Tablets**; **Spirulina Powder**; **Spirulina Tablets**

ALOE PURA ⊘✓✂1995
Aloe Vera Colon Cleanse; Aloe Vera Digestive Aid; Super Strength Aloe Vera Tablets; X5 Acid Aloe Vera Digestive Aid Tablets; *Aloe Vera Juice:* Cranberry Flavour, Maximum Strength, Pineapple & Papaya Flavour, Wildberry Flavour

AQUASOURCE ™☺⊘✓
Bifidus Complex & Klamath Lake Algae 90 Vegetable Capsules; **Cell Power - Instant Nutrition**; **CoQ10 Complex w Chromium Polynicotinate & Algae 30 Vegetable Capsules**; **Digestive Enzymes & Klamath Lake Algae 60 Vegetable Capsules**; **Green Energy - Algae & Hawaiian Spirulina & Alfalfa 75 & 300 Vegetable Capsules**; **Klamath Lake Algae 60 & 120 Vegetable Capsules**; **Klamath Lake Algae Powder 50g & 150g**; **Klamath Lake Algae Suspended in Organic Apple Juice 60ml**; **Lactobacillus Acidophilus & Klamath Lake Algae 90 Capsules**; **Lighten-Up! Advanced Meal Replacement w Algae - Vanilla Flavour**; **Start Easy Pack (Klamath Lake Algae 50 Vegetable Capsules, Digestive Enzymes & Klamath Lake Algae 60 Vegetable Capsules, Lactobacillus Acidophilus & Klamath Lake Algae 50 Vegetable Capsules, Bifidus Complex & Klamath Lake Algae 50 Vegetable Capsules)**; **Sun Power - Instant Nutrition**; **Super Antioxidant w Pycnogenol 60 Vegetable Capsules**

ARKOPHARMA (UK) LTD ☺⊘✓
Allercaps; Basikol; Ecoprostan; Ginseng Forte; Phyto Soya; Phyto Soya Double Potency; *Arkocaps:* Alfalfa, Artichoke, Bamboo Gum, Bilberry Leaves, Black Cohosh, Californian Poppy, Cherry Stalk, Common Plantain, Cranberry + C, Damiana, Devil's Claw High Potency, Feverfew, Ginger, Ginkgo Biloba, Great Burdock, Green Tea, Guarana, Hawthorn, Ispaghula, Milk Thistle, Nopal Cactus, Olive Leaf, Phyto Slim, Phytocalm, Phytocold, Phytomenopause, Phytomenopause Value, Phytorelax, Pineapple, Rhodiola, Siberian Ginseng, St John's Wort, Stinging Nettle, Vegetable Charcoal, Witch Hazel; *Hair & Nails:* Cheveux

Plus/Hair Plus, Forcapil; *Health From The Sun:* Organic Fiproflax, Organic Flax Lignan Gold, Organic Flax Liquid Gold, Total EFA - Veg/Lignan; *Oils in Gelatin Free Capsules:* Evening Primrose, Natural Vitamin E, Organic Flax, Pumpkin Seed Oil & Saw Palmetto, Starflower; *Slimming:* 4.3.2.1. Shape Up, Exolise, Mincifit Body Shaper Gel; *Sport & Energy Products:* 4.3.2.1. Energy

BEAUTY NATURALS (MARTHA HILL) ❶⊘✓
Eye Bright Vision Support Formula; Nails & Skin Nutrient Formula

BIO-HEALTH LTD ☺⊘✓
V-caps: Super Kelp & Vitamins, Super Rutin & Buckwheat

BIOFORCE
Herbamare; Kelp Tablets

BRUNEL HEALTHCARE ⊘✓ 1992
Vertese: Omega 3+6+9 Oils; *Vertese Capsules:* Evening Primrose Oil, High Strength Evening Primrose Oil (1000mg)

CAMBRIDGE BIOCEUTICALS ™☺⊘✓
Bio-Kult; **Duo-Kult**

CYTOPLAN ™
A Vitamins: **Beta Carotene**; *B Vitamins:* **Biotin**, **Choline Bitartrate Powder**, **Folic Acid**, **Multi B Extra**, **Niacin (Vitamin B3)**, **P. A. B. A. (Para-Amino-Benzoic Acid)**, **Pantothenic Acid (Vitamin B5)**, **Phosphatidyl Choline**, **Pyridoxine (Vitamin B6)**, **Riboflavin (Vitamin B2)**, **Thiamin (Vitamin B1)**, **Vitamin B12**; *C Vitamins:* **Ascorbic Acid Powder**, **Calcium Ascorbate Powder**, **Vitamin C + Bioflavonoids**, **Vitamin C + Bioflavonoids (Ascorbic Acid)**, **Vitamin C + Bioflavonoids (Calcium Ascorbate)**, **Vitamin C Extra**; *Colon Cleanse:* **Cytocleanse**, **Psyllium Husk Powder (340g/142g)**; *E Vitamins:* **Vitamin E**; *Minerals:* **Calcium**, **G. T. F. Chromium**, **Iron/Molybdenum**, **Magnesium**, **Magnesium Citrate (Vegicaps)**, **Potassium**, **Potassium Citrate (Vegicaps)**, **Selenium**, **Zinc Extra**, **Zinc Orotate**, **Zinc/Copper**; *Multi-Formulations:* **Anti Oxidant Plus CoQ10**, **Antioxidant plus Q10**, **Antox**, **CMB Formula**, **Cytoplex (Multi Vitamins & Chelated Minerals)**, **Dantox (High B6 MVM plus 3 Amino Acids)**, **Euro Formula (Multi Vitamin/Mineral)**, **Foundation Formula 1**, **Foundation Formula 2**, **Karoshil (Solace)**, **Nourish Bar - Orange Carob**, **Nourish Bar - Orange Carob (Pack of 3)**, **Nourish Bar - Plain**, **Nourish Bar - Plain (Pack of 3)**, **P5P Extra**, **Super B Extra**, **Trace Mineral Complex**; *Nutritional Support:* **Aloe Vera Gel - Topical Application**, **Aloe XL Inner Leaf**, **Aloe XL Whole Leaf**, **Bromelain - Proteolytic Digestive Enzyme**, **Cyto-Biotic Active**, **Cyto-Vite**, **Cyto-Zyme**, **Evening Primrose Oil (Vegicaps) - GLA 10%**, **Flaxseed Oil - Vegicaps - Omega 3 0.5ml/500mg**, **Fos-a-**

Dophilus, Phospholec (Super-Strength Lecithin), Probiotic Plus (30/60), Siberian Ginseng; *Organic Herbs:* **Organic Echinacea, Organic Garlic, Organic Gingko Biloba, Organic Saw Palmetto, Organic Valerian**; *Phytofood™ & Phytomed™:* **Cherry-C, Eye-Cyt, Phyto-Flavone, Phytofood™ Calcium, PhytoMins, Phytoshield, Phytox - Phyto-Antioxidant**; *Vegan:* **D-Glucosamine HCl**

DEVA NUTRITION ™☺
Deva Coenzyme Q10; **Deva Omega-3 DHA**; **Vegan Glucosamine HCL**

ESSENTIAL OIL COMPANY ☺⊘
Cool Oil Organic Omega Blend

GRANOVITA UK LTD ☺⊘✡✂
Evening Primrose Oil

GREEN PEOPLE CO. ™⊘
Omega 3 & 6 Sprinkle; *Capsules:* **Echinacea, Meno Pause Formula, Milk Thistle, Organic Femme Skin Beauty Formula, Seaweed, Sexy Greens - Men, Sexy Greens - Women, Siberian Ginseng**; *Liquids:* **Hawthorn & Artichoke Formula, Omega 3 & 6 Fuel 1:1, Omega 3 & 6 Fuel 3:1**

HEALTH + PLUS ™⊘
Acidophilus; **Agnus Castus**; **Aloe Vera Juice**; **Amino L-Arginine**; **Amino L-Glutamine**; **Amino L-Lysine**; **Amino L-Methionine**; **Amino L-Tyrosine**; **Ascorbic Acid Powder 250g**; **Bilberry w Eyebright**; **Black Cohosh**; **Brewer's Yeast**; **Calcium Ascorbate + Ascorbic Acid Powder 250g**; **Calcium Ascorbate Powder 250g**; **Cats Claw**; **Chelated Iron**; **Chewable Vit C 500mg**; **Chromium Picolinate**; **Citri-Trim Plus**; **Digest Plus**; **Dong Quai**; **EPO Liquid**; Fibre Gum; **Folic Acid**; FOS (Fructooligosaccharides); **Ginger Root**; Glucosamine; **Gotu Kola**; Homocysteine Complex; **Kelp 300mg**; **Konjac Fibre**; **Konjac Fibre Powder**; **Korean Ginseng**; **Lecithin Granules**; **Magnesium L'Aspartate**; **Megadophilus**; **Milk Thistle**; **MSM**; **Multi Probiotic**; Octacosanol; **Organic Selenium**; Phase Two; **Potassium 100mg**; **Premier Garlic**; **Psyllium Seed Husk Fibre**; **Saw Palmetto + Zinc**; **Selenium**; **Selenium 200mcg**; **Sodium Ascorbate Powder**; **Spirulina**; **St. John's Wort**; **Tribula Plus**; **Tyro Tan**; **Whole Grape**; **Zinc**; **Zinc Citrate**; *Liquid Essential:* **Beta Carotene 15mg, Co Enzyme Q10, E400, Lecithin 550mg, Lycopene Plus**; *Liquiforce Traditional Plant Tinctures:* **Agnus Castus, Bilberry, Black Cohosh, Cats Claw, Chamomile, Dandelion, Devil's Claw, Echinacea, Elderberry, Feverfew, Ginger, Ginkgo Biloba, Goldenseal, Gotu Kola, Hawthorn, Horsechestnut, Horsetail, Marigold, Milk Thistle, Nettle, Red Clover, Sage, Saw Palmetto, Slippery Elm Formula, St. John's Wort, Uva Ursi, Valerian, Wild Yam**

HEALTHQUEST LIMITED ™⊘✓
Supplements: **Body Shield, Chill Out, Lift, Man, Nutri-Aid, Woman**

HEALTHY AND ESSENTIAL ™
Essential Woman; Forti Flax; Omega Man; Omega Twin

HERBS HANDS HEALING LTD ™⊘✓
Exclusive suppliers of Dr Schulze's Superfood in the UK

HERBS OF GRACE ™⊘✓
Bleckman Formulae: **All**; *Blended Herbs:* **All**; *Fluid Extract Blends:* **All**; *Glycerites:* **All**; *Phytobiophysics Flower Formulae:* **All**; *Single Fluid Extracts:* **All**; *Single Herbs:* **All**

HIGHER NATURE PLC ™⊘✓
Acidobifidus; Advanced Brain™ Food Formula; Advanced Optimum Nutrition Formula; AGE Antioxidant; Alka-Clear (Powder & Capsules); Aloe Gold (Cherry/Cranberry); Aloe Gold (Natural); Alpha; Asta; Awake™ Food Formula; B-Vital; Betaine HCL; Bio Minerals; Boswellia & Devil's Claw; Bromelian; Butterbur; Calma-C; Candiclear 350; Cat's Claw; Cat's Claw Tea Bags; Chill™ Food Formula; Chlorella; Citricidal Liquid; Co-Enzyme Q10; Coloclear; ConcenTrace® Trace Mineral Drops; Connect®; Dinochews; Dong Quai & Agnus Castus; Echinacea & Black Elderberry; FOS; FreeCarb; Get Up & Go!; Glutamine Capsules; Glutamine Powder; H Factors; HCA; Herbal Aloe Gold Ear Drops; Herbal SpringClean; High PC Lecithin Granules; High Potency Vitamin B12 200mcg; High Strength Mexican Yam; ImmuneC®; IntestAid IB; Lactogest; Lysine 500mg; Lysine-C; Mega Potency Ginkgo 6000; Menophase; Milk Thistle & Artichoke; Mood™ Food Formula; Muira Puama & Damiana Aphrodisiaca; Neversnore; Nucell® Support; Ocean Kelp; Olive Leaf Extract; Osteofood; Paraclens; Phosphatidyl Serine; Premenstrual Complex; Probiogest; Probiomints; Rhodiola & Ashwagandha; Rosehips C 1000; Saw Palmetto & Pygeum Bark; Serotone 5HTP; Sheep's Sorrel Complex; St John's Wort; Sublingual Zinc; Super Strength Cranberry; Super Strength Supergar 8000; Supergest; Superphyte; Sx; The Sher Skin Support Formula; Vegetarian Glucosamine Hydrochloride; Vinpocetine; VisualEyes; X Factors; *ColoClear Extra:* **Capsules, Powder**; *MSM:* **Capsules, Crystals, Joint & Muscle Balm, Tablets**; *Omega Nutrition:* **Pumpkin Seed Butter**; *Omega Nutrition Organic:* **Apple Cider Vinegar, Hi-Lignan Nutri-Flax**; *Sambucol®:* **Liquid (Sorbitol), Lozenge**; *True Food®:* **All Man, Beta Carotene, GTF Chromium, Maxi Co-Q10, Soyagen, Super Potency Soyagen, Supernutrition Plus, Wise Woman**

HOLLAND AND BARRETT RETAIL LTD
Powder: BF Creatine, Brewer's Yeast, Creatine; *Tablets:* All Natural Amino-600, Chinese Chlorella, Natural Brewers Yeast 470mg, Spirulina 500mg

JARROW FORMULAS INC.
Amino Acids: L-Arginine, L-Glutamine (All except Capsules), Liquid L-Camitine; *Athletic Formulas:* Crea Surge - Mango/Guava, Creatine Monohydrate, Creatine Surge, Ribiso Powder, Tribulus Complex; *Ayurvedic Products:* Ashwagandha 3%, Gymnema-75, Maxi-Boz, Nimbin (Nimbicidin), Phyllantus, Stimuliv; *Body Optimizers:* Alpha GPC Veggie Caps, Glucose Optimizer; *CO-Q10 & Other Antioxidants:* Alpha Lipoic Acid Tablets, Alpha Lipoic Sustain 300 - 60 Tablets, Antioxidant Optimizer, CholesTame, Homocysteine PF (Methyl Donors), Melatonin Sustain, MSM 1000 Tablets, MSM Skin Gel + ALA +C, MSM Sulfur Powder, NattoMax Veggie Caps, SAM-e 200, SAM-e 400mg, TMG 500 Tablets, TMG Crystals Powder; *Garlic, Fibers, Digestive Enzymes:* Bromelain 1000, Citrus Pectin Powder, Gentle Fibensis, Lactase Enzyme, Nutri-Flax Fiber; *Germanium:* Germanium Powder; *Green, Fruit & Super Foods:* Berry High Powder, Green Defense Powder, Green Tea 5:1, Yaeyama Chlorella + Barley Tablets, Yaeyama Chlorella Powder, Yaeyama Chlorella Tablets; *Lipid Fatty Acid, Lecithin, Vinegar:* Essential Balance (All except Capsules), Flax Max 12fl oz; *Protein, Diet & Food Formulas:* Fermented Soy Essence, Glycemic Strawberry, Glycemic Vanilla, Iso-Rich Soy, Iso-Rich Soy + Greens, Lo Han Sweet, Xylipure Xylitol

KUDOS VITAMINS AND HERBALS LTD ⃠ ✓
Acidophilus plus Bifidus; Allerplex (Allergy Defence Formula); Bone Density Support Formula; CircuPlex Formula; Co Enzyme Q 10 40mg; Cranberry Complex; Digestive Enzymes; Evening Primrose Oil; Eye Bright; Garlic & Parsley (Reduced Odour); Hair Nutrient Formula; Kava Kava 900mg; Kudos 24 Multi-Active Age Management Complex; LivoPlex™; Maca 900mg; MenoPlex Formula; Nails & Skin Nutrient Formula; PineOxenol™; PMS Formula; Rhodiola 900mg; Soya Isoflavones; *Free Form:* Amino Acid Complex Plus B6, L-Arginine/L-Ornithine 250mg/250mg, L-Carnitine L-Tartrate 250mg, L-Cysteine 500mg, L-Glutamine 500mg, L-Lysine 500mg, L-Methionine 500mg

LIFEPLAN PRODUCTS LTD ™ ⃠ ✓
Acetyl L Carnitine & Alpha Lipoic Acid; **Agnus Castus**; **Biotin 2.5mg**; **Brewers Yeast**; **Calcium Pantothenate - 250mg**; **Caprylic Acid**; **Chamomile Blend**; **Cranberry Extract - 200mg**; **Culture Care - 28g**; **Damiana Leaf Capsules**; **Dandelion Root**; **Devils Claw - 500mg**; **Echinacea - 1000mg Time Release**; **Echinacea - 360mg**; **Enzyme Plus**; **Eyebright**; **Feverfew**; **Fibre - 440mg**; **Folic Acid**; **Golden Seal - 420mg**;

Hair Care Nutrients; Hawthorn; High Strength Odour Controlled Garlic - 300mg; Lutein; Nettle Leaf & Eyebright & Echinacea; Omega Blend Oil; Parsley Piert Powder - 125mg; Prune and Senna; Pycnogenol - Maritime Pine Bark Extract - 300mg; Raspberry Leaf; Red Clover; Rutin; Sage; Saw Palmetto; Sea Kelp w Added Calcium - 400mg; Siberian Ginseng High Strength - 600mg; Slippery Elm; Soyplus - Soya Isoflavones w Folic Acid; St. John's Wort Extract - 333mg; Standardised Extract of Ginger - 50mg; Standardised Extract of Milk Thistle - 175mg; Super Multinutrient; Swiss Hayflower; Thiamine 100mg; Valerian; Valerian Formula; Valerian Passiflora & Hops; Vegetarian Glucosamine; Women's Multinutrient; *Capsules:* **Guarana Powder, Nettle Powder**

LINPHARMA HERBAL PRODUCTS ™
Easigest; Echinacea Plus Nasturtium; Husk; Nitebalm; Winterbalm

MAXIMUSCLE LTD
CLA 90 Capsules; GH Kick; Glutamax Neutral; NO2; *Creatamax:* 300, 8000GL Fruit Punch, 8000GL Orange

NATURE'S AID LTD ⊘✓
Acetyl-L-Carnitine; Alpha Lipoic Acid; Brewers Yeast; Conc. Garlic 400mg; Cranberry; Devil's Claw; Kelp; Pycnogenol; Soya Isoflavones

NATURE'S OWN LTD ™
Cherry-C; Choline; *A Vitamins:* **Betacarotene (50/100)**; *B Vitamins:* **Biotin, Choline, Folic Acid, Niacin (Vitamin B3), P. A. B. A. (Para-Amino-Benzoic Acid), Pantothenic Acid (Vitamin B5), Pyridoxine (Vitamin B6), Riboflavin (Vitamin B2), Thiamin (Vitamin B1), Vitamin B Complex Plus (30/50/90), Vitamin B Complex Plus Vitamin C (30/50), Vitamin B12**; *C Vitamins:* **Ascorbic Acid Powder, Bioflavonoid Complex + C (50/100), Calcium Ascorbate Plus Bioflavonoids (30/50/100), Vitamin C w Bioflavonoids (30/50/100)**; *Digestive Aids:* **Bromelain - Proteolytic Digestive Enzyme, Fos-a-Dophilus, Probiotic Plus (20/30/60), Psyllium Husk Powder**; *E Vitamins:* **Vitamin E150 (30/50), Vitamin E300**; *Lifestyle:* **Executive, Fifties, Senior Citizens, Shift Workers, Smokers, Students, Working Men, Working Women**; *Minerals:* **Calcium (50/30), G. T. F. Chromium, Iron/Molybdenum, Magnesium, Manganese, Phytofood™ Calcium (30/60), Potassium, Selenium 100mcg Elemental, Selenium 200mcg Elemental (30/50), Zinc Orotate 100mg (50/100), Zinc/Copper (30/50)**; *Multi-Formulations:* **CMB Formulation, Dolomite 500mg, Karoshil, Multivitamin & Mineral (30/60/100)**; *Nutritional Support:* **Brewers Yeast (BPC), Evening Primrose Oil 10% GLA - Vegicaps (30/90), Flaxseed Oil**

- Organic Oil - Vegicaps, Kelp Plus - High Iodine Natural Multi Mineral, Organic Garlic (Vegicaps) Powdered Whole Garlic, Rutin, Siberian Ginseng - Whole Powdered Root; *Vegan:* **D-Glucosamine HCl**

NATURE'S REMEDIES ⊘ ✓
Zotrim

NESTLÈ
Build up Soup: Vegetable

NEWAYS INTERNATIONAL UK LTD ™
Green Qi

NUTRISPORT ⊘ ✓
90+ Protein Vegan; Creatine Powder

OPTIMA HEALTH & NUTRITION ⊘ ✓ ✂1995
Maxicol Capsules - For Bowel Health; Maxicol - For Bowel Health; *ESI Laboratories:* Echinacea 512mg Tablets, Echinacea Alcohol-free Liquid Extract, Echinacea Effervescent Tablets w Rosehip & Acerola, Echinacea High Potency Liquid Extract, Echinacea High Potency Vegcaps, Echinacea Throat Spray - Mint Flavour, Lecithin Granules; *Herbalforce:* Menolife Vegcaps - Original Herbal Complex for Women; *Liquid Evening Primrose Oil:* Lemon, Natural

PHYTO PRODUCTS LTD ☺
Schoenenberger Plant Juices: Artichoke, Beetroot, Birch, Carrot, Celery (Pyrrolizidine Alkaloid Free), Dandelion, Echinacea, Elderberry, Fennel, Ginkgo, Hawthorn, Horsetail, Manna Fig w Senna, Parsley, Potato, Radish Black, Ribwort, Rosemary, St. John's Wort, Stinging Nettle, Thyme, Valerian, Yarrow

PITROK LTD ⊘ ✓
Tofupill

POWER HEALTH PRODUCTS ⊘ ✓
Aloe Vera Supplements: 10000 Double Strength, Juice Drink 99.7%; *Cranberry Products:* Juice 1675mg w Vitamin C 100mg Sugar Free, Juice Concentrate Drink Mix, Juice Double Strength 4500mg; *GLA Supplements:* Borage (Starflower) Oil Liquid Cold Pressed, Evening Primrose Oil Liquid Cold Pressed; *Herbal Supplements:* Alfalfa 500mg, Bilberry 2500mg, Black Cohosh 350mg, Bromelain 10mg & Papain 100mg, Butterbur Root Powder 100mg, Cat's Claw 34mg, Echinacea 300 (Standardised 4% extract), Mexican Wild Yam 500mg, Olive Leaf 450mg, Rhodiola 500mg, Saw Palmetto (4:1 extract) 1000mg & Uva Ursi 100mg, Senna 37.5mg (7.5mg Sennosides), Soya Isoflavones Kudzu Root & Red Clover, Super Ginkgo Plus (w Green Buckwheat & Vit E); *Lifestyle Supplements:* Alpha Lipoic Acic 200mg, Alpha Lipoic Acid 200mg & L-Carnitine 500mg, Co Enzyme Q10 30mg; *Mineral Supplements:* Chromium Picolinate 200mcg, Kelp 500mg; *Multivitamin & Mineral Supplements:* Power ACE Super Antioxidant;

Supplements for Slimmers: Citrin 500 500mg (250mg HCA), Spirulina 500mg

POWER SPORT ⊘ 🐇
General Health Products: Soya Protein Powder Containing Amino Acids - Natural

PRINCIPLE HEALTHCARE ™ ☼
Bilberry Tablets; **Co Enzyme Q10 30mg VegaGels TM**; **Cranberry Tablets 200mg**; **Evening Primrose Oil 1000mg VegaGels TM**; **Folic Acid 400mcg Tablets**; **Ginger Tablets**; **Odourless Garlic 2mg VegaGels TM**; **Sea Kelp Tablets**; **Super B Complex Tablets**

PROTEXIN ™☺⊘ 🐇
Balance; Balance +; Project; Restore; Vitality

QUEST VITAMINS ⊘ 🐇
Agnus Castus; Bilberry; Black Cohosh 40mg Extract Tablets; Cats Claw 250mg Extract Tablets; Coenzyme Q10 30mg; Cranberry 200ml Extract Tablets; Devil's Claw; DL-Phenylalanine; Don Quai 250mg Extract; Echinacea; Enzyme Digest; Feverfew; Ginger; Ginkgo Biloba; Green Tea; Hawthorn 250mg Extract Tablets; Kava Kava; Kyolic Garlic 100/350/600 & Liquid; L-Arginine; L-Glutamine 500mg; L-Lysine; L-Ornithine 500mg; L-Phenylalanine 500mg; L-Tyrosine 500mg; Lactase; Milk Thistle; Non-Dairy Acidophilus Plus; Rhodiola 250mg Extract Tablets; Saw Palmetto; Senna; Siberian Ginseng; St John's Wort; Synergistic Boron; Uva Ursi; Valerian

RAWCREATION LTD ☺
MSM Powder; O-Mega-Zen3 Vegan DHA; OxCgen; Vegan Brain Pack

RELIV UK ™ 🐇 ⊘
Reliv Classic 504g

RHEMA UK LTD ❶⊘ 🐇 ✂
Bio-Kult Probiotic; *Klamah Blue Green Algae:* Powder, Tablets, V-Cap

SAGE ORGANIC LTD ™☺⊘ 🐇
Echinacea Formula; **Healthy Man**; **Healthy Woman**; **Menopause**; **Pregnancy**; **St John's Wort**; **Vitality 50+**

SAVANT DISTRIBUTION LTD ™❶⊘ 🐇
Beyond Greens; L-Glutamine Powder; **Omega 3 Basic**; Silver Colloid Liquid; **Synergy Spirulina**

SEAGREENS ™☺⊘ ☼
Ascophyllum Fine Granules: **Everyday Iodine Capsules**; *Mixed Wrack:* **Food Capsules**

SOLGAR VITAMINS LTD 🐇 ⊘
Alfalfa; Antioxidant Free Radical Modulators; Beta 1 3 Glucans; Brewers Yeast; Broccoli; Bromelain; Cardiovascular Support; Certified Organic Garlic; Cholesterol Factors; Energy Modulators; Glucose Factors; GSH Modulators; Homocysteine Modulators; Hydroxy

Citrate; Ipriflavone; Iso Soy; Lactase; Lipotropic Factors; Lutein Lycopene Carotene Complex; Lycopene Carotenoid Complex; Maximised Caprylic Acid; Microbial Modulators; MSM 1000mg; Natural Cranberry Extract w Vitamin C; Octacosanol; Phosphatidyl Serine; Prostate Support; Quercetin; Reishi Shiitake Maitake Mushroom Extract; Soya Lecithin '95' Granules; Spirulina; Super Concentrated Isoflavones; Vegan Digestive Enzymes; Vegan Digestive Modulators; *Co Q10:* 120mg, 200mg, 60mg; *Full Potency (FP) Herbs:* All; *Herbal Complexes:* All; *Standardised Full Potency (SFP) Herbs:* All

SOLO NUTRITION LTD
Chromium Polynicontinate Complex; D-Tox Formula; Echinacea Complex; Ester C 500mg + Bioflavonoids; Evening Primrose Oil plus Borage Oil; Ginkgo Biloba; Korean Ginseng; Milk Thistle Herb & Seed; Rhodiola Root; Saw Palmetto Berry Complex; Siberian Ginseng; St John's Wort; Super Acidophilus w F. O. S; Zincfifty

THORNCROFT
Thorncroft Cordials & Herbal Fusions: Cranberry & Hibiscus, Elderflower, Nettle, Pink Ginger, Rosehip

TREE-HARVEST
Maca; Spirulina; Wolfberries

UDO'S CHOICE ™
Ultimate Oil Blend: **Evening Primrose Oil**

VEGA NUTRITIONALS ™
Agnus Castus 300mg High Potency; **Aller-G Formula**; **Aloe Vera 500mg High Potency**; **Amino Complex plus B6**; **Anti-Oxidant Formula**; **Beta Carotene 170mg Dunaliella Salina**; **Biotin 1000mcg**; **Brain Fuel Amino Acids & Vitamins & Ginkgo Biloba**; **Calcium Citrate**; **Calcium Magnesium Zinc plus Boron**; **Cardiohealth Support**; **Cat's Claw 1000mg High Potency**; **Cellulite Vitamins & Herbs & Amino Acid**; **Champignon plus Fos & Chlorella & Spirulina**; **Chelated Calcium 500mg**; **Cholestatin Formula**; **Choline plus Inositol 250mg/250mg**; **Chromium Polynicotinate 200mcg Yeast Free**; **Co-enzyme Q10 30mg Extra High Potency**; **Colloidal Minerals w Kelp**; **Cran-biotic plus Caprilic Acid**; **Devil's Claw 300mg High Potency**; **Digestive Enzymes**; **Dong Quai 750mg High Potency**; **Echinacea 750mg High Potency**; **Energiser Amino Acids plus Herbs**; **EPO + B6 + Mexican Yam 250mg**; **Ester-C Complex**; **Feverfew 750mg High Potency**; **Folic Acid 400mcg**; **Garlic (Deodorised) 400mg High Potency**; **Gastro-eze Formula**; **Gentle Vitamin C 1000mg (Calcium Ascorbate)**; **Ginkgo Biloba 750mg High Potency**; **Ginseng (Siberian) 1700 Complex**; **Hair-Skin-Nails Formula**; **Hi-Active Control Formula**; **Inflam-eze Formula**; **Iron Bisglycinate 50mg non Constipating**; **Kelp & Greens**

Formula; **Maxijoint Formula**; **Memory + Formula**; **Menopause Formula**; **Milk Thistle 200-Complex**; **Multi Antioxidant**; **Multi Detox Formula**; **Multigluco T Factors w Karella**; **Nico-Quit Herbal Support**; **Non Dairy Acidophilus plus Bifidus Complex**; **Opti-care 20:20 Formula**; **P.A.B.A Para Aminobenzoic Acid 300mg**; **Panax Ginseng (Korean) 800 Complex**; **Paracidal Formula (Neem)**; **Pine Bark Extract 30mg**; **PMS B6 Epo Zinc Minerals & Herbs**; **Pre-Natal Formula**; **Prostate Formula**; **Psyllium Fibre 450mg**; **Pyridoxal '5' Phosphate 25mg**; **Selenium 200mcg Yeast Free**; **Slimaide Hydroxy-Citric Acid & Chromium**; **Soya Lecithin plus Starflower Oil (Omega 3+6)**; **Spectrum Adult (Multi Vitamin)**; **St John's Wort 333-Complex**; **Valerian 900-Complex**; **Vegatonic Herbal Formula**; **Vegra-forte (Export only)**; **Vein Support**; **Vitalize-Regenerative Formula**

XYNERGY HEALTH PRODUCTS
CoEnzyme-A; Spirolight Bars; *Lifestream:* Barley Grass & Ginger, Biogenic Aloe Vera Juice, Biogenic Aloe Vera Vegicaps, New Generation Spirulina; *Optimum Source:* Chlorella; *Pure Planet:* Ginseng Plus Spirulina, Organic Spirulina, Red Marine Algae + Spirulina; *Seagreens:* Culinary Ingredient, Everyday Iodine, Table Condiment; *Sweet Wheat - Freeze Dried Wheatgrass Juice:* Standard, VegiCaps; *Synergy Company:* Pure Synergy, Vita Synergy for Men, Vita Synergy for Women

INSECT REPELLENTS

ABSOLUTELY PURE ™
Kettlecare: **Herbal Bugless Oil**

AMPHORA AROMATICS LTD 1998
Bugs Away Insect Repellent Spray

BAY HOUSE AROMATICS 1978
Insect Repellent Gel

BEAUTY THROUGH HERBS 1990
Insect Barrier: Cream, Spray

BIOFORCE
Equineem Spray; Neemcare

BURT'S BEES
Natural Remedies: Herbal Insect Repellent

FINEMOOD LTD
Push-up Sticks: Insect Repellent

HIMALAYA UK LTD
Colibri

KOBASHI ™
Head Lice Repellent; *Luxury Lotions:* **Insect Repellent**

NEAL'S YARD REMEDIES ⦸
Bug Buster Comb

NEW SEASONS ☺⦸
Buzz Off Insect Repellent

OPTIMA HEALTH & NUTRITION ⦸ 1995
Thursday Plantation Tea Tree Walkabout: Lotion, Roll-On

XYNERGY HEALTH PRODUCTS ⦸
India Tree Herbal Insect Repellent; *India Tree:* Tea Tree Herbal Lotion

REMEDIES

ABSOLUTE AROMAS ™⦸
Ord River: **Tea Tree Antiseptic Cream 50ml**

ABSOLUTELY PURE ™⦸
Earthbound Organics: **Anti-Cellulite Oil**; *Kettlecare:* **Acne Serum**, **Anti-Blemish Rose Haqzel Astringent**; *Pure Essentials:* **Head Lice Remedy**, **Sinus Relief**; *Pure Essentials - Oils:* **Acne Facial**, **Arthritis**, **Cellulite**, **Eczema**, **Psoriasis**, **Psoriasis Scalp**, **Stretch Mark**

ACE NUTRITION LTD. ☺⦸ 1995
Vegicaps: Echinacea (Fresh Freeze-Dried), Feuerfew (Fresh Freeze-Dried), Garlic (Fresh Freeze-Dried), Ginkgo Biloba, Saw Palmetto (Fresh Freeze-Dried), St. John's Wort (Fresh Freeze-Dried)

AINSWORTHS HOMEOPATHIC PHARMACY
Homeopathic Remedies: All (Pills & Coarse Granules)

AMPHORA AROMATICS LTD ⦸ 1998
Aromatherapy Sprays: Antiseptic, Body De-Stress, Body Revitalise, Face Freshener, Foot Reviver, Mind De-Stress

ARKOPHARMA (UK) LTD ☺⦸
Activox Winter Remedies: Mint & Eucalyptus Lozenges, Spray; *Essential Oil Roll-Ons:* Migrastick, Teenstick

AROMA CRYSTAL THERAPY ⦸
Everyday Stress Gel; Nature's First Defence

ARTEL ALLERGY PRODUCTS
Herbal Relief: Breathe Free Herbal Spray, Herbal Headache Relief, Herbal Pain Freeze Spray, Herbal Sinus Relief, Hot Tamale Joint & Muscle Relief

BAY HOUSE AROMATICS ⦸ 1978
Herbal Candies: Cinnamon & Clove, Cough Assortment, Eucalyptus, Ginger & Orange, Ginseng, Lavender, Lemon Balm, Liquorice & Aniseed, Peppermint

BENNETT NATURAL PRODUCTS ⦸
Obbekjaers Peppermint: Powder, Pure Oil of Peppermint, Tablets

BERWITZ HOMEOPATHIC REMEDIES FOR PEOPLE ☺⦸
Assisi + Berwitz Homeopathic Remedy Cream: Burn Cream, First Aid Cream,

Psoriasis Cream, Rheumatism Cream, Tea Tree Cream, Varicose Vein Cream

BIO-HEALTH LTD ☺⊘✓
'Pure-fil' V-caps: All, Evening Primrose Oil, Iceland Moss, Melissa Leaf, Raspberry Leaf Tablets, Willow Bark, Wormwood

BIOFORCE
Aesculus Forte; Aesculus Gel; Arnica Gel; Avena Sativa; Biosnaky Seed Range; Bowel Essence; Calendula Complex; Comfrey Cream; Comfrey Gel; Concentration Essence; Confidence Essence; Craving Essence; Devil's Claw; Echinacea Complex; Echinacea Cream; Emergency Essence; Equine Essences; Equineem Soothing Lotion; Female Essence; Ginkgo Biloba; Ginsavena; Golden Grass Tea; Ivy-Thyme Complex; Knotgrass Complex; Linoforce; Luffa Complex; Luffa Nasal Spray; Male Essence; Menosan Tablets; Milk Thistle Complex; Milk Thistle Tablets; Mood Essence; Nature-C; Neemcare Oil; Night Essence; Passiflora Complex; Relaxing Essence; Silicea; Solidago Complex; Tormentil Complex; Urticalcin; Uva-Ursi Complex; Valerian-Hops Complex; Viola Tricolor; Wheat Germ Oil; Yarrow Complex; *Jan de Vries Range:* Aloe Vera Complex, Black Cohosh, Feverfew, Ginger, Marum Verum, Peppermint Complex, Vinca Minor, Vitality Essence

CAMILLA HEPPER LTD ⊘✓ ✂1987
Aromatherapy Oils: Hair Loss Treatment, Relaxing Bath, Soothing Bath, Tension; *Herb Ointments:* Comfrey, Leg & Vein

CEDAR HEALTH LTD
Bio-Strath Elixir; Linatox; Padma 28; *Pure Plan:* Apple + Green Tea, Gel, Original + Green Tea

CHIRALI OLD REMEDIES
Damp-Heat Cream; Dry Skin Cream; Itching Skin Cream; Muscle & Joint Soothing "Bi" Cream; Wild Yam Cream

COTSWOLD HEALTH PRODUCTS ☺⊘☼
Liquorice Juice Sticks; *Natural Herb V-caps:* Devils Claw, Echinacea, Ginko Biloba, Milk Thistle & Dandelion, St John's Wort, Valerian

DOLMA ™☺❶⊘✓👁✂
Miscellaneous Products: **Avasafab Antiseptic Cream**

DR HADWEN TRUST ☺❶⊘✓
Muscle & Joint Lotion

ESSENTIAL OIL COMPANY ☺⊘✓👁
Nitebalm Organic Herbal Tincture; *Thermotherapy - Microwaveable Heated Gifts:* Beddy-Bear Bed Warmer, Cherry Stone Pillow, Henry Warmheart Teddy Bear, Hot-Bunny Bed Warmer, Hot-Pak Rectangular Wheat Soother, Slippies Microwave Slippers

GREEN DOT GUIDES ⊘✓
Pain Ease Patch; *Tofupill:* Manage the Menopause

HEALTHPOL ☺⊘✓
Delacet Scalp & Hair Cleanser (Lice/Nits Solution)

HEALTHY HERBS ✓⊘☼
Aloe Vera Gel; Balance-the-Chanes; Musc Ease Gel; Raven of Tinctures

HERBS HANDS HEALING LTD ™⊘✓
Herbal Snuff; *Bowel Cleanse:* Olive & Artemisia Formula, Organic Cloves (Whole), Walnut & Wormwood Formula, Worming Heal Pack; *Colds & Chest Support:* Cherry Bark & Elderberry Syrup, Onion & Horseradish Elixir; *Digestive Assistance:* Cleanse & Balance Herb Tea, Digestion Heal Pack, Meadowsweet Herb Tea, Meadowsweet Tincture; *Ears, Eyes & Mouth:* Dr. Christopher's B & B Ear Formula; *For all Menopausal Stages:* Chamomile & Vervain Formula, Siberian Ginseng Tincture, Valerian & Passionflower Formula, Vitex & Black Cohosh Formula (Menopause); *Fungal Overload:* Pau d'Arco Bark Tea, Pau d'Arco & Chamomile Formula; *Heart & Circulatory Health:* Ginger & Hawthorn Formula, Ginkgo & Rosemary Formula, Hawthorn Tincture; *Heart & Circulatory Heath:* Prickly Ash & Rosemary Formula; *Hormone Assistance for Men:* Saw Palmetto & Damiana Formula; *Immune Stimulation:* Echinacea & Thyme Formula, Echinacea Tincture, Immuno Herbal Tea; *Immune Tonics:* American Ginseng & Astragalus Formula, Gentian & Liquorice, Siberian Ginseng & Liquorice, Siberian Ginseng Tincture; *Immune Travel Support:* Olive & Artemisia Formula; *Immunity & Allergies:* Immune Heal Pack, Juniper & Eyebright Formula; *Kidney & Bladder Health:* Dandelion & Marshmallow Formula, Nettle Leaf Tea; *Kidney Cleanses:* 28 Day Kidney Cleanse, One Day Kidney Cleanse; *Lazy Bowel:* Barberry Capsules, Chamomile & Cascara Capsules, Organic Linseed Seeds, Organic Psyllium Husks; *Liver Cleanses:* 28 Day Liver Cleanse, One Day Liver Cleanse; *Lungs & Breathing:* Breathe & Clear Herbal Tea, Mullein & Eucalyptus Formula; *Menstrual Help:* Agnus Castus & Raspberry Formula (Premenstrual), Agnus Castus Tincture, Crampbark Tincture, Menstruation Heal Pack, Parsley & Cornsilk Herb Tea, Squaw Vine & Fennel Formula (Monthly Cycle); *Muscles, Joints & Tendons:* Angelica & Meadowsweet Formula, Body Ease Herbal Tea, Castor Oil Pack Kit, Deep Tissue Oil; *Nervous System Health & Support:* Nerve Heal Pack; *Night Support:* Evening Peace Herbal Tea; *Prostate Support:* Saw Palmetto & Damiana Formula; *Skin Support:* Cleavers & Burdock Formula, Skin Guard Water; *Soothing & Nurturing the Bowel:* Chamomile Flowers Tea, Gentian & Liquorice Formula, Marigold & Crampbark Formula, Slippery Elm & Marshmallow Powder; *Useful Tonics for both Sexes:* American Ginseng & Astragalus Formula, Milk Thistle & Dandelion Formula; *Uterine Cleansing:* Marshmallow & Squaw Vine Pessaries

HERBS OF GRACE ™⊘✓
Miscellaneous: **Colloidal Silver Spray**

HOLLAND AND BARRETT RETAIL LTD
Aloe Vera Juice Drink; Damiana Leaves Capsules or Liquid; DGL Chewable Liquorice; Diet Aid; Echinacea Golden Seal Root; Extra Energy; Herbal Authority Oats Avena; Inner Fresh; Pure Gar Odour-Controlled Garlic; *Chewable Tablets:* All Natural Pineapple Bromelain; *Cough Syrup:* Chesty; *Liquid Extract:* Cranberry, Dong Quai, Echinacea, Ginkgo-Bilboa, Golden Seal Root, Guarana, Japanese Oil of Peppermint, Milk Thistle, Mullein Leaf, Peppermint, Saw Palmetto, Siberian Ginseng, St. Johns Wort, Valerian Root; *Oils:* Optimum Blend, Peppermint; *Powder:* Oil of Peppermint; *Tablets:* Alfalfa 500mg, Celery Seed 600mg, Chlorophyll & Mint Chewable, Choline, Cider Vinegar, Citrimax, Citrus Bioflavonoids 1000mg, DLPA 500mg, Dolomite, Eye-Vites, Gotu Kola 250mg, Green Barley Grass 500mg, Guarana 800mg, Horse Chestnut, Natural Amino 1000mg, Papaya Enzyme Chewable, Raspberry Leaf Extract 640mg, Siberian Ginseng, Taurine 500mg

J. L. BRAGG LTD ☺⃠
Bragg's Medicinal Charcoal Biscuits & Tablets

JARROW FORMULAS INC.
Herbal Formulas: Black Cohosh, Ginkgo Biloba Tablets, Larix 1000, Liquid Ginkgo Biloba 50:1, Marapusma, PycnOlive, Resveratrol Synergy

KOBASHI ™☺⃠
Roller Balls: First Aid, Relax & Sleep, Stress Buster, Study, Travel

KUDOS VITAMINS AND HERBALS LTD ⃠
Aloe Vera 20000mg of Juice; Black Cohosh 900mg; Cat's Claw 900mg; ClensoPlex™; Devils Claw 900mg; Dong Quai 900mg; Echinacea 900mg; Feverfew 900mg; Ginkgo Biloba 900mg; Korean Ginseng 900mg; Milk Thistle 900mg; Phyto-Nutrient Complex; Saw Palmetto; Siberian Ginseng 900mg; St John's Wort 900mg; Valerian 900mg

MARIGOLD HEALTH FOODS ❶⃠
Golden Temple Ancient Herbal Formula: Bedtime, Breathe Deep, Calming, Cold Season, De-tox, Ginger Lemon, Men's Stomach-Ease, Revitalize, Throat Comfort, Women's

MEADOWSWEET LTD ™☺⃠
Nature Power Range: **Muscle & Joint Lotion**

NAPIERS HERBAL HEALTH CENTRE
BPT Formula; Bug Buster Lotion; Cellulite Gel; Composition Essence; Duncan Napier's Cough Remover; Gentian Bitters; Joint-Ease; Lobelia Cough Syrup; Napiers Detox Plan; Nettle Blend (Anti-Hayfever); Sinus Rub; Special Mixture No.7; *Compounds:* Birch Herbal, Bladderwrack, Buchu, NC, Skullcap, Thuja (for Warts), Withania; *Creams:* Bug Buster, Capsicum &

Ginger, Thuja; *Liquid Formulas:* Herbal Tonic (Stress-Relief), Valerian, Willow Bark; *Oil Blends:* Circulation, Mullein Formula, Muscle Ache, Sleepy Time; *Powders:* Psyllium & Slippery Elm, Slippery Elm; *Pregnancy Oils:* Stretch Mark, Wheat Germ; *Tinctures:* Arnica & Comfrey, Echinacea, Ginkgo Extract 2:1, Hawthorn, Salvia, Vitex; *Traditional Herbal Products:* Organic Single Tinctures, Tincture Formulations

NATURAL BY NATURE OILS ☺⊘✓👁✂1974
Purely Lavender: Oblong Comfort Cushion, Relaxing Eye Pillow, Square Comfort Cushion

NATURE'S AID LTD ⊘✓
Agnus Castus; Aloe Vera 50mg; Bilberry; Black Cohosh; Boldo; Boswellia; Cat's Claw; Dong Quai; Echinacea; Feverfew; Ginger; Ginkgo Biloba; Horse Chestnut; Korean Ginseng; Milk Thistle; MSM; Passiflora; Red Clover; Rhodiola; Saw Palmetto; Siberian Ginseng; St Johns Wort; Traditional Herbal Bronchial Balsam; Uva Urst; Valerian; Wild Yam

NEAL'S YARD REMEDIES ⊘✓
Aloe Vera Cooling Spray; Aloe Vera Juice; American Ginseng; Aroma Stone; Aroma Stream; Ashwaghanda; Aspinevin Pump; Astragalus; Australian Bush Flower Remedies; Bach Flower Remedies; Bentonite Clay; Cellulose Herb Bags; Chinese Angelica; Citronella Formula; Codonopsis; Dang Gui; Dang Shen; Dead Sea Salts; Emulsifying Wax; Fleeceflower; Floradix; Flower Essence Blends; Fuller's Earth; Gan Cao; Ginseng; Gou Qi Zi; Green Clay; He Shou Wu; Healing Herbs; Herbs; Homeopathic Remedies; Huang Qi; Kaolin; Liquorice; Lycium Fruit; North American Flower Essences; Pumice Stone; Qi Yang Shen; Rehmannia Root; Relief Formula; Ren Shen; Rosewater; San Qi Ginseng; Shi Di Huang; Shizandra; Siberian Ginseng; Vegetable Glycerine; Witchazel; Wu Wei Zi; Xi Yang Shen; *Aromatherapy for:* Balance, Breathing Easy, Energy, Passion, Relaxation; *Capsules:* Vegecaps; *Macerated Oil:* Arnica, Calendula, Calendula, Comfrey, Mullein, St John's Wort; *Oils:* Apricot Kernel, Detox Toning, Evening Primrose, Ginger & Juniper Warming, Inhalation, Organic Almond, Sweet Almond; *Ointments:* Comfrey, Rhus Tox & Ruta; *Remedies to Roll for:* Energy, Night Time, Passion, Travel; *Spritzer:* Calm, Renew, Zest; *Tea Blend:* After Dinner, Bladder Soothing, Calming, Clear Lung, Cold & Flu, Detox, Hayfever, Night Time, Purifying, Winter Warming, Women's Tonic; *Tincture Blend:* Bladder Soothing, Cold & Flu, De-stress, Detoxing, Hayfever, Men's Tonic, Menopause, Women's Tonic; *Tinctures:* Chinese Herbal, Homeopathic

OPTIMA HEALTH & NUTRITION ⊘✓✂1995
Thursday Plantation Tea Tree: 15% Oil Lotion, Antiseptic Cream, Antiseptic Ointment, & Eucalyptus Inhalant

PASSION FOR LIFE PRODUCTS
Audiclean - Ear Cleansing Spray; Gassex Tablets - Natural Remedy to Aid Digestion; Liv.52 Tablets - Designed to Protect the Liver; Prost 8 Pro Tablets - Herbal Formulation to Aid Prostate Health; Snoreeze - Snoring Remedy; *Pilex - Natural Balanced Formula for Haemorrhoids:* Cream, Tablets

PHYTO PRODUCTS LTD ☺
Fluid Extracts: All; *Fresh Organically Grown Tinctures:* All; *Galenicals:* Garlic Juice, Vegetable Glycerine; *Infused Oils:* Comfrey, Marigold, St. John's Wort; *Standardised Extract:* Ginkgo Biloba; *Syrups:* Marshmallow, Thyme & Liquorice, Wild Cherry; *Tablets:* Garlic, Rutin & Vitamin C; *Tablets - 200mg:* Agnus Castus, Cramp Bark, Damiana, Devils Claw, Echinacea, Ginger, Ginkgo, Ginseng (Korean), Hawthorn, Kelp, Passiflora, Prickly Ash, Slippery Elm, St. John's Wort, Wild Yam; *Tablets - 50mg:* Golden Seal; *Tablets - Complex:* Buchu & Dandelion, Celery, Helonias, Papaya & Charcoal, Valerian, White Willow; *Tinctures:* All

PURPLE FLAME AROMATHERAPY ⦸
Tea Tree Pessaries

QUINESSENCE AROMATHERAPY ☺❶⦸
Essential Oil Synergies: After Flight, Anti-Pollen, Anti-Virus, Antiseptic, Breathe Ease, Cellulite, Energising, Foot Ease, Head Ease, Immune Optimise, Joint Mobility, Menopause, Muscle Ease, Pre-Menstrual, Problem Skin, Relaxing, Restful Sleep, Sinus, Stress, Uplifting

SCENT BY NATURE ☺⦸ ✂1986
Ainsworths Flower Remedies: Bach Rescue Remedy, Single Bach Flower Remedies; *Green Clay:* Fine Powdered, Ready-to-Use, w Organic Lemon Supplement

SCOTTISH HERBAL SUPPLIES ™☺❶⦸
Clays; **Herbal Alcoholic Tinctures**; **Vegetable/Herbal Ointments**

THE HUMANE RESEARCH TRUST ☺⦸
Assisi & Berwitz Homeopathic Remedy Creams: Anal Itching, Arnica, Athletes Foot, Cuts & Sores, Dry Skin Cream, Healing, Itching Eczema, Wart

THE ORGANIC HERB TRADING COMPANY ⦸☼
Organic Medicinal Tinctures: All except Propolis

TREE-HARVEST ⦸
Arboretum Space Spray; Gemmotherapy; Spagyric; Tree Companion; *Pulse Points:* Elderberry, Lavender, Linden, Mate, Pau d'Arco, Rose, Willow; *Tree Essences:* All

WELEDA ⦸ ✂1985
Aconitum/Bryonia; Archangelica Comp; Aurum/Prunus; Aurum/Valeriana Co; Avena Sativa Comp; Belladonna/Chamomile;

Chamomile/Nicotiana; Conchae 5% Comp; Medicinal Gargle; Melissa Comp; Ol Rhinale; Onopordon Comp A; Onopordon Comp B; Rhinodoron Nasal Spray; Silicea Comp; WCS Dusting Powder; *Drops:* Chamomilla 3X, Choleodoron, Cough, Feverfew 6X, Menodoron, Rheumad. 102A; *Elixir:* Birch, Blackthorn, Cough; *Granules:* Chamomila 3X; *Homeopathic/Herbal Remedies:* All (Request Vegan Version); *Lotions:* Calendula, Combudoron, Larch Resin, Skin Tone; *Massage Balms:* Arnica, Calendula; *Ointments:* Antimony prp

WELLFOODS LTD ⦸✓

Linda Kearns Cake - The wholly natural approach to relieving the symptoms of the menopause: Cherry, Cranberry, Date & Walnut, Original Raisin, Tropical

XYNERGY HEALTH PRODUCTS ⦸✓

Aloe 99: Gel; *Aztec Nopal & Neem:* Neem Capsules, Neem Oil, Neem Salve, Neem Tincture, Nopal Capsules; *Kiwiherb:* Black Cohosh & Sage, Calendula Ointment, Comfrey Ointment, Echinacea Root Extrcat, Echinacea Thyme & Liquorice, Ginger & Kawakawa, Mashmallow & Mullein, Meadowsweet Aniseed, Milk Thistle & Dandelion, Valerian Root Extract; *Lifestream:* Biogenic Aloe Vera Gel + Vit E, Biogenic Aloe Vera Mist

VITAMINS & MINERALS

BIO-HEALTH LTD ☺⦸✓

Buffered C Crystals; *V-caps:* B Complex (High Potency & Yeast-free), Bio-Caps Multivitamin & Mineral, Bio-E, Extra Calcium, Extra Iron, Extra Magnesium, Extra Mineral Complex, Extra Selenium, Extra Zinc, Super Kelp & Vitamins, Vitamin C - 500mg (Buffered), Vitamin C - 500mg w Bioflavonoids

BRUNEL HEALTHCARE ⦸✓ 1992

Vertese Capsules: High Strength Natural Vitamin E

CYTOPLAN ™

Cyto Gold 60/120

DEVA NUTRITION ™☺✓

Vegan Multivitamin

HIGHER NATURE PLC ™⦸✓

Calcium Ascorbate; **Chromium Polynicotinate 200mcg**; **Folic Acid 400mcg**; **High Stability Colloidal Silver**; **Multi without Iron**; **Sea Calcium**; **Selenium 200mcg**; **Ultra C Plus**; **Vitamin B12 200mcg**; **Zinc**; *True Food®:* **B Complex**, **B6**, **C**, **Calcium & Magnesium**, **Easy Iron**, **Magnesium**, **Natural Vitamin E**, **Selenium**, **Zinc**

HOLLAND AND BARRETT RETAIL LTD

Absorbable Magnesium; Amino Acid Chelated Manganese; B - 50 (Vitamin B Complex); Beta-Carotene Capsules; C

Liquid; C w Bioflavonoids (plus Rose Hips); Chelated Zinc Lozenge w Zinc Gluconate; L-Carnitine; L-Tyrosine; *Chewable Tablets:* Acerola C w Bioflavonoids, C - 500mg w Rose Hips; *Oils:* E - Oil Natural; *Powder:* Pure Vitamin C; *Tablets:* B - 100 (Vitamin B Complex), B-1 100mg, B-12, B-2 100mg, B-6, B-Complex & B-12, Biotin, Boldo, C - w Rose Hips, C-500mg Buffered, C-Complex w Bioflavonoids, Calcium Magnesium Boron, Caprylic Acid 350mg, Chelated Boron 3mg, Chelated Copper, Chelated Zinc 15mg w Copper, Chromium Picolinate, Complete B, Effervescent Vitamin C, Folic Acid, GTF Chromium 200mcg, High Strength Zinc 15mg, Iron 15mg, L-Glutamine 500mg, Magnesium 250mg, Niacin B-3, Paba, Pantothenic Acid, Potassium Chelated 99mg, Rutin, Selenium, Selenium Seven Day Souper Cabbage Diet, Selenomethionine 200mcg, Silica Complex, Vitamins for the Hair, Zinc Chelated, Zinc Gluconate, Zinc Picolinate 25mg

JARROW FORMULAS INC.
Basic Mineral & Bone Formulas: BioSil (All except Capsules), CalMag Citrates 2:1, Magnesium Optimizer, Vegetarian Bone-Up; *Basic Vitamins:* Buffered TLC (Vitamin C), Calcium Ascorbate Buffered C, Detox C, Inositol Powder, IP6 Powder, Methylcobalamin B12 Lozenges, Vitamin C Powder; *Multi Vit/Mineral Paks/Women's:* Multi E-Z Powder, Women's Multi

KUDOS VITAMINS AND HERBALS LTD ⃠ ✓
Antioxidant Nutrient Formula; Calcium/Magnesium/Zinc Balanced Formulation; Chromium GTF; Iron (Amino Acid Chelate) 30mg; Magnesium (200mg) plus Potassium (100mg); Multi-Mineral Complex; Natural Source Beta Carotene; Natural Vitamin E 200iu/400iu (dry); Prenatal Nutrient Formula; Q100 Multi-Vitamin & Mineral; Q200 Multi-Vitamin & Mineral w Coenzyme Q10; Vitamin B Complex 50mg; Vitamin B12 & Folic Acid; Vitamin B6 & Zinc; Vitamin C 500mg; Vitamin C plus Bioflavonoids; Zinc 20mg (Citrate); Zinc 50mg (Gluconate)

LIFEPLAN PRODUCTS LTD ™⃠ ✓
Boron Triple Source Trace Mineral; **Buffered Vitamin C w Rosehip & Acerola & Citrus Bioflavonoids - 500mg**; **Calcium & Magnesium - 500mg Powdered Dolomite**; **Calcium & Magnesium - 800mg Powdered Dolomite**; **Chewable Vitamin C - 100mg**; **Chewable Vitamin C High Strength w Acerola & Bioflavonoids - 500mg**; **High Strength Vitamin B6 - 100mg**; **Multi Minerals**; **Triple Source Magnesium**; **Vitamin B12 - 1000mcg**; **Vitamin B12 - 25mcg**; **Vitamin B6 - 50mg**; **Vitamin C & Zinc**; **Zinc - 10mg**

LIVING EARTH EUROPE ™
Major Mineral Mix + Trace Minerals; **Natures Body High Multi Vitamin**

Mineral & Amino Acid Powder; **Water Soluble Calcium w Magnesium**

MATTHEW CLARK PLC ⊘
Sanatogen: Original, w Iron

NATURE'S AID LTD ⊘ ✓
B & C; Calcium; Chromium Picolinate; Folic Acid; Magnesium & Boron; Vit B Complex; Vit B6 50 + 100mg; Zinc Gluconate; Zinc Picolinate; *Vit C:* 200mg, 500mg, 500mg Sugar Free, Low Acid, Time Release

NATURE'S OWN LTD ™
Euro Gold 30/90

NDS HEALTHCARE ⊘ ✓
Antioxidant Plus; Antioxidant w Trace Minerals; B-Complex Plus; Calcium; Essential Fatty Acids; G.T.F. Chromium Plus; Iron Plus; Magnesium Plus; Probiotic; Selenium; Vitamin C; Vitamin E; Zinc Plus; Zinc w Vitamin C

POWER HEALTH PRODUCTS ⊘ ✓
Mineral Supplements: Calcium 400mg, Hi Zinc 2mg Elemental, Iron - Amino Acid Chelate 14mg, MSM 1000mg, Oral Zinc 25mg (3.5mg Elemental), Potassium 200mg + Vitamin C 50mg, Selenium 100mcg & Zinc 2mg, Xtra Zinc 15mg Elemental; *Multivitamin & Mineral Supplements:* Multimineral & Zinc; *Vitamin Supplements:* B Complex 100% RDA, B12 500mcg, B6 100mg, Calcium Pangamate (B15) 50mg, Calcium Pantothenate (Vitamin B5) 500mg, Ester C® 500mg, Folic Acid 400mcg, Vitamin C 1000mg w Citrus Bioflavonoids, Vitamin C 500mg Orange w Betacarotene Chewable, Vitamin C Powder (Drink Mix)

PRINCIPLE HEALTHCARE ™ ✪
Calcium 400mg/Vitamin D2 2.5mcg Blackcurrant Tablets; **Magnesium 150mg Tablets**; **Synthetic Vitamin E 200iu VegaGels TM**; **Synthetic Vitamin E 400iu VegaGels TM**; **Vitamin B12 100mcg Tablets**; **Vitamin C 500mg Chewable Tablets**; **Zinc 15mg Tablets**

QUEST VITAMINS ⊘ ✓
Bio C Complex (Vitamin C & Bioflavinoids); Buffered C; Cal-Mag Plus; Chewable Vitamin C; Energy Nutrient Complex; Folic Acid w B Vitamins; Heart Nutrient Complex; Mega B-100 Timed Release; Mega B-50; Multi B Complex; Multiminerals; Pre-Natal Folic Acid; Super Mega B + C; Super Once A Day Vegan (Multi Vitamin & Minerals); Synergistic Iron; Synergistic Magnesium; Synergistic Selenium; Synergistic Zinc; Vitamin B12 500mcg; Vitamin B6 50mg; Vitamin C 1000mg Timed Release; Vitamin C 500mg

RHEMA UK LTD ❶ ⊘ ✓ ✂
Alpha Guard V-caps

SAVANT DISTRIBUTION LTD ™ ❶ ⊘ ✓
Ferrogreen Iron

SEVEN SEAS ™⊘

One-a-Day Multivitamins plus Minerals for Vegetarians & Vegans

SOLGAR VITAMINS LTD ⊘

B1 500mg; B6 50mg; Choline; Choline/Inositol; Dry Vitamin A Tablets; Folacin (Folic Acid); Inositol; Kelp Tablets; Megasorb B12 Nuggets 5000mcg; Niacin; Niacinamide; No-Flush Niacin; Oceanic Silica; P-5-P; PABA; Pantothenic Acid; Selenium; Vitamin K 100mcg Tablets; *Amino Acids:* All; *Antioxidants:* All except Pycnogenol 30mg; *B12:* 1000mcg, 100mcg; *Calcium:* Chelated, Chewable Wafers, Magnesium; *Calcium Magnesium:* Boron, Chelated 1:1, Citrate, Zinc; *Chelated:* Copper, Manganese, Molybdenum, Solamins; *Chromium:* Picolinate 100mcg, Picolinate 500mcg, Polynicotinate; *Fibre Products:* All; *Iron:* Chelated, Gentle; *Magnesium:* Chelated, Chelated w Calcium 2:1, Citrate, w B6; *Potassium:* Amino Acid Complex, Gluconate, Magnesium Aspartate; *Vitamin B Complexes:* All; *Vitamin C:* All; *Vitamin E:* 165mg (200iu), 330mg (400iu), 495mg (600iu), 83mg (100iu), Liquid, w Selenium; *Zinc:* 50mg, Chelated, Flavo, Picolinate

SOLO NUTRITION LTD ❶⊘

Advanced Vitamin B Complex; ZincFifty

VEGA NUTRITIONALS ™⊘

Magnesium Citrate; **Natural Vitamin E 400iu 335mg dry**; **Vitamin B & C Complex**; **Vitamin B Complex**; **Vitamin B1 100mg (Thiamine)**; **Vitamin B12 1000mcg**; **Vitamin B2 100mg (Riboflavin)**; **Vitamin B3 No Flush (Nicotinamide)**; **Vitamin B5 200mg (Calcium Pantothenate)**; **Vitamin B6 plus p-5-p 100mg**; **Vitamin B6 plus p-5-p 50mg**; **Vitamin C 1000mg**; **Vitamin C 1000mg SR**; **Vitamin C 1500mg**; **Vitamin C 500mg plus Bioflavinoids**; **Vitamin E 200iu 134mg dry plus Selenium Yeast Free**; **Zinc C Formula**; **Zinc Citrate 50mg**; **ZM3 Multivitamin & Minerals**; **ZMM High Potency Multi Mineral Complex**

XYNERGY HEALTH PRODUCTS ⊘

Synergy Company: Pure Radiance C

NOTES

■ **Alternatives** including herbalists, homoeopaths (but see **homoeopathy**, below), acupuncturists and remedies available from health/wholefood shops and chemists, may be useful in place of animal-tested synthetic drugs.

■ **Beta-carotene and vitamin D2:** see FOOD NOTES, page 106.

■ **Capsules** are often made from gelatine, but Vegicaps™ are an increasingly popular animal-free alternative.

■ **Contraceptives** may have been tested on animals or contain animal-derived ingredients:

■ **Condoms** are usually made from latex, in which case casein (a milk protein) will usually have been used as a processing aid. Condomi (available from The Vegan Society) is the only known animal-free brand in the UK.

■ **Oral contraceptives** may contain lactose (milk sugar) and / or magnesium stearate (possibly animal-derived).

■ **Drugs** may or may not contain animal-derived ingredients, but will have been tested on animals at some stage in production.

■ **Homoeopathic remedies** are derived from plant, mineral or animal substances. Tablets usually contain lactose, although sucrose may be used instead. There are many other animal-derived ingredients that are used in homeopathic products, including snake venom, bee venom and bee pollen. Many homeopaths, however, have a good working knowledge of veganism and should, where possible, be able to help locate animal-free alternatives.

■ **Prescriptions:** In order for a medicinal product to be allowed onto the UK market, it must have marketing authorisation, also known as a product licence. However, doctors can lawfully prescribe unlicensed drugs. Theoretically, this means that, providing an animal-free product is available, a GP can prescribe it. However, doing so increases the doctor's personal liability, should anything go wrong; many doctors are, therefore, reluctant to prescribe unlicensed alternatives.

VEGAN

BABY, INFANT & CHILDCARE

FOOD & DRINK

BICKIEPEGS LTD ☺⊘
Teething Biscuits for Babies

COW & GATE
Finger Foods: Organic Pure Baby Rice Cakes, Truly Fruit Bar - Apple, Truly Fruit Bar - Plum; *Jar Meals - Desserts from 4 months:* Apple & Peach, Apple & Pear; *Jar Meals - Desserts from 7 Months:* Apple Crumble w Strawberries, Apple Mango & Banana, Mixed Fruit; *Jar Meals - First Tastes from 4 months:* Apple Purée, Carrot Purée; *Jar Meals - Main Courses from 4 months:* Garden Vegetables, Vegetable Casserole; *Organic Jar Meals - Breakfasts from 4 months:* Apple & Peach; *Organic Jar Meals - Breakfasts from 7 months:* Apple & Cherry Muesli, Fruity Porridge; *Organic Jar Meals - Desserts from 4 months:* Banana & Apricot Dessert, Dutch Apple Pudding, Mango & Passionfruit Purée; *Organic Jar Meals - Desserts from 7 months:* Apple Banana & Peach Melba, Banana & Pear Compote, Summer Fruit Compote; *Organic Jar Meals - Main Courses from 4 months:* Butternut Squash Purée, Lentil & Vegetable Bake; *Organic Packet Meals:* Pure Baby Rice; *Organic Packet Meals - Breakfasts from 4 months:* Apple & Banana Muesli, Red Berry Compote; *Packet Meals:* Pure Baby Rice; *Packet Meals - Breakfasts from 4 months:* Sunshine Banana; *Packet Meals - Desserts from 4 months:* Apple & Banana Pudding, Summer Fruit Salad; *Packet Meals - First Tastes from 4 months:* Apple & Strawberry, Potato & Cauliflower

EMPIRE FOODBROKERS LTD ⊘
Beech-Nut Baby Food

FARLEY'S ™⊘
Soya Infant Formula 450g/900g

HIPP ORGANIC BABY FOODS ⊘
Stage 1 From 4 Months - Breakfasts: Apple & Mixed Cereal; *Stage 1 From 4 Months - Desserts:* Apple & Banana Purée, Apple & Blueberry Dessert, Apple & Grape Dessert, Apple & Pear Pudding, Apricot & Apple CompÙte, Banana & Peach Dessert, Banana w Rice Cereal, Fruit Pots Apple Banana & Peach, Fruit Pots Apple & Pear, Peach Dessert, Summer Fruit Dessert, William Christ Pears; *Stage 1 From 4 Months - Dried Varieties:* Apple/Orange/Banana, Baby Rice, Banana Porridge, Mashed Potato/Rosemary; *Stage 1 From 4 Months - Juices & Drinks:* Apple & Grape Juice, Apple Juice & Mineral Water, Apple Pineapple & Banana Juice, Fennel Drink, Mixed Fruit Juice, Mixed Fruit Juice w Mineral Water; *Stage 1 From 4 Months - Vegetables:* Carrots & Sweetcorn, Mixed Vegetables, Pumpkin w Rice, Tender Carrots & Potatoes; *Stage 2 From 7 Months - Desserts:* Tropical Fruit Salad

HOLLE BABY FOODS ⦸ ✓
Baby Rice Porridge; Millet Porridge; Oat Flake Porridge; Semolina Porridge; Spelt Porridge

PETER RABBIT ORGANICS ⦸
All

TRUUULY SCRUMPTIOUS ORGANIC BABY FOOD LTD. ☼
Medium Pots - Sweet (6+ months): Apple & Mango, Apple Pear & Kiwi, Pear Banana & Apricot; *Small Pots - Savoury (4+ months):* Butternut Squash, Carrot Parsnip & Swede, Potato Courgette & Pea, Sweet Potato; *Small Pots - Sweet (4+ months):* Apple Peach & Banana, Apple & Pear; *Small Pots - Sweet (5+ months):* Apple & Apricot

FOOTWEAR & CLOTHING

ANIMAL AID ☺❶⦸✓ ✂1976
Children's Outdoor Fleece Jackets

GREEN SHOES ⦸✓
The Children's Collection: Bar Sandal, Bridge Sandal, Buckle Boot, Dart Shoe, Ivy Boot, Lace Up Boot, T-Bar Sandal

VEGANSTORE.CO.UK ™☺⦸❶✓
No Bull: Cortina Children's Boot

HEALTH CARE

ABSOLUTELY PURE ™⦸✓✂
Caribbean Blue: **Baby Sun Shield**

BIO-HEALTH LTD ☺⦸✓
Junior Bio-Caps Multivitamin & Mineral

BIOFORCE
Child Essence; Echinacea Junior

CYTOPLAN ™
Multi-Formulations: **Children's Multex, Nourish Drink Children's Formula**

HIGHER NATURE PLC ™⦸✓
Omega Nutrition Organic: **Essential Balance Junior**

HOLLAND AND BARRETT RETAIL LTD
Cough Syrup: Junior; *Liquid Extract:* Echinacea for Juniors, Echinacea Golden Seal Root for Juniors

NATURE'S OWN LTD ™
Multi-Formulations: **Children's Multivitamin & Mineral**

NEAL'S YARD REMEDIES ⦸✓
Tea Blend: Children's Cooling

TOM'S OF MAINE ⦸✓✂
Natural Children's Nasal Decongestant: Daytime Formula, Night-Time Formula

XYNERGY HEALTH PRODUCTS ⦸✓
Kiwiherb: Childrens Chamomile,

Childrens Echinacea; *Sweet Wheat - Freeze Dried Wheatgrass Juice:* Sweet Kid

NAPPIES

BIO-D CO. LTD.™☺⃠ ✂1983
Nappy Fresh

GREEN DOT GUIDES ⃠
Eco Disposable Nappies; Organic Washable Nappy System; Waterproof Overpants

TOILETRIES ETC

ABSOLUTELY PURE ™⃠ ✂
Earthbound Organics: **Baby's Soap**; *Pure Essentials - Oils:* **Baby Massage**, **Cradle Cap**

AMPHORA AROMATICS LTD ⃠ ✂1998
Goodnight Sleeptight Massage Oil; *Bubble Bath:* Goodnight Sleeptight, Happy Hopper, Honey Bear's Treat

ARTEL ALLERGY PRODUCTS
Mums & Baby: Baby Wash, Lavender Oatmeal Baby Soap, Tropical Spice Massage Oil

BURT'S BEES ⃠
Baby Bee: Apricot Baby Oil; *Natural Remedies:* Doctor Burt's Toothpaste - Children's

CAPITELLI OILS ™☺ ⃠
Mother & Baby Oils: **Dolci Bambini (1-6 Months)**, **Dolci Bambini (6 Months +)**

DR HADWEN TRUST ☺❶⃠
Baby Cream; Baby Soft Bubble Bath; Gentle Baby Lotion; Mandarin & Lavender Hair & Body Wash; Mandarin & Vanilla Body Lotion; Mandarin & Vanilla Bubble Bath

ESSENTIALLY YOURS LTD ™⃠
My Baby: **Baby Lotion**, **Bubble Bath**, **Hair & Body Shampoo**, **LYB Body Lotion**, **Massage Oil**, **Nappy Cream**

GREEN DOT GUIDES ⃠
Baby Wipes

GREEN PEOPLE CO. ™⃠
Baby Lotion; **Baby Wash**; *Organic Babies:* **Baby Wash - Chamomile**; *Organic Children:* **Bath & Shower Gel**, **Conditioner**, **Shampoo**, **Spearmint & Aloe Vera Toothpaste**, **Toothpaste - Mandarin**, **Top to Toe Lotion**

KISS MY FACE ⃠ ✂
Kiss Kids: Grape Jelli Bubblewash

KOBASHI ™☺⃠ ✂
Luxury Lotions: **Baby Lotion**

LAVERA ™
basis sensitiv: **Baby & Children Sun Screen SPF 25**

MALIBU HEALTH PRODUCTS LTD ⃠
High Protection Sun Lotion: SPF30

Disappearing Coloured Spray for Kids, SPF30 Spray for Kids

MEADOWSWEET LTD ™☺⦸✓
Babycare Range: **Baby Cream, Baby Lotion, Baby Soft Bubble Bath**

NAPIERS HERBAL HEALTH CENTRE ✓
Children's Oil Blend; *Cream:* Infant Starflower; *Skin Creams:* Calendula, Infant Starflower

NATRACARE ☺❶⦸✓
Baby: Bathe - 78% Organic, Lotion - 70% Organic, Organic Massage Oil - 100% Organic, Shampoo - 78% Organic

NATURAL ORGANICS ™
Baby

NATURAL WOMAN ⦸✓
Earth Friendly Baby: Chamomile Shampoo & Bodywash, Lavender Cleansing Bar

NATURALLY GIFTED ™
Lavender Baby Soap

NEAL'S YARD REMEDIES ⦸✓
Baby Massage Oil

PURPLE FLAME AROMATHERAPY ⦸✓
Concentrated Oil Blends: Comfort Kidz

SEVEN WIVES NATURAL BODYCARE ™⦸✓
Baby Cleanser; Baby Cream; **Mother & Baby Cleansing Bar**

TISSERAND AROMATHERAPY PRODUCTS ™
Baby Bliss: **Gentle Cleansing Bar, Gently Foaming Bath Wash, Nursery Oil For Vaporisation, Soft Soothing Lotion, Soft Touch Massage Oil**

TOM'S OF MAINE ⦸✓✂
Natural Honeysuckle Baby Shampoo; Natural Soap for Children; *Natural Fluoride Toothpaste for Children:* Outrageous Orange, Silly Strawberry

URTEKRAM ⦸✓✂
Children's Shampoo; Children's Soap; *Body Lotion:* Children; *Children's:* Body Lotion, Conditioner; *Conditioner:* Children; *Pure Balance:* Shampoo - Children

WELEDA ⦸✓✂1985
Children's Tooth Gel; *Calendula Baby Range:* Oil

NOTES

- **Animal-free children's shoes** can be difficult to find. Veganstore.co.uk sells a small range, and Green Shoes can supply made-to-order children's shoes. Some high street chains may be willing to provide information about the materials used in their shoes. See the FOOTWEAR & CLOTHING NOTES (page 222) for more general information on finding vegan shoes.

- **Baby wipes** often contain lanolin, which is derived from wool.

- **Farley's Soya Infant Formula** is the only known animal-free complete infant formula available in the UK.

- **Information on real nappies** can be obtained from the Women's Environmental Network, which runs Real Nappy Week, see *www.wen.org.uk/rnw* for details or call the Real Nappy Helpline on 0845 8500606.

- **The Vegan Society** produces a range of information on raising vegan children, including *Raising your Vegan Infant - With Confidence* by State Registered Dietitian, Sandra Hood – visit *www.vegansociety.com/shop* or call 01424 427 393 for details. See 'SUGGESTED READING' (page 315) for further resources.

FOOTWEAR & CLOTHING

BELTS, WALLETS, BAGS ETC

ANIMAL AID ☺❶⊘✓✂1976
Briefcase; Hemp Wallets; Polar Fleece Boston Tea Hat; *Buckle Belt:* Gold Plated, 'Old Gold', 'Silver', Solid Brass

CAROL NICHOLSON (SOLE TRADER) ™☺❶✓⊘
Cotton Shopping Bags

ETHICAL WARES ☺❶✓
Bags: Fair Trade Rainbow Shoulder Bag; *Belts:* Black Gold-Plated Buckle, Black Old Gold Buckle (Tarnished), Black Silver Half Buckle, Black Solid Brass Buckle, Black Solid Square Silver Buckle, Brown Old Gold Buckle (Tarnished), A, B, C, D, E

FREERANGERS ™☺✓
Accessories: **Alex Belt**, **Aragon Belt**, **Bow Bag**, **Conker II Rucksack**, **Credit Card Holder**, **Full Wallet**, **Galadriel Belt**, **Guitar Strap**, **Half Wallet**, **Lucy Bag**, **Molly Bag**, **Palm Pilot Case**, **Prairie Belt**, **Purse**, **Sporran**, **Strider Belt**, **Zoe Bag**

THE VEGAN SOCIETY ™☺❶✓
Cotton Shopping Bag

VEGANLINE ☺❶
30mm Macho Belt & Chrome Buckle; Cleat Belt; Hemp Canvas Wallets

VEGANSTORE.CO.UK ™☺⊘❶✓
Faux Leather Briefcase; Vegan Shopper Bag; *Accessories:* **Wallet**, **Watch Strap**; *Ecolution:* Hemp Bi Fold Wallet, Hemp Tri Fold Wallet; *No Bull Belts:* Business, Vegan Logo

VEGETARIAN SHOES ☺
Record Bag; Shoe Laces; Wallet; *Belts:* Jeans, Select, Solo, Suit, X Belt

VIVA! ☺❶⊘✓
Black Dress Belt; Black & White 'Truth Belt'; Brown Suit Belt; Drawstring Bag; Mono Strap Rucksack; Wallet; Web Belt w Vegan Buckle

CLOTHING

ANIMAL AID ☺❶⊘✓✂1976
Arctic Fleece Jacket; Hemp Socks; Open Hem Sweatshirt; Skinny Fit Micro Fleece Jacket; Zip Up Hooded Sweatshirt; *T-Shirts:* All

DR HADWEN TRUST ☺❶⊘✓
Faux Suede Jackets: Classic Fitted, Luxury; *Tees:* 'Fluffy' (Bunny), 'Haring Along' (Rabbit)

MARLO ❶✓
Cardigan; Jersey Cotton Trousers; Rib Vest; Vest; *3/4 Sleeve T-Shirt:* Slash Neck Fitted, V Neck 3/4 Sleeve; *Long Sleeve T-Shirt:* Breton, Fitted, Hooded, Man/Woman Loose Fit, Rib Fitted; *Short Sleeve T-Shirt:* Fitted, Man/Woman

Loose Fit, Rib Fitted; *Sweatshirt:* Sweatshirt, Weight Breton, Weight Hood, Weight Hooded Dress; *T-Shirt:* Scoop Neck

PEOPLE TREE LTD ⃠
Organic Cotton: Hats, Skirts, T-Shirts, Trousers, Underwear

ROGUE DEVELOPMENT ™☺⃠
Ballistic Cat Knots; **Cat Knots**; **Double Six**; **Rogue Six**; **T-Shirts**

THE VEGAN SOCIETY ™☺❶
Enamel Badge; *T-Shirt:* Adults' 'Go Vegan', Against Animal Tasting, Kids' 'Go Vegan', Vegan 4 the Animals, Vegan 4 the Planet

VEGANLINE ☺❶
Hemp T-Shirts; Leather-like Jackets; Waterproof Breathable Socks

VEGANSTORE.CO.UK ™☺⃠❶
Faux Leather Gloves; T-Shirts; Tofu Totty Shirt; Vegan Definition Shirt; **Vegan Definition T-Shirt**; *No Bull Jackets:* **Camden**, **Harley**, **London**, **Soho**

VEGETARIAN SHOES ☺
Cow T-Shirt; *Black Gloves:* Gents, Ladies; *Jackets:* Angel, Biker-style, Box, Cutie, Dean, Ladies Reefer, Skipper, Tina; *Jeans:* Black, Fake Leather

VIVA! ☺❶⃠
T-Shirts & Sweatshirts: All

FOOTWEAR - GENERAL

ANIMAL AID ☺❶⃠ ✂1976
Carol Boot; Chandler Boot; Court Shoe; Jasmin Shoe; Milano Boot; Out of Step Shoe; Palma Pump; Ranger Walking Boot; Scandinavian Boot; Sorrento Sandal; Tallulah Mule; Tibet Boot; Tie Shoe; Women's Laced Ankle Boot; Zip Up Boot; Zippy Boot; *Leisure Boots:* Buckland, Hartland, Trekking, Tyneham

BEYOND SKIN LTD ™☺
Gabi; **Jenny**; **Jo Jo**; **Lou Lou**; **Olivia**; **Phoebe**; **Suzy**

DR HADWEN TRUST ☺❶⃠
Court; Ember; Gibson; Jasmin; Onyx Mule; *Boots:* Buckland, Carol, Dealer, Derby, Desert, Hartland, Ranger, Trekking, Tyneham, Women's Zip Suedette; *Sandals:* Ebony; *Shoes:* Megan, Monk, Oxford, 'Suede' Gibson; *Slippers:* Men's & Ladies' Fleece & Faux Suede

EARTH FOOTWEAR ™
Vegan Casuals: **Aspen**, **Breeze**, **Breeze 2**, **Delight**, **Duet**, **Dune**, **Eden**, **Forest**, **Gidget**, **Intrigue**, **Jasmine**, **Jubilee**, **Kharma**, **Kharma 2**, **Magnetism 2**, **Melissa 2**, **Miami**, **Mirage**, **Navigator & Navigator 2**, **Newport**, **Nova**, **Oasis**, **Orion 2**, **Samea**, **Shirley**, **Solar**, **Tofu**, **Woodland**

ETHICAL WARES ☺❶
All That Jazz; Arizona (Black & Brown); Black Cat; Bobby Shoe; Buckland;

Buckle Boot; Captain Swing; Carol Boot; Chandler; Chelsea Boot; Chukka Boot; Closed Toe Sandal; Court Shoe; Creeper; Dealer; Dept X; Derby; Desert Boot; Ember; Gibson; Hans Blix; Hartland; Jasmin Shoe; Joe Shoe; Jungle Shoe; Jupiter; Laced Ankle Boot; Liberator; Megan Shoe; Milano; Mindy; Misty Boot; Monk; New Balance 1006; New Balance 753; New Balance 765; New Balance 834; Onyx Mule; Out of Step; Oxford; Oz Boot; Poor Jean; (Positively) No Comment; Ranger; Rebel Rebel; Respect; Safety Boot; Scandinavian; Sky Mule; Sky Strap; Sling Back Shoe; Spaff Flopps; Springer Sandal; 'Suede' Gibson; Susie Boot; T-Bar Shoe; Tibet; Tie Shoe; Tolerance; Tregaron; Trekking; Tyneham; U Tramp; Weald 2; Wild Cat; Zip Suedette Boot; Zippy

FREERANGERS ™☺

Ladies: **Alder Shoe**, **Ash Sandal**, **Beech Shoe**, **Birch Shoe**, **Clover Shoe**, **Drifter Shoe**, **Ebony Shoe**, **Fern Shoe**, **Fig Sandal**, **Heather Clog**, **Jess Boot**, **Laurel Shoe**, **Lily Shoe**, **Lucy Shoe**, **Meg Mule**, **Shell Mule**, **Snowflake Mule**; *Mens:* **Bracken Shoe**, **Crag Shoe**, **Dale Mule**, **Dene Mule**, **Drifter Shoe**, **Elm Sandal**, **Glen Boot**, **Heather Clog**, **Maple Shoe**, **Pine Shoe**

GREEN DOT GUIDES ⃠

Hemp Shoes: Men's Lace-up Ankle Boot, Men's Lace-up Classics, Women's Lace-up Ankle Boot

GREEN SHOES ⃠

The Boot Collection: Belstone, Brutus Calf, Brutus Knee High, Buckle, Dartmoor, Field, Pie Crust, Polly; *The Sandal Collection:* 2 Piece Toggle, Bridge, Clasp, Denbury, Eclipse Mule, Hope, Mule; *The Shoe Collection:* Bar Sandal, Dartmoor Shoe, Eclipse Lace, Eclipse Strap, Pump

GUAT SHOES

Men's Styles - Lorica: Derby, Desert Boot, Lace Up, Loafer, Men's Sandal, Short Boot, Stroller; *Women's Styles - Lorica:* Buckle Shoe, Button Boot, Calf Boot, Cross-Over Sandal, Desert Boot, High Bar, Ladies Loafer, Peep-Toe Sandal, Plaited Sandal, Short Boot, Slide, Slip-on, Sticky-Bar Sandal, Stroller, Stroller Boot, T-Bar Sandal, Women's Lace-up, Women's Sandal

NATURAL SHOE STORE

City Collection Woven Fabric Espadrille; *Birkenstock Vegan Sandals:* Arizona, Boston Clog, Milano; *Comfort:* Slipper Style Shoe; *Earth Shoes:* Solar; *Grand Step:* 1979043, 1979089, CP08 Hemp Hi-Top; *Komodo:* Hemp Boot, Thong Sandals w Grass Footbed & Tyre Sole; *Vegetarian Shoes:* 502, Ladies Loafer

PEOPLE TREE LTD ⃠

Sandals

ROGUE DEVELOPMENT ™☺⃠

Creeper Shoes; **Gimp Boots**; **Gimp Shoes**

VEGANLINE ☺❶
Denim Flip-Flop; Equity Sandal; Garmont Hikers w Waterproof Breathable Socks; Rigger; *Blizzard Boot:* Black, Black Velcro, Dark, Dark Velcro; *Bouncing:* Boot, Shoe; *Court Shoe:* Beige, Black, Blue, Dark Brown, Embroidered Strap, Gloss Black, Matt Black, Patch, White; *Crochet Open-Toe:* Gold, Grey; *Loafer:* Elastic Side, Patch; *Mesh Loafer:* Black Suede, Black Vinyl, Brown Suede, Grey Snake, Thick Sole; *Mule:* Black, Burgundy Snake, Grey Snake, Pink Snake, Sailor Girl; *Safety:* Boots, Shoes; *Sandal:* Braided, Dr Zeuss, Strap Diamond, Toe Post Folk; *Shoes:* Agatha Christie, Black Suede, Brown Suede, Sailor Girl, Sensible, Upper Class

VEGANSTORE.CO.UK ™☺⃠❶
Ecolution: Hemp Dress Shoe; *Faux Real:* 2121 Shoe, Carnaby Boot, Milano Boot, Palma Pump, Roma Boot, Skyline Clog, Skyline Slip, Sophisto Sandal, Sorrento Sandal, Stellar Sandal, Tallulah Mule; *No Bull:* Bella Loafer, **BFB Shoe**, Comfort Court, **Diva Boot**, **Double Soul Shoe**, **Executive Shoe**, Executive Shoe, Kitty Kat Boot, Leon Loafer, Madison Boot, **Men's Brogue**, **Oxford Shoe**, Parma Boot, Polar Boot, Rimini Shoe, Savage Hiking Boot, Seville Gibson, Starlet Boot, Trekky All Terrain, Twister Boot, **Urban Legend Shoe**, **Zip Up Boot**

VEGETARIAN SHOES ☺
Airseal Boots: 14-Eye w Steel Toe, 20-Eye w Steel Toe, Boulder, Chelsea, Engineers w Steel Toe, Para w Steel Toe, Range, Redstone; *Airseal Shoes:* 3-Eyelet, Bump w Steel Toe, Padded Collar, T-Bar Sandal; *Birkenstock Sandals:* Arizona, Boston Clog-style, Milano; *Boots:* Combat, Cyber Biker, Derby, Desert, Jodhpur, Logga, Site Boot w Steel Toe; *Everyday Shoes:* Canyon Sandal, Chunky Gibson, Chunky Monk, Creeper, Hemp Skate, Kalahari, Mariner, Wombat; *Men's Boots:* Alex, Mikey; *Men's Shoes:* Brogu, Broker, Casino, City, Dylan Slip-on, Johnny Loafer, Montana, Office, Oxford, Square-Toe Loafer; *Walking Boots:* Approach Shoe, Nevis Boot, Trail Boot, Veggie Trekker; *Women's Boots:* Emma, Hi, Jenny, Jo, Metro; *Women's Sandals:* Comfort, Daisy, Lucy; *Women's Shoes:* Black Pump, Judy, Kelly, Marrakesh Mule, Simple Loafer, Stephanie, Tab

FOOTWEAR - SPORTS

ANIMAL AID ☺❶⃠ ✂1976
Sonic Sneaker; Training Shoe 753

DR HADWEN TRUST ☺❶⃠
New Balance: 765, High Performance 1006

NATURAL SHOE STORE
Grand Step: CP11 (Hemp Sneaker); *Vegetarian Shoes:* 6+3 X Trainer

VEGANLINE ☺❶
Hiker: Mens, Womens; *Safety:* Trainer Look-alikes; *Trainer:* Abstract, Ararat Olive, Bullet, Kings Cross, Mesh, Rufus Blue Black, Rufus Olive, Swift

VEGANSTORE.CO.UK ™☺⃠❶✔
Faux Real: Shirlaine Sneaker; *No Bull:* Mesa Shoe, Pump Sneaker, San Diego Sneaker, Sonic Sneaker, Stripe Sneaker

VEGETARIAN SHOES ☺
Cheetah Trainers: Navy/Reflective, Red/Reflective, White/Green, White/Navy; *Everyday Shoes:* Street Sneaker

WATERPROOFERS, POLISHES & CLEANERS

ETHICAL WARES ☺❶✔
Nikwax: Cleaning Gel, Fabric & Leather, Waterproofing

REALLY WORKS ™☺⃠✔✂
White Shoe Trainer/Tennis/Golf Shoe Restorer

VEGANSTORE.CO.UK ™☺⃠❶✔
No Bull: Shoe Polish

VEGETARIAN SHOES ☺
Black Animal-Friendly Polish; Clear Animal-Friendly Dubbin; Insoles

NOTES

■ **Footwear:** Quality animal-free footwear is generally available only by mail order from specialist companies. Vegetarian Shoes has a shop in Brighton, which is worth a visit if you are nearby. Cheap non-leather styles are stocked by many high street retailers. It has become common practice to use synthetic adhesives, but it is difficult to obtain guarantees.

■ **Running and training shoes:** many sports footwear companies stock models made entirely of non-animal materials but commonly are unable to guarantee, or are unwilling to ascertain, that the adhesives used are non-animal. Be wary of the term 'synthetic leather'; it may well describe a non-leather material but it *may* also indicate leather that has been treated differently to 'normal' leather! 'Nubuck' is leather; chlorenol (otherwise known as 'Hydrolite' or 'Durabuck') is non-leather, animal-free and tends to be more expensive.

■ **Textiles:** Under The Textile Products (Indications of Fibre Content) Regulations 1986, the term 'textile fibres' may include wool from sheep or lamb; wool or hair from alpaca, llama, camel, cashmere goat, angora goat, angora rabbit, vicuna, yak, guanaco, beaver or otter; horse, goat or other animal hair — with or without an indication of the kind of animal; silk from the silkworm; protein obtained from natural protein substances regenerated and stabilised through the action of chemical agents.

HOME & OFFICE

AIR FRESHENERS

DR HADWEN TRUST ☺❶⊘✓
Pot Pourri (w Reviver Oil): Bouquet of Roses, Orange & Cinnamon

ESSENTIAL OIL COMPANY ☺⊘✓👁
Aroma-Fan: Portable 2 Speed Fan Diffuser; *Aroma-Stone:* Stone Vaporiser

FINEMOOD LTD ⊘✓
Fragrant Oils (Add to Pot Pourri): Camella, Cedarwood, Cottage Garden, Dewberry, Jasmine, Lavender, Mediterranean, Mexican Vanilla, Opium, Peachtree, Red Rose, Sicilian Lemon, Spiced Orange, White Musk, Wild Rose, Yuletide; *Pot-Pourri:* Lavender, Mexican Vanilla, Red Rose, Yuletide; *Room Fragrancers (Sprays):* Apple Orchard, Chinese Magnolia, Freesia, Lavender, Passion Flower, Peach Tree, Wild Rose

L'OCCITANE EN PROVENCE ✓👁
Linen Water: Lavender, Linden, Rose, Verbena; *Perfumed Sachet:* Amber, Candied Fruits, Winter Forest; *Room Spray:* Amber, Candied Fruits, Cinnamon Orange, Clementine, Eau des 4 Reines, Eau des Vanilliers, Green Tea, Lavender, Madagascan Vanilla, Magnolia, Orange Blossom, Orange Flower, Winter Forest; *Solid Perfume:* L'Oranger; *Solid Perfume Cubes:* Candied Fruit, Eau d'Azur, Eau des Vanilliers, Winter Forest

NATIONAL TRUST ENTERPRISES LTD ⊘✓✂1998
Room Spray: Lavender, Rose

NATURAL BY NATURE OILS ☺⊘✓👁✂1974
Natural Room & Shoe Fresheners: Calico Lavender, Calico Lavender & Clove, Calico Lemon Scented Gum, Calico Rose Geranium & Lavender, Check Lemon Scented Gum, Floral Lavender, Floral Rose Geranium & Lavender; *Vapourizing Oils:* Aromatic Woods, Breathe-Ease, Bug-a-Way, Calming Moods, Christmas Spice, Citrus Fresh, Exotic Moods, Fresh Fields, Hay-a-Way, Meditation, Mountain Breeze, Oriental Spice, Quiet Night, Refreshing, Revitalizing, Romantic Evening, Summer Bouquet

PURPLE FLAME AROMATHERAPY ⊘✓
Pure Resin Pearls: Benzoin, Frankincense, Myrrh

QUINESSENCE AROMATHERAPY ☺❶⊘✓👁
Mood Enhancers: Arabian Nights, Autumn Meadows, Celestial Dream, Elemental Forest, Fantasia, Forbidden Fruit, Illuminessence, Moonflower, Persian Rose, Purple Valley, Secret Garden, Tranquilla, Wild Passion

TREE-HARVEST ⊘✓
Rare Gums & Resins: All

WOODS OF WINDSOR ☺✓
Linen Spray: Lavender, True Rose; *Perfumed Drawer Liners:* Forget Me

Not, Lavender, Lily of the Valley, Mimosa, Orange Spice, True Rose; *Perfumed Drawer Sachet:* Lavender, Lily of the Valley, Mimosa, Orange Spice, True Rose; *Perfumed Wardrobe Sachet:* Lavender, Lily of the Valley, Mimosa, Orange Spice, True Rose; *Room Spray:* Forget Me Not, Lavender, Lily of the Valley, Mimosa, Orange Spice, True Rose; *Vaporising Oil:* Forget Me Not, Lavender, Lily of the Valley, Mimosa, Orange Spice, True Rose

BLEACHES

ASTONISH ☺ ✂
Bathroom Range: Active Bleach - Tablets

ECOVER ™⊘
Bleach

BRUSHES

ASTONISH ☺ ✂
Furniture Care Range: Dust Buster (+ Optional Extension Handle)

CANDLES & INCENSE

AMPHORA AROMATICS LTD ⊘ ✂1998
Essential Oil Candles; *Incense Sticks:* Cedarwood, Frankincense, Gardenia, Honeysuckle, Jasmin, Lavender, Lemon, Neroli, Patchouli, Rose, Sandalwood, Ylang Ylang

ESSENTIAL OIL COMPANY ☺⊘
Night Lights (Unscented); *Aroma-Sticks:* All; *'Lily Flame' Luxury Candles:* All

FINEMOOD LTD ⊘
Frank the Dog: Dog Tired, Don't Resign Relax, Goodnight Frank, Never Ever Again, Stiff as a Bone, Survive Revive Get Lucky, Tonights the Night

HIMALAYA UK LTD ☺ ✂
Encens d'Auroville

KOBASHI ™☺⊘ ✂
Misc: **Burner-Vapourisers**

L'OCCITANE EN PROVENCE
Incense Cones: Cinnamon Orange, Clementine, Green Tea; *Incense Leaves:* Verbena Harvest; *Incense Sticks:* Cinnamon Orange, Eau des 4 Reines, Eau des Vanilliers, Lavender Harvest

NEAL'S YARD REMEDIES ⊘
Night Lights (White); White China Burners; *Incense:* Tibetan

PERFUMERS GUILD LTD, THE ☺❶⊘
Scented Candles: Hyacinth & Bluebell

PRICE'S PATENT CANDLES LTD
Altar: All; *Citronella:* All; *Dinner:* All except Large Resin Venetian Holder, Small Resin Venetian Holder; *Fragrance:* All; *Fresh Air:* All; *Fun:* All except Resin Flower Holder on Stick, Resin Cone

Holder on Stick, Resin Triangular Holder on Stick, Resin Square Tealight Holder, Resin Round Tealight Holder; *Heritage:* All except Beeswax Dinner, Beeswax Pillar; *Household:* All; *Luxury:* All; *Provence:* All; *Special Occasions:* All; *Time:* All

PURPLE FLAME AROMATHERAPY ⊘
Aromatherapy Candles: All

SCENT BY NATURE ☺⊘ ✂1986
Incense & Resin: Incense Holders & Oil Burners, Pure Tree Resins

SHEARER CANDLES ⊘
Candles: All

SIMPLY SOAPS ™⊘❶ ✂
India; **Love**; **Mesopotamia**; **Om**

THE VEGAN SOCIETY ™☺❶
Candle

TISSERAND AROMATHERAPY PRODUCTS ™
Candles: **In Perpetuum**, **In Toto**

TREE-HARVEST ⊘
Pure Plant Wax Candles: Aromatherapy Pure Coconunt & Palm Oil w Essential Oils, Dinner Candles, Glasspot

WOODS OF WINDSOR ☺
Aroma Candles: Aromatherapy Lavender; *Incense Cones:* Aromatherapy Lavender, Lavender, Lily of the Valley, Orange Spice, True Rose; *Solid Incense Sticks:* Orange Spice

CARPET PRODUCTS

ASTONISH ☺ ✂
Floor & Carpet Range: Carpet & Upholstery Shampoo, Instant Carpet & Upholstery Shampoo, Machine Carpet Shampoo

DRI-PAK LTD ☺❶⊘ ✂1997
Elco: Carpet Shampoo

CLEANERS - GENERAL

ASTONISH ☺ ✂
Bathroom Range: Acrylic Cleaner, Bathroom Cleaner, Cream Cleaner - Orange Fresh, Cream Cleaner - Original, Cream Cleaner - w Bleach, Enamel Cleaner, Glass & Tile Cleaner, Shower Self Cleaner; *Germ Killers:* Anti Bacterial Cleanser, Mould & Mildew Remover; *Glass, Ceramic, Tile & Household Range:* Household Antibacterial Paste Cleaner, Orange Household Paste Cleaner, Window Cleaner; *Kitchen & Cookware Range:* Ceramic Hob Cleaner, Kitchen Cleaner, Oven & Cookware Cleaning Paste, Oxy Plus, Oxy Plus Gel, Stainless Steel Cleaner, Stainless Steel Cream Cleaner; *Special Cleaners:* Orange Power Multi-Surface, Silver Cleaner

BIO-D CO. LTD. ™☺⊘ ✂1983
Glass & Mirror Cleaner; **Multi-Surface Cleaner**

CELLANDE MIDLANDS ☺⊘
Glass & Plastic Cleaner for Computers Spectacles etc

DRI-PAK LTD ☺❶⊘ 1997
Liquid Soda Multipurpose Cleaner; *Aqua Softna:* Washing Machine Descaler, Water Softener Powder & Tablets, Water Treatment

ECOLINO ™⊘
All-Purpose Cleaner

ECOVER ™⊘
Cream Cleaner; **Heavy Duty Cleaner**; **Limescale Remover**; **Multi-Surface Cleaner**; **Natural Citrus Cleaner & Degreaser**; **Squirteco**

GREEN PEOPLE CO. ™⊘
Home Care: **Micro-Fibre Cleaning Cloth**, **Multi-Purpose Cleaner (Concentrated)**, **Organic Aroma Clean**

HERBS HANDS HEALING LTD ™⊘
Home & Kitchen Cleaner

HOMECARE PRODUCTS ☺⊘
Bar Keepers' Friend - Powerful Powder; Bath Brite - Bath & Sink Descaler; Copper Glo - Powder Copper Cleaner; Four Hob Hotplate Polish; Hob Brite - Ceramic Hob; Homecare Stainless Steel; Shiny Sinks - Cream

LIBERON WAXES LTD
Brass & Copper Cleaner; Cold Patination Pre-Treatment; Fullers Earth Cleaning Powder; Ring Remover

OSMO UK Ltd ❶⊘
Gard Clean Green Growth Remover; Liquid Wax Cleaner

REALLY WORKS ™☺⊘
Home & Office: De-Greaser Deodoriser, Super Concentrated Cleaner, Wild Apple Concentrated Cleaner

RUSTINS LTD
Stain Blocker - Seal that Stain

URTEKRAM ⊘
Uniren Multi Cleaner

CLEANERS - INDUSTRIAL

REALLY WORKS ™☺⊘
Cleaners: Graffiti Remover

DISHWATER PRODUCTS

ASTONISH ☺
Dishwashing Range: 2 in 1 Dishwasher Tablets, Limescale Appliance Remover, Rinse Aid, Super Concentrate Dishwasher Liquid

DRI-PAK LTD ☺❶⊘ 1997
Opal: Dishwasher Cleaner, Granular Salt, Rinse Aid; *Opal Automatic Dishwasher Detergents:* Liquid, Powder, Tablet

ECOLINO ™⊘
Rinse Aid

ECOVER ™⃠✓
Dishwasher Tablets; **Rinse Aid**

FAITH PRODUCTS LTD ❶⃠✓✂ 👁1978
Clear Spring Cleaning Products: Dishwasher Gel, Rinse Aid

URTEKRAM ⃠✓✂
Uniren Dishwashing

DISINFECTANTS

ASTONISH ☺✓✂
Germ Killers: Antiseptic Disinfectant, Germ Clear Disinfectant

CAURNIE SOAPERIE ☺⃠✓👁✂
DES: Disinfectant

FABRIC CONDITIONERS

BIO-D CO. LTD. ™☺⃠✓ ✂1983
Fabric Conditioner

ECOLINO ™⃠✓
Fabric Softener

ECOVER ™⃠✓
Fabric Conditioner

FLOOR PRODUCTS

ASTONISH ☺✓✂
Floor & Carpet Range: No Rinse Floor Cleaner, Non Slip Floor Polish, Wood Floor Cleaner

ECOVER ™⃠✓
Floor Soap

LIBERON WAXES LTD ✓
Floor: Cleaner, Protector, Sealer, Wax; *Floor Oil:* Maintenance, Natural; *Floor Varnish:* Natural Finish, Traditional; *Laminate Floor:* Cleaner, Sealer; *Stone Floor:* Cleaner, Sealer, Shine

OSMO UK Ltd ❶⃠✓
Wash & Care Floor Cleaner

RUSTINS LTD
Floor Oil; *Acrylic Floor Coating:* Gloss, Satin; *Clear Plastic Floor Coating:* Gloss, Satin; *Floor Dye - Quick Drying:* Blue Haze, Country Pine, English Oak, Green Haze, Rich Mahogany, White Haze; *Floor Shine:* Laminated, Wood Cork & Vinyl; *Polyurethane Floor Sealer:* Gloss, Satin; *Slip Resistant Floor Coating:* Satin

FURNITURE & OTHER POLISHES

ASTONISH ☺✓✂
Furniture Care Range: Orange Oil Furniture Polish; *Special Cleaners:* Brass & Copper Cleaner

BIO-D CO. LTD. ™☺⃠✓ ✂1983
General Purpose Polish

LIBERON WAXES LTD ✓
Polish: Brass & Copper, Silver; *Polishing Mitts & Cloth:* Brass, Silver

GENERAL

CALCH TY-MAWR LIME LTD
Natilin: Flax Fibre Insulation Batts & Rolls

CAROL NICHOLSON (SOLE TRADER) ™☺❶✓⊘
Handcrafted Greetings Cards; **Reusable Gift Wrap**

LABEL IT OR LOSE IT ™
Vegan Label

TISSERAND AROMATHERAPY PRODUCTS ™
Lavender Products: **Lavender Head Cooling Cushion**, **Organic Lavender Wheat Cushion**

PAINT BRUSHES - DIY

LIBERON WAXES LTD ✓
Foam Applicators

OSMO UK Ltd ❶⊘✓
Quality Brushes & Polishing Pad

RUSTINS LTD
Brush Cleaner: Wet Brushes; *Brush Restorer:* Hard Brushes

PAINT, VARNISHES, WOODSTAINS ETC

AGLAIA NATURAL PAINTS
Balsam Lacquer Thinner; Boric Salt Impregnation; Fermentation Alcohol; Linseed Oil Primer; Wood Protection Brown

ECOS PAINTS ☺⊘☼✓✂
Ecos Garden Spectrum Shed & Fence Treatment: All; *Exterior Woodstains:* All; *Interior Woodstain Varnishes:* All; *Odourless Solvent-Free Organic Paints:* All

GREEN BUILDING STORE ⊘
All except Thermafleece Insulation, Primasol & Ecosol Emulsions & Colourisers, Water Based Varnish, Primer for Water Based Varnish, Hard Floor Wax, Borax Timber Preservative, Boracol 20

GREEN PAINTS
All

LA TIENDA
Earth & Mineral Pigments: All

LIBERON WAXES LTD ✓
Burnishing Cream; Fine Wood Stripper; Finishing; Haematite; Honing Oil; Iron Paste; Knotting; Liquid Paraffin; Lubricating Wax; Pumice Powder; Rottenstone; Sanding Sealer; Van Dyck Crystals; Wax & Polish Remover; Wood

Bleacher; *3-Part Touch Up Pens:* All; *Antique Varnish:* All; *Concentrate Spirit Dyes:* All; *Concentrated Water Based Dyes:* All; *Designer Metallic Varnish:* All; *Earth Pigments:* All; *Exterior Oils:* Decking, Garden Furniture; *Fine Paste Wax (Black Bison):* All; *Grain Filler:* All; *Hardwearing Varnish:* All; *Interior Oils:* Boiled Linseed, Pure Tung, Raw Linseed, Teak; *Liquid Wax (Black Bison):* All; *Natural Finish Varnish:* All; *Palette Wood Dyes:* All; *Spirit Wood Dyes:* All; *Tint & Wax:* All; *Touch Up Pens:* All; *Wood Filler:* All; *Wood Stopping:* All

OSMO UK Ltd ❶⃠✓
Brush Cleaner & Thinner; Paint-Remover; Wood Filler; Wood Protector; Wood Reviver; *Exterior Country Colour:* All; *Exterior One Coat Only:* All; *For Exterior Woods:* Clear Oil Wood Finish, Fence & Garden Stain, Wood Oils, Wood Stain & Preservation, WR Base Coat; *Interior Hardwax Oil:* For Floors, Special Floor Finish, White Foundation; *Interior Wood Wax Finish:* Clear Extra Thin, Opaque, Transparent; *Opaque Gloss Exterior Wood Stain:* All

REALLY WORKS ™☺⃠✓✂
Home & Office: Adhesive Remover

RUSTINS LTD
Aluminium Paint; Bitumen Black; Blackboard Black Quick Dry; Bleach for Wood; Cellulose Thinners; Clear Metal Lacquer; Danish Oil; Methylated Spirits; Rust Remover; Stove Black; Strypit Paint & Varnish Stripper; Teak Oil; Turpentine Pure; Wallpaper Remover; Yacht Varnish; *Acrylic Varnish - Quick Dry:* Clear Gloss, Clear Matt, Clear Satin; *Coloured Varnish - Gloss or Satin Quick-Drying:* Antique Pine, Dark Oak, Mahogany, Oak, Pine, Rosewood, Teak, Walnut; *Exterior Varnish - Water Based, Quick Drying:* Clear Gloss, Satin; *Exterior Woodstain - Gloss or Satin (Water Based, Quick Drying):* Dark Oak, Light Oak, Mahogany, Medium Oak, Teak, Walnut; *Flexterior - Flexible Exterior Satin Finish:* Clear, Dark Oak, Mahogany, Teak; *Grainfiller:* Mahogany, Natural, Oak, Teak; *Linseed Oil:* Boiled, Raw; *Metal Primer:* Red Oxide; *Paint:* Black Gloss, Black Matt, Black Satin, Brick & Tile - Matt Red, Brilliant White Gloss, Gold, Step & Tile - Gloss Red; *Paint Driers:* Terebene; *Plastic Coasting & Hardener:* Ceramic Glaze; *Plastic Coating:* Hardener, Outfit, Thinners; *Plastic Coating & Hardener:* Black or White, Gloss, Matt; *Plastic Wood:* Mahogany, Natural, Teak, White; *Polyurethane Varnish:* Clear Gloss, Clear Matt, Clear Satin; *Polyurethane Varnish Stain:* Gloss, Satin; *Primer:* Aluminium Wood, Pink - Lead Free, White - Lead Free; *Primer & Undercoat:* White; *Radiator Enamel:* Satin, White Gloss; *Radiator Enamel - Quick Drying:* Satin, White Gloss; *Sealer:* MDF - Quick Drying; *Small Job Paint:* White Undercoat, White Wood Primer; *Small Job Paint - Gloss:* Black, Buckingham Green, Buttercup, Chocolate, Delphinium, Lilac, Mandarin; *Small Job Paint -Gloss:* Oxford Blue; *Small Job Paint - Gloss:* Poppy, White; *Timberlife -*

Water-Based Fence & Shed Treatment: Dark Oak, Light Oak, Mahogany, Medium Oak, Teak, Walnut; *Undercoat:* White - Lead Free; *Wood Dye:* Antique Pine, Brown Mahogany, Dark Oak, Dark Teak, Ebony, Light Oak, Light Teak, Medium Oak, Pine, Red Mahogany, Walnut; *Woodstopping:* Exterior White, Mahogany, Natural, Oak, Teak

TOILET PRODUCTS

ASTONISH ☺ ✂
Bathroom Range: Toilet Bowl Cleaner

BIO-D CO. LTD. ™☺⊘ ✂1983
Toilet Cleaner

ECOLINO ™⊘
Toilet Cleaner

ECOVER ™⊘
Toilet Cleaner

HERBS HANDS HEALING LTD ™⊘
Bathroom Deep Cleaner

URTEKRAM ⊘ ✂
Uniren Toilet Cleaner

WASHING POWDERS, STARCH ETC

ASTONISH ☺ ✂
Fabric & Laundry Range: 2 in 1 Liquid Laundry Detergent, Colour Boosters, Crease Clear Starch, Fabric Freshener, Large Lint Remover, Limescale Prevention, Oxy Plus, Stain Bar, Stain Remover, Whites Booster

BIO-D CO. LTD. ™☺⊘ ✂1983
Laundry Liquid; **Washing Powder**

DRI-PAK LTD ☺❶⊘ ✂1997
Soap Flakes; Soda Crystals; *Elco:* Laundry Powder, Soda Crystals - Sodium Carbonate Decahydrate

ECOLINO ™⊘
Auto-Laundry Liquid; **Washing Powder**; **Wool-Wash**

ECOVER ™⊘
Biological Washing Powder; **Biological Washing Tablets**; **Concentrated Washing Powder (Non Biological)**; **Liquid Clothes Wash**; **Stain Remover**; **Washing Tablets**; **Wool Wash**

FAITH PRODUCTS LTD ❶⊘ ✂1978
Clear Spring Cleaning Products: Laundry Liquid

NATIONAL TRUST ENTERPRISES LTD ⊘✂1998
Linen Spray

REALLY WORKS ™☺⊘ ✂
Oxygen Stain Remover; Pre Wash Dirt & Stain Remover

WASHING UP PRODUCTS

ASTONISH ☺ ✂

Dishwashing Range: Tea Coffee & Stain Remover; *Kitchen & Cookware Range:* Pan Rack & Fryer Tablets, Scouring Pads

BIO-D CO. LTD. ™☺⊘ ✂1983
Washing Up Liquid

CAROL NICHOLSON (SOLE TRADER) ™☺❶ ⊘**Cotton Dishcloth Kits; Ready Knitted Dishcloth**

CAURNIE SOAPERIE ☺⊘ ✂

Washup Liquid: Organic Lemongrass Washup Liquid

ECOLINO ™⊘
Dishwashing Powder; Washing-Up

ECOVER ™⊘
Washing-Up Liquid Lemon Scent w Aloe Vera

FAITH PRODUCTS LTD ❶⊘ ✂1978

Clear Spring Cleaning Products: Washing Up Liquid

POLYCO LTD ⊘

Skincare Velvet (PVC Household Gloves)

REALLY WORKS ™☺⊘ ✂

Sink & Drain Cleaner

NOTES

■ **Adhesives** may be processed from hide, bones, fish or dairy products such as casein. Non-animal adhesives are based on starch, cellulose, natural rubbers, or inorganic substances based on silicone. The trend is towards using cheaper, synthetic materials.

■ **Banknotes** are produced from cotton fibre and linen rag, without the use of gelatine.

■ **Beds and mattresses** generally contain synthetic materials, such as acrylic, viscose, polyester, polypropylene, nylon or acetate. However, wool may be used in some mattresses.

■ **Pillows and duvets** are often stuffed with feathers, but increasingly polyester is used instead.

■ **Ceramics, glass, pottery:** Bone china goods contain around 50% bone. Porcelain, *plain* sanitary items (toilets, cisterns, sinks, etc) and *plain* earthenware glazed mugs (the glazes used are inorganic pigments made from minerals) appear to be animal-free. However, if a motif is added, it may be fixed with animal-derived glues. Glass consists of silica (in the form of sand), sodium oxide, calcium oxide, magnesium oxide and aluminium oxide, and appears to be animal-free.

■ **Envelope adhesives** are usually animal-free. However, some of the adhesives used on self-seal envelopes contain casein.

■ **Fabric dyes** for home use are usually synthetic and are often tested on animals. 'Natural' dyes are more likely to contain animal substances, such as cochineal / carmine.

■ **Floor coverings** made from PVC may be manufactured using possibly animal-derived stearates as stabilisers and stearic acid as a lubricant during certain production processes.

■ **Furniture** may contain synthetic or plant-based fibres (e.g. nylon, acrylic, polyester or cotton) or animal-derived materials, including leather, suede, wool, animal hair (especially horse) or feathers. Adhesives are commonly synthetic.

■ **Incense sticks** may contain gelatine or other animal substance as a binder.

■ **Match heads** contain gelatine, which is used as a binder.

■ **Paint** may contain casein or shellac and the ingredients may have been animal-tested.

■ **Paper** is usually sized (enhances the resistance of paper to liquid penetration and provides surface strength, stiffness and a glaze to the finished sheet) with starch derived from maize, wheat, potatoes or rice, but gelatine is still used for high-grade paper products. Casein is sometimes used as a binder in high quality food board and art papers. Some very specialist grades may contain chitin / chitosan.

■ **Postage stamps:** the gum on British stamps is animal-free, consisting of polyvinyl alcohol (petroleum based) and dextrin (from starch).

■ **Rubber:** Natural rubber is made from latex (sap obtained from rubber trees) combined with other materials, including the following which could be animal-derived: carbon black (E153), glycerol (E422), salts of fatty acids (E470), stearic acid (E570), calcium stearate (E572). Synthetic rubbers are made from oil and a combination of chemicals.

■ **Rubber gloves** may involve the use of milk casein as a processing aid in the latex.

■ **Water filters** contain charcoal, usually vegetable-based.

ANIMAL CARE

FOOD & FOOD SUPPLEMENTS

DENES NATURAL PET CARE LTD ⊘🐈
Baked Biscuits: Fresh Breath, Low Calorie, Wholegrain

GREEN ARK ANIMAL NUTRITION ☺⊘🐈
Organic Dog Cereal Mix

GROOMERS LTD ⊘🐈
Evening Primrose Oil; Pure Garlic Oil

HIGHER NATURE PLC ™⊘🐈
Animal Aloe; **OmegaPet Kibble for Dogs**

SEAGREENS ™☺⊘☼
Mixed Granules: **Equine Granules**, **Pet Granules**

THE VEGAN SOCIETY ™☺❶🐈
Vegecat; Vegecat pH; Vegekit

VEGEPET ☺❶⊘🐈
Vegecat Kibble Mix; Vegedog

VIVA! ☺❶⊘🐈
Dog Chew Bones

YARRAH ORGANIC PET FOOD ❶⊘🐈
Chewing Bones; Duo Snacks Vegetarian; Vegetarian Dog Biscuits; Vegie Ears; *DOG Alu Cup:* Vegetarian w Vegetables; *Multi Dog Biscuits:* Natural, Seaweed & Yeast

HEALTH & CARE PRODUCTS

BIOFORCE
Animal Essences Range

GREEN ARK ANIMAL NUTRITION ☺⊘🐈
Green Food Supplement; Herbal Tonic; Herbie Wellbeing; Rhino; Slippery Elm Gruel; *Powders:* Pure Garlic, Pure Seaweed, Raspberry Leaf

GROOMERS LTD ⊘🐈
Evening Primrose Oil Coat Spray; Groom & Detangle Spray; Ridx Flea Spray; *Shampoos:* Aloe Jojoba, Banana & Mango, Evening Primrose Oil, Medicated w Tea Tree Oil, Pina Colada w Coconut Oils, Puppy, Ridasect Flea, Seaweed & Cucumber, Tangerine & Grapefruit

JARROW FORMULAS INC.
Pet Oil: For Cats, For Dogs

MASON'S PRODUCTS ☺⊘🐈 ✂1976
Dog Oil for Massaging (For Dogs Horses & Humans)

OPTIMA HEALTH & NUTRITION ⊘🐈 ✂1995
Thursday Plantation Tea Tree: Dog Shampoo

RED STAR NATURAL LIQUID SOAPS LTD ™☺⊘✔👁✂
Dog Shampoos - Hard Bar: Sexy Rexy; *Dog Shampoos - Liquid:* Minty Muttley

SCENT BY NATURE ☺⊘✔✂1986
Bioforce Flower Remedies: Flower Remedies for Animals

THE HUMANE RESEARCH TRUST ☺⊘✔
Tea Tree Coat Conditioner for Dogs & Cats; *Assisi Homeopathic Remedies for Pets:* Euphrasia Eye Drops, Five Flower Remedy, Sore Paws Ointment, Verbascum Ear Drops; *Natural Drops:* Ear, Eye; *Natural Grooming Lotions:* Cats, Dogs, Small Animals; *Shampoos:* Aromatic for Dogs, Cats, Tea Tree for Dogs & Cats, Tea Tree for Dogs & Cats, Tea Tree for Dogs & Cats

NOTES

■ The inclusion of an 'Animal Care' section should not be construed as indicating support for the pet industry or ownership of pet (companion) animals. Pets exist solely for human gain — in the case of the pet trade: financial; in the case of pet owners: pleasure — and their freedom is necessarily restricted. In the quest for the 'perfect' pet, breeds of dog, cat, bird and fish have, through genetic manipulation, been created with 'aesthetically-pleasing' deformities. Many animal-free shoppers find pet ownership incompatible with their animal rights philosophy and those who find themselves caring for animals often do so because tens of thousands of domestic animals are unwanted and would otherwise be destroyed.

For information on feeding your cat or dog on a vegan diet, see *www.vegansociety.com*

GARDEN & LEISURE

ARTS & CRAFTS

AGLAIA NATURAL PAINTS
Artists' Filler Paste

CRAYOLA ☺
All

DALER ROWNEY LTD
Artists' Brushes: Cryla, Dalon, Series 260 270 & 280; *Cryla :* All except Ivory Black, Raw Sienna, Burnt Sienna & Middle Grey; *Designer's Gouache:* All except Neutral Grey 2, Lamp Black, Cool Grey 1,2,3 & Warm Grey 1,2,3; *F.W. Artist Inks:* All; *Georgian Oil Colours:* All except Ivory Black, Prussian Green & Vandyke Brown (Hue); *Painting Surfaces & Equipment:* All except Saunders Waterford Paper, Canvas Panels & Rabbit Skin Size; *Pearlescent Liquid Acrylic Inks:* All; *Rowney Block Printing Colours (Water Based & Oil Based):* All; *System 3 Colours:* All except Raw Sienna

LIBERON WAXES LTD
Antiquing Fluid; Belt Cleaners; Carnauba Wax Flakes; Whiting; Woodturning Stick; *Gilding & Framing Products:* Fontenay Base, Gilt Varnish, Metal Leaf

WINSOR & NEWTON
Bockingford Water Colour Paper; *Acrylic & Oil Mediums & Varnishes:* All; *Artisan Water Mixable Oil Colour:* All except Ivory Black; *Artists' Acrylic Colour, Finity:* All except Ivory Black, Payne's Gray; *Artists' Oil Colour:* All except Blue Black, Carmine, Ivory Black; *Artists' Oilbar:* All except Ivory Black, Payne's Gray; *Artists' Pigment:* All except Ivory Black, Carmine; *Artists' Soft Pastels:* All; *Brushes:* All except Series 7, Series 16, Series 7 Miniature, Series 3A Designer's Sable, Cirrus Kolinsky Sable, Pure Squirrel Pointed Wash Brushes, Pony & Goat Hair Mop, Goat Hair Mop Brushes, Sceptre Gold II, Artists' Hog, Winton Hog, Azanta Hog; *Calligraphy Inks:* All; *Cotman Water Colour:* All except Viridian Hue, Raw Umber, Ivory Black; *Designers' Gouache:* All except Ivory Black, Raw Sienna, Winsor Green, Spectrum Yellow, Intense Blue, Sky Blue, Purple Lake, Prussian Blue, Linden Green, Grenadine, Flame Red, Burnt Umber, Bengal Rose, Primary Blue, Lamp Black, Spectrum Violet; *Galeria Flow Formula Acrylic Colour:* All except Ivory Black, Payne's Gray; *Griffin Alkyd Fast Drying Oil Colour:* All except Ivory Black; *Water Colour Mediums:* All except Ox Gall, Lifting Preparation; *Winton Oil Colour:* All except Ivory Black, Raw Umber

CLEANERS - OUTDOOR

ASTONISH ☺
Car Care Range: All Weather Screen Wash, Back to Black, Engine Degreaser, Fabric Fresh, Glass Clear, Interior

Cleaner, Mini Duster, Pre-Wash Car Treatment, Travel Mate Range, Vinyl Trim & Dashboard Cleaner, Wash & Wax, Watermate, Wheel Cleaner

HOMECARE PRODUCTS ☺⊘✔
BBQ Cleaner; Patio & Path Cleaner; Wooden Garden Furniture Cleaner

LIBERON WAXES LTD ✔
Garden Furniture Cleaner; Rust Remover

REALLY WORKS ™☺⊘✔✂
Block Paving Cleaner & Restorer

GARDENING & COMPOST PRODUCTS

GROWGANIC ☺⊘✔☼
Growganic Seaweed Plant Feed: Extract, Tablets

LIVING EARTH EUROPE ™
Easy Green Sprouter

ORANGE-MATE INC
Hydro-Garden Wholesale Supplies: All except Earth Juice, Oxy Magic

Seagreens ™☺⊘☼
Mixed Granules: **Agricultural Granules**, **Garden Granules**; *Mixed Wrack:* **Agricultural Puree**

GLUES, STICKY TAPE ETC

AGLAIA NATURAL PAINTS
Cork & Structural Adhesive

LIBERON WAXES LTD ✔
Super Wood Glue

VEGANSTORE.CO.UK ™☺⊘❶✔
Weldbond: Multi Purpose Glue

SMOKING PRODUCTS

ARKOPHARMA (UK) LTD ☺⊘✔
Nicotine Free Herbal Cigarettes: NTB Cigarettes, NTB Cigarettes Peppermint

SWEDISH MATCH
Catch: Licorice Portion Mini; *Catch White:* Licorice Portion Large; *CatchDry:* Licorice Portion Mini, Lychee Portion Mini; *Ettansnus:* Lös ; *Generalsnus:* Lös, Portion Large, Portion Maxi, Portion Mild Large, Portion Mini, White Portion Large; *Göteborgs Prima:* Fint; *Göteborgs Rapé:* Lös; *Grovsnus:* Lös, Portion Large, Portion Maxi, White Portion Large; *Probe:* Lös, Portion; *Rallarsnus:* Lös; *Röda Lacket:* Lös; *Tre Ankere:* Portion, Portion Mini

NOTES

■ **Musical instruments:** All modern guitar strings are made from metal or nylon. Guitar picks are now made of plastic. The heads of most modern percussion instruments are non-animal 'skin'. 'World percussion' instruments are usually still made with animal skins. All Remo heads are animal-free.

■ **Photographic film and papers** (the resulting photographs) contain gelatine. However, digital cameras are now as affordable as traditional cameras and many of the types of paper available for printing photographs are animal-free (check with individual manufacturers to be sure).

■ **Plasticine** contains tallow (see GLOSSARY OF ANIMAL SUBSTANCES page 295).

■ **Tennis balls** contain wool.

■ **Vegan-organic or stockfree gardening** is becoming more and more popular; see USEFUL ADDRESSES page 309 for details of the Vegan-Organic Network, or visit www.vegansociety.com for more information.

■ **Video cassette / audio tapes** appear to be animal-free.

SUPERMARKETS

FOODS

BREADS, ROLLS, PIZZA BASES ETC

Bilash Naan Bread: Garlic & Coriander, Plain; *Bueno:* Tortilla Wraps; *Crofters:* Fruit Loaf; *La Boulangerie:* Part Baked Baguettes, Part Baked Batons; *Meierbaer:* Sunflower Seed Bread, Whole Rye Bread; *Morning Fresh:* Crumpets, Farmhouse Rolls - White, Fruit Loaf; *Romano:* Ciabatta Rolls, Ciabatta Rolls w Herbs, Classic Ciabatta, Focaccia Spolverate; *Spinaca Bread:* Thick White Sliced; *Stone Mill:* Finger Rolls, Potato Farls, Splitz Rolls; *Village Bakery:* Baps - Brown, Burger Buns, Crusty Stick, Finger Rolls, Sesame Burger Buns, Small Loaf - White, Small Loaf - Wholemeal, White Bloomer, White Buns, White Floured Baps, White Poppy Seeded Rolls, Wholemeal Buns, Wholemeal Rolls Topped w Bran & Oats; *Village Green:* Bagels, Crusty White Loaf, Crusty Wholemeal Loaf, Farmhouse Loaf - White, Farmhouse Loaf - Wholemeal, Gold Soft White Rolls, Gold Soft Wholemeal Rolls, White Muffins

BREAKFAST FOODS

Balanced Lifestyle: Peach & Apricot Bites; *Harvest Morn:* Breakfast Biscuits, Cornflakes, Pecan & Maple Crunch, Strawberry Crunch, Wheat Bisks; *New Day:* Choco Hoops, Chocorice, Crisp Rice, Malt Wheaties

CAKES & CAKE MIXES

Holly Lane: Jammy Devil Mini Tarts

CONFECTIONERY & SWEET SNACKS

Complimints; *Fresh & Free Chewing Gum:* Active Cassis Sugar Free, White w Calcium

COOKING AIDS - SAVOURY

Quixo: Onion Gravy Granules

COOKING AIDS - SWEET

Vitality: Sweetener

CRACKERS, CRISPBREADS ETC

Bisca: Crisp Rolls; *Snack Rite:* Cream Crackers

DESSERTS

Dominion: Fruitino's

DIPS & DRESSINGS

3 Gourmet Dips; *Centanni Salad Dressing:* Basil, Garlic & Chilli, Oregano, Original; *Centanni Salad Vinaigrette:* Balsamic, Basil, Lemon, Tomato; *Worldwide:* Fat Free French Salad Dressing

'ICE CREAMS', SORBETS ETC

Crazy Crocodile: Assorted Finger Lollies, Freezepops; *Macey's:* Freeze Pops; *Milfina:* Freshly Squeezed Orange Juice Lollies

PICKLES, SAUCES, VINEGARS ETC

Bramwells: Apple Chutney w Real Ale, Beetroot Chutney, Caramelised Onion Chutney, Chunky Apple Sauce, Dill

Mustard Sauce, Flame Roast Tomato Chutney, Hot English Mustard, Mint Sauce, Wholegrain Mustard; *Centanni:* Red Balsamic Vinegar; *Centanni Balsamic Vinegar:* Red, White; *Colway:* Extra Hot Summer Ketchup, Squeezy Brown Sauce, Squeezy Tomato Ketchup; *Masterchef Packet Sauce Mix:* Lamb Hotpot, Shepherd's Pie; *Newland:* Sweet Pickle; *Worldwide:* BBQ Marinades, Chilli Mixed Gourmet Sauce, Garlic Mixed Gourmet Sauce, Lime Curry Marinade, Mexican Mixed Gourmet Sauce

SAVOURIES - CANNED/BOTTLED
Corale: Premium Baked Beans

SAVOURIES - CHILLED/FRESH
Green Olives Marinated w Provencale Herbs; *Antipasti:* Marinated Artichokes, Marinated Sundried Tomato Strips, Semi-Dried Marinated Tomatoes; *Balanced Lifestyle:* Pasta Meals - Rigatone/Spicy Vegetable

SAVOURIES - DRIED
Bilash: Vegetable Mexican Beanfeast; *Farmwood:* Sage & Onion Stuffing; *Jade Instant Noodles:* Curry; *Snack Noodle:* Beef & Tomato, Spicy Curry

SAVOURIES - FROZEN
Champion: Potato Wedges, Roasting Potatoes

SEASONAL FOODS
Grandessa: Christmas Jam - Brandy, Christmas Jam - Cognac, Christmas Jam - Rum; *Holly Lane:* Deep Filled Mince Pies, Hot Cross Buns, Super Luxury Xmas Pudding, Top Iced Mince Pies

SNACKS - SAVOURY
Balanced Lifestyle: Sweet Thai Flavour Crisps; *Damora Rice Crackers:* Original, Seaweed; *Kettle Cook - Balanced Lifestyle:* Salsa & Mesquete; *Snack Rite:* Snackers; *Snack Rite Crisps:* Ready Salted, Salt & Vinegar; *Snack Rite Snacks from Around the World:* Bhaji Bites, Tex Mex Wedges

SPREADS - SWEET
Citora Marmalade: Fine Cut Lime, Thick Cut Grapefruit; *Grandessa:* Strawberry High Fruit Spread; *Overture Spread:* Blackberry, Forest Fruit, Peach, Strawberry

DRINK

ALCOPOPS
Tamova Twist/Rum Burst: Rum & Lemon, Rum & Pineapple, Vodka & Orange; *Tamova Vodka Mixer:* Black Ice, Blueberry, Cranberry, Purpleberry

BEERS
Saracen Pills 4 x 440ml; *Brasserie:* Premium French Stubby; *Breda:* Royal Lager; *Sainte Etienne:* Belgian Premium Lager

CIDERS & PERRIES
Taurus: Dry Cider, White Cider

SOFT
Ambience Juice Drink: Red Grape, White Grape; *Ameristar:* Diet Cola, Premium Cola, Premium Diet Cola, Premium Diet Lemonade, Premium Lemonade; *Austins:* No. 1 Traditional Summer Drink; *Clear Sensation:* Red Apple Flavoured Still Water; *Crazy Crocodile:* Banana Milkshake Mix, Chocolate Milkshake Mix; *Del Rivo:* Ambient Orange Juice, Apple Juice, Apple & Raspberry Drink, Grapefruit Juice, Orange Juice, Pineapple Juice, Premium Apple & Mango Juice, Premium Orange Juice w Juicy Bits, Tropical Juice; *Explosade:* Sports Drink; *Hyberry:* Apple High Juice, Blackcurrant, Lemon Fruit & Barley Squash, Orange High Juice, Peach Fruit & Barley Squash, Pink Grapefruit Fruit & Barley Squash, Tropical High Juice; *Macey's:* Milkshake Mix - Strawberry; *Moreton Hills Balanced Lifestyle:* Peach Flavoured Sparkling Spring Water; *Solesta:* Blackcurrant Juice; *Sunsqueeze Crush:* Diet Orange, Diet Pineapple & Grapefruit, Lemon, Lemon & Lime, Orange, Pineapple & Grapefruit, Sparkling Orange; *Topstar:* Iron Brew, Iron Brew Diet, Sugar-free Lemonade; *Westdales:* Dandelion & Burdock, Diet Cloudy Lemonade, Diet Dandelion & Burdock, Ginger Beer

SPIRITS & APÉRITIFS
Amaretto Aurelia; Napoleon Brandy; Ouzo; Pre-Mixed Spirits Rum & Orange; *Cocobay:* Rum & Coconut; *Glen Orrin:* 6 Year Old Malt Whisky; *Highland Earl:* Whisky; *Orsini:* Sambuca; *Oscars:* Peach Schnapps; *Southern Belle:* Bourbon Liquor Spirit

WINES - WHITE
Budavar: Chardonnay; *Christkindl:* Gluhwein; *Cromwell:* British Fortified Wine; *St Amandus:* Liebfraumilch

FOODS

BISCUITS
Bourbon Creams; Fruit Shortcake; Ginger Nuts; Morning Coffee; Rich Tea Fingers; Smartprice Cookie Mix; *Smartprice:* Ginger Nut Biscuits

BREADS, ROLLS, PIZZA BASES ETC
10 Flour Tortillas; 6 Flour Tortillas; Chapatis; Crumpets; Fruit Malt Loaf; Hovis Medium Sliced Wheatgerm Bread; Pain Rustique Twin Pack; Sandwich Baguette Granary; Traditional French Baguette; White Muffins; *Bakers Gold Thick Sliced Loaf:* White, Wholemeal; *Big Loaf:* Medium White, Thick White; *Bread Mixes:* Garlic & Rosemary Foccacia, Multigrain Loaf, Pizza Base, White Loaf; *Brown Bread:* Granary Malted, Smartprice Medium Sliced; *Extra Special:* Black Pepper Ladder Bread; *Fresh For a Week Medium Sliced Bread:* White, Wholemeal; *Good For You Bagels:* Cinnamon & Raisin, Onion, Plain, Sesame Seed; *Pitta Breads:* Garlic, Smartprice, White, Wholemeal; *White Bread:* Danish Soft & Light Thick Cut, Extra Thick Sliced, Medium Sliced (Square Cut), Organic Sliced, Scottish Batch Sliced, Smartprice Medium Sliced, Smartprice Thick Sliced, Thick Sliced (Square Cut), Wholesome Medium, Wholesome Thick; *Wholemeal Bread:* Medium Sliced (Square Cut), Organic Sliced, Thick Sliced (Square Cut)

BREAKFAST FOODS
Apricot Wheats; Bran Flakes; High Bran; Organic Bran Flakes; Organic Corn Flakes; Ready Oats; Sultana Bran; *Muesli:* Good For You Fruit, Wholewheat; *Smartprice:* Bran Flakes, Corn Flakes, Crispy Rice Cereal

'BURGERS','SAUSAGES', 'MEAT' SLICES ETC
Meat Free Savoury Mince (Less Than 2% Fat)

CONFECTIONERY & SWEET SNACKS
Smartprice: Lollipops, Mint Humbugs

COOKING AIDS - SAVOURY
Stuffing Mix: Apple & Herb, Apricot & Orange, Parsley Lemon & Thyme, Sage & Onion, Sage & Onion (Less than 1% Fat), Smartprice Sage & Onion

COOKING AIDS - SWEET
Crumble Topping; *Dessert Sauce:* Extra Special Raspberry & Drambuie; *Extra Special Dessert Sauce:* Orange & Cointreau; *Marzipan:* Golden, Smartprice Golden, White; *Ready to Roll Icing:* Standard, White

CRACKERS, CRISPBREADS ETC
Black Pepper Bread Sticks; Cracker Selection; Cream Crackers; Water Biscuits; *Ready to Eat Pappadums:* Plain, Spicy

DESSERTS
6 Brandy Snap Baskets; Raspberry Topping; *Deli:* Pease Pudding;

Vegetarian Jelly Crystals: Lemon, Orange, Strawberry

DIPS & DRESSINGS
Chilled: Salsa Dip; *Dressings:* Creamy French, French; *Good for You Dressings:* Oil Free Vinaigrette, Tomato & Herb; *Houmous:* Fresh; *Salsa:* Bean

GRAVIES & STOCKS
Onion Gravy; *Smartprice:* 10 Vegetable Stock Cubes

'ICE CREAMS', SORBETS ETC
Lollies: Kids Rocket, Orange Juice; *No Added Sugar Lollies:* Blackcurrant Flavoured, Kids, Lemon Flavoured, Orange Flavoured

PASTRY
36 Vol Au Vents; Shortcrust Mix; Smartprice Shortcrust Mix; *Pastry:* Puff

PICKLES, SAUCES, VINEGARS ETC
Beetroot: Baby in Sweet Vinegar, Cooked & Pickled, Crinkle Cut, Crinkle Cut in Sweet Vinegar, Sliced in Malt Vinegar, Smartprice Sliced in Malt Vinegar, Sweet Baby; *Chutney:* Extra Special Mango, Onion, Spiced Fruit, Tomato; *Condiments:* Bramley Apple Sauce, Cranberry Sauce, Extra Special Cumberland Sauce, Extra Special Fresh Mint Jelly, Mint Sauce; *Cooking Sauces:* Black Bean, Goan Curry, Good for You Sweet & Sour, Mediterranean Tomato, Rogan Josh, Sweet & Sour, Sweet & Sour w Extra Pineapple, Vindaloo; *Curry Paste:* Medium, Mild; *Deli:* Mini Gherkins, Silverskin Onions; *Gherkins:* Baby in Sweet & Sour Vinegar, Pickled in Sweet & Sour Vinegar; *Glazes:* Cranberry & Onion, Garlic & Rosemary, Lemon & Ginger; *Jelly:* Redcurrant; *Mexican Sauces:* Barbecue; *Mustard:* Coarse Grain Hot & Crunchy, Dijon Smooth & Hot, English, French Mild & Distinctive, Garlic, Wholegrain Balsamic; *Onions:* Hot & Spicy Chilli; *Organic Cooking Sauces:* Sweet & Sour, Tomato & Herb; *Packet Casserole Sauce Mixes for Cooking:* Beef in Ale, Sausage; *Pasta Sauces:* Fresh Napoletana, Napoletana, Original Bolognese, Smartprice Bolognese, Spicy Tomato, Sundried Tomato, Tomato & Chunky Vegetable, Tomato & Garlic, Tomato & Mushroom; *Piccalilli:* Mustard, Sweet; *Pickle:* Brinjal, Extra Special Lime, Mixed, Sandwich Tangy Spread, Sweet Harvest; *Pickled Onions:* Silverskin, Smartprice Sweet, Sweet, Tikka Flavoured; *Relish:* Sweetcorn; *Sauces:* Barbecue, Barbeque Ketchup, Brown, Smartprice Tomato Ketchup, Smartprice Tomato Ketchup Squeezy, Squeezy Brown, Sticky BBQ, Texan Style BBQ, Tomato Ketchup, Tomato Ketchup Squeezy, Yellow Bean & Cashew Nut; *Stir Fry Sauces:* Garlic & Chilli, Reduced Fat Sweet & Sour; *Vinegar:* Cider, Distilled Malt, Malt, Red Wine, Smartprice Malt, White Wine

PIES & PASTIES
Smartprice: 2 Apple Pies

SAVOURIES - CANNED/BOTTLED
Bombay Potato; Mixed Bean Salad; Tomato & Chilli Pizza Topper; Vegetable Balti (Medium); *Healthy Choice:* Chick Pea Dahl (Mild); *Smartprice:* Baked Beans, Spaghetti in Tomato Sauce, Spaghetti Loops, Vegetable Curry; *Spaghetti:* Loops In Tomato Sauce

SAVOURIES - CHILLED/FRESH
Marinated Corn on the Cob Chunks; Mixed Vegetable & Mushroom; Organic Golden Vegetable Rice; Potato Wedges w Olive Oil & Rock Salt; Potato Wedges w Parsley & Oil; Thai Curry Kit Prepack; Vegetable Rice Salad; *Aloo:* Mushroom, Potato; *Bhajis:* 12 Mini Onion, 12 Mini Onion (Cookie Bag), 6 Onion, Mini Onion, Mini Vegetable, Onion, Vegetable; *Extra Special:* Ratatouille; *Good For You:* Beetroot Salad, Mediterranean Cous Cous, Pasta & Sundried Tomato Salad, Roasted Red Pepper Arrabiata, Spanish Style Potatoes, Spiced Rice Salad, Sun Dried Tomato Pasta Salad, Tex Mex Rice, Vegetable Balti & Pilau Rice, Vegetables w Balsamic Dressing; *Pakora:* Achari, Broccoli, Mixed Vegetable, Onion, Tomato, Vegetable; *Samosas:* Vegetable; *Spring Rolls:* Mini Vegetable, Vegetable; *Stir Fry:* Chinese Style, Exotic, Mixed Pepper, Mushroom & Vegetables

SAVOURIES - DRIED
Fajita Dinner Kit; *Instant Noodle Snacks:* Good for You Chicken Chow Mein Flavour, Good for You Mediterranean Tomato Flavour, Paprika Chicken Flavour, Smartprice Beef & Tomato Flavour, Smartprice Chicken & Mushroom Flavour, Smartprice Spicy Curry Flavour, Spicy Curry Flavour; *Instant Pasta Break Snacks:* Tomato & Herb

SAVOURIES - FROZEN
Garlic Mushrooms; Garlic & Rosemary Roast Potatoes; Hot & Spicy Onion Rings; Micro Chips; Nut Cutlet; Onion Bhaji & Vegetable Samosa Pack x15; Oriental Vegetable Stir Fry; Potato Croquettes; Potato Waffles; *3 Way Cook Chips:* Straight Cut; *Bhajis:* Onion; *Frying Chips:* Crinkle Cut, Smartprice Straight Cut, Steak Cut; *Good for You:* Potato Wedges, Roast Potatoes, Straight Cut Oven Chips; *Oven Chips:* American Fries, Steak Cut, Straight Cut; *Samosas:* Vegetable

SNACKS - SAVOURY
Dry Roasted Peanuts; Poppadums; Ready Salted Crisps; Roasted Salted Pistachios; *Extra Special:* Handcooked Crisps w Seasalt; *Smartprice:* Lightly Salted Tortilla Chips, Ready Salted Crisps; *Tortilla Chips:* Lightly Salted Round, Regular

SOYA AND OTHER 'MILKS'
Soya Milk: Sweetened w Apple Juice, Unsweetened Organic

SPREADS - SAVOURY
Yeast Extract; *Tapenade:* Extra Special Roasted Red Pepper & Tomato

SPREADS - SWEET
Jam: Apricot, Blackcurrant, Organic Strawberry, Seedless Raspberry, Smartprice Mixed Fruit, Smartprice Strawberry, Strawberry; *Jelly:* Bramble; *Marmalade:* Extra Special Pink Grapefruit, Fine Cut Lime Shred, Fine Cut Orange (25% Less Sugar), Fine Cut Orange Shred, Organic Orange, Shredless Orange, Smartprice Orange, Thick Cut Orange; *Preserve:* Ginger

DRINK

BEERS
Lager: Belgian, French, German, Shandi

'HOT'
Drinking Chocolate

SOFT
Bitter Lemon; Diet Iron Brew; Diet Lemonade; Dry Ginger Ale; Ginger Ale; Iron Brew; Just Cola; Just Cola w Vanilla; Just Diet Cola; Just Diet Cola w Citrus; Kids Lemonade; Lemonade; Soda Water; *Blue Charge Energy Drink:* Diet, Diet Cranberry, Standard; *Breakfast Juice:* Pure Orange & Grapefruit w Bits; *Chilled Juice:* Cranberry Drink, Grape Apple & Raspberry from Concentrate Drink, Orange & Grapefruit, Pure Apple From Concentrate, Pure Grapefruit, Pure Orange & Banana, Pure Orange Smooth from Concentrate, Pure Orange w Juicy Bits from Concentrate, Pure Orange w Mango Puree from Concentrate, Pure Pineapple, Smartprice Orange; *Cordial:* Blackcurrant, Elderflower & Lemon, Peppermint; *Flavoured Spring Water:* Rebalancing - Cranberry w Natural Extracts of Ginger & Lemongrass, Up Lifting - Tangerine & Lime w Natural Extracts of Guarana & Ginseng; *Flavoured Spring Water Drink - Still:* Cranberry, Mango & Guava, Raspberry w Green Tea Extract, Sicilian Lemon; *Flavoured Water:* Grapefruit & Mandarin, Strawberry & Vanilla; *Fruit Crush:* Berry (No Added Sugar), Citrus, Summer, Tropical; *Fruit Juice Drink:* Cranberry & Raspberry; *High Juice:* Apple Squash, Blackcurrant, Cranberry & Apple, Florida Orange, Summerfruits Squash, Tropical Squash, White Grape & Peach Squash; *Indian Tonic Water:* Standard, Twist Lemon Flavour; *Juice:* Pure Apple, Pure Grapefruit, Pure Orange & Pineapple, Pure Orange w Bits, Pure Pineapple; *Juice Drink (w Added Vitamins ACE & Calcium):* Orange, Tropical; *Kids Chilled No Added Sugar Juice Drink:* Apple Pear & Blackberry, Orange Pineapple & Banana; *Kids No Added Sugar Juice Drink:* Apple & Blackcurrant, Cherry Berry, Orange; *Kids Sugar Free Totally Bubbly:* Appleade, Cherryade, Lemonade, Limeade, Orangeade; *Low Calorie:* Bitter Lemon, Ginger Ale; *Low Calorie Indian Tonic Water:* Standard, Twist Lemon Flavour, Twist Lime Flavour; *No Added Sugar Crush:* Apple & Blackcurrant, Citrus Berries, Orange & Pineapple; *No Added Sugar Flavoured Spring Water:* Apple & Mango,

Blackberry & Elderflower, Calm Lemon & Vanilla, Lemon & Lime; *No Added Sugar Fruit & Barley Juice Drink:* Orange, Peach & Apricot; *No Added Sugar Fruit Juice Drink:* Cranberry; *No Added Sugar High Juice:* Apple & Blackcurrant Squash, Apple & Strawberry Squash; *No Added Sugar Juice Drink:* Apple & Blackcurrant & Barley, Pink Grapefruit & Barley, Summerfruits (Added Vits ACE & Calcium); *No Added Sugar Squash:* Apple, Apple & Blackcurrant, Blackcurrant, Forest Fruits, Lemon & Lime, Orange, Orange & Pineapple, Smartprice Apple & Blackcurrant, Strawberry, Strawberry Fruit; *Organic Juice:* Apple, Orange; *Smartprice:* Tonic Water; *Smartprice Juice:* Pure Apple, Pure Grapefruit, Pure Orange, Tomato; *Smoothies:* Orange Mango & Banana, Pineapple Banana & Pear, Strawberry Banana & Guava; *Spring Water Drink:* Peach Flavour (No Added Sugar); *Squash:* Apple & Blackcurrant, Lemon & Lime, Lime Cordial, Orange (10% Fruit), Orange & Pineapple; *Traditional Style:* Cream Soda, Dandelion & Burdock, Diet Lemonade, Ginger Beer, Lager Shandy, Lemonade

SPIRITS & APÉRITIFS

Dandelion & Burdock; Gin; Raspberry & Vanilla; *Smartprice:* Whisky

WINES - RED

Argentinian: Malbec, Malbec Reserve, Red Select Blend, Red Wine; *Bulgarian:* Cabernet Sauvignon; *French:* Beaujolais, Chateauneuf Du Pape Red Wine, Claret, Cotes Du Rhone Villages, Minervois, Reserve Claret; *Italian:* Chianti, Valpolicella; *South African:* Reserve Pinotage; *South African Cape:* Merlot, Pinotage, Red; *USA Californian:* Red Wine, Reserve Zinfandel, Sweet Red, Zinfandel

WINES - ROSÉ

Australian: Medium Rose; *USA Californian:* Rose

WINES - WHITE

Australian: White Wine; *Chilean:* Chardonnay, Reserve Sauvignon Blanc; *French:* Chenin Blanc Demi-Sec, Muscadet, Vin de Pays Chardonnay; *Italian:* Frascati, Frascati Selezione, Orvieto Abbocatto, Soave, Soave Classico; *South African Cape:* Chardonnay, Chenin Blanc, Created for Curry White (Semillon/Chardonnay), Reserve Sauvignon Blanc, Sauvignon Blanc, White; *USA Californian:* Chardonnay, Reserve Chardonnay, White Wine

FOODS

BISCUITS
Bourbon Creams; Fruit Shortcake; Ginger Nuts; Morning Coffee; Nice; Oatens; Rich Tea; Rich Tea Finger; Shortcake

BREADS, ROLLS, PIZZA BASES ETC
Baps; Bun Crown; Ciabatta Rolls; Currant Buns; Finger Rolls; Grande Mange Blanc Rolls; Kibbled Seed Loaf; Luxury White Batched Rolls; Malted Grain Rolls; Nettle Bread; Olive Ciabatta; Olive Pave; Petit Parisienne; Rustique Elat Rolls; Soft White Rolls; Spiced Fruit Buns; Split Rolls; Sub Rolls; Teacakes; Tomato Foccacia; White Bread; Wholemeal Rolls; *Part-Baked:* Brown Loaf, French Flute, Vienna Stick, White Loaf; *Pitta Bread:* Garlic & Coriander, White, Wholemeal; *Take & Bake:* Homecrust Sandwich Loaf, Small White Baguette, White Petit Pain, Wholemeal Loaf, Wholemeal Petit Pain

CAKES & CAKE MIXES
White Iced Buns

COOKING AIDS - SAVOURY
Sage & Onion Stuffing Mix

DIPS & DRESSINGS
Dijon Mustard; English Mustard

PICKLES, SAUCES, VINEGARS ETC
Brown Sauce; Cranberry Sauce; Mint Sauce; Redcurrant Jelly; Sweet Pickle; Sweet & Sour Sauce; Tomato Ketchup; *Cooking Sauces:* Rogan Josh; *Pasta Sauce:* Napoletana, Original, w Mushrooms, w Peppers; *Pickled:* Baby Beetroot, Gherkins, Red Cabbage, Sweet Onions; *Vinegar:* Cider, Distilled Malt, Malt, Red Wine, White Wine

SAVOURIES - CANNED/BOTTLED
Beans in Tomato Sauce; *Budgens & HP:* Healthy Beans in Tomato Sauce

SAVOURIES - CHILLED/FRESH
Beansprout & Vegetable Stir Fry; Bombay Potato; Family Stir Fry; H&S Wedges; Mushroom Dopiaza; Mushroom Stir Fry; Roast Potatoes w R&T; Sticky Rice; Vegetable Jalfrezi; Vegetable Samosas; Vegetable Spring Rolls; *Salads:* Chefs, Crunchy, Crunchy w Peppers, Herb, Organic Rocket, Rocket, Seasonal, Sweet Crunchy, Sweet Mix, Tatsoi

SAVOURIES - FROZEN
Hot & Spicy Wedges; Oven/Fry Frozen Chips

SEASONAL FOODS
Christmas Puddings; Hot Cross Buns

SNACKS - SAVOURY
Crisps: Ready Salted; *Nuts:* Salted Peanuts; *Nuts - Roasted & Salted:* Cashews, Pistachios

SPREADS - SWEET
Mincemeat; *Conserves & Jams:* Apricot,

Blackcurrant, Bramble, Raspberry, Strawberrry; *Jellies:* Lemon, Lime; *Orange Marmalade:* Fine, Shredless, Thick

DRINK

SOFT

American Cola; American Diet Cola; American Ginger Ale; Apple & Blackcurrant; Bitter Lemon; Cream Soda; Diet Lemonade; Diet Tonic; Lemonade; Pink Lemonade; Shandy; Soda Water; Tonic Water w a Twist of Lemon; Traditional Diet Lemonade; Traditional Lemonade; Whole Orange; *Juices - Ambient:* Cranberry, English Apple, Pineapple, Pink Grapefruit, Pure Orange; *Juices - Chilled:* Cloudy Apple, Cranberry, Florida Orange, Grapefruit, Pineapple, Pure Apple, Pure Orange; *No Added Sugar:* Apple & Blackcurrant, Cherryade, Lemon, Orange Lemon & Pineapple, Orangeade, Whole Orange

SPIRITS & APÉRITIFS

Cognac; Gin; Port Wine; Prince Royal Brandy; Vodka

WINES - WHITE

Bordeaux Blanc Sec; Bordeaux Sauvignon Blanc

FOODS

BISCUITS
Bourbon Creams; Country Crunch; Cream Crackers; Digestive; Fruit Shortcake; Ginger Nuts; Lemon Puffs; Morning Coffee; Nice; Plain Chocolate Ginger Thins; Rich Tea; *Crackers:* Water Biscuits - High Baked

BREADS, ROLLS, PIZZA BASES ETC
12 Crumpets; 4 Currant Buns; 4 Fruited Teacakes; 4 Plain Muffins; 4 Potato Breads; 4 Potato Cakes; 6 Fruited Teacakes; 8 Burger Buns; 8 Crumpets; Ciabatta; Pizza Base Mix; *Baps:* 4 Large Malted, 4 Large White, 6 Burger Buns w Sesame Seeds, 6 Sliced Burger Buns w Sesame Seeds, 8 Burger Buns w Sesame Seeds; *International:* 4 Ready to Eat Poppadums; *Loaves:* Bakers Choice Medium White, Bakers Choice Medium White N. Ireland, Brown - Medium Sliced, Danish Medium, Danish Thick, Everyday White, Everyday Wholemeal Medium, Gold Malted Grain - Thick Sliced, Gold White Thick, Gold Wholemeal - Thick Sliced, Long Life White Medium, Longer Life White - Thick Sliced, Medium Sliced Wholemeal, Thick Sliced Wholemeal, White, White Extra Thick N. Ireland, White - Extra Thick Sliced, White Sliced, Wholemeal - Medium Sliced; *Naan Breads:* 2 Spicy Garlic, Garlic & Coriander, Meal Solutions Plain, Plain; *Pitta Bread:* 6 Garlic, 6 Plain, Healthy Living 6 Wholemeal; *Ready to Bake:* 2 Baguettes, 6 Petit Pain; *Rolls:* 12 Morning, 4 Premium White, 4 Wholemeal Deli Style, 6 Finger, 6 Morning, 6 White, 6 Wholemeal, 8 White, Bakers Choice White, Scottish White; *White Part Baked:* 2 Baguettes, Petit Pain

BREAKFAST FOODS
Bran Flakes; Choco Hoops; Everyday Frosted Flakes; Everyday Muesli; Fruit & Nut Muesli; Healthy Living Porridge Oats w Wheatbran; High Fibre Bran; Instant Hot Oat Cereal; Malt Crunchie Cereal; Maple & Pecan Crisp; Mixed Fruit Muesli; Perfect Choice; Porridge Oats; Strawberry Crisp; Sultana Bran; Wholewheat Biscuits

CAKES & CAKE MIXES
6 Assorted Jam Tarts; Crumble Mix; Fairy Cake Mix; Luxury Sponge Cake Mix; Rock Cake Mix; Scone Mix; Shortcrust Pastry Mix

CONFECTIONERY & SWEET SNACKS
American Hard Gums; Assorted Fruit Flavour Lollies; Flying Saucers; Fruit Drops; Fruit Jellies; Fruit Sherbet Mix; Orange & Lemon Slices; Rose & Lemon Flavour Turkish Delight

COOKING AIDS - SAVOURY
Golden Breadcrumbs; *Stuffing Mixes:* Parsley & Thyme, Sage & Onion

COOKING AIDS - SWEET
Custard Powder; Cut Mixed Peel; Glace

Cherries; Granulated Sweetener; Lemon Juice; Mincemeat; Ready To Roll Icing; Ready to Roll White Icing; *Baking:* Yu-Lade, Yu-Lade - Ginger; *Fruit Fillings:* Apple, Apple & Blackberry, Blackcurrant, Red Cherry; *Marzipan:* Golden, White

CRACKERS, CRISPBREADS ETC
Melba Toast

DESSERTS
Frozen: Everyday Twin Apple Pies

DIPS & DRESSINGS
Salsa; Salsa Dip; Spiced Tomato & Onion; *Bag Salads:* Chardonnay Flavour Salad Dressing, French Dressing, Mint Drizzle, Pasta Salad, Spiced Orange Salad Dressing, Truly Irresistible Mango & Chilli Dressing; *Dressings:* French, Very Low Fat Vinaigrette; *Dressings - Low Cal:* Virtually Fat Free Vinaigrette; *Mustard:* Dijon, French

GRAVIES & STOCKS
Vegetable Gravy: Browning, Mix

'ICE CREAMS', SORBETS ETC
10 Orange Juice Lollies; 10 Rocket Lollies; *Sugar Free Mini-Pops:* Orangeade

PICKLES, SAUCES, VINEGARS ETC
Apple Sauce; English Mint Sauce; English Mustard; Fairtrade Bramley Apple Sauce w Kentish Cider; Fairtrade Cranberry Sauce w Port; Mint Sauce; *Brown Sauce:* Brown Sauce, Everyday, Squeezy Bottle; *Chutneys:* Mango Chutney; *Clear Pickled Onions:* Silverskin, Standard, Strong; *Cook In Sauce:* Black Bean, Healthy Living Sweet & Sour, Jalfrezi, Rogan Josh, Sweet & Sour; *Fresh Pasta Sauces:* Organic Tomato & Basil; *Gherkins:* Baby in Vinegar, Pickled; *Pasta Sauces:* Arrabbiata, Garlic & Onion, Healthy Living, Hot & Spicy, Mushroom, Napoletana, Organic Tomato & Basil, Spicy Red Pepper, Sun-Dried Tomato & Basil, Sundried Tomato Vodka & Chilli, Tomato & Herb, w Mushrooms; *Pickled Beetroot:* Baby, Sliced, Sweet Crinkle Cut; *Pickled Onions:* Sweet; *Pickles:* Sandwich, Sweet; *Red Cabbage:* Sweet Pickled; *Relish:* Barbeque, Hamburger, Onion, Sweetcorn; *Tomato Ketchup:* Everyday, Squeezy, Standard; *Vinegar:* Distilled Malt, Malt

SAVOURIES - CANNED/BOTTLED
Ratatouille Provencale; *Baked Beans:* in Reduced Sugar & Salt Tomato Sauce, In Tomato Sauce, Organic in Tomato Sauce; *Spaghetti:* Everyday, In Reduced Sugar & Salt Tomato Sauce, In Tomato Sauce, Organic in Tomato Sauce, Rings In Tomato Sauce

SAVOURIES - CHILLED/FRESH
Ready to Roast Potatoes; *Deli:* Beetroot Salad, Bombay Potato, Croutons, Hot & Spicy Potato Wedges, Mammoth Green Olives (52%) (stone in) in a Lemon Marinade, Mini Onion Bhaji, Mini Vegetable Samosa, Mini Vegetable Spring Roll, Mixed Leaf Salad,

Moroccan Style Cous Cous, Mushroom Provencale, Onion Bhaji, Pilau Rice, Potato Wedges, Stuffed Olives, Vegetable Samosa, Vegetable Spring Rolls; *Ethnic Snacks:* Onion Bhajis, Party Mini Bhaji Selection w Dip, Vegetable Samosas; *Meal Solutions - Indian:* Aloo Saag, Bombay Potatoes, Fragrant Pilau Rice, Peshwari Rice, Pilau Rice; *Meal Solutions - Snacks:* 6 Mini Spring Rolls; *Potato Wedges:* Garlic & Herb, Party Pack; *Ready Meals - Oriental:* Vegetable Spring Rolls 4; *Snack Salads:* Gourmet Pasta Salad, Premium Moroccan Style Cous Cous; *Stir Fry:* Black Bean, Mixed Vegetable, Sichuan, Sweet & Sour, Szeuchan; *Variety Salads:* Beetroot, Pasta & Pepper, Pasta & Tomato, Three Bean

SAVOURIES - DRIED
Instant Mashed Potato; *Nuts:* Bombay Mix, Roasted Salted Pistachios; *Savoury Rice:* Barbecue Flavour, Biryani, Chicken Flavour, Curry, Mixed Vegetable, Mushroom, Pilau

SAVOURIES - FROZEN
Breaded Vegetable Rings; Golden Vegetable Rice; Italian Style Vegetable Stir Fry; Mini Spring Roll Selection; Oriental Style Mixed Vegetable Stir Fry; Oven Crunchies; *Fry Chips:* Everyday Straight Cut, Steak Cut; *Frying Chips:* Crinkle Cut, Steak Cut; *Microwave Chips:* Crinkle Cut; *Onion Rings:* Breaded; *Oven Chips:* American Style 3-way Cook, Crinkle Cut, Crinkle Cut 3-way Cook, Everyday, Healthy Living Reduced Fat, Steak Cut 3-way Cook, Straight Cut, Straight Cut 3-way Cook; *Potato Products:* Hash Browns, Hot & Spicy Wedges, Party Mini Rostis, Plain Cut Wedges, Roast Potatoes, Waffles, Wedges; *Potatoes:* Crispy, Roast

SEASONAL FOODS
6 Deep Filled Mince Pies; *Nuts:* Xmas Roasted & Salted Pistachios; *Xmas Puddings:* Premium, Rich Fruit

SNACKS - SAVOURY
Chilli Tortilla Chips; Dry Roasted Peanuts; Mini Poppadums; Ready Salted Potato Rings; *Nuts:* Assorted Mixed Nuts & Raisins, Mixed Nuts & Raisins, Mixed Nuts & Raisins - 2003, Roasted Salted Cashews, Roasted Salted Mixed, Roasted Salted Peanuts & Cashew Nuts, Roasted Salted Pistachios; *Peanuts:* Large Roasted Salted, Large Salted, Roasted Salted; *Potato Crisps:* Organic Ready Salted, Smoky Bacon Flavour (Single Bag within Multi), Trad Ready Salted, Trad Salt & Vinegar; *Ready Salted:* Crunchy Sticks

SOUPS
Broth & Soup Mix; Organic Vegetable; Potato & Leek; Thick Vegetable; *Packet:* Calorie Counter Cup Soup Minestrone

SOYA AND OTHER 'MILKS'
Organic Unsweetened Soya Drink; UHT Sweetened Soya Drink; *Soya Drink:* Organic Sweetened, Unsweetened

SPICES
Cajun Style Seasoning; Chinese Style Seasoning; Mediterranean Style Seasoning; Mexican Style Seasoning; Thai Style Seasoning; *Curry Powder:* Hot, Mild

SPREADS - SAVOURY
Yeast Extract

SPREADS - SWEET
Bramble Jelly; Ginger Conserve; *Jam:* Apricot, Blackcurrant, Damson, Everyday Mixed Fruit, Orange & Ginger, Plum, Raspberry, Raspberry Seedless, Strawberry; *Marmalade:* 3 Fruits, Coarse Cut Orange, Everyday Thin Cut Orange, Fine Cut Orange, Orange Jelly - Thin Cut, Orange Shredless, Sweet Orange, Thick Cut Orange, Thin Cut Lemon; *Premium Soft Set Conserve:* Apricot, Blackcurrant, Raspberry, Red Cherry, Strawberry

DRINK

ALCOPOPS
Glitz Black Ice: Vodka Blend; *Glitz Ice:* Orange, Vodka Blend - Blueberry, Vodka Blend - Crystal; *Glitz Imperial:* Black, Blackcurrant, Lemon, Orange, Watermelon

BEERS
Best Bitter; Mild; Organic Ale; Strong Premium Ale; Summer Breeze Ale; Traditional Bitter; Wheat Beer; *Lagers:* Belgian Premium, French Premium, Premium, Spanish Premium, Superstrength

CIDERS & PERRIES
Tillington Hill Premium Reserve Dry Cider

'HOT'
Drinking Chocolate

LOW & NON-ALCOHOLIC
Lemonade Shandy

SOFT
Apple & Raspberry from Concentrate Drink; *American Dry Ginger Ale:* Low Calorie, Standard; *Bitter Lemon:* Low Calorie, Standard; *Carbonates:* Cloudy Lemonade, Cola Flavour Drink, Cream Soda, Dandelion & Burdock, Everyday Lemonade, Ginger Beer, Orangeade, Soda Water, Sparkling Apple Juice, Sparkling Apple Juice from Concentrate, Standard Lemonade; *Cola:* Everyday, Standard; *Cordials:* Apple & Blackcurrant Flavour Drink, Blackcurrant Flavour, Lime w Sugar & Sweeteners, Mixed Fruit Flavour Drink, Whole Lemon Flavour Drink, Whole Orange Flavour Drink; *Crush:* Pink Grapefruit; *Diet Carbonates:* Cloudy Lemonade, Cola, Lemonade; *Everyday:* Low Calorie Orange Drink, Orange Lemon & Pineapple Flavour Drink; *Everyday No Added Sugar:* Orange Lemon & Pineapple Flavour Drink; *High Juice:* Apple, Apple Squash, Blackcurrant, Orange, Pineapple &

Grapefruit, Tropical Fruit; *Indian Tonic Water:* Low Calorie, Standard, w a Twist of Lemon, w a Twist of Lime, w Lemon; *Juice:* Apple, Tomato; *Juice Drink:* Citrus, Cranberry, Sparkling Cranberry w Spring Water; *Juice Drinks:* Apple & Blackcurrant, Apple & Mixed Berry, Cranberry, Fairtrade Orange From Concentrate, Tropical; *No Added Sugar:* Orange Drink, Orange Drink w Sweeteners, Strawberryade, Summer Fruits Flavour Fruit & Barley Drink; *No Added Sugar Barley Water:* Pink Grapefruit; *No Added Sugar Carbonates:* Caffeine Free Cola, Cherryade w Sweeteners, Cola, Cola w Sweeteners, Lemonade w Sweeteners, Limeade w Sweeteners, Orange & Peach Fruit Juice Drink, Raspberryade, Strawberryade w Sweeteners; *No Added Sugar Cordials:* Apple & Blackcurrant Flavour Drink, Apple Flavour Drink, Lemon & Lime, Strawberry, Whole Orange Flavour Drink; *No Added Sugar Diet Carbonates:* Cherryade, Lemonade, Limeade, Orangeade; *No Added Sugar Diet Crush:* Apple, Grapefruit, Lemon & Lime, Orange, Pineapple & Grapefruit; *No Added Sugar Fruit & Barley Drink:* Peach & Apricot Flavour, Pink Grapefruit Flavour; *No Added Sugar Juice Drink:* Orange & Peach Still, Tropical, Tropical w Sweeteners; *No Added Sugar Juice Drinks:* Apple & Strawberry, Apple & Strawberry w Sweeteners, Blackcurrant, Blackcurrant w Sweeteners; *No Added Sugar One Shot Bottles:* Apple & Blackcurrant Fruit Juice Drink, Apple & Blackcurrant Still Juice Drink; *Orange Juice:* Everyday Pure, Fair Trade (Smooth), Freshly Squeezed, Pure Florida from Concentrate w Juicy Bits, Pure from Concentrate; *Pure Juice:* Orange & Pineapple, Pineapple; *Pure Juice from Concentrate:* Apple, Florida Pink Grapefruit, Grapefruit, Pineapple; *Sparkling Spring Water:* Elderflower & Lime; *Sparkling Spring Water Drink:* Apple & Blackberry, Lemon & Lime, Orange & Cranberry, Peach, Raspberry

SPIRITS & APÉRITIFS

Napoleon Brandy; Premium Fair Trade White Rum; Premium London Dry Gin; Premium Scotch Whisky; Premium Triple Distilled Vodka; Scotch Whisky; *Delaney's:* Irish Cream, Irish Whiskey

WINES

Australian Grenache 2003; Bin 66 Argentinian Viognier Reserve; Cape American Oak Pinotage; Chilean Old Vines Carignan; Frascati Superiore; Jacaranda Hill Semillon; Lighthouse Point Malbec; Moscato Frizzante; Orvieto Classico; Orvieto Classico 2003; Primitivo Sangiovese; Primitivo Sangiovese 2002; Soave; *British Fortified Wine:* Cream, Medium Dry, Pale Cream, Pale Dry; *Fair Trade:* Oaked Semillon 2002; *Organic:* French Vin de Pays d'Oc

WINES - FRUIT

Ginger; Green Ginger

WINES - RED

Australian Red Wine; Cape Boo Bridge Shiraz; Cape Shiraz Reserve; Chilean Cabernet Sauvignon; Chilean Cabernet Sauvignon Reserve; Chilean Merlot; Corbières Rouge; Cotes du Rhone; Cyprus Island Vines Red Wine; Cyprus Mountain Vines Cabernet Sauvignon; Cyprus Mountain Vines Semillon; Elephant Trail Shiraz Pinotage; Jacaranda Hill Shiraz; Long Slim Chilean Cabernet Merlot; Rioja Cuvee Nathalie; Romanian Prairie Merlot 2000; Swirling Skirts Argentinian Bonarda Shiraz Famatina Valley; Underworld Shiraz Viognier; Vin de Pays d'Oc Cabernet Sauvignon 2003; Vin de Pays d'Oc Fruity Red Wine; Vin de Pays d'Oc Merlot; Vin de Pays d'Oc Shiraz 2003; Vin de Table Red; *Fair Trade:* Cape Affinity Red, Cape Cabernet Sauvignon, Shiraz Reserve; *Laid Back Ruby:* Ruby Cabernet, Ruby Cabernet 2002, Ruby Cabernet 2003; *Organic:* Tierra Sana Tempranillo

WINES - ROSÉ
Cape Ha-de-da Rose; Vin de Pays d'Oc Shiraz Rosé 2003; Vin de Pays d'Oc Syrah Rosé 2001; *Fair Trade:* Chilean Merlot Rosé 2004

WINES - SPARKLING
Bucks Fizz; Tempranillo Sparkling Red Wine 2003; Tempranillo Sparkling Red Wine 2004

WINES - WHITE
Australian Orange Sauvignon Blanc Reserve 2000; Australian White Wine; California Chardonnay Colombard The Big Chill; California Chardonnay Colombard The Big Chill 2003; California Starlight Coast Chardonnay; California Starlight Coast Zinfandel; Cape Chardonnay Reserve - Seal Bay; Cape Oak Aged Chenin Blanc; Cape White; Catalan Chardonnay Jaume Serra - Barrel Fermented; Chilean Chardonnay; Chilean Chardonnay Reserve; Corbières; Elephant River Colombard Cardonnay; Hungarian Chardonnay 3 litre; Hungarian White; Lambrusco Bianco; Long Slim Chilean Chardonnay Semillon; Reserve Côtes du Rhone Blanc 2003; Sicilian White; South Australian Chardonnay; Vin de Pays d'Oc Cotes des Gascogne 2003; Vin de Pays d'Oc Chardonnay 2003; Vin de Pays du Jardin de la France Sauvignon Blanc 2003; *Fair Trade:* Cape Chenin Blanc 2003, Cape Chenin Blanc 2004, Cape Unity White; *Organic:* Cape Soleil Chardonnay, French Vin de Pays d'Oc Chardonnay Sauvignon Blanc, French Vin de Pays d'Oc Chardonnay Sauvignon Blanc, French Vin de Pays d'Oc Chardonnay Sauvignon Blanc

TOILETRIES

BATH & SHOWER
Liquid Shower-Premium: Body Wash - Refreshing

FOODS

BISCUITS
Bourbon Creams

BREADS, ROLLS, PIZZA BASES ETC
Crumpets; Danish Toaster Soft & Light Loaf; Garlic Slices; Harvester Garlic Baguettes; Large Brown Baps; Large White Baps; Part-Baked Loaf; Softbake French Sticks; White Muffins; *Homebake:* White Dinner Rolls; *Pitta Bread:* Garlic, Standard, White; *Premium Sliced White Bread:* Medium, Thick; *Rolls:* Hot Dog, Organic Crisp, White; *Sliced White Bread:* Medium, Thick; *Sliced Wholemeal Bread:* Medium, Thick

BREAKFAST FOODS
Cornflakes; Good Choice Fruit & Nut Cereal; Muesli; *Great Value:* Wheat Bisks

CAKES & CAKE MIXES
Treacle Tarts

DESSERTS
Strudel: Apple, Woodland Fruit

DIPS & DRESSINGS
Houmous Dip

'ICE CREAMS', SORBETS ETC
Non Melting Strawberry Jelly Sticks; Water Ice Push Ups; *Great Value:* Assorted Ice Lollies; *Kids Crew:* Assorted Rocket Lollies, Cola & Lemonade Ice Breakers, Orange & Blackcurrant Ice Breakers; *Lollies:* Assorted Fruit, Orange Juice, Orange & Raspberry Spiral, Rocket, Sourz, Sweet Shop Water Ice; *Sorbet:* Blackcurrant, Lemon

PICKLES, SAUCES, VINEGARS ETC
Brown Sauce; Tomato Ketchup; *Cooking Sauces:* Balti Curry, Beef in Ale, Black Bean, Chilli, Curry, Sweet & Sour; *Pasta Sauces:* Tomato Garlic & Onion, Tomato & Herb, Tomato & Mushroom; *Sauces:* Curry, Red Wine Casserole, Sweet & Sour

PIES & PASTIES
Great Value: Apple Pies

SAVOURIES - CHILLED/FRESH
Mediterranean Pasta Salad; Onion Bhajis; Party All Year Spring Roll Selection; Sweet n Sour Vegetables

SAVOURIES - FROZEN
Breaded Onion Rings; Crispy Battered Onion Rings; Hash Browns; Indian Takeaway Pilau Rice; Oriental Mix; Potato Wedges; Southern Fried Potato Wedges; Tex Mex Potato Wedges; Vegetables & Savoury Rice; *3 Way Cook Chips:* Crinkle Cut, Steak Cut, Straight Cut; *Chips:* American Style Slim Fries, Southern Fried; *Fry Chips:* Crinkle Cut, Steak Cut, Straight Cut; *Great Value:* Microwaveable Chips, Potato Waffles, Straight Cut Oven Chips; *Kids Crew:* Mini Potato Waffles, Snakes & Ladders

Potato Shapes, Spooky Potato Shapes; *Oven Chips:* Best Ever, Good Choice, Jumbo, Probably The Best, Steak Cut, Straight Cut; *Potato:* Croquettes, Noisettes, Traditional Roast; *Potatoes:* Crispy, Garlic & Herb Roast, Roast

SNACKS - SAVOURY
Great Value: Ready Salted Crisps

SPREADS - SWEET
Jam: Blackcurrant, Strawberry; *Marmalade:* Thick Cut, Thin Cut

DRINK

SOFT
Chilled Juice: Orange, Pure Apple, Smooth Orange & Grapefruit, Tropical Fruit; *Great Value:* Low Calorie Lemonade

FOODS

BISCUITS
Butter Puffs; Ginger Snaps; *Digestive:* Biscuits, Reduced Fat, Reduced Sugar High Fibre; *Rich Tea:* Biscuits, Finger Biscuits, Reduced Fat

BREADS, ROLLS, PIZZA BASES ETC
2 Half Ciabatta; Bagel; Ciabatta; Olive Fougasse; Wheatgerm; *Batch:* Seeded Unsliced; *Bloomers:* Multiseed; *Breads:* Mediterranean Style, Sundried Tomato; *Bruschettine:* Cracked Black Pepper, Green Olive, Lightly Salted, Mediterranean Style; *Count On Us:* Granary Thick Sliced, Soft Grain Bloomer; *Pittas:* 12 Mini, 8 Standard, 8 Wholemeal; *Premium White:* Medium, Thick; *Ready to Bake:* 3 Half Baguettes, 8 Crusty Rolls; *Rolls:* 4 Ciabatta, 4 Green Olive, 4 Panini

BREAKFAST FOODS
Fruit & Nut Muesli: Count On Us, Luxury, Organic; *Muesli:* Unsweetened Fruit & Bran

CAKES & CAKE MIXES
Cinnamon Ring Doughnut

COOKING AIDS - SWEET
Lemon Juice from Concentrate

CRACKERS, CRISPBREADS ETC
Biscuits for Cheese Selection 100g; Oatcakes; Rice & Oat Bran Cakes

DESSERTS
2 Summerfruit Puddings; *Compote:* Strawberry & Raspberry, Summerfruit; *Dessert Sauces:* Raspberry; *Jelly:* Raspberry

DIPS & DRESSINGS
Tomato Salsa; *Count On Us Dressings:* Balsamic Vinegar Roasted Garlic & Herb, Fire Roasted Tomato & Basil, Lemon & Watercress, Sweet Chilli; *Dressings:* Balsamic Vinegar & Caramelised Fig, Moroccan; *French Dressings:* Classic, Reduced Fat, Standard; *Houmous:* Organic, Reduced Fat, Spicy Red Pepper, Standard

GRAVIES & STOCKS
Concentrated Vegetable Stock

'ICE CREAMS', SORBETS ETC
8 Juicily Fruity Lollies; Lemon & Lime Flavour Spring Water Tube; *Extremely Fruity Sorbet:* Mango, Raspberry

PICKLES, SAUCES, VINEGARS ETC
Old Piccalilli; Old Tomato Ketchup; Sundried Tomato Paste; *Chutneys:* Apple Cider & Date, Autumn Plum, Date & Tamarind, Old Traditional Fruit, Organic Apple Date & Lemon, Organic Tomato w Smoked Garlic, Spiced Mango, Sweet Mango; *Cooking Sauces:* Tomato & Basil; *Curry Sauces:* Piri Piri, Vindaloo; *Marinade:* Chinese Barbecue, Fragrant Thai, Moroccan; *Organic Sauces:* Roasted Red Pepper & Olive, Roasted Tomato & Oregano; *Pasta Sauces:* Tomato & Herb; *Pickles:* Sweet Aubergine; *Pour Over Pasta Sauces:* Tomato & Chilli; *Relish:* BBQ, Peri Peri, Red Pepper & Onion, Tomato; *Sauces:* Dark Soy, Hot Peri Peri, Sichuan, Stir Fry, Sweet Chilli Ginger,

Sweet & Sour; *Stir Through Pasta Sauces:* Green & Black Olive, Roasted Italian Vegetable, Sicilian Gourmet, Sundried Tomato & Garlic

SAVOURIES - CANNED/BOTTLED
Baked Beans; Cannelini & Borlotto Beans in Olive Oil w Gralic & Red Wine Vinegar

SAVOURIES - CHILLED/FRESH
12 Falafel; 2% Fat Couscous & Roasted Vegetables; Chunky Chips; Crispy Wedges; Curly Fries; Mushrooms a la Grecque; Oven Fries; Roasted Artichoke Hearts in Extra Virgin Olive Oil; Roasted New Potatoes w Garlic & Rosemary; Roasted Red & Yellow Peppers; Savoury Vegetable Rice; *Count on Us:* Chunky Chips; *Global Meal Solutions:* Frites; *Mediterranean Style:* Vegetables; *Olives:* Kalamata, Large Marinated Selection, Marinated Selection, Queen Green; *Salads:* 1% Fat Beetroot, 2% Fat 3 Bean, 3 Bean, Herb, Italian Style, Rice Lentil & Roast Aubergine, Salad Bowl; *Stir Fry:* Mixed Mushroom, Vegetable & Beansprout

SAVOURIES - FROZEN
Chips: Crinkle Cut, Just Bake, Microwaveable Crinkle Cut; *Fries:* American Style Coated, Catering, Curly; *Mediterranean Style:* Potatoes & Vegetables

SNACKS - SAVOURY
Salt & Pepper Pretzels; *Count On Us:* Lightly Salted Baked Potato Crisps; *Crinkle Crisps:* Ready Salted; *Crisps:* Ready Salted; *Handcooked Crisps:* Eat in Lightly Salted, Lightly Salted, Lightly Salted Red Duke Of York, Sea Salt & Balsamic Vinegar, Sea Salt & Crushed Black Pepper, Sea Salt Lemon & Coriander; *Handcooked Ridge Crisps:* Chargrilled Steak & Onion Flavour, No Added Salt; *Potato Crisps:* Beef & Onion Flavour; *Potato Sticks:* Ready Salted; *Pretzel Sticks:* Lightly Salted; *Reduced Fat Crinkle Crisps:* Ready Salted; *Rings:* Beef & Onion, Ready Salted; *Roasted & Salted:* Cashews, Luxury Nut Assortment, Peanuts, Peanuts & Cashews; *Squares:* Ready Salted; *Tortilla Chips:* Lightly Salted

SOUPS
Chunky 3 Bean; Chunky Winter Vegetable; Gazpacho; Minestrone; Provencal; Spicy Red Lentil & Tomato; Tomato & Basil; Tomato & Fresh Basil; *Count On Us:* Tomato & Roasted Red Pepper

SPREADS - SAVOURY
Chargrilled Aubergine Pesto

SPREADS - SWEET
Conserve: Blackcurrant, Raspberry, Red Cherry; *Marmalade:* Coarse Cut Seville Orange, Medium Cut Blood Orange, Medium Cut Mandarin, Medium Cut Ruby Red Grapefruit, Medium Cut Seville Orange, No Peel Orange

DRINK

SOFT
Pineapple Juice

FOODS

BISCUITS

Bourbons; Coconut Crumble Creams; Fruit Digestives; Fruit Shortcakes; Ginger Snaps; Ginger Thins; Lebkuchen Plain Chocolate Heart Biscuits; Lemon Thins; Morning Coffee; Nice; Organic Digestives; Reduced Sugar Digestive Fingers; Rich Tea Fingers; Rich Teas; Rustics; Shortcake Biscuits; *Be Good To Yourself:* 25% Less Fat Rich Teas, Less Than 10% Fat Ginger Snaps, Less than 9% Fat Raspberry Flavour Fruit Roll Biscuits; *Low Price Biscuits:* Chocolate Chip, Rich Tea

BREADS, ROLLS, PIZZA BASES ETC

12 Crumpets; 2 Premium Mixed Rolls; 2 Sundried Tomato & Basil Mini Focaccia; 24 White Snack Rolls; 3 Ready To Bake Baguettes - White; 4 Large Teacakes; 4 Potato Farls; 8 Crumpets; 8 Potato Farls; Be Good To Yourself Less Than 3% Fat Malted Brown Sliced Bread w Added Fibre; Ciabatta Crispbread; Deep Pan Pizza Base; Pizza Base Mix Twin Pack; Plain White Bread; Premium Gold White Thick Sliced; Scottish Square White Medium Sliced; Tex 'n' Mex 12 Flour Tortillas; Way to 5 Focaccia Filled w Red & Green Peppers Marinated in Basil Oil; *12 Packs:* Finger Rolls; *13 Packs:* Longer Life White Buns; *14 Packs:* Sliced White Baps; *15 Packs:* Sliced Wholemeal Baps; *4 Pack Baps:* Giant Malted; *4 Pack Muffins:* Premium White Muffins; *4 Pack Rolls:* Premium White Country Style; *5 Pack Baps:* White Giant; *5 Pack Muffins:* Spiced White; *5 Pack Rolls:* White Hotdog; *6 Floury Batch Rolls:* Malted Floury Batch Rolls; 6 *Pack Baps:* Wholemeal Giant Baps; 6 *Pack Muffins:* White; 6 *Packs:* Burger Buns; *7 Floury Batch Rolls:* White; *7 Packs:* Currant Buns; *8 Floury Batch Rolls:* Wholemeal; *8 Packs:* Finger Rolls; *9 Packs:* Potato Cakes; *Be Good To Yourself Less Than 2% Fat w Added Fibre:* 4 White Rolls, White Sliced Bread, Wholemeal Sliced Bread; *Bread Mixes:* Garlic & Rosemary Focaccia, Mixed Grain, Sunflower Brown; *Crumpets:* 9 Finger; *Instore Bakery Bread:* Harvestgrain, White Bloomer, White Farmhouse, White Sandwich, White Split Tin, Wholemeal; *Instore Bakery Organic Bread:* Malted Grain, White, Wholemeal; *Longer Life Sliced Bread:* White Medium, White Thick, Wholemeal Medium, Wholemeal Thick; *Low Price:* 12 White Rolls, Sliced White Bread, Wholemeal Bread Medium Sliced; *Organic:* 4 White Rolls, 4 Wholemeal Rolls Topped w Linseed & Sesame Seeds, Potato & Roasted Onion Plait, Premium White Thick Sliced, Premium Wholemeal Thick Sliced, Raisin Pumpkin & Sunflower Seed Batch, Ready To Bake 2 Half Ciabatta, Soft White Batch, Soft Wholemeal Batch, Stoneground Wholemeal Medium Sliced, White Medium Sliced, Wholemeal Cob Loaf w Oatflakes & Rye; *Pittas:* 10 Mini White, 10 Standard, 6 Organic White, Garlic,

Sesame, Wholemeal; *Ploughman's:* 4 White Rolls, 4 Wholemeal Rolls, Mixed Pack; *Ready To Bake:* 9 Petit Pains - White, Green Olive & Thyme Focaccia, Tomato & Basil Twist; *Ready To Cook Pizza Bases:* 12" Pizzeria, Deep & Crispy, Thin & Crispy; *Sliced Brown Bread:* Medium, Thin; *Sliced White Bread:* Extra Thick, Medium, Thick, Thin; *Sliced Wholemeal Bread:* Medium, Thick; *Taste The Difference:* 4 Currant Buns, Golden Wholemeal Thick Sliced, Premium Gold Malted Brown Thick Sliced, Wholemeal Multigrain Thick Sliced; *Taste The Difference Ready To Bake:* 1 Ciabatta & 1 Black Olive Ciabatta, 2 Half Ciabatta, 3 Sfilatino, 4 Ciabatta Rolls, Black Olive Ciabatta, Ciabatta

BREAKFAST FOODS
Apricot Wheats; Hi Fibre Bran Cereal; Hot Oat Cereal; Low Price Cornflakes; Malties; Mini Wheats; Natural Bran; Puffed Wheat; Raisin Wheats; *Be Good To Yourself Less Than 4% Fat Multigrain Cereal w Cranberries &:* Apple, Blueberries; *Breakfast Topper:* Fruit, Nut Mix; *Freefrom Muesli:* Fruit & Nut, Tropical; *Muesli:* Be Good To Yourself Less Than 4% Fat, Fruit & Spice, No Added Salt or Sugar Deluxe, No Added Salt or Sugar Wholewheat; *Organic:* Cornflakes, Fruit & Fibre; *Wholewheat:* Biscuits, Miniflakes, Miniflakes w Tropical Fruit

CAKES & CAKE MIXES
6 Real Fruit Jam Tarts; Mini Organic Strawberry Tarts; Treacle Tart; *6 Low Price:* Apple Pies; *7 Low Price:* Raspberry Flavour Tarts

CONFECTIONERY & SWEET SNACKS
12 Party Lollies; Flying Saucers; Nutty; Pear Drops; Sherbet Cocktails; *Freefrom 5 Cereal Bars:* Fruity

COOKING AIDS - SAVOURY
Chestnut; Fast Action Dried Yeast; Roasted Garlic & Garden Herbs; *Breadcrumbs:* Golden, Natural; *Special Recipe Stuffing Mix:* Apple & Herb; *Stuffing Mix:* Parsley Thyme & Lemon, Sage & Onion

COOKING AIDS - SWEET
Crumble Topping; Custard Powder; Cut Mixed Peel; Easy Ice Ready To Roll Icing; Luxury Mincemeat; Stem Ginger in Sugar Syrup; *Almond Marzipan:* Natural, Traditional; *Blue Parrot Café Squeezy Ice Cream Sauces:* Apricot & Banana, Strawberry; *Fruit Fillings:* Apple, Apricot, Black Cherry, Blackcurrant, Red Cherry, Rhubarb; *Glacé:* Cherries, Cherries w Natural Colour, Cherry Halves, Ginger, Luxury Mixed Fruits, Multi Coloured Cherries; *Ice Cream Sauces:* Orange & Grand Marnier, Summer Fruit; *Slendasweet Sweetener:* Granular, Tablets

CRACKERS, CRISPBREADS ETC
Butter Puff Biscuits; Harvest Grain Crackers; High Bake Water Biscuit; Light & Crispy Crackers; Oat Thin Biscuits; Wholemeal Krispwheat

Crispbread; *Biscuits:* Thai Style Sesame Seed & Coconut, Thin & Crisp Sesame & Onion; *Cream Crackers:* Be Good To Yourself, Standard, w Sesame Seeds; *Grissini Italian Breadsticks:* Sesame Seed, Standard, Torinesi Thin Italian; *Oatcakes:* Organic Highland, Rough, Traditional Highland

DESSERTS
Taste The Difference Summerfruit Pudding; *Blue Parrot Café Fruit in Jelly:* Peaches in Orange Flavoured Jelly, Peaches & Pears in Strawberry Flavoured Jelly; *Freefrom Dairy Free Custard:* Chocolate Flavour, Vanilla; *Frozen Strudel:* Apple, Apple & Mincemeat, Woodland Fruit; *Fruity Jelly:* Mandarin & Pineapple, Strawberry & Raspberry; *Way To Five Jelly:* Mixed Berry, Tropical Fruit

DIPS & DRESSINGS
Fresh Roasted Aubergine Dip; Tex 'n' Mex Medium Taco Seasoning Mix; Thai Chilli Dipping Sauce; *Be Good To Yourself Dressings:* 90% Fat Free, 90% Fat Free Squeezy Bottle w Sugar & Sweetener, French, Hot Lime & Coconut, Less Than 5% Fat Vinaigrette Fresh, Raspberry, Tomato & Red Pepper, Vinaigrette; *Classic Vinaigrette Dressings:* Balsamic, French; *Dressings:* French, Fresh French, Fresh Lime & Coriander, Porcini; *Houmous:* Be Good To Yourself 50% Less Fat, Fresh, Fresh Roast Red Pepper, Organic; *Organic Dressings:* French, Tomato & Herb; *Salsa:* Fresh, Hot & Fiery, Thick & Chunky; *Taste The Difference Dressings:* Green Olive, Moroccan, Roasted Red Pepper, Tomato Chipotle & Smoked Paprika

GRAVIES & STOCKS
12 Vegetable Stock Cubes; Fresh Vegetable Stock; Gravy Powder; Vegetable Stock Pot

'ICE CREAMS', SORBETS ETC
Blue Parrot Café Ice Lollies: 10 Real Fruit Juice No Added Sugar Assorted, 10 Real Fruit Juice Rocket, Assorted Organic Apple & Organic Blackcurrant, Frozen Concentrated Jaffa Orange Juice; *Ice Lollies:* 10 Real Fruit Juice, 10 Real Orange Fruit Juice, 6 Fizzy, Taste The Difference Mango & Passionfruit; *Sorbet:* Lemon, Mango, Strawberries & Champagne

MARGARINES, FATS, OILS ETC
Organic Olive Spread; *Dairy Free Soft Spread:* Plain, w Garlic & Herbs; *Freefrom Dairy:* Low Fat Vegetable Spread 38% Fat, Vegetable Spread 70% Fat

PASTRY
Frozen Authentic Greek Filo Pastry (uncooked); Puff Pastry; *Fresh Pastry:* Filo, Ready Rolled Puff Perfect for Sweet & Savoury Recipes; *Shortcrust Pastry:* Mix, Ready Rolled

PICKLES, SAUCES, VINEGARS ETC
Gherkins in Vinegar; Red Cabbage in Sweet Vinegar; *Antipasto:* Artichokes,

Mixed Peppers, Sun-Dried Tomato, Wild Mushroom; *Balsamic Vinegars:* of Modena, Taste The Difference Apple, Vintage of Modena, w Cranberry, w Fig & Lime, w Raspberry; *Be Good To Yourself Italian Sauces:* Less Than 1% Fat Tomato & Herb for Pasta & Bolognese, Less Than 5% Fat Mediterranean Chargrilled Pepper Stir-In; *Be Good To Yourself Less Than 1% Fat Cooking Sauce:* Barbeque, Chilli Con Carne, Red Wine; *Blue Parrot Café Italian Sauces:* Bruschetta Topping, Pizza Topping Tomato & Vegetable, Tomato & Red Pepper Pasta; *Chutney:* Apple Raisin & Date, Chargrilled Aubergine w Spices, Flame Roasted Tomato & Pepper, Hot & Spicy Mango, Mango Plum & Ginger, Mild Mango, Organic Tomato, Peach, Pineapple Caraway & Cumin, Redcurrant & Red Onion w Balsamic Vinegar, Special Selection Hot Mango, Special Selection Tomato, Strawberry & Black Pepper; *Cooking Sauces:* Arrabbiata, Be Good To Yourself Less Than 5% Fat Balti, Bengali Hot & Sour Kari, Chair de Tomate, Cornichons in Sweet Vinegar, Gujarati Red Pepper Ras, Hot Chilli Con Carne, Keralan Shacuti, Madras, Medium Chilli Con Carne, Mushroom Pasta, Ratatouille Provencale, Rogan Josh, Siciliana, Sun Dried Tomato & Vinegar Stir-In, Tomato & Herb Pasta, Tomato & Moroccan Spice Tagine; *Cous Cous Sauce:* Chickpea Pinenut & Garlic, Moroccan Seven Vegetable, Roasted Red Pepper Tomato & Garlic; *Flavours of The Orient Sauce:* Dark Soy, Light Soy, Sweet & Sour, Szechuan Sweet & Sour; *Freefrom Sauces:* Korma, Mushroom White Wine & Dijon Mustard, Sun Dried Tomato & Basil, Tikka Masala; *Fresh Cooking Sauces:* Arrabbiata, Aubergine & Carrots, Be Good To Yourself 95% Fat Free Napoletana, Napoletana, Roasted Red Pepper Pasta Dressing, Way to Five Roasted Red Pepper w Tomatoes; *Fresh Indian Cooking Sauces:* Jalfrezi, Madras, Saag Masala; *Glaze:* Cranberry & Thyme Whiskey, Orange & Rosemary, Redcurrant Brandy & Juniper; *Jelly:* Cider & Sage, Cranberry & Apple w Thyme, Mint, Redcurrant; *Low Price:* Pickled Onions, Sliced Beetroot, Sweet Pickle; *Marinades:* French, Garlic & Herb, Italian, North African, Sticky BBQ, Sun Dried Tomato, Thai, Tomato & Herb, West Indian; *Mustard:* Chilli, Dijon w Tarragon, English, French Dark, French Dijon, German Style, Wholegrain, Wholegrain w White Wine; *Olives:* 12 Par Dry Black, Greek Green, Kalamata, Kalamata Pitted, Organic Tomato Ketchup; *Olives in Brine:* Pitted Black, Pitted Green, Pitted Queen Stuffed w Red Jalapeno, Queen, Sliced Black; *Organic Vinegars:* Balsamic, Malt, White Wine; *Piccalilli:* Dijon, Plain, Sweet; *Pickle:* Beetroot, Hot, Sweet; *Pickled:* Onions, Onions in Hot & Spicy Vinegar, Red Cabbage, Silverskin Onions, Sweet Pickled Onions; *Relish:* Barbecue, Onion, Sweetcorn, Tomato, Tomato & Chilli; *Sandwich Gherkins:* in Chilli & Mustard Vinegar, in Sweet Vinegar; *Sauce for Pasta & Bolognese:* Mushroom, Onion & Garlic; *Special Selection Mustard:* Balsamic, Suffolk;

Special Selection Olives: Alexandria Hot Spiced Black, Kalamata & Green, Kalamata w Marjoram; *Special Selection Vinegars:* Champagne Wine, Chianti Red Wine, Normandy Cider, Tarragon Wine, Vinsanto Wine, Vintage Balsamic of Modena; *Stir Fry Sauces:* Black Bean, Cantonese Black Bean, Ginger & Lemongrass, Tamarind & Lime, Thai Kaffir Lime Chilli & Basil; *Sweet & Sour Stir Fry Sauce w Crispy Vegetables:* Extra Pineapple, Plain, Spicy; *Table Sauces:* Apple & Ginger, Bramley Apple, Brown, Cranberry, Dill w Mild Sweet Mustard, Fresh Mint, Fruit, Hot Onion w Chilli, Italian Hot Tomato Ketchup, Italian Tomato Ketchup, Low Price Brown, Low Price Ketchup, Mint, Mint w Flame Roasted Garlic

SAVOURIES - CANNED/BOTTLED
Bombay Potatoes; Chickpea Dhal; Country Vegetable w Herb Dumplings Casserole; Meatfree Spaghetti Bolognese; Organic Spaghetti in Tomato Sauce; *Baked Beans in Tomato Sauce:* Curried, Low Price, Organic, Reduced Sugar Reduced Salt w Sugar & Sweetener, Standard; *Mixed Beans:* in Mild Chilli Sauce, in Spicy Pepper Sauce; *Mushy Peas:* Chip Shop Style, Low Price, No Added Colour, Standard

SAVOURIES - CHILLED/FRESH
Gourmet Mediterranean Style Cous Cous; Indian Steamed Basmati Rice; Mediterranean Roasted Vegetables in Balsamic Vinegar & Herb Dressing; Southern Indian Lime Rice; Spinach & Moong Daal; Sweet Potato & Green Pea Bonda; Taste The Difference Sunblush Tomatoes w Wild Rice; Way to 5 Spaghetti in a Cherry Tomato & Basil Sauce; Wheat w Roast Vegetables; *Be Good To Yourself:* 95% Fat Free Pasta & Vegetable Salad, Crunchy Green Salad w Lime & Coriander Dressing, Mint Ebly, Seeded Carrot Slaw; *Be Good To Yourself Less Than 5% Fat:* Beetroot Salad, Cous Cous w Crunchy Vegetables, Grape Salad, Penne Arrabbiata, Potato & Herb Salad, Vegetable Curry w Rice; *Cantonese:* 6 Mini Vegetable Spring Rolls, Fresh Oriental Chow Mein, Premium Stir Fry; *Deli Counter:* Felafel, Inari Block, Large Onion Bhaji, Mini Onion Bhaji, Thai Vegetable Spring Rolls, Vegetable Samosa; *Deli Counter Olives:* Jumbo Green w Garlic Basil & Lemon, Pitted Black, Summer, w Coriander & Lime; *Deli Counter Salads:* 95% Fat Free Italian Style Tomato, Beetroot Carrot & Mandarin, Ebly & Chickpea, Italian Style Pasta, Noodle & Vegetable, Panzella & Pasta Snack, Sweetcorn & Black Bean, Three Bean; *Deli Counter Taste The Difference:* Marinated Artichokes, Mixed Antipasti, Sunblush Tomatoes; *Deli Counter Taste The Difference Olives:* Blond w Cumin & Chilli, Cocktail of Mixed, Green Stuffed w Pimento, Kalamata Greek, Mixed Stuffed Green w Pimento Black Olive & Almonds, Naturally Ripened Black, Pitted Green; *Eastern Indian:* Aubergine Masala, Bengali Pilau Rice, Mushroom & Spinach Tikki, Vegetable Jalfrezi Curry;

Food To Go: 3 Colour Pilau Rice, Aloo Tikki, Aunt Bessie's Crispy Roast Potatoes, Boiled Basmati Rice, Bombay Potato, Mini Vegetable Samosa, Pilau Rice, Spinach & Moong Daal, Spinach Pakora; *Freefrom Ricebowl:* Chinese 5 Spice, Tikka Masala; *Noodles:* Chinese Stir Fry Thread, Deli Counter Teriyaki, Fresh 'n' Ready Washed & Ready to Cook Stir Fry, Singapore Thread, Thread; *Northern Indian:* 3 Colour Pilau Rice, Mushroom Pilau Rice, Pilau Rice, Tadka Daal; *Rice:* Roasted Spice, Thai Coconut w Mango, Thai Sticky, Turmeric & Lemon; *Western Indian:* Bombay Potato, Vegetable Dhansak Curry

SAVOURIES - DRIED

Cous Cous Quick Snack Tomato & Roasted Vegetable; Freefrom Spring Onion & Cheese Flavoured Mash Potato Pot; *Fortified Pasta:* Blue Parrot Café Tricolore Shells for Kids w Calcium & Iron, Fusilli for Active Living; *Instant Noodles:* Chicken, Chicken Curry, Sweet & Sour, Thai Green Curry, Vegetable

SAVOURIES - FROZEN

Blue Parrot Café Golden Rice w Vegetables; Breaded Onion Rings; Bubble & Squeak; Crispy Coated Garlic Mushrooms; Jacket Wedges; King Edward Roast Potatoes; Thai Style Rice w Stir Fry Vegetables; *Be Good To Yourself:* 96% Fat Free Oven Chips, Roast Potatoes; *Chinese:* Stir Fry Vegetables w Soy Sauce, Takeaway 4 Vegetable Spring Rolls; *Fry Chips:* American Style, Crinkle Cut, Low Price; *Indian Takeaway:* Gobi Aloo Saag, Onion Bhajis & Vegetable Samosas, Pilau Rice; *Oven Chips:* American Style, Crinkle Cut, Homestyle, Low Price, Organic Straight Cut, Steak Cut Only 5% Fat, Straight Cut Only 5% Fat

SEASONAL FOODS

6 Hot Cross Buns; Organic Mince Pies

SNACKS - SAVOURY

Be Good To Yourself Olive Oil & Sea Salt Baked Potato Chips; Bombay Mix; Les Mignons French Onion Flavour Croutons; Lightly Salted Traditional Pan Fried Crisps; Mini Poppadoms; Onion Rings; Organic Tomato Flavour Knobbles; Plain Ready to Eat Pappadums; Pretzel Thins; Salt & Vinegar Twirls; Sea Salt Popcorn; The Original Yo! Sushi Veggie Snack; Tomato & Basil Mini Grissini; *American Style Pretzels:* Salted, Sea Salt & Cracked Pepper; *Ready Salted Crisps:* 12 Pack, 6 Pack, Be Good To Yourself 25% Less Fat, Be Good To Yourself 6 Pack, Crunchy Sticks, Lift Offs, Potato Chips, Potato Rings, Potato Squares, Potato Triangles, Twirls; *Taste The Difference Crisps:* Charlotte Lightly Salted Traditional Pan Fried, Cracked Black Pepper Olive Oil, Rosemary Olive Oil, Sage Onion & Thyme Traditional Pan Fried, Vegetable Pan Fried; *Tortilla Chips:* Big Chilli Flavour, Cool Salted, Organic Blue Corn Lightly Salted

SOUPS

Extra Thick Vegetable; Fresh Tomato & Basil; Italian Range Tomato w Basil;

Italian Ribollita Vegetable; Taste The Difference Fire-Flamed Tomato & Red Onion; *Organic:* Leek & Potato, Tomato & Basil, Tuscan Bean

SOYA AND OTHER 'MILKS'
Soya UHT Alternative to Dairy Milk: Sweetened w Added Calcium, Unsweetened

SPREADS - SAVOURY
Freefrom Pesto: Green, Red

SPREADS - SWEET
Special Selection Hand Made Orange Marmalade w Whisky

TOFU, TEMPEH, MISO ETC
Tofu Soya Bean Curd

DRINK

BEERS
Biere des Flandres; Biere des Moulins des Flandres; Diat Pils; *Lager:* Belgian Super Strength, German Pilsner, Premiere Gold, Spanish Cerveza; *Taste The Difference:* Bavarian Style Wheatbeer, Kolsch Style Lager, Viennese Style Amber Lager

CIDERS & PERRIES
Cider: Strong, Strong Dry, Vintage; *Taste The Difference Cider:* Medium Dry, Medium Sweet

'HOT'
Cocoa; Drinking Chocolate; Fair Trade Drinking Chocolate

LOW & NON-ALCOHOLIC
German Low Alcohol Lager; Low Alcohol Cider; Shandy

SOFT
Cream Soda; Dandelion & Burdock Flavour Drink; Fiery Ginger Beer; Ginger Beer; Low Price Orange Drink; Mr Men Low Pear & Blueberry Drink; Premium Bitter Orange; Root Beer; Soda Water; *Bitter Lemon:* Diet Bitter Lemon, Premium, Standard; *Blue Parrot Café Flavoured Spring Water:* Apple, Banana, Blackcurrant, Orange, Peach, Strawberry; *Blue Parrot Café Organic Juice Drinks:* Apple & Blackcurrant, Apple & Strawberry, Tropical; *Blue Parrot Café Squash:* Apple, Apple & Blackcurrant, Apple & Strawberry, Tropical; *Caledonian Flavoured Spring Water:* Blackcurrant & Apple, Lemon & Lime, Peach & Orange, Sparkling w a Dash of Lemon; *Classic Cola:* Caffeine Free Diet, Diet, Standard; *Cola:* Diet, Low Price, Standard; *Cool Crush:* Apple, Lemon & Lime, Orange, Pineapple & Grapefruit; *Coolers:* Exotic, Mango, Raspberry; *Cordial:* Blackcurrant, Cherry, Cranberry & Raspberry, Lime w Ginger & Aromatic Bitters, Raspberry & Vanilla, Redcurrant & Lime, Taste The Difference Blackcurrant w Star Anise; *Diet:* Dandelion & Burdock, Ginger Beer; *Diet Cool Crush:* Lemon & Lime, Orange, Pineapple & Grapefruit; *Fizz:*

Apple, Cherry, Lime, Orange; *Flavoured Sparkling Spring Water:* Apple & Cherry, Apple & Cucumber, Elderflower & Pear, Grapefruit, Lemon & Lime, Mulled Mandarin & Cranberry, Orange & Mango, Peach, Strawberry & Vanilla; *Flavoured Still Spring Water:* Forest Fruits, Tropical Fruit; *Ginger Ale:* American, Diet American, Dry, Premium American, Premium Dry; *High Juice Squash:* Apple, Apple & Blackcurrant, Lemon, Orange, Peach, Pineapple, Pink Grapefruit, Reduced Sugar Orange Squash, Summer Fruits, Tropical Fruits; *Ice Tea:* Lemon, Orange, Peach Green Tea; *Juice Drink Plus:* C & E, Citrus Plus Fibre, Grape Cranberry & Raspberry + Calcium & Magnesium, Orange Carrot & Banana + Vitamins A; *Juice Drinks:* Apple, Apple Redcurrant & Lime, Aronia & Raspberry, Blood Orange & Nectarine w Vitamins A & E, Blue Parrot Café Apple & Strawberry, Cloudy, Cloudy Diet, Cranberry, Cranberry & Orange, Diet, Exotic, Freefrom Added Sugar Apple 'C', Fruit Cocktail, Lemonade, Low Price, NAS Cranberry & Raspberry, NAS Orange, Orange, Regular, Standard, Summerfruits, Tropical Fruit, White Grape & Peach; *Low Sugar Juice Drinks:* Apple, Apple & Blackcurrant, Apple & Strawberry, Cherry, Cranberry, Cranberry & Apple, Cranberry & Orange, Orange, Tropical; *Low Sugar Squash:* Apple & Blackcurrant, Grapefruit, Lemon & Lime, Mixed Fruits, Orange, Orange Lemon & Pineapple, Orange & Mango, Whole Lemon, Whole Orange; *Mood Drink:* Invigorate, Pick Me Up, Stress Less; *Smoothies:* Banana Orange & Coconut, Orange Passionfruit & Carrot Post-Party, Orange Strawberry & Guava, Organic Orange & Mango, Pineapple Banana & Mango, Raspberry Banana & Peach; *Squash:* Apple & Blackcurrant, Blackcurrant, Orange Lemon & Pineapple, Whole Lemon, Whole Orange; *Still No Added Sugar Cloudy Drinks:* Apple & Rhubarb, Grapefruit, Lemon, Pink Lemon; *Tonic Water:* Diet Indian, Diet w a Dash of Lemon, Indian, Indian w a Dash of Lemon, Premium Indian, Premium Low Calorie Indian, Premium Low Calorie w a Twist of Lemon; *Traditional Style:* Cream Soda, Diet Dandelion & Burdock, Lemonade - Made w Real Lemons; *Way To 5 100% Fruit Smoothie:* Pineapple Mango & Lime, Raspberry & Boysenberry

SPIRITS & APÉRITIFS

Dry Fino Sherry; Vodka; VSOP Grand CRU Cognac; *Brandy:* French, Spanish; *Gin:* Blackfriars, Dry London; *Rum:* Dark, Superior Dark, Superior White, White; *Whisky:* Blended, Claret Finish, Cognac Finish, Finest Old Matured, Highland, Islay, Kentucky Straight Bourbon, Sherry Cask, Single Malt Irish, Speyside

FOODS

BISCUITS
Bourbon Creams; Fruit Shortcake; Ginger Crunch; Morning Coffee; Rich Tea Finger; Shortcake; *Kwik Save:* Bourbon Creams, Fruit Shortcake, Ginger Nuts, Morning Coffee, Nice, Rich Tea, Rich Tea Fingers; *Makes Sense:* Bourbon Creams, Ginger Nut; *Simply:* Ginger Nuts

BREADS, ROLLS, PIZZA BASES ETC
Currant Buns; Danish Soft White Bread; Organic Crispbread; Pizza Base Mix; Premium Soft Batch Bread; Scottish Plain Bread; Softgrain Sliced Bread (All Sizes); Spiced Fruit Buns x 4; Teacakes; White Burger Baps; *Bake Off:* Sunflower & Poppy Seed Batard; *Baps:* Large White x 4, Soft White, White Burger, Wholemeal; *Bread:* Tomato & Basil; *Farmhouse:* Soft Loaf; *French Style Baguettes:* Harvester, White; *Kwik Save Naan Bread:* Garlic & Coriander, Plain; *Kwik Save Simply:* Brown Bread - All Slice Sizes, White Bread; *Long Life:* Premium Wholemeal, Sliced White, White Bread, Wholemeal Bread - All Slice Sizes; *Makes Sense:* Brown Bread (All Sliced Sizes), White Sliced Bread (All Slice Sizes); *Naan Bread:* Plain; *Petit Pain:* Harvester, White; *Pitta Bread:* White, Wholemeal; *Rolls:* 12 Soft White, 6 Soft White, Malted Brown, White Finger, White Giant Finger; *So Good:* Ciabatta Loaf, Ciabatta Sticks; *Wholemeal Bread:* All Slice Sizes

BREAKFAST FOODS
Choco Hoops; Malted Wheats; Wheat Biscuits; *Kwik Save:* Fruit & Nut Muesli, Wheat Biscuits; *Kwik Save Simply:* Bran Flakes, Corn Flakes, Frosted Flakes, Wheat Biscuits; *Makes Sense:* Corn Flakes; *Muesli:* Fruit & Nut, Luxury Fruit, Wholewheat

CAKES & CAKE MIXES
Apple Pies ISB; *Funky Food Factory:* 9 Mini Assorted Jam Tarts

CHOCOLATE
Chocolate Mint Crisps; *So Good:* Continental Plain Chocolate

CONFECTIONERY & SWEET SNACKS
American Hard Gums; Chocolate & Caramel Numbers; Clear Fruits; Fruit Sherbets; Sugared Almonds; *Kwik Save:* Clear Fruits

COOKING AIDS - SAVOURY
Stuffing: Apple & Herb, Sage & Onion

COOKING AIDS - SWEET
Crystallised Stem Ginger; Custard Powder; Cut Mixed Peel; Glace Cherries; *Mincemeat:* Luxury w Brandy & a Hint of Orange, Traditional

CRACKERS, CRISPBREADS ETC
Cream Crackers; Water Biscuits; *Breadsticks:* Classic, Sesame; *Healthy Selection:* Brown Rye Crispbread

DIPS & DRESSINGS
Roasted Red Pepper Houmous; *Dips:* Fresh Extra Hot Salsa, Fresh Salsa, Salsa,

Sweet Chilli (for Thai Meal Bag for Two); *French Dressings:* Reduced Fat, Standard; *Fresh Dressings:* French; *Good Intentions:* Roasted Red Pepper & Basil Dressing; *Kwik Save:* Salsa Dip; *Relish:* Tomato & Onion (Part of Fresh Indian Dips Multipack); *So Good:* Balsamic Dressing; *Tex Mex:* Spicy Potato Wedges

'ICE CREAMS', SORBETS ETC
10 Double Lickers; 10 Orange Flavour Ice Lollies; Rocket Lollies; *Kwik Save:* Orange Flavour Lollies, Rocket Lollies

PASTRY
Short Crust Pastry Mix

PICKLES, SAUCES, VINEGARS ETC
Apple & Calvados Sauce; Deli Mixed Olive & Pickle Selection; Hot Chilli Sauce; Malt Vinegar; Medium Chilli Sauce; Plum & Sesame Sauce; Redcurrant Jelly; Sweet Piccalilli; Sweet Pickle; Sweet Pickled Baby Beetroot; Sweet Pickled Crinkle Cut Beetroot; Sweet Pickled Onions; Sweet Pickled Sliced Beetroot; Tomato Ketchup (Glass & Plastic Bottles); *Basics:* Malt Vinegar, Tomato Ketchup; *Chutneys:* Mango (Part of Fresh Indian Dips Multipack); *Healthy Selection Pickled:* Sliced Beetroot, Sweet Sliced Beetroot; *Italian Sauce:* Tomato & Basil; *Makes Sense:* Brown Sauce, Sweet Pickled Onions; *Mustard:* English, Piccalilli; *Pasta Sauce:* Traditional, w Chunky Vegetables, w Mushrooms, w Onion & Garlic, w Peppers; *Pickled:* Onions, Red Cabbage, Silverskin Onions; *Pickles:* Lime (Part of Fresh Indian Dips Multipack); *Sauces:* Bramley Apple, Brown, Cranberry, Mint, Rogan Josh Curry Culinary, Sweet & Sour Culinary

SAVOURIES - CANNED/BOTTLED
Pimiento Stuffed Green Olives; Ratatouille; Reduced Sugar & Salt Baked Beans in Tomato Sauce; Spaghetti Rings in Tomato Sauce; Wholewheat Spaghetti In Tomato Sauce; *Baked Beans:* In Tomato Sauce; *Basics:* Spaghetti in Tomato Sauce; *Spaghetti:* Short Cut In Tomato Sauce

SAVOURIES - CHILLED/FRESH
4 Vegetable Spring Rolls; Bombay Potato (Part of Meals to Go Meal Deal); Delicately Flavoured Pilau Rice; Exotic Style Stir Fry; Onion Bhajis; Pilau Rice (Part of Curry to Go Meal Deal); Thai Sticky Rice (Part of Thai Bag Meal for Two); Thai Vegetable Spring Rolls (Part of Thai Bag Meal for Two); Vegetable Samosa Deli Counter; Vegetable Samosas; *Indian:* Bombay Potato; *Mini Indian Selection:* Celebrations Vegetable Samosa, Onion Bhaji, Onion Bhajis Deli Counter, Vegetable Pakora, Vegetable Samosas Deli Counter; *Onion Bhajis:* Deli Counter; *Oriental Selection:* Mini Vegetable Spring Rolls, Sweet & Sour Vegetable Parcels; *Thai Range:* Thai Meal for Two - Sticky Rice; *Vegetable Spring Rolls:* Single

SAVOURIES - DRIED
Sundried Tomato Cous Cous; *Kwik Save Instant Noodles:* Chicken; *Savoury Rice:* Curry; *Simply:* Instant Noodles - Beef

SAVOURIES - FROZEN
American Fries; Roast Potatoes; *Chips:* Crinkle Cut, Steak Cut, Straight Cut; *Kwik Save:* Breaded Onion Rings; *Kwik Save 3 Way Cook Chips:* American Fries, Steak Cut, Straight Cut; *Kwik Save Oven Chips:* Straight Cut; *Kwik Save Simply:* Deep Fry Straight Cut Chips; *Makes Sense Chips:* Deep Fry Straight Cut; *Onion Rings:* Breaded

SEASONAL FOODS
Standard Hot Cross Bun; Xmas Line - Shallow Fill Mince Pies x 6

SNACKS - SAVOURY
Large Roasted Salted Peanuts; Luxury Roast Salted Mixed Nuts; Luxury Unsalted Mixed Nuts; Mixed Nuts & Raisins; Potato Sticks; Roast Salted Cashew Nuts; *Crisps:* Hand-Cooked Slightly Salted; *Kwik Save Crisps:* Ready Salted, Roast Chicken; *So Good:* Sea Salt & Balsamic Vinegar Flavour Crisps; *Tortilla Chips:* Chilli Flavour, Lightly Salted

SOUPS
Scotch Broth Soup Mix

SPREADS - SWEET
Conserve: Apricot, Blackcurrant, Raspberry, Strawberry; *Kwik Save Conserve:* Apricot, Raspberry, Strawberry; *Kwik Save Jam:* Apricot, Blackcurrant, Raspberry, Seedless Raspberry, Strawberry; *Kwik Save Marmalade:* Lemon Shred, Thick Cut Orange, Thin Cut Orange; *Kwik Save Simply:* Medium Cut Orange Marmalade, Mixed Fruit Jam, Strawberry Jam; *Makes Sense:* Medium Cut Orange Marmalade, Strawberry Jam; *Pure Fruit Jam:* Apricot, Blackcurrant, Raspberry, Seedless Raspberry, Strawberry; *Pure Fruit Marmalade:* Fine Cut Orange, Lemon Shred, Medium Cut Orange, Orange Shred, Thick Cut Orange; *So Good:* Apricot Conserve, Blackcurrant Conserve, Raspberry Conserve, Strawberry Conserve

DRINK

BEERS
Biere de Belgique; French Premier Lager; German Pilsner

LOW & NON-ALCOHOLIC
Kwik Save: Shandy

SOFT
100% Pure Squeezed Florida Pink Grapefruit Juice; Cloudy Lemonade; Cream Soda; English Apple Juice; Freshly Squeezed Orange Juice; Ginger Beer; Lime Juice Cordial; Orange & Peach Drink; Organic Orange Juice; Pressed English Apple Juice; Pure Apple Juice; Pure Florida Orange Juice; Pure Grapefruit Juice; Pure Orange Juice; Pure Orange Juice w Bits; Pure Pineapple Juice; Pure Smooth Orange Juice; Pure Unsweetened Florida Orange Juice; Pure Unsweetened

Orange Juice Smooth; Tomato Juice; *American Ginger Ale:* Low Calorie, Standard; *Basics:* Pure Orange Juice; *Bitter Lemon:* Low Calorie, Standard; *Cola:* Original, Original Caffeine Free Diet, Original Diet; *Hi-Juice Drink:* Apple, Pink Grapefruit; *High Juice Drink:* Blackcurrant, Orange; *Indian Tonic Water:* Low Calorie, Low Calorie w Lemon, Low Calorie w Lime, Standard; *Juice Drink:* Apple & Grape, Apple w Sweeteners, Blackcurrant w Sweeteners, Cranberry, Cranberry w Sweeteners, Strawberry w Sweeteners, Tropical Fruit; *Juice Drink Multipack:* Apple w Sweeteners, Blackcurrant w Sweeteners, Orange w Sweeteners; *Kwik Save:* American Ginger Ale, Apple Juice, Bitter Lemon, Cloudy Diet Lemonade, Cloudy Lemonade, Cream Soda, Dandelion & Burdock, Diet Lemonade, Ginger Beer, Lemonade, Orange Juice, Orange Juice w Bits, Pineapple Juice, Pure Orange Juice; *Kwik Save Flavoured Spring Water Drink - Slightly Sparkling:* Cranberry, Lemon & Lime, Peach; *Kwik Save High Juice Drink:* Apple, Blackcurrant, Orange; *Kwik Save Indian Tonic Water:* Low Calorie, Standard; *Kwik Save No Added Sugar:* Blackcurrant Flavour Drink, Cherryade, Limeade, Orangeade, Strawberryade; *Kwik Save No Added Sugar Squash:* Apple & Blackcurrant, Lemon, Whole Orange; *Kwik Save Original Cola:* Diet, Standard; *Kwik Save Simply:* Cola, Lemonade, Orange Drink, Pure Apple Juice, Pure Orange Juice; *Kwik Save Squash:* Apple & Blackcurrant, Orange, Whole Orange; *Lemonade:* Cloudy Diet, Diet, Standard; *Makes Sense:* Cola, Lemonade, Orange Drink, Pure Orange Juice; *No Added Sugar:* Apple Crush, Cherryade, Limeade, Orangeade, Pink Grapefruit Fruit & Barley Drink, Strawberryade; *No Added Sugar Squash:* Apple, Apple & Blackcurrant, Lemon, Strawberry, Tropical Fruit, Whole Orange; *Orange Juice Drink:* w Sweeteners; *Slightly Sparkling Spring Water Fused w:* Cranberry, Grapefruit, Lemon & Lime, Peach; *Sparkling Juice:* Apple, Red Grape, White Grape; *Squash:* Apple & Blackcurrant, Lemon, Lemon & Lime, Orange, Orange & Pineapple

HEALTHCARE

FOOD SUPPLEMENTS

ACE Balance

FOODS

BISCUITS
Nairns Savoury Biscuit Selection; *Finest:* Stem Ginger Cookies; *Organic:* Shorties; *Value:* Digestive

BREADS, ROLLS, PIZZA BASES ETC
12 Crumpets; 4 Potato Farls; 6 Currant Buns; 6 Teacakes; 6 Tomato & Herb Tortilla Wraps; 8 Crumpets; 8 Potato Farls; 9 Value Crumpets; Ciabatta; Olive Ciabatta; Only 6.0g Carbohydrate per Slice Loaf; Organic Malt Loaf; Pizza Base Mix; *Bagels:* 5 Organic; *Baps:* 4 Large Wholemeal, 6 Large White; *Buns:* 12 Stayfresh White; *Finest:* 4 Everything Bagel, Campaillou Bread, Caramelised Garlic & Rosemary Foccacia, Cracked Black Pepper Bruschetinne, Crusty Malted Wheat Bread, Crusty Wholemeal Bread, Light Rye Bread, Mini Sundried Tomato & Basil Focaccia, Plain Ciabatta, Potato & Rosemary Bread; *Muffins:* 4 Demerara Sugar, 4 Oven Bottom, 6 White; *Naan Bread:* 2 Plain, 4 Mini Garlic & Coriander, Value; *Part Baked:* Ciabatta Bread; *Premium White Bread:* Extra Thick Sliced, Medium Sliced; *Premium Wholemeal Bread:* Medium Sliced, Thick Sliced; *Premium Wholesome White Bread:* Medium Sliced; *Rolls:* 12 Soft White, 4 Ciabatta, 4 Focaccia, 4 Panini, 6 Soft White, 6 White Morning, 6 Wholemeal; *Standard Brown Bread:* Medium Sliced; *Standard White Bread:* Medium Sliced, Stayfresh Medium Sliced, Stayfresh Thick Sliced, Thick Sliced, Toaster Extra Thick Sliced; *Value Packs:* 4 Teacakes; *White Danish Bread:* Medium Sliced, Thick Sliced; *Wholemeal Bread:* Stayfresh Medium Sliced, Stayfresh Thick Sliced

BREAKFAST FOODS
Multigrain Hoops; Puffed Wheat; Scottish Porridge Oats + Wheat Bran; Tropical Feast; *Healthy Living:* Muesli, Wheat Biscuits; *Kids:* Choco Hoops, Malt Wheats; *Multigrain Flakes:* Apple & Cranberry; *Organic:* Bran Flakes; *Value:* Cornflakes, Frosted Flakes, Rice Snaps

CAKES & CAKE MIXES
6 Value Apple Pies; Luxury Crumble Mix; *Jam Tarts:* Assorted, Value Raspberry Flavour

CHOCOLATE
Choc Gift Stacking Boxes; Fairtrade Plain Chocolate; Free From Chocolate

CONFECTIONERY & SWEET SNACKS
American Hard Gums; Fizzy Strawberry Lances; Fruit Sherbets; Peppermint Fresh Breath Strips; *Cereal Bars:* 5 Healthy Living Cranberry & Blackcurrant

COOKING AIDS - SAVOURY
Sage & Onion Stuffing Mix; *Finest:* Herb Stuffing Mix

COOKING AIDS - SWEET
Mincemeat; Mincemeat Cherries, Almonds & Brandy; *Glace Cherries:* French, Natural Coloured

CRACKERS, CRISPBREADS ETC
50% Reduced Fat Cream Crackers; High Baked Water Biscuits; Plain Mini Poppadoms; *Breadsticks:* Original, Original Mini; *Crackers:* Multigrain; *Finest:* Italian Olive Breadsticks, Scottish Oatcakes w Cracked Black Pepper; *Free From:* Savoury Snack Rice Cakes; *Rice Cakes:* BBQ, Salt & Vinegar, Salt & Vinegar Snack Minis

DESSERTS
Strudel: Apple, Woodland Fruit

DIPS & DRESSINGS
Dips: Sweet & Sour; *Finest:* Mango Salsa Dip; *Finest Dipping Oils:* Balsamic, Chilli & Garlic, Italian Herbs; *Houmous:* Healthy Living, Organic, Roasted Red Pepper; *Salad Dressing:* Healthy Eating, Healthy Eating Oil Free French, Healthy Living French, Healthy Living Tomato & Basil, Mustard & Tarragon; *Salsa Dip:* Cool

GRAVIES & STOCKS
Vegetable Gravy Granules; Vegetable Stock Cubes; *Value:* Vegetable Stock Cubes

'ICE CREAMS', SORBETS ETC
Lollies: Assorted 10 Real Fruit, Finest Fresh Squeezed Orange Juice, Kids Assorted Fruit, Rocket; *Sorbet:* Mango

MARGARINES, FATS, OILS ETC
Dairy Free Sunflower Spread

PICKLES, SAUCES, VINEGARS ETC
Corn Maryland Style Relish; Fruity Brown Sauce; Mint Jelly; Pickled Red Cabbage; *Chinese Cooking Sauce:* Finest Blackbean Stirfry, Value Sweet & Sour; *Chutney:* Curried Fruit, Finest Apple & Flame Roasted Tomato & Garlic, Hot Mango, Mango, Peach; *Finest:* Baby Beetroot Red Wine & Oregano, Mint Jelly w Rosemary, Onions Chillies & Smoked Mesquite, Silverskin Onions Lemon & Black Pepper; *Finest Glaze:* Balsamic, Mustard Maple & Whisky, Roast Garlic Lemon & Thyme; *Finest Sauce:* Mustard & Dill, Peking Sweet & Sour, Rough Chop & Roast Red Pepper, Sundried Tomato Garlic & Basil, Tomato Garlic & Chilli; *Finest Stir Fry Sauce:* Lemon & Ginger, Yellow Bean & Ginger; *Finest Tapenade:* Green Olive w Lemon & Garlic, Sweet Red Pepper; *Fresh Organic Sauce:* Arrabiata, Napoletana; *Healthy Living Sauce:* Sweet & Sour; *Indian Cooking Sauces:* Madras, Rogan Josh; *Ketchup:* Reduced Sugar & Salt; *Mustard:* Burgess English, Dijon, Finest Horseradish, Finest Smoked Garlic, Finest Wholegrain Peppercorn, Wholegrain; *Onions:* Sweet Silverskin in Vinegar; *Pasta Sauce:* Original; *Piccalilli:* Finest Spicy Indian, Finest Three Mustard, Sandwich, Standard, Sweet; *Pickle:* Original, Sandwich; *Pickled Onions:* Hot & Spicy, Sharp Silverskin, Sweet Silverskin, Traditional; *Relish:* Finest Chunky Beetroot, Onion, Tomato & Chilli; *Sauce:* Sweet & Sour; *Sauce for Pasta:* Chunky Vegetable, Healthy Eating, w Onion & Garlic; *Sauces:* Bramley Apple, Brown (Bottle/Squeezy), Fresh Garden Mint Sauce, Fruity, Mint, Ready To Serve Mint Squeezy, Smooth Bramley Apple, Value Brown, Value

Mint Sauce; *Stir Fry:* Black Bean Sauce, Family Pack, Mixed Pepper, Sweet Chilli Sauce, Szechuan Sauce, Value Veg, Vegetable; *Tomato Ketchup:* Value; *Vinegar:* Cider, Malt, Red Wine, White Wine

SAVOURIES - CANNED/BOTTLED
Bruschetta Topping; Bubble & Squeak; Lentil Dahl; Mixed Veg Chilli; Olive Salad Mix; Pimento Stuffed Olives in Brine; Ratatouille Provencale; Saag Aloo; *Baked Beans:* Healthy Living, Value; *Spaghetti:* In Tomato Sauce, Long Cut, Rings In Tomato Sauce; *Value:* Vegetable Chilli

SAVOURIES - CHILLED/FRESH
6 Onion Bhajis; Large Mixed Bhaji Pack; Large Pakora Pack; New York Style Healthy Eating Potato Wedges; Onion Bhajis; Roasted Winter Vegetables; Vegetarian Chilli & Rice; *Finest:* Chunky Chips, Four Bean Salad, Kalamata Olives, Queen Green Olives, Ready to Bake Vegetable Seln Chilli; *Healthy Living:* Roast Potatoes, Roasted Winter Vegetables; *Mini:* Onion Bhaji; *Olive Bar:* Black & Green Olives in Chilli & Thyme, Chargrilled Mixed Peppers, Garlic Stuffed Olives, Greek Mammoth Green Olives, Greek Olives in Lemon & Garlic, Kalamata Olives, Lemon Olives in Ginger & Lemongrass, Mixed Olives in Chilli & Basil, Moroccan Olives in Lemon & Coriander, Pitted Collosal Olives & Roasted Vegetables, Queen Green Olives w Sundried Tomatoes, Sundried Tomatoes; *Salad Bar:* Italian Salad, Mushroom a la Greque; *Stir Fry:* Beansprout & Veg

SAVOURIES - DRIED
Value: Instant Mash, Spicy Curry Quick Snack

SAVOURIES - FROZEN
American Style Fries; Breaded Onion Rings; Crispy Potatoes; Party Mini Rostis; Steakhouse Fry Chips; *Fry Chips:* Crinkle Cut, Straight Cut; *Healthy Living:* Low Fat Roast Potatoes; *Oven Chips:* American Style, American Style Thin Fries, Crinkle Cut

SEASONAL FOODS
6 Organic Mince Pies; Valentine's Lovetokens

SNACKS - SAVOURY
Organic Ready Salted Crisps; Potato Chips; Ready Salted 30% Less Fat Crisps; Roasted Salted Mixed Nuts; Roasted Salted Nut Assortment; Thick & Crunchy Texas BBQ; *Finest:* Fragrant Thai Herb Crisps, Roasted Salted Cashew & Macadamia Nuts; *Value:* Tortilla Chips

SOUPS
Organic: Tomato & Basil

SOYA AND OTHER 'MILKS'
Fresh Soya Milk: Sweetened; *Organic Soya Drink:* Sweetened, Unsweetened

SPREADS - SWEET
Finest Conserve: Apricot, Blackcurrant,

Raspberry, Red Cherry, Strawberry; *Jam:* Organic Raspberry, Organic Strawberry, Plum, Raspberry, Strawberry; *Jelly:* Bramble; *Marmalade:* Fine Cut Breakfast, Fine Cut Lemon Shred, Fine Cut Orange, Fine Cut St Clements, Finest Sweet Orange w Drambuie, No Peel Lemon Jelly, No Peel Orange Jelly, Organic Fine Cut, Thick Cut Orange, Value Orange; *Preserve:* Finest Ginger

DRINK

'HOT'

Instant Lemon Tea Granules

LOW & NON-ALCOHOLIC

Traditional Style Lemonade Shandy

SOFT

Finest Morello Cherry Crush; Lime Juice Cordial; No Added Sugar Appleade; Sugar Free Strawberryade; Traditional Style Ginger Beer; *Active Glucose Drink:* Orange, Orange Energy, Sparkling Orange, Standard; *Aqua:* Orange & Peach Flavour Detox, Strawberry Mineral Max; *Chilled Finest Crush:* Mango & Passionfruit, Orange & Raspberry, Summer Fruit, Tropical; *Chilled Juice Drink:* Apple & Raspberry, Cranberry, Orange & Banana, Summer Fruits; *Chilled Kids Juice Drink:* Apple & Blackcurrant, Orange & Pineapple; *Chilled Orange Juice:* Smooth, w Bits; *Cola:* Standard, Sugar Free; *Finest:* Blackberry Redberry & Mulberry Cordial, Indian Tonic Water, Mexican Key Limecrush, Tonic Water w Lemon; *Finest Freshly Squeezed Orange Juice:* & Grapefruit, Smooth, w Bits; *Flavoured Springwater:* Apple, Cranberry, Grapefruit, Lemon & Lime, Raspberry; *Healthy Eating No Added Sugar Juice Drink:* Cranberry & Orange, Orange, Orange w Calcium; *High Juice No Added Sugar Squash:* Blackcurrant; *Juice Drink:* Apple & Elderflower, Forest Fruits, Orange & Peach, Pear & Raspberry, Raspberry & Strawberry, Tropical; *Kick Stimulation Drink:* Diet w Cranberry, Standard; *Kids Flavoured Water:* Banana & Vanilla; *Kids High Juice Squash:* Orange & Pineapple; *Kids Juice:* Orange & Banana; *Kids Juice Drink:* Apple & Strawberry, Blackcurrant, Orange & Peach; *Lemonade:* Diet, Organic, Sparkling, Standard, Sugar Free, Value, Value Sugar Free; *Mix It:* Lemon Ice, Pina Colada; *Mixers:* Indian Tonic Water; *No Added Sugar Fruit & Barley:* Peach, Pink Grapefruit; *No Added Sugar Healthy Eating:* Orange; *No Added Sugar Healthy Eating Juice Drink:* Apple; *No Added Sugar Juice Drink:* Apple, Apple & Blackcurrant, Apple & Strawberry, Sourpear Drops, Tropical Orange; *No Added Sugar Squash:* Mixed Fruit, Orange, Tropical; *Organic Crush:* Apple, Grapefruit, Orange; *Pure Juice:* Exotic, Fair Trade Orange, Florida Orange & Grapefruit, Grapefruit, Orange w Bits, Tomato, Tropical; *Spring Water Hint of:* Apple & Raspberry, Blackberry & Grape, Cherry & Cranberry, Elderflower & Lemon,

Grapefruit, Lemon & Lime, Orange, Peach; *Squash:* Value Low Calorie Orange, Whole Lemon, Whole Orange; *Still Spring Water:* Apple, Cranberry, Grapefruit, Lemon & Lime, Raspberry; *Sugarfree:* Cherryade, Orangeade; *Traditional Style:* Ginger Beer, Lemonade Shandy; *Value:* Low Calorie Apple & Blackcurrant Drink; *Value Juice Drink:* Orange

FOODS

BISCUITS

Bourbons; Clown Face; Fruit Shortcake; Gromit; Morning Coffee; Organic Ginger; *Rich Tea:* Biscuits, Fingers, Low Fat

BREADS, ROLLS, PIZZA BASES ETC

6 Finger Crumpets; Daktyla; Danish Toaster; Feuille de Campagne; Mixed Olive Petit Pave; Mixed Olive Rustique; Pain Cirque; Pain Vivant; Paysan Rustique; Potato & Herb Knot; Pretzel; Spanish Seeded Gallego; Tomato Petit Pave; *Bagels:* 4 Organic, 5 Caramelised Onion & Poppyseed, 5 Cinnamon & Raisin Bagel, Plain Bake Off; *Bake-Off Breads:* Baguette, Flute, Granary Baton, Grand Rustique, Organic Baguette, Organic Brown Bread, Organic Heyford Wholemeal, Organic Heyford Wholemeal Long Tin, Organic White Bread, Pain Au Levain, Pain Rustique, Petit Pain, Poppy Knot, Rustique Flat, White Farmhouse; *Bake-Off Sun:* Granary Tin, Malted Sandwich, White Bloomer, White Farmhouse, White Long Split Tin, White Long Tin, White Tin, Wholemeal Farmhouse; *Baps:* 4 Giant White, 4 Giant Wholemeal, 6 White Floured, 6 Wholemeal; *Bread:* Ascot Brown Thin, Boule, Farmhouse Malted Batch, Granary Malted Tin, Hovis Wheatgerm, La Buche du Nord, Malted Farmhouse, Malted Tin, Mediterranean Olive, Mixed Olive Pave, Organic Malted Wheat Tin, Pave Lillois, Pet Parisienne, Scarpetta, Sliced Richly Fruited, Soft Grain Thick, Sundried Tomato Pave, Walnut; *Brown Bread:* Ascot Medium; *Buns:* 6 Sesame Seed Burger; *Ciabatta:* Italian, Mediterranean; *Focaccia:* Trio, w Rosemary; *Food Explorers:* 4 White Rolls; *Frozen Bread:* 3 Half Baguettes; *Granary:* Malted Brown Sandwich, Sesame, Thick; *Grand Mange:* Blanc, Paysan; *Organic Bread:* German Recipe Rye, Malted White Long Tin, Premium Thick, Traditional White, Traditional Wholemeal, White Medium; *Pane:* All'Olio, Rustico; *Pitta Bread:* 6 Standard; *Premium:* Thick Wholemeal w Seeds, White Medium, Wholemeal, Wholemeal Medium, Wholemeal Thick; *Premium Bread:* White Thick; *Rolls:* 2 Paninis, 4 Loose White, 4 Loose Wholemeal, 4 Malt, 4 Old Fashion White, 4 Organic Brown, 6 White Snack, 8 White Finger, Ciabatta, Crusty, French, White Crusty, White Soft; *Rye:* Light w Caraway Seed; *White Bread:* Bloomer, Farmhouse, Farmhouse Batch, Farmhouse Crusty Batch, French Stick, Medium, Organic Farmhouse, Organic Long Tin, Organic Old Fashioned, Organic White Tin, Poppy Farmhouse, Poppy Seed, Sandwich, Seeded Farmhouse, Soft Sandwich Tin, Sour Doughbread, Split Tin, Thick, Tin; *Wholemeal:* Batch, Farmhouse, Long Tin, Medium, Oat & Seed, Organic Heyford Long Tin, Stoneground Tin Organic Flour; *Wholemeal Bread:* Organic, Organic Heyford Tin, Organic Old Fashioned, Organic Stoneground Farmhouse, Sandwich, Soft Sandwich Tin, Tin

BREAKFAST FOODS
Blackberry & Cranberry Crisp; Chocolate Hoops; High Fibre Bran; Malted Wheats; Maple & Pecan Crisp; Multigrain Hoops; Porage Oats & Bran; Triple ChocNutCrisp; Wholemeat Cereal Biscuits; *Food Explorers:* Chocolate Nut, Hot Oat Cereal, Toffee Caramel; *Hot Oat:* Original, Variety; *Muesli:* Cranberry, High Fibre, Luxury Fruit, Luxury Fruit & Nut, Maple & Nut, Orchard Fruit, Organic, Tropical; *Perfect Balance:* Multi Flake Cereal

CAKES & CAKE MIXES
Apple & Blackberry Pie; Apple Pie; Assabee; Baklava; Boukage; Kulwuskur; Strawberry & Rhubarb Pie; Treacle Tart; *Family Pie:* Apple, Apple & Blackberry

CHOCOLATE
After Dinner Gift; After Dinner Mints; Choc Brazil Nuts; Chocolate Covered Ginger; Continental Plain Chocolate; Mint Thins; Peppermint Creams; Plain Chocolate Cocoa Dusted Walnuts

CONFECTIONERY & SWEET SNACKS
Clear Mints; Crystal Stem Ginger; Fruit Jellies; Marzipan Fruits; Mint Imperials

COOKING AIDS - SAVOURY
Lightly Salted Croutons

COOKING AIDS - SWEET
Cut Mixed Peel; Glace Cherries; Raspberry Sauce; *Marzipan:* Golden, White; *Mincemeat:* Cranberry & Port, Traditional

CRACKERS, CRISPBREADS ETC
Celery Seed Biscuits; Cream Crackers; High Bake; Rye & Sesame Biscuits; *Breadsticks:* Perfect Balance, Traditional; *Food Explorers:* Mini Breadsticks; *Oatcakes:* Organic, Scottish; *Perfect Balance Ricecake:* Lo Salt, No Salt; *Poppadums:* 8 Spicy, 8 Standard; *Thins:* Poppy & Sesame

DESSERTS
Food Explorers: 4 Peach & Jelly, Mandarin & Pineapple; *Kids:* 2x Mixed Fruit, 2x Peach Pot; *Organic Fruit Compote:* Red, Yellow; *Puddings:* 4 Summer, Bistro 2 Summer, Family Summer, Summer, Winter

DIPS & DRESSINGS
Horseradish Cream; Salsa Dip; *Dressings:* Balsamic Pepper, French, Mustard & Dill, Pepper & Balsamic; *Houmous:* Lemon, Organic, Red Pepper, Reduced Fat; *Perfect Balance Dressings:* French, Passionfruit & Pineapple; *Perfectly Balanced Dips:* Roasted Pepper

'ICE CREAMS', SORBETS ETC
Ice Lollies: Juice, Orange Juice

PICKLES, SAUCES, VINEGARS ETC
Balsamic Glaze; Gherkins; Shallots; *Beetroot:* Baby, Sliced, Sweet Baby, Sweet Sliced; *Chutney:* Apple & Walnut, Hot Mango, Mango, Spiced Peach; *Chutneys:* Caramelised Onion, Roasted Vegetable, Spicy Onion, Tomato; *Food Explorers:* Pasta Sauce; *Jelly:* Mint, Redcurrant & Port; *Marinades:* BBQ, Thai, Tomato & Chilli; *Mustard:*

Dijon, English, French, Wholegrain; *Onions:* Balsamic, Traditional, w Spices; *Organic Perfectly Balanced Sauce:* Sweet & Sour; *Pasta Sauce:* Arrabbiatta, Original; *Perfect Balance Pasta Sauce:* Funghi, Napoletania; *Perfect Balance Sauces:* Balti; *Perfectly Balanced Cooking Sauce:* Chilli; *Perfectly Balanced Sauces:* Jalfrezi, Tomato & Herb; *Piccalilli:* Mustard, Sweet; *Pickled:* Onion, Silverskin Onions, Sweet Onion; *Relish:* Garlic, Salsa; *Sauce:* Apple, Cranberry, Mint, Plum & Ginger; *Sauces:* BBQ, Cajun, Sweet & Sour, Teriyaki; *Soy Sauce:* Dark, Japan, Light, Teryaki; *Tapenade:* Olive & Lemon, Sundried Tomato; *Tomato Ketchup:* Organic, Reduced Sugar, Squeezy, Standard; *Vinegar:* Balsamic, Cider, Malt, White Wine

SAVOURIES - CANNED/BOTTLED
Ratatouille; Rosti Swiss Style Potatoes; Spaghetti in Tomato Sauce; Spaghetti Rings; Vegetable Chilli; *Baked Beans:* Perfect Balance; *Beans:* Organic Baked Beans, Spicy Tomato; *Coucous:* Tomato & Onion

SAVOURIES - CHILLED/FRESH
4 Vegetable Samosas; 6 Onion Bhajis; 6 Vegetable Spring Rolls; Black Rice w Mango; Bombay Potatoes; Borettane Onions; Garlic & Rosemary Potatoes; Grilled Artichoke Hearts; Grilled Aubergines; Grilled Courgettes; Grilled Mushroom Trio; Grilled Peppers; Grilled Shallots; Marinated Red Peppers; Masala Dal; Onion Bhajis; Organic Falafel; Puy Lentils & Tomato; Roast Potatoes; Roasted Peppers; Roasted Vegetable Coucous; Sweet & Sour Pumpkin; Thai Fragrant Rice; Thyme Roasted Tomatoes; Vegetable Biryani; Vegetable Dhansak; Vegetable Jalfrezi; Vegetable Masala; Vegetable Spring Rolls; *Olives:* a la Grecque, Almond, Black & Green w Herbs, Greek Kalkidis, Kalamata, Kalamata Greek, Large Green Stuffed, Mediterranean, Mixed Stuffed, Pimento Stuffed, Stuffed Green; *Perfectly Balanced:* Red Peppers; *Pilau Rice:* Lemon, Spinach & Carrot, Standard, w Spinach; *Rice:* Couscous, Thai Fragrant; *Salads:* Bean, Beetroot, Carrot Courgette & Coriander, Cucumber, Mediterranean, Moroccan Couscous, Noodle, Pasta & Vegetable, Pea Apricot & Pepper, Potato & Onion, Spicy Mexican Bean, Tabbouleh, Tarragon Bean, Tomato, Vegetable

SAVOURIES - FROZEN
Coated American Fries; Diced Potato; Potato Rosti; Spicy Jacket Wedges; *Chips:* Crinkle Cut Oven, Fry, Organic Oven, Oven, Reduced Fat Oven, Steak Cut Oven

SEASONAL FOODS
Hot Cross Buns: 12 White, 4 Perfectly Balanced, 6 White

SNACKS - SAVOURY
Bombay Mix; Exotic Mix; Low Salt Tortillas; Onion Rings; Poppadums; Potato Rings Ready Salted; Potato Sticks; Vegetable Chips; *Crisps:* Chilli & Tomato, Hand-Cooked Sea Salt, Low Fat Crinkle, Ready Salted, Salt & Vinegar, Sea Salt Lemon & Thyme, Sea

Salt Organic; *Pretzels:* Large Salted, Salt & Black Pepper, Selection; *Roasted & Salted Nuts:* Almonds, Cashews, Luxury Mixed, Macadamias, Organic Cashews, Organic Mix, Organic Peanuts, Peanuts, Pecans; *Tortilla Chips:* Blue Corn, Organic, Yellow Corn

SOUPS
Chunky 3 Bean; Chunky Minestrone; Gazpacho; Tomato & Basil; *Perfect Balance:* Mediterranean Vegetable, Tuscan Bean

SOYA AND OTHER 'MILKS'
Rice Drink w Calcium; *Organic Soya Milk:* Sweetened, Unsweetened; *Soya Milk:* Sweetened

SPREADS - SWEET
Conserve: Apricot, Black Cherry, Blackcurrant, Ginger, Greengage, Morello Cherry, Raspberry, Strawberry, Victoria Plum; *Fresh Marmalade:* Grapefruit, Lemon, Orange; *Jam:* Apricot, Raspberry, Seedless Raspberry, Strawberry; *Marmalade:* 3 Fruits, Orange & Ginger, Organic Thin, Pink Grapefruit, Reduced Sugar, Seville Orange Thick, Seville Orange Thin, Shredless; *Organic Conserve:* Cherry; *Organic Continental Conserve:* Apricot, Blackcurrant, Raspberry, Strawberry; *Organic Marmalade:* Seville Orange; *Reduced Sugar Jam:* Apricot, Blackcurrant, Strawberry

TOFU, TEMPEH, MISO ETC
Organic Tofu

DRINK

'HOT'
Cocoa Powder; Drinking Chocolate; Organic Drinking Chocolate

SOFT
Bitter Cranberry; Bitter Lemon; Cola; Cream Soda; Diet Cola; Fiery Ginger Beer Light; Orange & Mango; Pressed English Apple Drink; Ruby Grapefruit; *Cordial:* Elderflower, Lime Juice; *Crush:* Raspberry & Lemon; *Flavoured Still Water:* Grape; *Flavoured Water:* Cranberry & Raspberry, Lemon & Lime, Scottish Water w Lemon, Scottish Water w Lime, Strawberry, White Grape; *Food Explorers Flavoured Still Water:* Lemon, Raspberry, Strawberry; *Food Explorers Juice:* Apple, Blackcurrant, Chilled Apple, Orange, Tropical; *Fruit Crush:* Berry; *Fruit Drink:* Apple & Cranberry, Apple & Elderflower, Apple & Raspberry, Cranberry, Orange & Mango; *Fruit Juice:* Apple & Elderflower, Exotic, Florida Pink Grapefruit, Grape Cherry & Cranberry, Orange & Banana, Orange & Mango, Orange & Passionfruit, Organic Pure Apple, Pure Apple, Pure Grapefruit, Pure Pineapple, Red Grape, Variety Pack, White Grape; *Ginger Ale:* American, Dry; *Ginger Beer:* Fiery, Light; *High Juice:* Apple, Blackcurrant, Blackcurrant Light, Cranberry & Blueberry, Grape & Peach, Lemon, Orange, Pink Grapefruit, Summer

Fruits, Tropical; *Lemonade:* Cloudy, Cloudy Light, Sparkling, Standard, Still, w Lemon; *Low Calorie:* American Ginger Ale, Bitter Lemon, Lemonade, Tonic Water; *NFC Fruit Juice:* Apple Pear & Blackcurrant, Orange & Banana, Pineapple; *No Added Sugar:* Apple & Blackcurrant, Lemon; *No Added Sugar Squash:* Grapefruit, Orange; *Orange Juice:* Florida, Florida Squeezed, Organic, Organic Freshly Squeezed, Premium Smooth, Premium w Bits, Pure, Pure Smooth, Smooth, Sunpride Pure; *Premium Fruit Juice:* Apple & Cranberry, Tomato; *Presse:* Lemon & Elderflower; *Presse Fruit Juice:* Apple, Tomato; *Pressed Fruit Juice:* Apple & Mango, English Apple, Tomato; *Sparkling Flavoured Water:* Mango; *Sparkling Juice:* Apple & Elderflower; *Spring Water:* Cranberry & Blueberry, Elderflower, Grapefruit; *Squash:* Orange; *Tonic Water:* Diet w Lemon, Low Calorie w Lemon, Standard, w Lemon

NOTES

■ NOT LISTED?

Some supermarkets have informed us that they are unable to provide vegan lists. These include Morrisons (including Safeway Stores) and Lidl. As with all manufacturers and retailers, they are most likely to improve their vegan customer service if they receive requests from vegans; once they realise the size of the vegan market they are more likely to act helpfully as they will perceive it to be in their interest.

Morrisons:

Customer Service
Department
Wm Morrison
Supermarkets plc
Parry Lane
Bradford
BD4 8TD

Telephone: 01274 356000

Lidl:

Lidl Customer Service
Department
Lidl UK GmbH
19 Worple Road
Wimbledon
SW19 4JS

Telephone: 0870 444 1234

■ THE HELPFUL

Some of the more enlightened supermarkets now take the step of marking their vegan own-brand products. Although there is no substitute for The Vegan Society's own trademark, this is a very welcome development and shows an increased recognition of the importance of vegans as a group of customers. In recent years, Sainsbury's, Tesco and the Co-op have all introduced their own system of vegan labelling, although at present this mostly applies only to food products.

■ WHAT'S MISSING?

Some supermarkets were unable to provide complete listings. The Co-op does not produce a vegan list for toiletries and cosmetics. Similarly some supermarkets, such as Tesco and Sainsbury's, do not carry lists of vegan wines. This does not mean, however, that such products do not exist, and if enough people requested such lists then it is likely these supermarkets could be persuaded to produce them.

■ UP-TO-DATE?

Supermarkets regularly change their suppliers, and sometimes will not update their lists accordingly. In particular, the vegan list supplied by Sainsbury's has not been updated since late 2002.

Contact details are provided for all companies listed, so if you have a query about a particular product, you may wish to contact the company directly. See COMPANY CONTACTS, page 323.

When updates are made to supermarket lists, they will be available from The Vegan Society or at *www.animalfreeshopper.com*

■ HUMANE COSMETICS STANDARD

The following supermarkets are approved by BUAV to use their Humane Cosmetics Standard on their own brand toiletries and cosmetics: the Co-op, Safeway Stores, Sainsbury's.

More information on the Humane Cosmetics Standard, see ANIMAL TESTING CRITERIA, page 298.

■ CIWF COMPASSIONATE SUPERMARKET OF THE YEAR AWARDS

Compassion in World Farming holds an annual awards ceremony for compassionate supermarkets. The winners in 2003/04 were as follows:

Compassionate Supermarket of the Year – Waitrose
Most Improved Compassionate Supermarket – Waitrose
Welfare Ideal-Most Advanced Supermarket – Marks & Spencer

For more information, contact Compassion in World Farming (see USEFUL ADDRESSES, page 309)

ANIMAL-FREE CRITERIA

To qualify for inclusion in the Animal free shopper, products must, as far as is possible and practical, be entirely free from animal involvement.

NO ANIMAL INGREDIENTS

The manufacture and/or development of the product, and where applicable its ingredients, must not involve, or have involved, the use of any animal product, by-product or derivative

SUCH AS:

• **animal-derived additives** — (see below) • **animal fibres** — angora, astrakhan, cashmere, mohair, wool • **animal milks** • **animal milk derivatives** — casein, caseinates, lactates, lactic acid, lactose • **bee products** — bee pollen, bee venom, beeswax, honey, propolis, royal jelly • **dairy products and by-products** — butter, cheese, whey, yoghurt • **eggs and their derivatives** (eg albumen, lecithin, lutein • **items obtained directly from the slaughter of animals** — fish (including anchovies), game and their derivatives (eg meat/fish extracts and stocks), poultry, meat • **marine animal products** — ambergris, capiz, caviar(e), chitin, coral, fish scales, fishmeal, isinglass, marine oils and extracts (eg fish oils, shark oil (squalene or squalane), seal oil, whale oil), natural sponge, pearl, roe, seal meat, shellfish, sperm oil, spermaceti wax, whale meat • **miscellaneous** — amniotic fluids, animal and fish glues, carmine/carminic acid, catgut, chamois, cochineal, crushed snails or insects, fixatives (eg musk, civet, castoreum) hormones (eg oestrogen, progesterone, testosterone) ivory, lanolin(e), oil of mink, parchment, placenta, silk, shellac, snake venom, some vitamins (eg D3), urea, vellum, and any carriers, processing aids or release agents containing/comprising substances of animal origin • **slaughter by-products** — animal fats (eg dripping, lard, suet, tallow), amino acids, aspic, bone, bone charcoal, bone meal, bristles, collagen, down, dried blood, fatty acid derivatives, feathers, fur, gelatin(e), glycerin(e)/glycerol, hair, hides (leather, suede etc), hoof & horn meal, oleic acid, oleoic oil, oleostearin, pepsin, proteins (eg elastin, keratin, reticulin), rennet, skins, stearates, stearic acid, stearin(e)

Vegetable, mineral or plant/mineral-derived synthetic forms of these substances are acceptable, as are microbiologically-fermented substances of plant origin.

NO ANIMAL TESTING

The development and / or manufacture of the product, and where applicable its ingredients, must not involve, or have involved, testing of any sort on animals conducted at the initiative of the manufacturer or on its behalf, or by parties over whom the manufacturer has effective control.

ADDITIVES

A food additive alters the properties of a basic foodstuff or mixture of foodstuffs for the purpose of achieving one, or a combination of, the following: aiding the production process, preserving, modifying consumer perception. The majority of additives possess no nutritive value.

All the countries of the European Union share a common list of additives. They are preceded with an 'E' to show they have been approved for use within the Union and must be displayed on the labels of all foods containing them. Some additives do not have E-numbers and therefore do not have to be declared. These include solvents, used to dilute other additives such as colourings and to extract flavours. Flavourings constitute the largest group of non-E additives.

Colourings and dyes that are approved for use in the cosmetics industry within the EU are also designated a Colour Index ('CI') number.

The addition of substances to modify food is by no means a new phenomenon. Salt, for example, has been used as a preservative since c3000BCE. However, the sheer number of additives available for use today, the routine and insidious use of animal-derived substances, the known health problems associated with some additives (including eczema, hyperactivity, nausea, allergies, asthma and migraine) — hazards of others that may yet come to light, and the totally unnecessary and morally objectionable requirement to test new additives on animals, all provide the animal free shopper with an incentive to avoid additive-containing products where alternatives are available.

Note: All products appearing in the Animal Free Shopper containing additives listed in the **POSSIBLY ANIMAL-DERIVED** category have been judged to be animal free on the basis of manufacturer/distributor declarations.

ANIMAL-DERIVED ADDITIVES

• **E120 (CI75470)** carmine/cochineal • **E542** edible bone phosphate • **E901** beeswax • **E904** shellac • **calcium mesoinositol hexaphosphate • lactose • sperm oil • spermaceti**

POSSIBLY ANIMAL-DERIVED

• **E101** riboflavin, lactoflavin, vitamin B_2 • **E101a** riboflavin 5'-phosphate • **E153** (believed animal-free version only may be used in food) carbon black, vegetable carbon • **E161(b)** lutein • **E161(g)** canthaxanthin • **E236** formic acid • **E237** sodium formate • **E238** calcium formate • **E270** lactic acid • **E322** lecithin • **E325** sodium lactate • **E326** potassium lactate • **E327** calcium lactate • **E422** glycerol (glycerine) • **E430** (believed to be no longer permitted in food) polyoxyethylene (8) stearate, polyoxyl (8) stearate • **E431** polyoxyethylene (40) stearate, polyoxyl (40) stearate • **E432** polyoxyethylene sorbitan monolaurate, polysorbate 20, tween 20 • **E433** polyoxyethylene sorbitan mono-oleate, polysorbate 80, tween 80 • **E434** polyoxyethylene sorbitan monopalmitate, polysorbate 40, tween 40 • **E435** polyoxyethylene sorbitan monostearate, polysorbate 60, tween 60 • **E436** polyoxyethylene sorbitan tristearate, polysorbate 65, tween 65 • **E470(a)** sodium, potassium and calcium salts of fatty acids • **E470(b)** magnesium salts of fatty acids • **E471** glycerides of fatty acids, glyceryl monostearate, glyceryl distearate • **E472(a)** acetic acid esters of glycerides of fatty acids, acetoglycerides, glycerol esters • **E472(b)** lactic acid esters of glycerides of fatty acids, lactylated glycerides, lactoglycerides • **E472(c)** citric acid esters of glycerides of fatty acids • **E472(d)** — tartaric acid esters of glycerides of fatty acids • **E472(e)** mono and diacetyltartaric acid esters of glycerides of fatty acids **E472(f)** mixed acetic and tartaric acid esters of mono- and di-glycerides of fatty acids • **E473** sucrose esters of fatty acids • **E474** sucroglycerides • **E475** polyglycerol esters of fatty acids • **E476** polyglycerol esters of polycondensed fatty acids of castor oil, polyglycerol polyricinoleate; polyglycerol esters of dimerised fatty acids of soya bean oil • **E477** propylene glycol esters of fatty acids; propane-1,2-diol esters of fatty acids • **E478** lactylated fatty acid esters of gylcerol and propane-1,2-diol • **E479(b)** thermally oxidised soya bean oil interacted with mono- and di-glycerides of fatty acids • **E481** sodium stearoyl-2-lactylate • **E482** calcium stearoyl-2-lactylate • **E483** stearyl tartrate • **E491** sorbitan monostearate • **E492** sorbitan tristearate, span 65 • **E493** sorbitan monolaurate, span 20 • **E494** sorbitan mono-oleate, span 80 • **E495** sorbitan monopalmitate, span 40 • **E570** fatty acids (including myristic, stearic, palmitic and oleic), butyl stearate • **E572** magnesium salts of fatty acids (including magnesium stearate); calcium stearate • **E585** ferrous lactate • **E627** guanosine 5'-disodium phosphate, sodium guanylate, disodium guanylate • **E631** inosine 5'-disodium phosphate, sodium 5'-inosinate • **E635** sodium 5'-ribonucleotide • **E640** glycine and its sodium salt • **E920** L-cysteine hydrochloride • **E1518** glyceryl mono-, di- and tri-acetate (triacetin) • **calcium hepatonate** • **calcium phytate** • **diacetin** • **glyceryl** • **leucine** • **monoacetin** • **oxystearin** • and **any unspecified flavourings**

GLOSSARY OF ANIMAL SUBSTANCES

A '*****' indicates that non-animal (synthetic, vegetable or plant/mineral-derived) versions/sources by the same name are known to exist.

• **albumen/albumin** egg white Use/s: food binder • **alpha hydroxy acids (AHAs)*** naturally occurring chemicals derived from fruit or milk Use/s: cosmetics • **ambergris** morbid concretion obtained from the intestine of the sperm whale Use/s: perfumes • **amino acids*** 'building blocks' of proteins • **amniotic fluid** fluid surrounding the foetus within the placenta Use/s: cosmetics • **amylase*** enzyme in saliva and pancreatic juice • **anchovy** small fish of the herring family. Often an ingredient of Worcester sauce and pizza toppings Use/s: flavour enhancer • **angora** fibre obtained from rabbits or goats Use/s: clothing • **aspic** savoury jelly derived from meat and fish Use/s: glazing agent • **astrakhan** skin of still born or very young lambs from a breed originating in Astrakhan, Russia Use/s: clothing • **beeswax (E901)** secreted by bees to produce combs Use/s: furniture and floor polishes, candles, cosmetics • **bone/bonemeal** animal bone Use/s: horticultural fertiliser, bone china ornaments, crockery, supplements • **brawn** boiled meat, ears and tongue of pig Use/s: foodstuff • **bristle*** stiff animal hair, usually from pigs Use/s: brushes • **calcium mesoinositol hexaphosphate** Use/s: baked goods, soft drinks, processed vegetables • **capiz** shell Use/s: lampshades • **carmine/carminic acid (E120)** red pigment obtained from cochineal Use/s: food and drink dyes • **casein** main protein of milk Use/s: cheese making • **cashmere** fine wool from the cashmere goat and wild goat of Tibet Use/s: clothing • **castoreum** obtained from the anal sex gland of the beaver Use/s: fixative in perfumes • **catgut** dried and twisted intestines of the sheep or horse Use/s: stringed musical instruments, surgical stitching • **caviar(e)** roe of the sturgeon and other fish Use/s: a relish • **charcoal*** charred bone or wood Uses: clarifying agent • **chitin** organic base of the hard parts of insects and crustacea eg shrimps, crabs Use/s: conditioners and skin care products, thickener and moisturiser in shampoos • **chamois** soft leather from the skin of the chamois antelope, sheep, goats, deer etc Use/s: cleaning cloth • **cholecalciferol** see **D3** • **civet** substance scraped from glands in the anal pouch of the civet cat Use/s: fixative in perfumes • **cochineal (E120)** dyestuff consisting of the dried bodies of scale insects. Used for making carmine Use/s: red food and drink colouring • **cod liver oil** oil extracted from the liver of cod and related fish Use/s: food supplement • **coral** hard calcareous substance consisting of the continuous skeleton secreted by coelenterate polyps for their support and habitation Use/s: ornaments • **collagen** constituent of connective tissue which yields gelatin(e) on boiling Use/s: cosmetics, sausage skins • **D3 (cholecalciferol)** vitamin derived from lanolin or fish oil Use/s: vitamin and food supplements • **deoxyribonucleic acid (DNA)*** controls protein synthesis/stores genetic information. Found in all animal and plant cells Use/s: cosmetics, genetically-modified organisms, shampoos • **down** underplumage of fowls (especially duck and goose) Use/s: filling quilts, pillows, sleeping bags, padded clothing • **dripping** melted animal fat Use/s: frying • **eider down** small, soft feathers from the breast of the eider duck Use/s: filling quilts • **elastin** protein uniting muscle fibres in meat Use/s: moisturiser in cosmetics • **fatty acids*** organic compounds: saturated, polyunsaturated and unsaturated • **feather** epidermal appendage of a bird Uses: fashion accessory, feather dusters • **felt*** cloth made of wool, or of wool and fur or hair Use/s: clothing • **gelatin(e)** jelly obtained by boiling animal tissues (skin, tendons, ligaments etc) or bones Use/s: confectionery, biscuits, capsules, jellies, photographic film, match heads • **glycerin(e)/glycerol (E422)*** clear, colourless liquid which may be derived from animal fats, synthesised from propylene or from fermentation of sugars Use/s: solvent for flavours, texture improver, humectant • **hide** animal skin (raw or tanned) Use/s: clothing and footwear, clothing accessories, upholstery • **insulin*** pancreas of cattle, sheep or pigs Uses: managing diabetes **isinglass** very pure form of gelatin(e) obtained from the air bladders of some freshwater fishes, especially the sturgeon Use/s: clarifying alcoholic drinks, jellies • **keratin** protein found in hair, horns, hoofs and feathers Use/s: shampoos and conditioners, fertiliser • **L'cysteine hydrochloride (E920)*** manufactured from animal hair and chicken feathers, or synthetically from coal tar Use/s: shampoo, improving agent for white flour • **lactic acid (E270)*** acid produced by the fermentation of milk sugar but also by fermentation in pickles, cocoa and tobacco Use/s: acidulant in confectionery, soft drinks, pickles and sauces • **lactose** milk sugar Use/s: tablet filler, sweetener, 'carrier' for flavouring agents — especially in crisps • **lanolin(e)** fat extracted from sheep's wool Use/s: cleaning products, an emollient and emulsifer used in cosmetics — especially lipsticks • **lard** fat surrounding the stomach and kidneys of the pig, sheep and cattle Use/s: culinary • **leather** tanned hide (mostly from cattle but also sheep, pigs, goats etc) Use/s: clothing and footwear, clothing accessories, upholstery • **lecithin (E322)*** fatty substance found in nerve tissues, egg yolk, blood and other tissues. Mainly obtained commercially from soya bean, peanut and corn Use/s: emulsifier in baked goods and confectionery • **lutein(E161(b))*** substance of deep yellow colour found in egg yolk. Obtained commercially from marigold Use/s: food colouring • **mohair** cloth or yarn made from the hair of the angora goat Use/s: clothing • **musk*** substance secreted in a gland or sac by the male musk deer Use/s: perfume • **oleic acid*** fatty acid occurring in animal and vegetable fats Use/s: soaps, cosmetics, ointments • **oleoic oil** liquid obtained from pressed tallow Use/s: margarines • **oleostearin** solid obtained from pressed tallow Use/s: soap and candle making • **oestrogen*** female sex hormone from cow ovaries or pregnant mares' urine Use/s: cosmetics, body building supplements, hormone creams • **parchment*** skin of the calf, sheep or goat, dressed and prepared for writing etc • **pearl** ('Mother of', or 'cultured') concretion of layers of pain-dulling nacre formed around a foreign particle within the shell of various bivalve molluscs, principally the oyster Use/s: jewellery and decorative • **pepsin** enzyme found in gastric juices Use/s: cheese making • **placenta** organ by which the foetus is attached to the umbilical cord Use/s: cosmetics • **progesterone*** sex hormone Use/s: hormone creams • **propolis** bee glue. Used by bees to stop up crevices and fix combs to the hive Use/s: toiletries and cosmetics • **rennet*** extract of calf stomach. Contains the enzyme rennin which clots milk Use/s: cheese making, junkets • **reticulin** one of the structural elements (together with elastin and collagen) of skeletal muscle • **ribonucleic acid (RNA)** * see **deoxyribonucleic acid (DNA)** • **roe** eggs obtained from the abdomen of slaughtered female fish Use/s: a relish • **royal jelly** food on which bee larvae are fed and which causes them to develop into queen bees Use/s: food supplement • **sable** fur from the sable marten, a small carnivorous mammal Use/s: clothing, artists' brushes • **shellac (E904)** insect secretion Use/s: hair spray, lip sealer, polishes, glazing agent • **silk** cloth made from the fibre produced by the larvae ('silk worm') of certain bombycine moths, the harvesting of which entails the destruction of the insect Use/s: clothing, cosmetics • **sodium 5'-inosinate** occurs naturally in muscle. Prepared from fish waste Use/s: flavour enhancer • **sperm oil** oil found in the head of various species of whales Use/s: candle making • **spermaceti wax** fatty substance found mainly in the head of the sperm whale, other whales and dolphins Use/s: medicines, candle making, cosmetics • **sponge*** aquatic animal or colony of animals of a 'low order', characterised by a tough elastic skeleton of interlaced fibres Use/s. bathing aid • **squalene/squalane*** found in the liver of the shark (and rats) Use/s: toiletries and cosmetics • **stearate*** salt of stearic acid Use/s: body building supplements • **stearic acid (E570)*** organic acid prepared from stearin • **stearin(e)*** general name for the three glycerides (monostearin, distearin, tristearin). Formed by the combination of stearic acid and glycerin; chiefly applied to tristearin, which is the main constituent of tallow or suet Use/s: medicines, skin softener in toiletries and cosmetics • **suede*** kid-, pig- or calf-skin, tanned Use/s: clothing and footwear • **suet*** solid fat prepared from the kidneys of cattle and sheep Use/s: cooking • **tallow** hard animal fat, especially that obtained from the parts about the kidneys of ruminating animals Use/s: soap and candle making • **taurine*** amino acid • **testosterone*** male hormone Use/s: body building supplements • **urea*** waste nitrogen formed in the liver and excreted by the kidneys Use/s: toiletries and cosmetics • **vellum*** fine parchment prepared from the skins of calves, lambs or kids Use/s: writing material • **vitamin A*** (retinol) derived from fish liver oil or egg yolk Use/s: cosmetics, food supplement • **velvet*** fabric made usually of silk but also rayon or nylon Use/s: clothing • **volaise** ostrich meat • **whey** residue from milk after the removal of the casein and most of the fat. By-product of cheese making Use/s: margarines, biscuits, crisps, cleaning products • **wool** hair forming the fleecy coat of the domesticated sheep (and similar animals) Use/s: clothing

ANIMAL TESTING CRITERIA

It remains the case that animal protection groups and manufacturers promote a number of variations on the 'not tested on animals' theme. Depending on one's perspective or strategy, all have their strengths and weaknesses.

The criterion used to complete the Animal Free Shopper recognises that most substances have been, and some may continue to be, animal tested and simply requires that a product's manufacturer, or 'related' company, has not initiated testing on either the finished product or, where applicable, the ingredients.

For those readers who prefer companies using either a fixed cut-off date or the Humane Cosmetics Standard (see below), an appropriate symbol (see **KEY**, see page iii) appears in the product listings after the company name.

HUMANE COSMETICS STANDARD

In response to pressure from animal protection groups and consumers across Europe, the European Parliament proposed a ban on the marketing of animal tested cosmetics (Directive 93/35). However, early in 1997, to widespread dismay, the European Union (EU) postponed its 1 January 1998 target date until into the new century. An international coalition of animal protection groups from across the EU and North America drew up an international Humane Cosmetics Standard and launched a major campaign calling on all manufacturers and retailers to adopt it.

Co-ordinated (in the UK) by the British Union for the Abolition of Vivisection (BUAV), the standard requires companies not to conduct, commission, nor be party to any animal testing either now or in the future, and to adopt a fixed cut-off date for ingredients testing. The cut-off date is chosen by the company, but must be before the date that it applies to join the standard.

FIXED CUT-OFF DATE

A company that has adopted a fixed cut-off date has a policy of using only ingredients that have not been tested on animals by, or at the initiative of, either it or its suppliers since a specified date. In addition, the company will not initiate animal tests on its finished products.

The Cosmetics Industry Coalition for Animal Welfare (CICAW) encourages cosmetic companies to adopt an animal testing fixed cut-off date — preferably 1976 (the year the EU required all new ingredients to be safety(animal)-tested).

See 'Vivisection' (page 30) for more details on animal testing.

GENETICALLY MODIFIED ORGANISMS

Of concern to the consumer wishing to avoid genetically modified organisms (GMOs), because of possible long-term effects on health or the implications of their release into the environment, is the presence in the UK food supply of GM soya, containing genes derived from a bacterium, a virus and a petunia. Soya is found in around 50% of all processed foods.

So far, there has been very little research to assess the health and safety implications of GMOs. The insertion of foreign genes can have many harmful unexpected effects: for instance the insertion of a Brazil nut gene into soya resulted in a reaction in people allergic to nuts. There is also a risk of increasing antibiotic resistance in bacteria. Critics warn of unexpected and irreversible effects on agriculture and biodiversity. They condemn the immorality of the 'patenting of life' — transgenic animals, plants and seeds. From a vegan perspective, even if no animal gene was used during the modification process, it is likely that animal-derived enzymes were employed.

GM material can cross species barriers to other crops and weeds, and once released it is impossible to 'clean up' any unforeseen consequences. Plants designed to kill 'pests' can kill beneficial insects as well and stimulate the development of resistance in the pests. Plants engineered for herbicide resistance will encourage increased use of chemicals. Most American farmers who have turned to GM crops seem to be getting yields no better than farmers growing traditional varieties. They also appear to be using similar quantities of pesticides.

The Soil Association believes that genetic modification has no place in the production of safe and healthy food. Organic farming systems aim to produce food with care for human health, the environment and animal welfare.

In keeping with its vegan ethic, The Vegan Society is totally against the use of animal genes or animal substances in the development and production of GMOs. The Vegan Society believes that all foods that contain, may contain, or have involved GMOs should be clearly labelled, and has signed up to the Five Year Freeze campaign for a moratorium on genetic engineering and patenting in food and farming.

OTHER ETHICAL CONSIDERATIONS

To qualify for inclusion in the Animal-Free Shopper a product need only be free of animal ingredients and animal testing. However, whilst avoiding products having direct animal involvement is a coherent and far-reaching ethical stance in itself, many animal-free shoppers choose to make purchase on a wide range of additional ethical considerations pertaining to humans, animals and the environment — such as:

- **vegan ownership** Some shoppers prefer to support those companies which are wholly or partly owned by vegans (see **KEY**, page iii)
- **product range** Many companies manufacture or distribute both animal and non-animal products. Given the choice, many animal-free shoppers prefer to buy from those companies whose entire range is animal-free (see **KEY**, page iii)
- **company activities** A number of companies manufacturing or distributing animal-free (and animal) products are involved directly in animal abuse — such as the meat and dairy industries.
- **company connections** Some seemingly innocuous companies have parent, sister or subsidiary companies which are involved directly in animal abuse.
- **company affiliations** Possible animal abuse affiliations include: The British Industrial Biological Research Association (BIBRA), Research Defence Society (RDS), The Countryside Alliance, Game Conservancy.
- **company sponsorships & donations** Common areas include animal-connected medical research and sporting events.
- **organised boycotts** Even large multi-national companies have ceased an objectionable activity when threatened with, or subjected to, a boycott campaign. Though not always successful, it is argued that boycotts are, nevertheless, a useful means by which to heighten public awareness.
- **use of by-products** The production of animal-free goods may involve the generation of by-products which are then employed for purposes the animal-free shopper would not normally support. Examples include: white flour — bran — animal feed; wheat etc — straw — animal bedding; linseed, rapeseed, soya — cake/meal — animal feed; sugar beet — pulp — animal feed.

- **pesticide use** – the excessive use of chemical pesticides and fertilisers damages the environment and kills wildlife. Many animal-free shoppers prefer to avoid contributing to the destruction of our countryside and instead chose organic products – we have printed these products in bold and highlighted those companies whose entire product range is organic (see **KEY** page iii).
- **genetically-modified organisms** See **GENETICALLY-MODIFIED ORGANISMS**, (page 299 and **KEY**, page iii).
- **microbiological testing -** in order to ensure the safety of their products, and to forestall damaging law suits which might arise following the discovery of a defect, many manufacturers test batches of their products for the presence of bacterial contaminants. The nutrient media 'fed' to the bacteria (in order to identify them) are commonly derived from the slaughterhouse or the dairy industry. Virtually all foodstuffs, and most toiletries and cosmetics, are subject to testing involving the use of animal derivatives. Unfortunately, animal-free shoppers cannot avoid microbiologically-tested foodstuffs, which not only include processed foods but also unprocessed fruits and vegetables — and even drinking water!

Recognising that human and animal rights are inextricably linked and that all life is dependent upon the well-being of the planet, the animal-free shopper might also wish to avoid companies involved in or with: cash crops, environmentally damaging practices, irresponsible marketing, land rights, low wages and poor conditions, and oppressive regimes.

As well as boycotting certain goods, many shoppers actively seek out products that promote a cleaner environment or seek to improve workers' rights. Organic and fair trade products are now available almost everywhere in the UK, with the number and variety of products increasing all the time. You can find contact details for organisations promoting these aspects of food production in the USEFUL ADDRESSES section, page 309.

FURTHER INFORMATION

The Ethical Consumer Research Association Unit 21, 41 Old Birley St, Manchester M15 5RF **t** 0161 226 2929 **w** www.ethicalconsumer.org **e** mail@ethicalconsumer.org Publishes *The Ethical Consumer*: a magazine providing information on companies behind brand names across a range of ethical issues — including 'Animal Testing', 'Factory Farming' and 'Other Animal Rights'.

ANIMAL FREE SHOPS

The outlets listed below are run by vegans and only stock vegan products

- **Devon** *Exeter Body Piercing* 17 Fore Street Centre, Fore Street, Exeter EX4 3AN **t** 01392 494 545 **e** info@exeterbodypiercing.co.uk **w** www.exeterbodypiercing.co.uk
- **Germany** *Vegan-Shop & Versand* Hohenstrasse 50, 60385 Frankfurt am Main **t** 00 49 69 440 989
- **Gwynedd** *Vegonia Wholefoods* 49 High Street, Porthmadog LL49 9LR **t** 01766 515 195 **e** vegonia@vegonia.worldonline.co.uk
- **Manchester** *Unicorn Grocery* 89 Albany Road, Chorlton, Manchester M21 0BN **t** 0161 861 0010 **e** office@unicorn-grocery.co.uk **w** www.unicorn-grocery.co.uk
- **Nottinghamshire** *Sumac Centre* 245 Gladstone Street, Nottingham NG7 6HX **t** 0845 458 9595 **e** sumac@veggies.org.uk **w** www.veggies.org.uk/sumac
- **West Midlands** *One Earth Shop* 54 Allison Street, Digbeth, Birmingham B5 5TH **t** 0121 632 6909

ONLINE SHOPS

- **Animal Aid** www.animalaid.org.uk/shop
- **Cruelty Free Shop** www.crueltyfreeshop.com
- **Ethical Wares** www.ethicalwares.com
- **Meadowsweet Ltd** www.meadowsweet.co.uk
- **Veganline** www.veganline.com
- **Vegan Society** www.vegansociety.com
- **Veganstore.co.uk** www.veganstore.co.uk
- **Vegetarian Shoes** www.vegshoes.com
- **Via Vegan Ltd** www.viavegan.com
- **VIVA**! www.viva.org.uk/shop
- **World's End Trading** www.worldsend.co.uk

CONTACT NETWORKS

BUSINESS

- **Vegan Business Connection** c/o Veggies, 245 Gladstone Street, Nottingham NG7 6HX **t** 0845 458 9595 **w** www.veggies.org.uk/vbc.htm
- **Vegan Village** Imaner House, 14 Wynford Grove, Leeds, Yorkshire (West Riding) LS16 6JL **t** 0113 293 9385 **w** www.veganvillage.co.uk

FAMILIES

- **Vegan Families Network** 35 Rectory Grove, Hampton, Middlesex TW12 1AH **t** 020 8941 8075
- **Vegan Family House w** www.veganfamily.co.uk
- **VegParents NW t** 020 8941 8075 **w** www.ukveggie.com/vegparentsnw

INTERNATIONAL

- **Vegan Society International Contact** c/o The Vegan Society, Donald Watson House, 7 Battle Road, St Leonards-on-Sea, East Sussex TN37 7AA **t** 01424 427 393 **w** www.vegansociety.com
- **International Vegetarian Union t** 020 8265 3277 **w** www.ivu.org
- **European Vegetarian Union** Friedhofstrasse, 1267693 Fischbach **t** 00 49 6305 993108 **w** www.europeanvegetarian.org
- **VegDining w** www.vegdining.com
- **Veggies' Animal Contacts Directory w** www.veggies.org.uk/acd
- **World Animal Net** 24 Barleyfields, Didcot, Oxfordshire OX11 0BJ **t** 01235 210 775 **w** www.worldanimal.net
- **America** American Vegan Society,56 Dinshah Lane, PO Box 369, Malaga, New Jersey 08328-0908 **t** 00 1 856 694 2887 **w** www.americanvegan.org
- **Australia** Vegan Society of Australia, P.O. BOX 85, Seaford, Victoria 3198 **t** 00 61 03 9776 4425 **w** www.veganaustralia.org
- **Austria** Vegane Gesellschaft Öesterreich, Waidhausenstrae 13/1, A 1140 Wien **t** 00 43 1 9291 4988 **w** www.vegan.at
- **Denmark** Vegana, Raadmand Steins Allé 45, 7, 2000 Frederiksburg **t** 00 45 7020 0510 **w** www.vegana.dk
- **Finland** Vegaaniliitto Ry, Hãmeentie 48, 00500 Helsinki, 217918-11297 Nordea **t** 00 358 50 344 9524 **w** www.vegaaniliitto.fi

- **Hong Kong** Hong Kong Vegan Society **w** www.ivu.org/hkvegan/
- **Indonesia** Indonesian Vegan Society **t** 00 62 8159 927 067 **w** www.i-v-s.org
- **Italy** Italian Vegan Society **w** www.vegetariani.it
- **Latin America** Latin American Vegan Society, Servidão do Nilton 412 Praia de Cacupé, 88050-170,Florianópolis SC **t** 00 55 48 235 1609 **w** www.ivu.org/latin-america.html
- **Luxembourg** De Vegabond, c/o Bote Postale 44, 3701, Rumelange **t** 00 352 567 231 **w** www.ivu.org/devegabond
- Netherlands Nederlande Vereniging Voor Veganisme, Postbus 19131, 350 DC Utrecht **t** 00 26 4420746 **w** www.veganisme.non-profit.nl
- **New Zealand** Veganz **w** www.veganz.pl.net
- **Spain** Asociación Vegana Española (AVE), Apartado Postal 478, 29740 Torre del Mar, Málaga **t** 00 95 251 3981 **w** www.ivu.org/ave
- **Sweden** Veganföreningen, Ulla Tröeng, Klövervägen 6, 647 30, Mariefried **t** 00 46 159 12 467 **w** www.vegan.se

LOCAL - ENGLAND

- **Birmingham Vegetarians & Vegans** – Warehouse Café, Allison St, Digbeth 4th Tues.7.30 pm *Barbara, 5 Esher Rd, Kingstanding, B44 9QJ, 0121 353 2442*
- **Blackpool Vegans –** *blackpoolvegans@btinternet.com, www.blackpoolvegans.makessense.co.uk*
- **Bournemouth Vegetarians & Vegans** – last Tues. 7.30 Wessex Tales Vegan Restaurant. *Harry, 01202 555712*
- **Brighton One World Group** (Brighton Vegans) – *Julie, 07909 505461, jules_5@hotmail.com*
- **Bristol Vegetarians & Vegans**, *Shane 0117 951 1199*
- **Cambridge Vegans** – 2nd Sat. 10.30am - 12, Rainbow café 2nd & 4th Mon., 7 India Centre veg café, Mill Rd. *Adam, 01223 520311, adam@gimp.org, www.vegancambridge.org.uk*
- **Chester & Clwyd Vegetarians & Vegans** – monthly *walk & bring-&-share. Brian, 01978 790442, indesigneko@aol.com*
- **Croydon Vegans** – *Tracey, 0208 655 3797, tracey@moosenet.free-online.co.uk*
- **Cumbria Vegans –** 2nd Thurs. 7.30. *Anita, 15 Challoner St, Cockermouth, CA13 9QS. 01900 824045, anita@yuvaorganicfoods.wanadoo.co.uk*
- **Devon Vegans –** *Judy, 01626 821451, grahamhill@liverton72.freeserve.co.uk*
- **Doncaster & Area Vegans & Vegetarians** – *Vivien, 01405 769730* (day only)
- **East Riding Vegans** – *monthly meals*, Hitchcock's, 8. *Mark, 01482 471119, mark@merrydowncontrolware.co.uk, www.merrydowncontrolware.co.uk/ervegans*

- **Essex Vegans** – 1st Tues., Brentwood School Sports Centre. *Karin, info@veggievision.co.uk, www.veganessex.org*
- **Gloucestershire Vegans,** *Vicky, 01666* 503892 *stephens-family@tiscali.co.uk*
- **Guildford Vegetarian & Vegan Soc.** – *01483 425040*
- **Harrow Vegans –** social & meals, all ages. *Julie, 0208 866 5278, fletcher_julie@hotmail.com, http://groups.yahoo.com/group/HarrowVeg/*
- **Herefordshire & Worcestershire Vegans –** last Sun *Bruce, 01684 541808, brucetanner@btopenworld.com, www.vegan3counties.org.uk*
- **Hertford and Welwyn Vegans** – *Joanne, 01992 534047, Kimberley1@tinyonline.co.uk*
- **Huddersfield & Area Vegans –** *Peter, 34 Stainecross Ave, 01484 304396*
- **Isle of Wight Vegetarians & Vegans** – 3rd Thurs. *Keeper's Lock, Youngswoods Way, Alverstone, Sandown, 01983 407098*
- **Kent Vegans** – *Ros, 59 Chapel Rd, Ramsgate, CT11 0BS, 01843 589027*
- **Lancashire Vegetarians & Vegans** (LancsVeg) – last Thurs. 8 City Deli, Preston, & lots more. *Maureen, 01706 222036, maureen.lancsveg@ntlworld.com, www.lancsveg.co.uk*
- **Leeds Vegetarians & Vegans** – socials & potluck lunches. *Natalie, 0113 248 4044 natalie@tharraleos.freeserve.co.uk*
- **Leicester Vegetarians & Vegans** – *Sue, 0116 240 4010, www.leicesterveggies.idps.co.uk*
- **Lincoln Vegans** – 21 May 7.30 Pasquale's. *Jacqueline, 07875721160, jackie.bs@btinternet.com*
- **London Lesbian Vegans** – *Kat 0207 243 8225, veganartist@onetel.com*
- **London Vegans** – last Wed. 6.30 Millman Street Community Rooms, WC1, & lots more. *7 Deansbrook Rd, Edgware, Middx, HA8 9BE*, tel/fax *0208 9311 904, info@londonvegans.org.uk, www.londonvegans.freeserve.co.uk*
- **Luton & Dunstable Vegans** – food and fun on 15th. *Rupert Kaye, 6 Friars Walk, Dunstable LU6 3JA, 01582 673228, rupertkaye@aol.com*
- **Manchester Vegan Society –** last Sat. 3, The Basement, off Piccadilly Gdns, children welcome. *0161 248 0055, keely.jolliffe@gmail.com*
- **ManVeg** (Manchester Vegetarians & Vegans) – 2nd Thurs. *Janet, 01925 728786* (after 4.30), *janet.harbottle@ntlworld.com, www.manveg.co.uk*
- **Milton Keynes Vegetarians & Vegans** – 2nd Wed. *meal*, Veggie World, Bletchley Centre & more. *Mark 01908 240903, veganman1961@yahoo.co.uk*
- **Norfolk Vegetarian & Vegans**, *Gabrielle, 01603 864415, vegerose@hotmail.com, www.vegfolk.co.uk*
- **Northants Vegans** – 2nd Tues. *David 01933 226682*
- **North Dorset Vegans –** *Rosie, veganrosie@hotmail.com*
- **North Lincs Vegans** – last Thurs. 7.30, Barnetby-Le-Wold, *01652 681900, john.bateman24@BTopenworld.com*

- **North Riding Vegetarians & Vegans** (also covers Co. Durham) – *meals & more. Patricia, 0845 458 4714 (after 7.30) patricia@p-m-t.freeserve.co.uk*
- **Northumbria Vegans & Vegetarians** – *Gordon, 0191 258 6793, gmforrest@tiscali.co.uk*
- **Nottingham Vegetarians & Vegans** – meals & more. *David, Veggies/Sumac Centre, 245 Gladstone St, NG7 6HX, 0845 458 9595 / 01629 814117, nvvs@veggies.org.uk*
- **OxVeg** – 1st Thurs. The Mitre. *Paul, 01235 769425, oxfordveg@ivu.org, www.ivu.org/oxveg/*
- **Rochester Area Vegans & Vegetarians –** *Sheila, 01634 220027, sheilamccrossan@hotmail.com*
- **Rugby Vegans –** *Andrea, 4 Keynes Dr, Bilton, Rugby, CV22 7ST, 01788 810805, therugbyvegan@yahoo.co.uk*
- **ScouseVeg** –– 1st Fri. Egg Café, L'pool, & lots more. *Jane 0151 933 1338, jane.ol@virgin.net, www.scouseveg.co.uk*
- **Sevenoaks Vegans** – *pub* 3rd Thurs. & *meals out Jackie, 01732 462183, JackieG@apc-plc.co.uk*
- **Sheffield Vegan Soc**. *C/o Recyc, 54 Upperthorpe Rd, S6 3EB, info@sheffieldvegansociety.org.uk www.sheffieldvegansociety.org.uk*
- **Shropshire Vegans** – Malcolm, *01952 432874, malc@c3173.freeserve.co.uk, www.shropveg.org.uk*
- **Snow Club** – booking for March '06 *Stephen & Sophie 0118 946 4858, www.veggiesnow.makessense.co.uk*
- **Southend Animal Aid Vegans** – 3rd Sat. 2.30 Cafe Pulse, Leigh Rd, Leigh. *Nicky, PO Box 211, Short St, Southend, SS1 1AA, 07092 001851, southendanimalaid@hotmail.com*
- **St Helens Vegans** – *22 Hope Cl, St Helens, WA10 2HL, 01744 614807*
- **Sussex University Vegans – new group being set up by Helen** for sharing & celebrating veganism, *07929 779139, hrm22@sussex.ac.uk*
- **Thames Valley Vegans & Vegetarians** – *meals out & more. Stephen & Sophie 0118 946 4858 www.tvvvs.makessense.co.uk*
- **Tunbridge Wells & Area Vegans** – 2nd Thurs. Raj Pavilion & more. *Mark*, day *01892 543048*, evening *01580 819391*, *mark.hanna@virgin.net*
- **Twickenham and Surrey Vegetarians & Vegans** – *Lesley, 0208 941 8075, Lesley@vegan4life.org.uk, http://groups.yahoo.com/group/TWandKTveg/?yguid=73160822*
- **Vegan Campaigns –** BM Box 2300, London, WC1N 3XX, *07796 774200, info@vegancampaigns.org.uk, www.vegancampaigns.org.uk*

- **Vegan Families Group** – events & mutual support for children & parents. *Lesley Dove, 35 Rectory Gr, Hampton, Middx, TW12 1AH, 0208 941 8075, Lesley@vegan4life.org.uk, http://groups.yahoo.com/group/VegParentsSE/*
- **Vegan Harlow** – *socials, meals, etc. Lian, info@veganharlow.co.uk, www.veganharlow.co.uk*
- **Veggiestudents –** website enabling students to meet and find veg*an things locally, *http://www.freewebs.com/veggiestudents/index.htm, veggiestudents@hotmail.com*
- **VegParentsNW** (Vegan & Vegetarian Parents North West) – social group for parents of babies, toddlers & pre-teens; e-mail advice & news group & events. *www.ukveggie.com/vegparentsnw, Lesley, 0208 941 8075*
- **West Gloucestershire Vegans**, *Barbara, 01594 833634*
- **York Vegans**, *Neil & Fiona, 01904 788038* or *0774 218 4249, yorkvegan@wynded.co.uk*
- **Young Indian Vegetarians & Vegans** – *Nitin Mehta, 226 London Rd, Croydon, CRO 2TF, 0208 686 6931, animalahimsa@yahoo.co.uk*

LOCAL - SCOTLAND

- **Aberdeen Vegans & Friends** – 1st Sat. *lunch*, Lemon Tree, Queen St/West North St. *George 07713 848663, georgerodger@f2s.com*
- **Glasgow Vegans** – 1st Sat. 3, Mono, King's Ct. *Jo, 0141 954 6519, gvn@hotmail.com, http://gvn.rhizomatics.org.uk*
- **Isle of Mull Vegans & Vegetarians** – monthly socials, rambles, picnics etc. for all ages, some in Oban. *Joanne, Tiree Cottage, Kintra, PA66 6BT, 0845 330 7442*

LOCAL - WALES

- **Chester & Clwyd Vegetarians & Vegans** – monthly *walk* & *bring-&-share. Brian, 01978 790442, indesigneko@aol.com*
- **Swansea Vegans** – 3rd Mon. 7, FMH Page St, *George, 01792 518773, george.barwick@ntlworld.com*

LOCAL - IRELAND

- **Clare, Galway, Limerick & Tipperary**, *Jacqueline Walsh, Bealkelly, Tuamgraney, Co. Clare, 061 923220, Jacqueline@mulvenna.org*

- **Dublin** – 1st Sat. St Andrew's Centre. *Gloria Bartolome, 21 Mask Green, Artane, Dublin 5, 086 346 8350, mystik@eircom.net, gloriair@eircom.net*
- **Co. Wexford** – various events in N. Wexford. *Mags & Ali, Gorey*, text/ring *087 689 7018, maggiann@eircom.net*
- **Co. Wicklow/S. Co. Dublin** – social events, nothing too serious. *Izzy*, ring/text *087 227 2049, contact@veganirish.com*

SOCIAL

- **Vegan Camp** c/o 245 Gladstone Street, Nottingham NG7 6HX **t** 0845 330 3918 **w** www.veggies.org.uk/vegancamp
- **Vegan Summer Gathering w** www.veganviews.org.uk/vsg
- **Vegan World Ventures** 4 Cameron Road, Seven Kings, Ilford, Essex IG3 8LA **t** 020 8220 2003
- **Vegetarian & Vegan Gay Group** 86 Caledonian Road, London N1 9DN **t** 020 7713 9063 **w** www.vvgg.freeserve.co.uk
- **Vegetarian Matchmakers** Concord House, 7 Waterbridge Court, Appleton Warrington, Cheshire WA4 3BJ **t** 01925 601 60 **w** www.veggiematchmakers.com
- **Veggie-Link** 42 Hawthorne Crescent, Findern, Derby DE6 6AN **t** 01283 703 809
- **Vegi Ventures** Castle Cottage, Castle Square, Castle Acre, King's Lynn Norfolk PE32 2AJ **t** 01760 755 888 **w** www.vegiventures.com

SPORT

- **Vegan Bodybuilding** PO Box 307, Brighton BN2 1HW **t** 07050 396 611 **w** www.veganbodybuilding.org
- **Vegetarian Cycling & Athletic Club** 13 Peers Lane, Shenley, Church End Milton Keynes, Buckinghamshire MK5 6BG **t** 01908 503 919 **w** www.geocities.com/vegetariancac

USEFUL ADDRESSES

ANIMAL EXPERIMENTS AND ALTERNATIVES

• **British Anti-Vivisection Asssociation** PO Box 73, Chesterfield, Derbyshire S41 0YZ **e** bava@blueyonder.co.uk **w** www.bava.pwp.blueyonder.co.uk • **British Union for the Abolition of Vivisection (BUAV)** 16a Crane Grove, Islington, London N7 8NN **t** 020 7700 4888 **e** info@buav.org **w** www.buav.org • **Doctors & Lawyers for Responsible Medicine** PO Box 302, London N8 9HD **t** 020 8340 9813 **e** dlrm@gn.apc.org **w** www.dlrm.org • **Dr Hadwen Trust** Dr Hadwen House, 84a Tilehouse Street, Hitchin, Hertfordshire SG5 2DV **t** 01462 436 819 **e** info@drhadwentrust.org.uk **w** www.drhadwentrust.org.uk • **FRAME** 96-98 North Sherwood Street, Nottingham NG1 4EE **t** 0115 958 4740 **e** frame@frame.org.uk **w** www.frame.org.uk • **Humane Research Trust** Brook House, 29 Bramhall Lane South Bramhall, Stockport Cheshire SK7 2DN **t** 0161 439 8041 **e** info@humaneresearch.org.uk **w** www.humaneresearch.org.uk • **Lord Dowding Fund for Humane Research** See National Anti-Vivisection Society • **National Anti-Vivisection Society** 261 Goldhawk Road, London W12 9PE **t** 020 8846 9777 **e** info@navs.org.uk **w** www.navs.org.uk • **Nurses' Anti-Vivisection Movement** PO Box 32, Matlock, Derbyshire DE4 3YJ **t** 01629 824 664 • **People Against Vivisection** **e** djurs@blueyonder.co.uk **w** www.sjne01487.pwp.blueyonder.co.uk • **Plan 2000** 234 Summergangs Road, Hull, Yorkshire (East Riding) HU8 8LL **t** 01482 786 855 **e** admin@eurosolve.com **w** www.eurosolve.com/charity/plan2000 • **Quest Cancer Research** Unit 3, Seedbed Business Centre, Pinnalles Road, Harlow, Essex CM19 5AF **t** 01279 451 359 **e** questcancer@btinternet.com • **Save the Newchurch Guinea Pigs (SNGP)** PO Box 74, Evesham, Worcestershire WR11 3WF **t** 01902 564 734 **e** info@liberation-now.org **w** www.liberation-now.org • **SPEAK Campaigns** PO Box 6712, Northampton NN2 6XR **t** 0845 330 7985 **e** info@speakcampaigns.org.uk **w** www.speakcampaigns.org.uk • **Stop Huntingdon Animal Cruelty** 6 Boat Lane, Evesham, Worcestershire WR11 4BP **t** 0845 458 0630 **e** info@shac.net **w** www.shac.net • **Uncaged** 9 Bailey Lane, Sheffield S1 4EG **t** 0114 272 2220 **e** info@uncaged.co.uk **w** www.uncaged.co.uk

BLOODSPORTS

• **Conservative Anti-Hunt Council** 38 Holway Avenue, Taunton, Somerset TA1 3AR **t** 01823 286 398 • **Hunt Saboteurs' Association** BM HSA, London, WC1N 3XX **t** 0845 450 0727 **e** info@huntsabs.org.uk **w** www.huntsabs.org.uk • **League Against Cruel Sports** 83-87 Union Street, London SE1 1SG **t** 0845 330 8486

e info@league.uk.com **w** www.league.uk.com • **National Anti-Hunt Campaign** 27 Old Gloucester Street, London WC1N 3XX **t** 0207 419 572 **e** nahc@nahc.freeeserve.co.uk **w** www.geocities.com/norwichsafe/antihunt.html **Pisces (Campaign for the Abolition of Angling)** BM Fish, London WC1N 3XX **t** 01792 464 176 **e** pisces@pisces.demon.co.uk **w** www.pisces.demon.co.uk

CIRCUSES & ZOOS

• **Captive Animals Protection Society** PO Box 573, Preston, Lancashire PR1 9WW **t** 0845 330 3911 **e** info@captiveanimals.org **w**www.captiveanimals.org

DEVELOPING WORLD

• **Help International Plant Protein Organisation (HIPPO)** The Old Vicarage, Llangynog, Carmarthen SA33 5BS **t** 01267 241 547 **e** hippocharity@aol.com • **Vegfam** The Sanctuary, Nr.Lydford, Okehampton, Devon EX20 4AL **t** 01822 820 203 **e** vegfam@veganvillage.co.uk **w**www.veganvillage.co.uk/vegfam

DIET / LIFESTYLE

• **All Raw Times w** www.rawtimes.com • **Bristol Cancer Help Centre** Grove House, Cornwallis Grove, Clifton, Bristol, Somerset BS8 4PG **t** 0845 123 2310 **e** info@bristolcancerhelp.org **w** www.bristolcancerhelp.org • **FRESH Network**, PO Box 71, Ely Cambridgeshire CB7 4GU **t** 0870 800 7070 **e** info@fresh-network.com **w**www.fresh-network.com • **Institute for Plant Based Nutrition** 333 Bryn Mawr Avenue, Bala, Cynwyd, Pennsylvania 19004-2606, USA **e** info@plantbased.org **w**www.plantbased.org • **International Vegetarian Union t** 020 8265 3277 **e** info@ivu.org **w** www.ivu.org • **London Vegetarian Info Centre** 2 Melcombe Gardens, Kenton, Middlesex HA3 9RH **t** 020 8204 1231 • **Movement for Compassionate Living** c/o Lenita, 31 Florence Avenue, Maidenhead, Berkshire SL6 8SJ • **Physicians Committee for Responsible Medicine** 5100 Wisconsin Avenue, NW Suite 400, Washington DC 20016, USA **t** 202 686 2210 **e** pcrm@pcrm.org **w** www.pcrm.org • **Vegan**

Information Network & ESCAPE PO Box 2801, Brighton BN1 3NH • **Vegan Views** Flat A15, 20 Dean Park Road, Bournemouth, Dorset BH1 1JB **e** info@veganviews.org.uk **w** www.veganviews.org.uk • **Vegan Village** Imaner House, 14 Wynford Grove, Leeds, Yorkshire (West Riding) LS16 6JL **t** 0113 293 9385 **e** postie@veganvillage.co.uk **w** www.veganvillage.co.uk **Vegetarian & Vegan Foundation** 8 York Court, Wilder Street, Bristol BS28QH **t** 0117 970 5190 **e** info@vegetarian.org.uk **w** www.vegetarian.org.uk • **Vegetarian Society** Parkdale, Dunham Road, Altringham, Cheshire WA14 4QG **t** 0161 925 2000 **e** info@vegsoc.demon.co.uk **w** www.vegsoc.org • **World Vegan Day** c/o The Vegan Society, Donald Watson House, 7 Batttle Road, St Leonards-on-sea, Sussex (East) TN37 7AA **t** 0845 458 8244 **w** www.worldveganday.org • **Young Indian Vegetarians** 226 London Road, Croydon CR0 2TF **t** 020 8686 6931 **e** animalahimsa@yahoo.co.uk

DIRECT ACTION

• **Animal Liberation Front Press Office** BM 4400, London WC1N 3XX **t** 07752 107 515 **e** alfpressoffice@yahoo.com • **Animal Liberation Front Supporters Group** BM 1160, London WC1N 3XX **t** 0870 138 5037 **e** info@alfsg.co.uk **w** www.alfsg.org.uk

FARMING & GROWING

• **Compassion in World Farming** Charles House, 5a Charles Street, Petersfield, Hampshire GU32 3EH **t** 01730 264 208 **w** www.ciwf.org.uk • **Fairtrade Foundation** Room 204,16 Baldwin's Gardens, London EC1N 7RG **t** 020 7405 5942 **e** mail@fairtrade.org.uk **w** www.fairtrade.org.uk• **Farm & Food Society** 4 Willifield Way, Golders Green, London NW11 7XT **t** 020 8455 0634 • **Farm Animal Welfare Network** Po Box 40, Holmfirth, Huddersfield, Yorkshire (West Riding) HD7 1QY **w** www.fawn.me.uk • **Henry Doubleday Research Association** • Ryton Organic Fardens, Coventry, Warwickshire CV8 3LG **t** 024 7630 3517 **e** enquiry@hdra.org.uk **w** www.hdra.org.uk • **National Organisation Working Against Live Exports** St Josephs, Souldern, Bicester, Oxfordshire OX6 9LA **t** 01869 345 243 • **Plants For a Future** Blagdon Cross, Ashwater, Beaworthy, Devon EX21 5DF **t** 01208 872 963 **e** webmaster@pfaf.org **w** www.pfaf.org • **Soil Association** Bristol House, 40-56 Victoria Street, Bristol BS1 6BY **t** 0117 314 5000 **e** info@soilassociation.org **w** www.soilassociation.org • **Sustain** 94 White Lion Street, London N1 9PF **t** 020 7837 1228 **e** sustain@sustainweb.org **w** www.sustainweb.org • **Veganic Garden Supplies/Information** c/o Weavers Way, Heath Farm Road, Worstead, North

Walsham, Norfolk NR28 9AH **t** 01692 404 570 • **Vegan Organic Network** 161 Hamilton Road, Longsight, Manchester, Lancashire M13 0PQ **t** 0161 928 3614 **e** veganorganic@riseup.net **w** www.veganorganic.net

FUR & LEATHER

• **Campaign Aginst Leather and Fur (CALF)** BM 8889 London WC1N 3XX **e** calf@alrob.freeserve.co.uk • **Campaign to Abolish the Fur Trade (CAFT)** PO Box 38, Manchester M60 1NX **t** 0845 330 7955 **e** caft@caft.org.uk **w** www.caft.org.uk

GENERAL

• **Advocates for Animals** 10 Queensferry Street, Edinburgh EH2 4PG **t** 0131 225 6039 **e** info@advocatesforanimals.org **w** www.advocatesforanimals.org.uk • **Animal Aid** The Old Chapel, Bradford Street, Tonbridge, Kent TN9 1AW **t** 01732 364 546 **e** info@animalaid.org.uk **w** www.animalaid.org.uk • **Animal Concern** PO Box 5178, Dumbarton G82 5YJ **t** 01389 841 639 **e** animals@jfrobins.force9.co.uk **w** www.animalconcern.com • **Animal Cruelty Investigation Group** PO Box 8, Halesworth, Suffolk IP19 0JL **e** mike@acigawis.freeserve.co.uk **w** www.acigawis.freeserve.co.uk • **Animal Defenders** See National Anti-Vivisection Society (Animal Experiments & Alternatives) • **Greenpeace UK**, Canonbury Villas, London N1 2PN **t** 020 7865 8100 **e** info@uk.greenpeace.org **w** www.greenpeace.org.uk • **IFAW** 8th Floor, 87-90 Albert Embankment, London SE1 7UD **t** 020 7587 6700 **e** info@ifaw.org **w**www.ifaw.org • **PETA Europe** PO Box 36668, London SE1 1WA **t** 020 7357 9229 **e** info@petauk.org **w** www.peta.org.uk • **Petsearch Register of Animals Lost & Found** Longhouse, 35 Church Lane, Melksham, Wiltshire SN12 7EF **t** 01225 705 175 **e** ukpetsearch@freeuk.com **w** www.ukpetsearch.freeuk.com • **Respect for Animals** PO Box 6500, Nottingham NG4 3GB **t** 0115 952 5440 **e** info@respectforanimals.org **w** www.respectforanimals.org • **RSPCA** Wilberforce Way, Southwater, Horsham, West Sussex RH13 7WN **t** 0870 335 999 **w** webmail@rspca.org.uk w **w**ww.rspca.org.uk • **VIVA!** 8 York Court, Wilder Street, Bristol, Somerset BS2 8QH **t** 0117 944 1000 **e** info@viva.org.uk **w** www.viva.org.uk • **World Society for the Protection of Animals** 89 Albert Embankment, London SE1 7TP **t** 020 7587 5000 **e** wspa@wspa.org.uk **w** www.wspa.org.uk • **World Wide Fund for Nature** Panda House, Weyside Park, Catershall Lane, Godalming GU7 1XR **t** 01483 426 444 **w** www.wwf-uk.org

MARINE ANIMALS

• **British Divers Marine Life Rescue** Lime House, Regency Close, Uckfield Sussex (East) TN22 1DS **t** 01825 765 546 **e** info@bdmir.org.uk **w** www.bdmlr.org.uk • **Cetacea Defence** PO Box 78, Shaftesbury, Dorset SP7 8ST **w** www.cetaceadefence.org • **Marine Conservation Society** Unit 3, Wolf Business Park Alton Road, Ross-on-Wye, Herefordshire HR9 5NB **t** 01989 566 017 **e** info@mcsuk.org **w** www.mcsuk.org • **Shellfish Network** Springside Forest Road, E Horsley, Leatherhead, Surrey KT24 5AZ **e** info@shellfishnetwork.org.uk **w** www.shellfishnetwork.org.uk • **Whale & Dolphin Conservation Society** PO Box 232, Melksham Wiltshire SN12 7SB **t** 0870 870 5001 **e** info@wdcs.org **w** www.wdcs.org

MISCELLANEOUS

• **McLibel Support Campaign** BM McSpotlight, London WC1N 3XX **e** info@mcspotlight.org w www.mcspotlight.org • **Vegan/Vegetarian Esperanto Group** Nant Yr Hafod Cottage Llandegla, Wrexham, Denbighshire LL11 3BG **t** 01978 790 442 **e** brianthesquirrel@compuserve.com • **Vegetarian Housing Association** PO Box 193, Hastings, East Sussex TN34 2WT **t** 01424 757 851 **e** office@veghousing.org.uk **w** www.veghousing.org.uk

PRISONERS' SUPPORT (ANIMAL RIGHT / VEGAN)

• **Vegan Prisoner Support Group** PO Box 194, Enfield, Middlesex EN1 4YL **t** 020 8292 8325 **e** info@vpsg.org **w** www.vpsg.org

RELIGIOUS

• **Anglican Society for the Welfare of Animals** PO Box 7193, Hook, Hampshire RG27 8GT **t** 01252 843 093 **e** feedback@aswa.org.uk **w** www.aswa.org.uk • **Animal Christian Concern** PO Box 70, Horsworth, Leeds LS18 5BG **t** 0113 258 3517 • **Catholic Concern for Animals** 36 Broad Oak Park, St Johns, Colchester, Essex CO4 4JY **e** ann.bates@lineone.net **w** www.catholic-animals.org • **Christian Ecology Link** 3 Bond Street, Lancaster LA1 3ER **t** 01524 33858 **e** info@christian-ecology.org.uk **w** www.christian-ecology.org.uk • **Christian Prayer Fellowship for the Protection of Animals** 5 Wemyss Place, Peebles EH45 8JT • **Jewish Vegetarian & Ecological**

Society 855 Finchley Road, London NW11 8LX **t** 020 8455 0692 **e** ijvs@yahoo.com **w** www.ivu.org/jvs • **Kindness Unlimited** The Old Vicarage, Llangynog, Carmarthenshire SA33 5BS **e** springoftruelife@aol.com • **Pagan Animal Rights Network** 110 Geoffrey Road, Brockley, London SE4 1NU

WILD ANIMALS

• **Born Free Foundation** 3 Grove House, Foundry Lane, Horsham, West Sussex RH13 5PL **t** 01403 240 170 **e** info@bornfree.org.uk **w** www.bornfree.org.uk • **British Hedgehog Preservation Society** Hedgehog House, Dhustone, Ludlow, Shropshire SY8 3PL **t** 01584 890 801 **e** bhps@dhustone.fsbusiness.co.uk **w** www.software-technics.com/bhps • **Care for the Wild International** The Granary, Tickfold Farm Kingsfold Sussex (West) RH12 3SE **t** 01306 627 900 **e** enquiries@careforthewild.com **w** www.careforthewild.org • **Fox Project** The Southborough Centre, Draper Street Southborough, Tunbridge Wells, Kent TN4 0PG **t** 01892 545 468 **e** fox@foxproject.org.uk **w** www.foxproject.org.uk • **International Primate Protection League (UK)** Gilmore House, 166 Gilmore Road, London SE13 5AE **t** 020 8297 2129 **e** enquiries@ippl-uk.org **w** ww.ippl-uk.org • **Jenita Fox Rescue** Oak Tree Cattery, Main Road, Colden Common, Winchester, Hampshire SO21 1TL **t** 023 8069 2309 • **London Wildlife Trust** Skyline House, 200 Union Street, London SE1 0LW **t** 020 7261 0447 **w** www.wildlondon.org.uk • **National Federation of Badger Groups** 2B Inworth Street, London SW11 3EP **t** 020 7228 6444 **e** elaine.king@nfbg.org.uk **w** www.badger.org.uk • **National Seal Sanctuary** Gweek, near Helston, Cornwall TR12 6UG **t** 01326 221 361 **e** seals@sealsanctuary.co.uk **w** www.sealsanctuary.co.uk • **Tiggywinkles**, **The Wildlife Hospital Trust** Church Farm, Aston Road, Haddenham, Aylesbury Buckinghamshire HP17 8AF **t** 01844 292 292 **e** mail@sttiggywinkles.org.uk **w** www.sttiggywinkles.org.uk

YOUTH GROUPS

• **Animal Aid Youth Group** See Animal Aid (General) • **Animal Defenders** See National Anti-Vivisection Society (Animal Experiments & Alternatives) • **Go Wild** See World Wide Fund for Nature (General) • **Junior Elefriends** See Born Free Foundation (Wild Animals) • **Junior RSPCA** See RSPCA (General) • **VC21** See Vegetarian Society (Diet/Lifestyle) • **Vegilantics** See Vegan Society magazine and website for details

SUGGESTED READING

A '*' before a title indicates it is available from the Vegan Society. These are all available online at www.vegansociety.com/shop or can be ordered by phone on 01424 427 393. For a pack containing a range of Vegan Society information resources and a current books and merchandise catalogue, send a SAE marked 'Info Pack' to: The Vegan Society, Donald Watson House, 7 Battle Road, St Leonards-on-Sea, East Sussex TN37 7AA.

Note: Many of the titles listed below are not written from an entirely animal-free viewpoint but are included on the basis of their educational or practical value.

ADDITIVES

- **A Consumer's Dictionary of Food Additives** Ruth Winter, Three Rivers Press(1999)
- **Animal Ingredients A-Z** The EG Smith Collective, AK Distribution (2004)
- **Food Additives, Nutrients and Supplements** Eileen Renders, Clear Light Publishing (1999)
- **The New E for Additives** Maurice Hanssen, HarperCollins (1987)

ANIMAL CARE

- **Vegetarian Cats and Dogs** James Peden, Harbingers of a New Age (1995)

ANIMAL EXPERIMENTS & ALTERNATIVES

- **Sacred Cows and Golden Geese** Jane Goodall & Dr C R Greek & J S Greek, Continuum International Publishing Group (2002)
- **Science on Trial: The Human Cost of Animal Experiments** Dr Robert Sharpe, Awareness Publishing (1994)
- **Slaughter of the Innocent** Hans Ruesch, Slingshot (2003)
- **Specious Science** C Ray Greek & Jean Swingle Greek, Continuum (2003)
- **Vivisection or Science: An Investigation into Testing Drugs and Safeguarding Health** Pietro Croce, Zed Books (1999)
- **Vivisection Unveiled: An Expose of the Medical Futility of Animal Experimentation** Dr Tony Page, Jon Carpenter (1997)

ANIMAL RIGHTS - LIBERATION & ETHICS

- **Animal Century: A Celebration of Changing Attitudes to Animals** Mark Gold, Jon Carpenter (1999)
- **Animal Liberation** Peter Singer, Ecco (2001)
- *** Animal Rights: A Very Short Introduction** David DeGrazia, Oxford University Press (2002)
- **Animal Rights — Extending the Circle of Compassion** Mark Gold, Jon Carpenter (1995)
- **Animal Welfare: A Cool Eye Towards Eden** John Webster, Blackwell Science (1995)
- **Animals' Rights** Henry Salt, Open Gate Press (1980)
- **Animals, Politics & Morality** Robert Garner, Manchester University Press (1993)
- **Born to be Wild** Juliet Gellatley, The Women's Press (2001)
- *** Campaign Against Cruelty** Alex Bourke and Ronny Worsey, Scamp Media (2001)
- **Caught in the Act: Feldberg Investigation** Melody MacDonald, Jon Carpenter (1994)
- **Free the Animals: The Story of the Animal Liberation Front** Ingrid Newkirk, Lantern Books (2000)
- *** Kids Can Save the Animals** Ingrid Newkirk, Warner Books (1991)
- *** Making Kind Choices** Ingrid Newkirk, St. Martin's Griffin (2005)
- **Morals, Reason and Animals** S. F Sapontzis, Temple University Press (1987)
- **The Case for Animal Rights** Tom Regan, University of California Press (2004)
- **The Dreaded Comparison: Human and Animal Slavery** Marjorie Spiegel, Gay Men's Press (1988)
- **The Pocketbook of Animal Facts & Figures UK** Caroline E. Clough & Barry Kew, Fourth Estate (1993)
- **The Savour of Salt: A Henry Salt Anthology** George and Willene Hendrick, Open Gate Press (1989)
- **The Silent Ark** Juliet Gellatley, HarperCollins (1996)
- **The Unheeded Cry: Animal Consciousness, Animal Pain and Science** Bernard E. Rollin, Iowa State University Press (1998)
- *** You Can Save the Animals** Ingrid Newkirk, Prima (1999)

BABIES & CHILDREN

- *** Raising your Vegan Infant - With Confidence** Sandra Hood, The Vegan Society (2005)
- *** Happy, Caring, Healthy & Sharing** – a book for young green vegans Graham Burnett, Land & Liberty (1991)

- * **Raising Vegan Children in a Non-Vegan World** Erin Pavlina, VegFamily (2003)
- * **Raising Vegetarian Children** Joanne Stepaniak & Vesanto Melina, Contemporary Books (2003)
  * **Vegan Infants Case Histories** Plamil Foods

CATERING

- * **Profit From Emerging Dietary Trends** John Hartley, Go Publish (2000)

CIRCUSES AND ZOOS

- **Animals in Circuses and Zoos - Chiron's World?** Marthe Kiley-Worthington, Aardvark Publishing (1997)
- **The Rose-Tinted Menagerie** William Johnson, Gay Men's Press (1990)

CONSUMERISM

- **The Good Shopping Guide** Charlotte Mulvey (ed.), The Ethical Marketing Group (2004)

COOKBOOKS

- * **A Vegan Taste of Eastern Europe** Linda Majzlik, Jon Carpenter (2004)
- * **A Vegan Taste of France** Linda Majzlik, Jon Carpenter (2003)
- * **A Vegan Taste of Greece** Linda Majzlik, Jon Carpenter (2003)
- * **A Vegan Taste of India** Linda Majzlik, Jon Carpenter (2002)
- * **A Vegan Taste of Italy** Linda Majzlik, Jon Carpenter (2001)
- * **A Vegan Taste of Mexico** Linda Majzlik, Jon Carpenter (2002)
- * **A Vegan Taste of North Africa** Linda Majzlik, Jon Carpenter (2003)
- * **A Vegan Taste of Thailand** Linda Majzlik, Jon Carpenter (2004)
- * **A Vegan Taste of the Caribbean** Linda Majzlik, Jon Carpenter (2001)
- * **A Vegan Taste of the Middle East** Linda Majzlik, Jon Carpenter (2002)
- * **Authentic Chinese Cuisine** Bryanna Clark Grogan, Book Publishing Company (2000)
- **Cook Vegan** Richard Youngs, Ashgrove Publishing (2001)
- **Cooking with PETA: Great Vegan Recipes for a Compassionate Kitchen** PETA, Book Publishing Company (1997)

- * **Fat-Free & Easy** Jennifer Raymond, Heart & Soul Publications (1997)
- **Green Gastronomy** Colin Spencer, Bloomsbury (1996)
- **Healing Foods Cookbook: The Vegan Way to Wellness** Jane Sen, HarperCollins (2000)
- * **Incredibly Delicious: Recipes for a New Paradigm** M. Katz, Gentle World (2003)
- * **Japanese Cooking** Miyoko Nishimoto Schinner, Book Publishing Company (1999)
- * **Kitchen Doctor – Vegan Cooking for Health** Nicola Graimes, Southwater (2003)
- * **More Fabulous Beans** Barb Bloomfield, Book Publishing Company (2003)
- * **Nonna's Italian Kitchen** Bryanna Clark Grogan, Book Publishing Company (1998)
- * **PETA Celebrity Cookbook** PETA (2002)
- * **Simple Treats** Ellen Abraham, Book Publishing Company (2003)
- **Simply Vegan** Debra Wasserman & Reed Mangels, Vegetarian Resource Group (US) (1999)
- * **So What Do You Eat?** Liz Cook (1999)
- **The Absolutely Animal-Free Cookbook** Wendy Turner, The Book Guild (1997)
- * **The Anglelica Home Kitchen** Leslie McEachern, Ten Speed Press (2003)
- * **The Artful Vegan** Eric Tucker with Bruce Enloe/desserts by Amy Pearce, Ten Speed Press (2003)
- **The Cake Scoffer** Ronny, Vegan International Cake Engineers (2000)
- * **The Cookbook for People Who Love Animals** Gentle World (1981)
- * **The Everyday Vegan** Dreena Burton, Arsenal Pulp Press (2003)
- **The Health Promoting Cookbook** Alan Goldhamer, Book Publishing Company (1997)
- * **The Joy of Vegan Cookery** Amanda Grant, Metro Publishing Ltd (2002)
- * **The Uncheese Cookbook** Joanne Stepaniak, Book Publishing Company (2003)
- * **The Vegan Cookbook** Alan Wakeman and Gordon Baskerville, Faber & Faber (1996)
- **The Vegan Gourmet: Full Flavor and Variety with over 100 Delicious Recipes** Susann Geiskopf-Hadler & Mindy Toomay, Prima Publishing (1999)
- * **The Whole Foods Diabetic Cookbook** Patricia Stevenson & Michael Cook & Patricia Bertron RD, Book Publishing Company (2003)
- * **Vegan** Tony Weston and Yvonne Bishop, Hamlin (2004)
- * **Vegan Baking** Linda Majzlik, Jon Carpenter (2000)
- * **Vegan Barbecues & Buffets** Linda Majzlik, Jon Carpenter (1999)
- * **Vegan Cooking** Eva Batt, Thorsons (1985)

- **Vegan Cooking for Everyone** Leah Leneman, HarperCollins (2003)
- *** Vegan Cooking for One** Leah Leneman, Thorsons (2000)
- *** Vegan Dinner Parties** Linda Majzlik, Jon Carpenter (1998)
- *** Vegan Feasts** Rose Elliot, Thorsons (2000)
- *** Vegan Rustic Cooking for all Seasons** Diana White, Vegan Organic Trust (2002)
- **Vegan Vittles: A Collection of Recipes Inspired by the Critters of Farm Sanctuary** Joanne Stepaniak, Book Publishing Company (1996)
- **Warming Up to Living Foods** Elysa Markowitz, Book Publishing Company (1998)

FARMING (ANIMAL PRODUCTION)

- **Do Hens Suffer in Battery Cages?** Michael Appleby, The Athene Trust, 5a Charles St, Petersfield, Hants GU32 3EH (1991)
- **The Meat Business - Devouring A Hungry Planet** Geoff Tansey & Joyce D'Silva (eds) Earthscan (1999)

FEMINISM & ANIMAL RIGHTS

- **Animals & Women: Feminist Theoretical Explorations** CJ Adams & J Donovan, Duke University Press (1995)

FOOD

- **Food For Free** Richard Mabey, Collins (2004)
- **Food Wars: The Global Battle for Mouths, Minds and Markets Tim Lang & Michael Heasman, Earthscan (2004)**
- **The Atlas of Food Erik Millstone & Tim Lang, Earthscan (2003)**

GARDENING

- *** Forest Gardening** Robert A de J Hart, Green Earth (1996)
- *** Permaculture: A Beginners Guide** Graham Burnett, Land & Liberty (2000)
- *** Sprout Garden** Mark M Braunstein, Book Publishing Company (1999)
- **The Gaia Natural Garden: Gardening in Harmony with Nature** Peter Harper, Jeremy Light & Chris Madsen, Gaia Books (2003)

GMOs

- **Animal Genetic Engineering: of Pigs, Oncomice and Men** Peter Wheale & Ruth McNally (eds.), Pluto Press (1995)
- **Genetic Engineering, Food and our Environment** Luke Anderson, Green Books (1999)
- *** Seeds of Deception** Jeffrey M. Smith, Green Books (2004)

NUTRITION & HEALTH

- *** 10 Days to Better Health** Kirsten Hartvig & Dr Nic Rowley, Piatkus Books (2003)
- *** Becoming Vegan** Brenda Davis & Vesanto Melina, Book Publishing Company (2000)
- **Detox Your World** Shazzie, Raw Creation (2003)
- **Diet, Life Expectancy and Chronic Disease: Studies of Seventh-day Adventists and other Vegetarians** Gary E Fraser, OUP (2003)
- **The Dietitian's Guide to Vegetarian Diets** Virginia Messina, Reed Mangels and Mark Messina, Jones & Bartlett Publishers (2004)
- *** Feel-Good Food** Susie Miller & Karen Knowler, The Women's Press (2000)
- *** Foods That Fight Pain** Neal Barnard, Bantam Books (1999)
- **Love Yourself, So Hate the Weight!** Brother Craig, Woodbridge Press (1996)
- *** Plant Based Nutrition and Health** Stephen Walsh PhD, The Vegan Society (2003)
- **The New Home Herbal: A Handbook of Simple Remedies** Barbara Griggs, Pan (1995)
- **Vegan Nutrition** Gill Langley, The Vegan Society (1995) – now out of print, but may be available second hand or from your local library
- **Vegan Nutrition: Pure & Simple** Michael Klaper MD, Book Publishing Company (1987)

QUOTATIONS

- **The Extended Circle: A Dictionary of Humane Thought** Jon Wynne-Tyson, Open Gate Press (1990)

REFERENCE

- **Animals' Contacts Directory** Veggies (2002/03)

TRAVEL

- **The New Spain - Vegan & Vegetarian Restaurants** Jean-Claude Juston, available from www.vegetarianguides.co.uk
- *** The Vegan Passport George Rodger (ed), The Vegan Society (2005)**
- *** Vegetarian Britain Alex Bourke, Vegetarian Guides (2005)**
- *** Vegetarian France Alex Bourke & Alan Todd, Vegetarian Guides (1998)**
- *** Vegetarian Europe Alex Bourke, Vegetarian Guides (2000)**
- *** Vegetarian London Alex Bourke, Vegetarian Guides (2005)**
- **Vegetarian Journal's Guide to Natural Foods Restaurants: In the U.S. and Canada Vegetarian Resource Group (2005)**
- **Vegan Guide to New York Rynn Berry, available from www.vegetarianguides.co.uk**
- **Vegetarian Nottinghamshire now available as an information sheet from Veggies Catering Campaign. See www.veggies.org.uk**
- **Vegetarian Guide to the Lake District published annually by Viva! www.viva.org.uk**
- **Vegetarian Oxfordshire Paul Appleby, available from www.ivu.org/oxveg**
- *** Vegetarian Visitor Annemarie Weitzel (ed.), Jon Carpenter (2005)**

VEGANISM & VEGETARIANISM

- *** Abundant Living in the Coming Age of the Tree** Kathleen Jannaway, MCL (1999)
- *** Being Vegan** Joanne Stepaniak, McGraw-Hill (2003)
- **Diet for a New America: How your Choices Affect your Health, Happiness & the Future of Life on Earth**, John Robbins, H J Kramer (1998)
- **Living Without Cruelty** Mark Gold, Green Print (1988)
- *** Plants for a Future** Ken Fern, Permanent Publications (1997)
- **The Food Revolution: How your Diet can Help Save your Life and our World** John Robbins, Conari Press (2001)
- **The Livewire Guide to Going, Being and Staying Veggie** Juliet Gellatley, Trafalgar Square Publishing (1997)
- *** The Vegan Sourcebook** Joanne Stepaniak & Virginia Messina, Lowell House Group (1998)
- *** Vegan Stories** Julie H Rosenfield (ed.), The Vegan Society (2002)
- *** Well Fed – Not An Animal Dead** Graham Burnett, Land & Liberty
- *** Why Vegan?** Kath Clements, Heretic (1995)

VERSE

- **No Room, Save in the Heart: Poetry and Prose on Reverence for Life- Animals, Nature and Human-kind** Ann C. Free, Flying Fox Printing (1986)
- *** 21st Century Toys** BJ Laprade, InfoDirect Ltd (1999)
- **Explicit Vegan Lyrics: The Little Book of Vegan Poems** Benjamin Zephaniah, AK Distribution (2000)
- **Talking Turkeys** Benjamin Zephaniah, Puffin Books (1995)

MAGAZINES

- **Agscene** CIWF, Charles Hse, 5a Charles St, Petersfield, Hants GU32 3EH
- **Animal Action** RSPCA, Causeway, Horsham, W Sussex RH12 1HG
- **Animal Times** PETA, PO Box 3169, London SW15 3ZG
- **Animals Defenders** 261 Goldhawk Rd, London W12 9PE
- **Arkangel** BCM 9240, London WC1N 3XX
- **Campaign Report** NAVS, 261 Goldhawk Rd, London W12 9PE
- **Ethical Consumer** ECRA Publishing, Unit 21, 41 Old Birley St, Manchester M15 5RF
- **FRESH** PO Box 71, ELY, CB7 4GU
- **Green Futures** 13-17 Sturton Street, Cambridge, CB1 2SN
- **HOWL** HSA, BM HSA, London, WC1N 3XX
- **New Consumer** 0800 389 4728
- **Outrage** Animal Aid, The Old Chapel, Bradford St, Tonbridge, Kent TN9 1AW
- **Pisces** BM Fish, London WC1N 3XX
- **Resurgence** Rocksea Farmhouse, St. Mabyn, Bodmin, Cornwall, PL30 3BR
- **Speak Out** SPEAK Campaigns, PO Box 6712, Northampton NN2 6XR
- **The Ecologist** PO Box 326, Sittingbourne, Kent ME9 8FA
- **The Vegan** The Vegan Society, Donald Watson Hse, 7 Battle Rd, St Leonards-on-Sea, E Sussex TN37 7AA
- **The Vegetarian** VSUK, Parkdale, Dunham Rd, Altrincham, Cheshire WA14 4QG
- **Vegan Views** 6 Hayes Ave, Bournemouth BH7 7AD
- **Viva! Life** 8 York Court, Wilder Street, Bristol, BS2 8QH
- **Wales Vegan** Montpelier, Llandrindod, Powys, Wales
- **Wildlife Guardian** LACS, Sparling Hse, 83-87 Union St, London SE1 1S

COMPANY CONTACT DETAILS

- **Aarhus United UK Ltd** www.aarhusunited.com/uk 01482 701 271
- **Absolute Aromas** www.absolute-aromas.com 01420 540 400
- **Absolutely Pure** www.absolutelypure.com 0870 760 6915
- **Ace Nutrition Ltd.** www.ace-nutrition.com 01753 544 002
- **Ainsworths Homeopathic Pharmacy** www.ainsworths.com 020 7935 5330
- **Aldi Stores Ltd** www.aldi-stores.co.uk 01827 711 800
- **All Seasons Health** www.allseasonshealth.com 01983 537 533
- **Alpro UK Ltd** www.alprosoya.co.uk 01536 720 605
- **Ambrosian Vegetarian Foods** www.synergynet.co.uk/ambrosian/our_range.htm 01283 225 055
- **AMI srl** www.aminews.net 00 39 049 780 1712
- **Amphora Aromatics Ltd** www.amphora-aromatics.com 0117 908 7770
- **Anglesey Natural Foods** www.quinova.co.uk 01248 422 011
- **Anheuser-Busch Europe Ltd** www.budweiser.co.uk 020 8332 2302
- **Animal Aid** www.animalaid.org.uk 01732 364 546
- **AquaSource** www.aquasourcealgae.com 01392 822 155
- **Arkopharma (UK) Ltd** www.arkopharma.co.uk 020 8763 1414
- **Aroma Crystal Therapy** www.aromacrystaleurope.com 07945 94478
- **Aromafoods** www.aromafoods.org.uk 0800 0744 876
- **Artel Allergy Products** www.artelallergyproducts.com 01279 876 901
- **Asda Stores Ltd** www.asda.com 0113 243 5435
- **Ashbourne Biscuits Ltd** www.ashbournebiscuits.co.uk 01335 342 373
- **Aston Manor Brewery Co Ltd** www.astonmanor.co.uk 0121 328 4336
- **Atlantic Seaweed** allanleys@hotmail.com 01438 213 194
- **Australian Nougat Company** www.ausnougat.com.au 07548 853 132
- **Avalon Vineyards** www.pennardorganicwines.co.uk 01749 860 393
- **Bakers Delight** www.bakers-delight.co.uk 01482 227 439
- **Barry M Cosmetics** www.barrym.com 020 8349 2992
- **Baxters of Speyside Ltd** www.baxters.co.uk 01343 820 393
- **Bay House Aromatics** www.bay-house.co.uk 01273 601 109
- **Beanies Health Foods** www.beanieshealthfoods.co.uk 01489 574 593

- **Beauty Naturals (Martha Hill)** www.beautynaturals.com 0800 980 6662
- **Beauty Through Herbs** www.bth.co.uk 01847 822 208
- **Bells of Lazonby Ltd** www.villagebakery.com 01768 898 347
- **Belvoir Fruit Farms** www.belvoircordials.co.uk 01476 870 286
- **Bendicks of Mayfair** www.bendicks.co.uk 01962 844 800
- **Bennett Natural Products** www.healthremedies.co.uk 01257 404 659
- **Beyond Skin Ltd** www.beyondskin.co.uk 01494 871 655
- **Bickiepegs Ltd** www.bickiepegs.co.uk 01224 790 626
- **Binney & Smith (Europe)** www.crayola.com 01234 360 201
- **Bio-D Co. Ltd.** www.biodegradable.biz 01482 229 950
- **Bioforce** www.bioforce.co.uk 01294 277 344
- **Bio-Health Ltd** www.bio-health.co.uk 01634 290 115
- **Black Sheep Brewery Plc** www.blacksheep.co.uk 01765 689 227
- **Blue Lotus** www.bluelotusproducts.com 0116 299 8122
- **Bodywise (UK) Ltd** www.natracare.com 01275 371 764
- **Bottlegreen Drinks Co** www.bottlegreen.co.uk 01453 874 000
- **Brake Bros** www.brake.co.uk 01233 206 000
- **British Bakeries** www.britishbakeries.co.uk 01753 857123
- **British Sugar plc** www.britishsugar.co.uk 020 7589 6363
- **Britvic Soft Drinks Ltd** www.britvic.co.uk 01245 261 871
- **Broadland Foods** 111 Great Barr Street, Birmingham, B9 4BB 0121 773 5955
- **Broughton Ales** www.broughtonales.co.uk 01899 830 345
- **Broughton Pastures Organic Fruit Wine** www.BroughtonPastures.co.uk 01442 823 993
- **Brunel Healthcare** www.bruhealth.co.uk 0117 949 7040
- **Buckfast Organic Bakery Ltd** Clive's Pies', Hamlyn House, Mardle Way, Buckfastleigh, Devon, TQ11 0NR 01364 642 279
- **Budgens Stores Ltd** www.budgens.co.uk 020 8422 9511
- **Burt's Bees** www.forever-natural.com 01628 898 410
- **Buxton Foods** www.stamp-collection.co.uk 020 7637 5505
- **Cadbury** www.cadbury.co.uk 0121 458 2000
- **Calch Ty-Mawr Lime Ltd** www.lime.org.uk 01874 658 249
- **Calder Valley Soap** www.uksoaps.net 01422 362 202
- **Caledonian Brewing Co** www.caledonian-brewery.co.uk 0131 337 1286
- **Caledonian Curry Co.** www.caledoniancurry.co.uk 01863 766 025

- **Calypso Soft Drinks** www.calypso.co.uk 01978 668 400
- **Cam International** www.soyahealth.co.uk 01432 360 216
- **Cambridge Bioceuticals** www.bio-kult.com 01353 723 234
- **Camilla Hepper Ltd** www.camillahepper.co.uk 01491 826 196
- **Capitelli Oils** www.capitelli-oils.co.uk 0131 661 7275
- **Carlsberg UK Ltd** www.carlsberguk.co.uk 01604 668 866
- **Carmel Food Ltd** www.carmel-food.com 020 8902 3002
- **Carol Nicholson (Sole Trader)** Round Lodge, Belstead Road, Ipswich, Suffolk IP2 9EH 01473 688 128
- **Cauldron Foods Ltd** www.cauldronfoods.co.uk 01275 818 448
- **Caurnie Soaperie** www.caurnie.com 0141 776 1218
- **Cedar Health Ltd** www.cedarhealth.co.uk 0161 483 1235
- **Celestial Designs Aromatherapy** www.btinternet.com/~aromashop 01745 550 411
- **Cellande Midlands** www.cellande.co.uk 0121 472 2903
- **Chegworth Valley Juices** www.chegworthvalley.com 01622 859 272
- **Chimans** sallyagarwal@yahoo.co.uk 01271 883 864
- **Chirali Old Remedies** www.cuppingtherapy.co.uk 020 8306 6736
- **Chocolate Society** www.chocolate.co.uk 020 7259 9222
- **Clearspring** www.clearspring.co.uk 020 8749 1781
- **Colora Henna** 217 Washington Avenue, Carlstadt, NY 07072, USA 00 1 201 939 0969
- **Community Foods Ltd** www.communityfoods.co.uk 020 8450 9411
- **Condomi Health UK Ltd** www.condomi.com 01260 295316
- **Co-operative Group Ltd** www.co-op.co.uk 0161 827 5688
- **Cooplands Ltd** Milethorn Lane, Doncaster, Yorkshire (South) DN1 2SX 01302 818 000
- **Cotswold Health Products** www.cotsherb.co.uk 01453 843 694
- **Cow & Gate** www.cowandgate.co.uk 01225 768 381
- **Culpeper Ltd** www.culpeper.co.uk 01223 894 054
- **D & D Chocolates** www.d-dchocolates.com 024 7637 0909
- **Daler Rowney Ltd** www.daler-rowney.com 01344 461 000
- **Daniel Field Direct** www.danielfield.com 0845 230 2124
- **Davenport Vineyards** www.davenportvineyards.co.uk 01892 852 380
- **Dees Caribbean Imports** deesimports@hotmail.com 020 8504 0489

- **Denes Natural Pet Care Ltd** www.denes.com 01273 325 364
- **Deodorant Stone (UK) Ltd** www.deodorant-stone.co.uk 01559 384 856
- **Deva Nutrition** www.devanutrition.com 00 1 781 632 7353
- **Dipak Foods Ltd** 25 Silverstone Drive, Leicester, LE4 7RR 0116 251 1300
- **Discovery Foods** www.discoveryfoods.co.uk 01494 464 460
- **Divine (The Day Chocolate Company)** www.divinechocolate.com 020 7378 6550
- **Dolma** www.veganvillage.co.uk/dolma 0115 963 4237
- **Doves Farm Foods Ltd** www.dovesfarm.co.uk 01488 684 884
- **Dr Hadwen Trust** www.drhadwentrust.org.uk 01462 436 819
- **Dragonfly Foods** www.beany.co.uk 01364 642 700
- **Dri-Pak Ltd** www.dripak.co.uk 0115 932 5165
- **Duerrs** www.duerrs.co.uk 0161 226 2251
- **Dunkerton's Cider Company** www.dunkertons.co.uk 01544 388 653
- **Duval-Leroy UK Ltd** www.duval-leroy.com 020 8982 4216
- **Earth Footwear** www.earth.us 00 1 781 893 7474
- **Ecos Paints** www.ecosorganicpaints.com 01524 852 371
- **Ecover** www.ecover.com 01635 528 240
- **Elizabeth Shaw Ltd** www.elizabethshaw.co.uk 0117 301 3300
- **Ella Drinks** www.bouvrage.com 01786 834 342
- **Empire Foodbrokers Ltd** www.empirefoodbrokers.com 020 8537 4080
- **Essence Serene** www.healthandbeautybymail.co.uk 01271 329 930
- **Essential Oil Company** www.eoco.org.uk 01256 332 737
- **Essential Trading Co-Operative Ltd** www.essential-trading.coop 0117 958 3550
- **Essentially Yours Ltd** www.essentially-yours.co.uk 01372 465 414
- **Ethical Wares** www.ethicalwares.com 01570 471 155
- **Faith Products Ltd** www.faithproducts.com 0161 764 2555
- **Fauser Vitaquellwerk KG** www.vitaquell.de 00 49 40 572 020
- **Fayrefield Foods** www.fayrefield.co.uk 01270 589 311
- **Finemood Ltd** www.shirleyprice.com 01455 615 466
- **First Foods Ltd** www.first-foods.com 01494 431 355
- **First Quality Foods** www.firstqualityfoods.co.uk 08707 771 910
- **First Quench** www.threshers.co.uk 01707 387 400
- **Fox's Biscuits** www.foxs-biscuits.co.uk 01924 444 333

- **Freerangers** www.freerangers.co.uk 01207 565 957
- **Fresh Foods Co Ltd** www.freshfood.co.uk 020 8749 8778
- **Fullers** www.fullers.co.uk 020 8996 2000
- **Funk Bubble** www.funkbubble.co.uk 07775 898 889
- **General Mills Berwick** Tweedside Trading Estate, Berwick-Upon-Tweed, Northumberland TD15 2UX 01289 307737
- **George Bateman & Son** mjcullimore@bateman.co.uk 01754 880317
- **Get Real Organic Foods** www.get-real.co.uk 01939 210 925
- **Gluten Free Foods Ltd** www.glutenfree-foods.co.uk 020 8953 4444
- **Golden Wonder** www.goldenwonder.com 01858 410 410
- **Gourmet Woodland Mushroom Ltd** www.gourmetmushrooms.co.uk 01751 475 900
- **GR Wright & Sons Ltd** www.wrightsflour.co.uk 020 8344 6900
- **Granovita UK Ltd** www.granovita.co.uk 01933 273 717
- **Green & Blacks** www.greenandblacks.com 020 7633 5900
- **Green Ark Animal Nutrition** www.greenark.co.uk 01706 212 086
- **Green Building Store** www.greenbuildingstore.co.uk 01484 854 898
- **Green Dot Guides** www.naturalcollection.com 01225 404 010
- **Green People Co.** www.greenpeople.co.uk 01444 401 444
- **Green Shoes** www.greenshoes.co.uk 01803 864 997
- **Green Shop** www.greenshop.co.uk 01452 770 629
- **Groomers Ltd** www.groomersshampoo.com 01635 581 958
- **Growganic** www.growganic.com 01380 871 050
- **Guat Shoes** www.guatshoes.co.uk 0114 268 6364
- **H J Heinz Co Ltd** www.heinz.co.uk 020 8573 7757
- **Haldane Foods Ltd** www.haldanefoods.co.uk 01908 211 311
- **Hanami Ltd** www.hanami.ie 00 353 1 671 3671
- **Hanley Food Group** www.vegpasty.com 01736 363 654
- **Harbourne Vineyard** www.harbournevineyard.co.uk 01797 270 420
- **Harvey Mercer** www.heartys.co.uk 01423 528 822
- **Health + Plus** www.healthplus.co.uk 01323 872 277
- **Healthpol** www.delacet.co.uk 020 8360 0386
- **Healthquest Limited** www.healthquest.co.uk 020 8424 8844
- **Healthy and Essential** www.healthyandessential.com 08700 536 000
- **Healthy Herbs** peterhh80@fsmail.net 01925 822 502

- **Hendersons (Sheffield) Ltd** www.hendersons-relish.co.uk 0114 272 5909
- **Herb UK Ltd** 11 Somerford Business Park, Wilverley Rd, Christchurch, Dorset BH23 3RU 01202 477 188
- **Herbs Hands Healing Ltd** www.herbshandshealing.co.uk 01379 608 201
- **Herbs of Grace** www.herbsofgrace.co.uk 01638 712 123
- **Hermitage Oils** www.hermitageoils.com 01274 565 957
- **Heron Quality Foods Ltd** www.glutenfreedirect.com 00 353 233 9006
- **Higher Nature Plc** www.higher-nature.co.uk 01435 883 484
- **Himalaya UK Ltd** www.himalaya-uk.com 020 8761 9250
- **Hipp Organic Baby Foods** www.hipp.co.uk 0845 050 1351
- **Holland and Barrett Retail Ltd** www.hollandandbarrett.com 024 7624 4400
- **Holle Baby Foods** www.drhauschka.co.uk 01386 792 622
- **Homecare Products** www.homecareproducts.co.uk 01473 832 020
- **Honesty Cosmetics Ltd** www.honestycosmetics.co.uk 01629 814 888
- **House of Life** Mercury House, Shipstones Business Centre, Northgate, New Basford, Nottingham NG7 7FN 07904 402 209
- **Humdinger Ltd** www.dairy-free.co.uk 01482 625 790
- **Iceland Frozen Foods PLC** www.iceland.co.uk 01244 842 842
- **Il Mangiar Sano** info@ilmangiarsano.com
- **Innocent Drinks** www.innocentdrinks.co.uk 020 8600 3939
- **Interbrew** www.interbrew.com 0870 24 111 24
- **International Partnership Ltd (Seagreens Division)** www.seagreens.com 0845 06 400 403
- **Isle of Bute Foods Ltd** www.scheese.co.uk 01700 505 357
- **J&D Black Ltd** sales@jdblack.co.uk 01252 344 010
- **J. L. Bragg Ltd** www.charcoal.uk.com 01473 748 345
- **James White** www.jameswhite.co.uk 01473 890 111
- **Jarrow Formulas Inc.** www.jarrow.com 00 1 310 204 6930
- **Jeremy's Soups** jeremyssoups@ukonline.co.uk 01768 353 311
- **Jethros** www.jethros.co.uk 01273 417 405
- **Jonathan Crisp** www.jonathancrisp.co.uk 01865 882 514
- **Jophiel®** www.jophieloils.com 0161 626 1549
- **Jordan (Cereals) Ltd** www.jordans-cereals.co.uk 01767 319 454
- **Jungle Passion Ltd** www.junglepassion.co.uk
- **Just Wholefoods** www.justwholefoods.co.uk 01285 651 910

- **Kelloggs** www.kelloggs.co.uk 0161 869 2000
- **Kent Cosmetics** enquiries@kentcos.com 01622 859 898
- **Kettle Foods** www.kettlefoods.co.uk 0800 616 996
- **Kingfisher Natural Toothpaste** www.kingfishertoothpaste.com 01603 630 484
- **Kiss My Face** www.kissmyface.com 01347 878 751
- **Kitchen Garden Preserves** www.kitchengardenpreserves.co.uk 01453 759 612
- **Kobashi** www.kobashi.co.uk 01392 217 628
- **Kudos Vitamins and Herbals Ltd** www.kudosvitamins.com 020 8392 6524
- **L'Occitane en Provence** www.loccitane.com 020 7907 0301
- **Label It or Lose It** www.labelitorloseit.com 07949 062 475
- **Laverana GmbH** www.lavera.co.uk 01557 814 941
- **Lawncourt Harvest Ltd** Unit 6A, Eastlands Road, Leiston, Suffolk IP16 4LL 01728 833 004
- **Leafcycle** www.leafcycle.co.uk 01398 331 808
- **Leeora Vegetarian Food** www.leeoravegetarianfood.co.uk 01206 514 966
- **Liberon Waxes Ltd** www.liberonwaxes.co.uk 01797 367 555
- **Life Food GmbH - Taifun-Tofuprodukte** www.taifun-tofu.com 00 49 7611 52100
- **Lifeplan Products Ltd** www.lifeplan.co.uk 01455 556 281
- **Lifestyle Healthcare Ltd** www.glutenfree.co.uk 01491 570 000
- **Lindt & Sprungli** www.lindt.com 01895 424 062
- **Linpharma Herbal Products** www.linpharma.com 01506 848 649
- **Little Salkeld Mill** www.organicmill.co.uk 01768 881 523
- **Living Earth Europe** www.soyafresh.co.uk 0845 330 6781
- **London Oil Refining Company Ltd** www.astonishcleaners.com 0113 236 0036
- **Lumen Foods** www.soybean.com 00 1 337 436 6748
- **Luscombe Organic Drinks** www.luscombe.co.uk 01364 643 036
- **Lush** www.lush.co.uk 01202 668 545
- **Lyme Regis Fine Foods Ltd** www.lymeregisfoods.com 01428 722 900
- **MacSween of Edinburgh** www.macsween.co.uk 0131 440 2555
- **Malibu Health Products Ltd** www.malibusun.com 020 8758 0055
- **Marigold Health Foods** sales@marigoldhealth.co.uk 020 7388 4515
- **Marks & Spencer** www.marksandspencer.com 0845 302 1234
- **Marlo www.marlo.co.uk** 01736 755 928
- **Mary Berry & Daughter** www.maryberry.co.uk 01494 813 113

- **Mason's Products** www.dogoil.co.uk 01706 379 817
- **Matthew Clark plc** www.mclark.co.uk 01275 836 100
- **Matthews Foods** www.matthews-foods.co.uk 0800 028 4499
- **Maxim Marketing Company** www.maximmarketing.co.uk 020 8998 2357
- **Maximuscle Ltd** www.maximuscle.com 01923 650 600
- **McCain Foods GB Ltd** www.mccain.com 01723 584 141
- **Meadowsweet Ltd** www.meadowsweet.co.uk 01449 676 940
- **Meridian Foods** www.meridianfoods.co.uk 01490 413 151
- **MH Foods Ltd** www.mhfoods.net 01322 337 711
- **Montagne Jeunesse** www.montagnejeunesse.co.uk 01792 310 306
- **Montezumas** www.montezumas.co.uk 01243 576 589
- **Mooncup Ltd.** www.mooncup.co.uk 01273 673 845
- **Mother Hemp Ltd** www.motherhemp.com 01262 421 100
- **Napiers Herbal Health Centre** www.napiers.net 0131 343 6683
- **National Trust Enterprises Ltd** www.nationaltrust.org.uk 0870 609 5381
- **Natura Organics** www.naturaorganics.com 01273 685 800
- **Natural by Nature Oils** www.naturalbynature.co.uk 01582 840 848
- **Natural Organics** www.organicsoap.net 020 8488 2469
- **Natural Shoe Store** www.birkenstock.co.uk 020 7602 2866
- **Natural Woman** www.natural-woman.com 0117 968 7744
- **Naturally Gifted** www.naturally-gifted.co.uk 0871 990 2121
- **Naturally ME Inc** www.naturalfeast.com 00 1 508 785 0027
- **Nature's Aid Ltd** www.naturesaid.net 01772 686 231
- **Nature's Own Ltd** www.natures-own.co.uk 01684 310 022
- **Nature's Remedies** www.naturesremedies.uk.com 01494 727 888
- **Naturemade Oasis** www.naturemade.co.uk 01769 573 571
- **Nature's Plate** www.naturesplate.co.uk 01392 413 578
- **Naturewatch** www.naturewatch.org 01242 252 871
- **NDS Healthcare** www.ndshealthcare.com 08700 11 11 88
- **Neal's Yard Remedies** www.nealsyardremedies.com 020 7627 1949
- **Nestlé** www.nestle.co.uk 0800 00 00 30
- **Network of Wholefood Wholesale Co-Operatives** now@essential-trading.co.uk 0117 958 3550
- **New Seasons** www.newseasons.co.uk 01235 821 110
- **Neways International UK Ltd** www.neways.co.uk 01480 861 764

- **Norfolk Lavender Ltd** www.norfolk-lavender.co.uk 01485 570 384
- **Nubian Care** www.nubiancare.co.uk 01332 366 144
- **Nutrisport** www.nutrisport.co.uk 01942 519 111
- **One With Nature** www.onewithnature.com
- **Optima Health & Nutrition** www.optimah.com 029 2038 8422
- **Orange-Mate Inc** www.hydrogarden.com 024 7661 2888
- **Organic Colour Company** www.herbatint.co.uk 020 8960 7968
- **Oscar Bars** www.oscarbars.com 01544 340 081
- **Oshadhi Ltd** www.oshadhi.co.uk 01223 242 242
- **OSMO UK Ltd** www.osmouk.com 01296 481 220
- **Panacea ApS** www.panacea.dk 00 45 48 27 7110
- **Pantri Nolwenn** pantri.nolwenn@talk21.com 0845 330 6193
- **Passion for Life Products** www.passionforlife.com 0800 096 1121
- **Pasta King (UK) Ltd** www.pastaking.co.uk 01626 334 480
- **Pataks Foods Ltd** www.pataks.co.uk 01942 272300
- **Patisserie Organic** www.patisserieorganic.co.uk 020 7482 1922
- **Paul's Tofu** 66-68 Snow Hill, Melton Mowbray, Leicestershire LE13 1PD 01664 560 572
- **People Tree Ltd** www.ptree.co.uk 020 7739 0660
- **Perfumers Guild Ltd, The** parfumjohn@aol.com 01923 260 502
- **Phyto Products Ltd** info@phyto.co.uk 01623 644 334
- **Phytofoods** pollysyred@onetel.net.uk 01547 510 242
- **Pitfield Brewery** www.pitfieldbeershop.co.uk 020 7739 3701
- **Pitrok Ltd** www.pitrok.co.uk 020 8563 1120
- **Plamil Foods Ltd** www.plamilfoods.co.uk 01303 850 588
- **Polyco Ltd** www.superglove.co.uk 020 8443 9000
- **Power Health Products** www.power-health.co.uk 01759 302 595
- **Price's Patent Candles Ltd** www.prices-candles.co.uk 01234 264 500
- **Principle Healthcare** clare.campbell@principlehc.com 01756 792 600
- **Probiotics International Ltd.** www.protexin.com 01935 822 921
- **Pure Soaps** www.puresoaps.co.uk 0776 201 8422
- **Pure Wine Company** www.purewine.co.uk 023 80 238 214
- **Purple Flame Aromatherapy** www.purpleflame.co.uk 01676 542 542
- **PZ Cussons UK Ltd** www.originalsource.co.uk 0161 491 8000
- **Queensland Government** www.export.qld.gov.au 020 7031 8108

- **Quest Vitamins** www.questvitamins.co.uk 0121 359 0056
- **Quinessence Aromatherapy** www.quinessence.com 01530 835 918
- **R J Foods Limited** www.rjfoods-flapjack.com 01202 481 471
- **Rainbow Flavours** andrewsmith771@hotmail.com 020 8670 9256
- **Rakusen's** www.rakusens.co.uk 0113 278 4821
- **Rawcreation Ltd** www.detoxyourworld.com 08700 113 119
- **RDA Organic** www.rdaorganic.com 020 8875 9740
- **red23.co.uk** www.red23.co.uk 01992 815 859
- **Red Bull Company Limited** www.redbull.com 020 7434 0100
- **Red Star Hand Crafted Soaps** swampys@gn.apc.org 01922 712691
- **Redbush Tea Co** www.redbushtea.com 0845 601 2658
- **Redwood Wholefood Company** www.redwoodfoods.co.uk 01536 400 557
- **Refresh UK plc** www.refreshuk.com 01225 715 170
- **Reliv UK** www.reliv.com/uk 01527 559 811
- **Ren** www.renskincare.com 020 7724 2900
- **Rhema UK Ltd** rhemauk@aol.com 020 8488 8111
- **Ritter Sport** www.ritter-sport.de 0715 797 268
- **Robert Cain & Company Limited** www.cainsbeers.com 0151 709 8734
- **Rocks Organic Cordials** www.rocksorganic.com 0118 934 2344
- **Rogue Development** www.roguedevelopment.co.uk 020 7274 7048
- **Rustins Ltd** www.rustins.co.uk 020 8450 4666
- **Ryvita** www.ryvita.co.uk 01202 743 090
- **Sacla** www.sacla.co.uk 01494 687 900
- **Sage Organic Ltd** www.sagenutritionals.com 01672 872 907
- **Sainsbury's Supermarkets Ltd** www.sainsburys.co.uk0800 636 262
- **Samuel Smith** High Street, Tadcaster, N Yorkshire, LS24 9SB 01937 832 225
- **SanchiSee Community Foods** 020 8450 9419
- **Savant Distribution Ltd** www.savant-health.com 0845 060 6070
- **Scent By Nature** www.scentbynature.net 01493 369 678
- **Scottish Herbal Supplies** Drimlabarra Herb Farm, Kildonan, Isle of Arran KA27 8SE 01770 820 314
- **Sedlescombe Organic Vineyard** www.englishorganicwine.co.uk 0800 9802884
- **Seeds of Change** www.seedsofchange.co.uk 01664 415 490
- **Serf to Surf UK** www.serftosurf.co.uk 0870 787 5688
- **Setalg www.setalg.com** 00 33 296 228 639

- **Seven Seas** www.seven-seas.ltd.uk 01482 375 234
- **Seven Wives Natural Bodycare** www.sevenwives.co.uk 01736 74 00 11
- **Shearer Candles** www.shearer-candles.com 0141 445 1066
- **Shepherdboy** www.shepherdboy.co.uk 0116 260 2992
- **Sheppy's Cider** www.sheppyscider.com 01823 461 233
- **Sikelia Ltd** sikeliauk@yahoo.co.uk 020 8788 0548
- **Simply Nature** www.simply-nature.co.uk 01580 201 687
- **Simply Organic** www.simplyorganic.co.uk 0131 448 0440
- **Simply Soaps** www.simplysoaps.com 01603 720 869
- **Skin Care Cafe Ltd** Old Bailey, School Road, Hurst, Berkshire, RG10 0BR 07977 209 692
- **Smilde** www.smildefood.uk.com 01892 669616
- **Smooth Brothers** www.smoothbrothers.com 00 353 879 278 826
- **Solano Trading** 11 Summer Hill, Frome, Somerset BA11 1LT 01373 473 809
- **Solgar Vitamins Ltd** www.solgar.com 01442 890 355
- **Solo Nutrition Ltd** www.solonutrition.co.uk 01273 628 747
- **Soma** www.somajuice.com 0870 950 7662
- **Somerfield** www.somerfield.co.uk 0117 935 9359
- **Source Foods** www.miso.co.uk 01495 371 698
- **Soya Health Foods Ltd** www.soya-group.com 0161 924 2214
- **Spa House Ltd** 2 Camden crescent, Bath, BA1 5HY 01225 316 140
- **Splash English Wines** www.splashwines.co.uk 01484 323 814
- **Spoff (Scotland) Ltd** www.spoff.co.uk 01349 854 290
- **Stiletto Foods** mrs.crimbles.cakes.@monomark.co.uk 020 8840 2244
- **Suma Wholefoods** www.suma.coop 0845 458 2290
- **Supercook** www.supercook.co.uk 0151 7068200
- **Swedish Match** www.swedishmatch.com 00 46 8 658 02 00
- **Swizzels Matlow Ltd** www.swizzels-matlow.com 0800 970 0480
- **Tanjero** www.tanjero.co.uk 0114 256 2977
- **Tesco** www.tesco.com 0800 505 555
- **The Booja Booja Company Ltd** www.boojabooja.com 01508 499 049
- **The Cocoa Tree (1657) Ltd** www.thecocoatree.co.uk 01548 580 009
- **The Durham Brewery Ltd** www.durham-brewery.co.uk 0191 377 1991
- **The Herbary** www.beansandherbs.co.uk 01985 844 442
- **The Humane Research Trust** www.humaneresearch.org.uk 0161 439 8041

- **The Innis & Gunn Brewing Company Ltd.** www.innisandgunn.com 0131 337 4420
- **The Organic Herb Trading Company** www.hambledenherbs.co.uk 01823 401 205
- **The Organic Spirits Company** www.junipergreen.org 01483 894 650
- **The Vege Chip Company** www.ajitas.com 00 61 7 55 250 670
- **The Vegan Society** www.vegansociety.com 0845 45 88244
- **Thorncroft** www.thorncroft.ltd.uk 01642 791 792
- **Thorntons Plc** www.thorntons.co.uk 0845 121 1911
- **Tisserand Aromatherapy Products** www.tisserand.com 01273 325 666
- **Tom Soya** www.tomsoya.com 01244 289 001
- **Tom's of Maine** www.tomsofmaine.com 00 1 207 985 2944
- **Traquair** www.traquair.co.uk 01896 831 370
- **Tree of Life UK Ltd** www.naturesstore.co.uk 01782 567 100
- **Tree-harvest** www.tree-harvest.com 01531 635 284
- **Triano Brands Limited** ron@trianobrands.co.uk 01704 870 764
- **Tropical Wholefoods** www.tropicalwholefoods.com 0191 548 0050
- **Trufree (Nutricia)** www.trufree.co.uk 01225 711 801
- **Truuuly Scrumptious Organic Baby Food Ltd.** www.bathorganicbabyfood.co.uk 01761 239 300
- **Turtle Island Foods** www.tofurky.com 00 1 541 386 7766
- **United Biscuits Ltd** www.unitedbiscuits.co.uk 01494 463 388
- **Urtekram** www.urtekram.dk 00 45 9854 2288
- **Vega Nutritionals** info@vegavitamins.co.uk 08452 267 300
- **Veganline** www.veganline.com 0800 458 4442
- **Veganstore.co.uk** www.veganstore.co.uk 01273 302 979
- **VegeFarm Corp** info@vegdist.co.uk 00 886 2214 93 189
- **Vegepet** www.vegepet.com 00 1 406 295 4944
- **Vegetarian Shoes** www.vegshoes.com 01273 691 913
- **Vegetarians Choice** 171 Merley Lane, Wimborne, Dorset BH21 3AG 01202 889 900
- **Veggies Catering Campaign** www.veggies.org.uk 0845 458 9595
- **Venture Foods Ltd** www.venturefoods.com 01743 289 133
- **Vinceremos Organic Wines** www.vinceremos.co.uk 0113 244 0002

- **Vindotco UK Ltd** www.reallyworks.co.uk 01652 652 444
- **Vintage Roots** www.vintageroots.co.uk 0118 976 1999
- **Virgin Wines Ltd**. www.virginwines.com 0870 164 2038
- **Visage International Partners Ltd.** ann.golding@visageinternational.com 01206 752 722
- **VIVA!** www.viva.org.uk 0117 944 1000
- **Waitrose** www.waitrose.co.uk 0800 188 884
- **Walkers Snack Foods Ltd** walkers.corpex.com/cr15p5/index.htm 0116 234 2345
- **Warburtons** www.warburtons.co.uk 01204 556 600
- **WDB Brands** www.wdbbrands.co.uk 01902 711 811
- **Weetabix Ltd** www.weetabix.co.uk 01536 722 181
- **Weleda** www.weleda.co.uk 0115 944 8222
- **Wellfoods Ltd** www.bake-it.com 01226 381 712
- **Westler Foods Ltd** www.westlerfoods.com 01653 693 971
- **Weston & Sons Ltd** www.westons-cider.co.uk 01531 66 0233
- **Wicken Fen** www.wickenfen.co.uk 01361 883 150
- **William Santus & Co. Ltd** www.uncle-joes.com 01942 243 464
- **Winsor & Newton** www.winsornewton.com 020 8424 3415
- **Woods of Windsor** www.woodsofwindsor.co.uk 0118 931 3820
- **Wrigley Co Ltd** www.wrigley.com 01752 701 107
- **Xynergy Health Products** www.xynergy.co.uk 01730 813 642
- **Yaoh** www.yaoh.co.uk 0117 923 9053
- **Yarrah Organic Pet Food** www.yarrah.com 00 31 341 439 850
- **York Foods** menieruk@infotelecom.es 01904 647 721
- **Yorkshire Hemp Ltd** www.yorkshirehemp.com 01924 375 475
- **Zedz Foods** www.zedzfoods.co.uk 0161 835 1442

INDEX

A

B

D

E

F

Q

R

S

T

U

V

NOTES

Membership / Renewal

THE Vegan SOCIETY

◯ I wish to become a member and support the work of the Vegan Society.

◯ I wish to renew my membership. Membership No. (if known)

....

Name:...Address:...

....Postcode:..............................

Tel:...email:..

Date of Birth: (for security purposes) ..../.........../.........

Occupation:..

A copy of the Society's rules (Memo & Articles of Association) can be viewed on our website or at our office. Alternatively you may buy a copy for £5.

◯ Please tick this box if you are a dietary Vegan. This entitles you to voting rights in the Society's elections if aged 18+.

◯ Please treat my membership subscription as Gift Aid. I have paid UK income or capital gains tax equal to the amount the Society reclaims.

◯ My income is less than £8000 per year and I qualify for the low income discount of 33%.*

◯ I wish to enrol other members of my household for an additional £7 each.**

Please give full names of additional members and specify if dietary vegan and / or under 18. (If more than six additional members please attach separate sheet.)

contiued overleaf ➲

Membership

Individual **£21**	
* Less **£7** low-income deduction (if applicable)	
** Add **£7** per additional household member	
Life **£350**	
Memo & Articles of Association **£5**	
Overseas: Europe +**£5** / Rest of World +**£7**	
Donation	
Total:	

How to pay

Payment must be made by credit card, sterling International money order or sterling cheque drawn on a British bank.

- **Cheque / PO** payable to *The Vegan Society*
- **Credit / Debit card** (below)
- **Direct Debit** ◯ Please send me a form
- **Website:** www.vegansociety.com

☐☐☐☐☐☐☐☐☐☐☐☐☐☐☐☐☐☐

Please debit my Visa / Mastercard / Visa Delta / Connect / Switch / Solo card number

Name on card:...Signature:...............................

Today's date........../........../........Start date:........./..........Expiry date........./.........

Switch Issue No.:.................

Please return to: **Membership Dept.**

The Vegan Society | Donald Watson House | 7 Battle Road

St Leonards on Sea | East Sussex TN37 7AA | UK.

Tel: **0845 45 88244** | Fax: **01424 717064**

Visit: **www.vegansociety.com** email: **membership@vegansociety.com**

This form may be photocopied